Language typology and syntactic description

Volume III
*Grammatical categories and the lexicon*

*Language typology and syntactic description* is published under the auspices of the Center for Applied Linguistics.

# Language typology and syntactic description

Volume III
*Grammatical categories and the lexicon*

Edited by
TIMOTHY SHOPEN
*Australian National University*

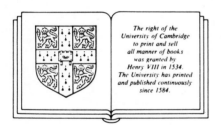

The right of the
University of Cambridge
to print and sell
all manner of books
was granted by
Henry VIII in 1534.
The University has printed
and published continuously
since 1584.

CAMBRIDGE UNIVERSITY PRESS

Cambridge
New York    Port Chester    Melbourne    Sydney

Published by the Press Syndicate of the University of Cambridge
The Pitt Building, Trumpington Street, Cambridge CB2 1RP
40 West 20th Street, New York, NY 10011, USA
10 Stamford Road, Oakleigh, Melbourne 3166, Australia

First published 1985
Reprinted 1987, 1990

Printed in Great Britain by the Athenaeum Press Ltd,
Newcastle upon Tyne

Library of Congress catalogue card number: 84-20028

*British Library cataloguing in publication data*

Language typology and syntactic description
Vol. 3. Grammatical categories and the lexicon
1. Grammar, Comparative and general – Syntax
I. Shopen, Timothy
415    P291

ISBN 0 521 26859 1 (hard covers)
ISBN 0 521 31899 8 (paperback)

# Contents

**Grammatical categories**

### 3 Inflectional morphology
STEPHEN R. ANDERSON
*University of California, Los Angeles*

## 4 Tense, aspect, and mood

SANDRA CHUNG
*University of California, San Diego*
*and*
ALAN TIMBERLAKE
*University of California, Los Angeles*

## 5 Deixis

STEPHEN R. ANDERSON *and* EDWARD L. KEENAN
*University of California, Los Angeles*

**Derivational morphology**

**6 Causative verb formation and other verb-deriving morphology**
BERNARD COMRIE
*University of Southern California*

**7 Lexical nominalization**
BERNARD COMRIE
*University of Southern California*
*and*
SANDRA A. THOMPSON
*University of California, Los Angeles*

# Acknowledgements

This work began at a conference on field work questionnaires initiated by Rudolph Troike at the Center for Applied Linguistics (CAL). The participants agreed that the best way to prepare for field work is to develop an idea of what to look for, and this led to the idea of a typological survey that could serve as a reference manual and a textbook for students.

Many people have helped us in the work that we now present. I will name only a few here. Rudolph Troike and John Hammer of CAL, and Alan Bell of the National Science Foundation did much to help in the organization of the project, and the National Science Foundation provided generous financial support without which the work would not have been possible. Diana Riehl of CAL was a reliable and capable intermediary in the complex administration of the project. Carmen Silva-Corvalan and Sandra Thompson deserve special thanks for their work at UCLA, while here in Australia many people provided help. The Australian National University has been very generous in its support of my work. I am grateful to Penny Carter and Julia Harding of Cambridge University Press for the careful work in the production of our books. Three people that have been especially helpful to me in the final stages of the editing are Edith Bavin, Jean Harkins, and above all, Rosemary Butt. My thanks to all.

Timothy Shopen
Canberra, Australia
*February 1984*

# Abbreviations for grammatical terms

The following are abbreviations for grammatical terms used frequently in the glosses for examples. Other abbreviations are explained as they are presented.

| | | | |
|---|---|---|---|
| ABS | Absolute | IRR | Irrealis |
| ACC | Accusative | IO | Indirect object |
| ACT | Actor | LOC | Locative |
| AG | Agent | NOM | Nominative |
| ART | Article | NZN | Nominalization |
| ASP | Aspect | NZR | Nominalizer |
| ASSOC | Associative | OBJ | Object |
| AUX | Auxiliary | OBL | Oblique |
| BEN | Benefactive | PART | Participle |
| CL | Classifier | PASS | Passive |
| COMP | Complementizer | PCL | Particle |
| COMPL | Completive | PERF | Perfective |
| COND | Conditional | PL | Plural |
| DAT | Dative | PREP | Preposition |
| DECLAR | Declarative | PRES | Present |
| DEF | Definite | PRO | Pro form |
| DEM | Demonstrative | PROG | Progressive |
| DET | Determiner | Q | Question marker |
| DO | Direct object | REFL | Reflexive |
| DU | Dual | REL | Relativizer |
| EMPH | Emphasis | RPRO | Relative pronoun |
| ERG | Ergative | SJNCT | Subjunctive |
| FUT | Future | SG | Singular |
| GEN | Genitive | SUBJ | Subject |
| HABIT | Habitual | TNS | Tense |
| IMP | Imperative | TOP | Topic |
| INCOMPL | Incompletive | VN | Verbal noun |
| INDIC | Indicative | I | First person |
| INF | Infinitive | 2 | Second person |
| INSTR | Instrumental | 3 | Third person |

# Introduction

*Grammatical categories and the lexicon* is the third of three volumes comprising the work *Language typology and syntactic description*. The first volume is *Clause structure* and the second is *Complex constructions*. Our purpose has been to do a cross-linguistic survey of syntactic and morphological structure that can serve as a manual for field workers, and for anyone interested in relating observations about particular languages to a general theory of language.

The first two chapters of the volume concern the notion of the word. The first is by Stephen Anderson on typological distinctions in word formation. Anderson examines the notion of structure in lexical items with a survey of important grammatical and typological notions that have been applied to word formation. He looks at word formation processes that include stem modification, derivation and compounding.

The second chapter is by Leonard Talmy on what he terms 'lexicalization patterns'. He explores the ways in which languages combine conceptual material into single words, most particularly into verbal roots, their inflections, and a unit that frequently accompanies verbs which he terms the 'satellite'. He proceeds to develop a typology along these lines with special reference to expressions of motion.

The next three chapters concern grammatical categories. The third chapter of the volume is by Stephen Anderson on inflectional morphology. He first clarifies the notion of inflection as a part of word formation and then surveys the grammatical categories encoded in inflections on the major parts of speech.

The fourth chapter is by Sandra Chung and Alan Timberlake on tense, aspect and mood. They take particular care to define the semantic notions involved and then exemplify a typology with sketches of some representative languages.

The fifth chapter is by Stephen Anderson and Edward Keenan on deixis. They concern themselves with person deixis, spatial deixis and temporal deixis. They consider deixis in respect to the speech act, and 'relativized deixis' which keys on other points of space and time established in the discourse.

The last two chapters of the volume are about derivational morphology. The first of these and the sixth of the volume is by Bernard Comrie on causative verb formation and other verb-deriving morphology. Most of the chapter looks at verb formation entailing a change in valency. He considers analytic, morphological and lexical causatives in detail and also considers verbs formed from verbs without a change in valency.

The last chapter of the volume by Bernard Comrie and Sandra Thompson is on lexical nominalization. They explore devices for forming nouns from verbs and adjectives, with a major part of the chapter on the 'action nominal'. They also look at devices for forming nouns from other nouns.

*Note:* References to chapters in all three volumes of *Language typology and syntactic description* are preceded by the volume number. For example: chapter III.1 (chapter 1, this volume), chapter II.3 (chapter 3, Volume II).

# 1 Typological distinctions in word formation

STEPHEN R. ANDERSON

## 0.0 Introduction

The chapters of this volume differ somewhat from much of what has preceded in Volumes I and II. While earlier chapters have been primarily devoted to principles of sentence construction, these chapters are concerned with the principles governing a language's *lexicon* or stock of words. The present chapter deals with the creation of word units out of smaller components, while chapter 2 treats the range of conceptual material that may be grouped together into a single such unit. Chapters 6 and 7 deal with two areas of word formation closely linked to syntactic structure: the formation of causative verbs and related patterns of verbal derivation; and the construction of nominalized forms corresponding to predicative structures.

## 0.1 *The lexicon*
Our concern here is with the formation of words, and more particularly with the notion of *stems*. Traditionally, the lexicon is thought of as a (more or less structured) list of the form- meaning correspondences (or signs) which speakers have made conventional. With only marginal exceptions, these associations are arbitrary: even onomatopoeic words are arbitrary, at least in part. The fact that English *ear* means what it does and functions as a noun does not follow from any general property of the language: any other combination of English sounds would do as well, or the language might lack such a word altogether. We can oppose this arbitrariness of the sign to other aspects of the word. Thus, given that *ear* is a noun, it follows from the syntax of English that it can appear as a subject, object, etc., but not as an (unsupported) predicate. Similarly, given that it has the phonetic shape /iɹ/, its plural /iɹz/ follows from the general properties of English inflection. This is not to say that it could not – like some lexical items – be exceptional in either morphology or syntax, but nonetheless the contrast is clear: morphology and syntax are areas of overall regularity, as opposed to the brute fact

that in English, *ear* denotes an ear. This fact is completely 'exceptional' in the sense that there is nothing else about the language from which it could have been predicted. Such arbitrariness is typical of the lexicon, which is to this extent the repository of what is idiosyncratic and unpredictable about linguistic forms.

If the lexicon is the locus of unpredictability in form–meaning associations, it follows that it cannot be limited to a list of words alone, but must also include some larger structures. Beyond specifying the forms and meanings of individual words, the lexicon need say nothing about the sentence *He bit my ear*: the structure follows from general principles of English syntax, and the meaning follows from equally general principles for the interpretation of such structures. In *Lend me your ear*, however (in the sense 'listen!'), the meaning of the whole is not *compositional*: that is, it is not a straightforward function of the meanings of its parts. This meaning has much the same arbitrary character as the definition of a simple word, and it is hard to see any principled basis for excluding such phrasal idioms from a lexicon as we have defined it above. Indeed, sometimes the form as well as the meaning of an idiom must be treated as lexical: the structure of *to and fro*, for example, is not syntactically regular in English, and its form as well as its meaning would seem to be a matter for lexical listing.

We will have nothing further to say about the problems of idiom formation here. Our focus is less on the arbitrariness of lexical information than on the possibility of finding some systematic internal structure to the list of forms; for that reason, we will concentrate on the most common kind of lexical form, thinking of the lexicon as a list of words, and ignore the fact that some larger structures ought properly to be included as well.

This brings up the problem of specifying what we mean by a *word*. As will be pointed out in the third chapter of this volume, there really is no satisfactory resolution of this classical problem, since it involves several mutually independent (and sometimes conflicting) criteria. At the risk of some circularity, we will assume that it is the grammatical sense of the notion 'word' (rather than, for example, the phonological notion) which is of interest. 'Words' in this sense are the lexical categories discussed as 'parts of speech' in chapter 1.1. This will include most of the things we usually write between spaces in English, but also some larger structures such as compounds. While there may be cases in which the boundary between 'words' in this sense is unclear, it would appear that the problems we wish to address here are not directly affected by this fact.

## 0.2 *The notion of 'structure' in lexical items*

There would be little to study in the domain of word formation principles if all of the items in the lexicon were like *ear* – arbitrary associations between a form and its meaning, where neither has internal structure that is relevant to the existence of the association. Besides such unanalyzable cases, however, other items in the lexicon (perhaps the majority) can be seen as 'partially motivated', in the sense that they involve (individually arbitrary) isolable parts combined in principled ways.

Consider the form *broken-hearted*, for example. It is not enough to list an association between the phonological sequence /browkənhaɹtəd/ and the meaning 'disconsolate'. We must relate the first part of the form to the independent word *broken* (and thus eventually to *break*), and the following part to the independent word *heart*. This is not simply because of the resemblance in sound and meaning (after all, we do not relate *hear* to *ear*, despite the phonetic resemblance and semantic connections between them). Somewhere in the lexicon can be found the information that *break X's heart* means 'render X disconsolate'; but it is probably the existence of other parallel formations (*long-lived*, *three-legged*, *open-mouthed*, etc.) that establishes our sense of a formal pattern into which this relationship fits. What interests us is the sort of principle by which the adjective *broken* (related to the verb *break*) and the noun *heart* are combined to yield the adjective *broken-hearted*.

A number of different processes can be seen at work in this example. *Broken* is related to *break* by a combination of internal vowel change and suffixation found in other deverbal adjectives (*melt/molten*) and participles (*steal/stolen*). It combines with *heart* to form a compound *broken heart*, from which an adjective is formed by adding the suffix *-ed* meaning 'having or endowed with (noun)' (not to be confused with the usual verbal past participle ending: contrast *a learnèd professor* 'one endowed with learning' with *a learned response* 'one which has been learned').

The individual components of the formation can all be seen abundantly elsewhere in the language; but still, the existence of a form *broken-hearted* is a partially arbitrary fact which must be listed in the lexicon. This is because even though we can say a great deal about *how* it is formed, given its components, we cannot predict with certainty *that* it will be formed. Exactly parallel to *break X's heart*, for example, we have *cook X's goose*, *X's goose is cooked*, etc., but no corresponding adjective *\*cooked-goosed*. The existence of the one but not the other is thus an idiosyncratic fact about the word stock of the language, while the principles by which either is (or could be) formed have a generality that goes beyond any particular item in the lexicon. It is in this sense that we can speak of lexical items as 'partially motivated', and about structure in the lexicon.

## 0.3  *Formal and functional aspects of word formation*

In III.3 we will treat principles by which words are built up of smaller pieces (called formatives), in connection with inflectional morphology. There we will note that it is to some extent artificial to distinguish between inflection and other sorts of morphological complexity, and the line is hard to draw. Our interest here, however, is not in the productive and syntactically relevant categories of inflection, but rather in the internal structure of the meaningful 'core' of the word. We will thus abstract away from those properties of a word's shape that are due to its membership in the inflectional categories considered in chapter 3 of this volume. Thus, we will not always be dealing with 'words' in the obvious sense: in a language like Latin, for example, when we remove the 'inflectional' material from most nouns, verbs, or adjectives, what remains is not a form that occurs independently in sentences in the language. For this reason, we will refer to a 'word' thus shorn of its inflectional markings as a *stem*, and the remainder of this chapter will be devoted to the study of stem formation processes.

The study of stem formation includes the traditional domain of *derivational morphology*, but it is not limited to this. The formation of compounds is not always considered together with derivational morphology, but in some languages this is an important way of creating new lexical items. A special case of compound formation is *incorporation* (usually by a verb, of its object or intransitive subject).

We can look at stem formation processes of any of these types from two points of view: formally, in terms of the effects of the process, or functionally, in terms of the relations between the items that the process describes. Consider derivation. The formation of English agent nouns like *owner*, *listener*, etc. can be viewed formally as the addition of the suffix *-er*, or functionally as establishing a relation between a verb and 'one who (verb)s [perhaps typically, or professionally]'.

When we have characterized both the formal and the functional sides of a particular kind of word formation, we can go on to assess its role in the system of the language. Here there are several points to consider: (1) does this formal process always express the same relation between forms? (2) are there other processes that also express this same relation? These two questions are relevant both to derivation and to compounding. Another issue of relevance to word formation processes of all types is: (3) given a form that satisfies the conditions on one term of the

Table 1.1. *Derivational relationships among some Russian verbs*

|  | I | II | III |
|---|---|---|---|
| 'sit' | sidet′ (sidi-) | i. sadit′ (sadi-)<br>sažat′ (sažaj-)<br>p. po-sadit′ (po-sadi-) | sadit′-sja (sadi-. . .-sja)<br><br>sest′ (sjad-) |
| 'lie' | ležat′ (leži-) | i. klast′ (klad-)<br>p. po-ložit′ (po-loži-) | ložit′-sja (loži-. . .-sja)<br>leč′ (ljag-) |
| 'stand' | stojat′ (stoi-) | i. stavit′ (stavi-)<br><br>p. po-stavit′ (po-stavi-) | stanovit′-sja<br>.(stanovi-. . .-sja)<br>stat′ (stan-) |

relation in question, how likely is it that the other term appears as well (i.e., how productive is the process)? At least one more question is relevant to derivation: (4) given that a derivational relation exists, which of the two forms is 'derived from' the other? The answers to all of these questions can be quite complicated, and lead us into other areas. Perhaps the most problematic of these issues is that of directionality of derivation.

In many instances, the direction of derivation is clear from the forms: one form has an affix that is lacking in the other, and can thus be considered to be derived from it. Often, however, one finds that each form has a different affix; or else that there is no segmentable formative that distinguishes them (the difference being based on vowel change, for instance). In such cases it is often difficult to decide whether one form should be derived from the other at all, or whether some sort of reciprocal derivation should be established, or perhaps both forms should be derived from some third form that does not exist separately as a word of the language.

To illustrate the range of problems that can occur, Table 1.1 shows three series of derivationally related Russian verbs. The first set is concerned with sitting position, the second with lying position, the third with standing position. Each series is divided into three subgroups, identified by the roman numerals.

Forms in I indicate a state (e.g. 'to be in a sitting position'); III entry into a state (e.g. 'to assume a sitting position'); and II the causative equivalent of III (e.g. 'to put someone/something into a sitting position'). Within II and III, both imperfective (i.) and perfective (p.) aspect forms are given with infinitive and non-past stems.

The semantic relations are perfectly regular; the formal relations are irregular in ways that involve most of the problems discussed above. Although aspect is usually considered an inflectional category in Russian, the formal complexity of paradigms involving aspectual affixes gives it a character more compatible with the notion of derivation. Aspectual pairs such as *sadit'-sja/sest'*, *ložit'-sja/leč'* and *stanovit'-sja/stat'* have formal relations well outside the usual scope of Russian inflectional morphology. In column II, one finds a regular formal and semantic relation between *sadit'* and *po-sadit'*, between *stavit'* and *po-stavit'*, but no formal relation between *klast'* and *po-ložit'*. From a formal point of view, *klast'* is a distinct lexical item, although its semantic function strongly calls for integration into the overall system shown in Table 1.1. Russian, incidentally, has no simple verb *\*ložit'*; the tendency for *sadit'* to be replaced by *sažat'* may soon mean that the simple verb *sadit'* will also be non-existent. Statements of the direction of derivation are complicated by vowel alternations (e.g. *lež/lož* 'lie') and alternation of theme suffixes (e.g. *-e-* and *-i-* in *sid-e-t'*, *sad-i-t'*), which means that different forms often contain exactly the same number of formatives. In some instances, direction of derivation seems to be readily dictated by morphological complexity (e.g. *po-sadit'* is derived from *sadit'* by prefixing *po-*, and *sadit'-sja* from *sadit'* by suffixing *-sja*). Generalization of these derivational processes, however, would suggest that the perfective in column III should be *\*po-sadit'-sja*, a form which, like *\*po-ložit'-sja* and *\*po-sta(no)vit'-sja*, does not exist: the actual form is *sest'*. Indeed, apart from the anomalous *klast'*, the forms *sest'*, *leč'*, and *stat'* contain fewer formatives than any of the other forms, having no theme suffix between the stem and the infinitive suffix *-t'*. Overall, then, it is not possible to say without reservation that the forms in column III are derived from the corresponding forms in column II.

The Russian examples in Table 1.1 illustrate the kind of formal complexity that one may find in common vocabulary. Much of word formation is far more orderly and regular than this, and we have concentrated on such examples below; but field workers should not be surprised if they find comparably idiosyncratic subparts of a word or stem formation system.

## 1.0 Typology of word formation processes

With the exception of the genetic relationships revealed by historical linguistics, distinctions in word formation processes have probably been the single most popular basis on which languages have been classified. We see the motivation for this when we compare languages such as Eskimo and Vietnamese, the former with exceedingly long and complex words, and the latter with nearly every word made up of one and only one formative (indeed, one syllable). The temptation is to take these obvious differences as the sole basis of a typological classification. We must recall, however, that the purpose of a typology is to uncover relations among phenomena. The discovery that language X differs from language Y in respect of property $p$ is only of typological interest if something follows from it: that is, if $p$ is always associated with some apparently distinct property $p'$, such that the discovery that X has $p$ will allow us to predict that it will also have $p'$. If we divide the languages of the world into those whose phonological inventory includes a glottal stop [ʔ] and those without this sound, for example, the resulting 'typology' is of little or no interest since neither class of languages seems to display any concomitant property worthy of note. Before basing a typological system on the nature of word formation, then, we must ask whether such a scheme will reveal properties of interest.

## 1.1 *Classical typological systems based on word formation*
When we consider the nature of (much of) traditional grammar, though, it is clear why a typology based on word formation processes should have been so appealing. In general, traditional studies could be divided into 'phonology' and 'grammar'; and 'grammar' in this tradition was composed almost exclusively of the principles of word formation (inflectional and derivational morphology, plus compounding). 'Syntax' in such works was generally just an appendix to the word formation rules, giving the 'uses of the cases, parts of speech, etc.'. The fact that languages can differ in the internal structure of words thus implies that there are distinctions to be made in the most central portions of such a grammar.

The systems of classification on morphological principles proposed in early work were numerous and varied, but they had in common a concentration on (a) the degree of internal complexity of words, in the sense of the number of formatives that make up a single word; and (b) the transparency of the boundaries between formatives (or, more specifically, the extent to which a discrete part of a word could be associated with each particular aspect of its meaning). The categories of such a schema are usually ranged along some single dimension. It is still quite common to hear the following: *isolating* languages tend to have a one to one ratio of formatives to words (paradigm example: Chinese); *agglutinating* languages have complex words formed by the juxtaposition of several formatives, with clear boundaries between them (paradigm example: Turkish); while *(in)flectional* languages have internally complex words which cannot easily be segmented into an exhaustive and non-overlapping string of formatives (paradigm example: Latin). In the study of the languages of North America (and elsewhere outside of Europe), researchers turned up many cases which did not appear to fit into this classification, and often added at least one further category for *polysynthetic* languages (paradigm example: Eskimo). These latter are similar to agglutinative languages in internal complexity and perhaps also segmentability, but with the added feature that some affixal material may represent semantic content of the sort usually reserved for independent stems (cf. the discussion below of Kwakw'ala).

It is clear that at least the central examples of these types differ significantly from one another, but that the classification corresponds to a single dimension of variability, or that it is possible (or useful) to classify the world's languages exhaustively and uniquely on this basis is much less self-evident. In fact, the majority of languages that have been studied to date each show some mixture of features associated with more than one of these types. More importantly, nothing much seems to follow from this classification: it has never been shown, for example, that languages with agglutinative properties share other features of a non-accidental sort that are not shared with non-agglutinating languages as well. For these reasons, the traditional terms do not seem to constitute any significant typology. At best, they furnish a convenient set of impressionistic labels for the surface forms of words. If taken in this spirit, the difficulty of providing substantive definitions for these language types need not worry typologists.

### 1.2 *Sapir's typology*
Concerned with the vagueness of traditional schemes for classifying languages, Sapir (1922) proposed a significantly more articulated set of categories. Instead of a single dimension, he discusses three independent parameters. The first of these is a major innovation, and concerns the type of concept represented in a word. All languages, he suggests, represent basic or concrete concepts (the primary meanings of nouns, verbs, and adjectives). They may also be said to require expression (perhaps by formal features of arrangement, such as word order, rather than by overt formatives) for 'pure relational' concepts: identification of basic grammatical relations such as subject and object, modifier and head, etc. These are (roughly) the categories we will characterize as 'relational' in the discussion of inflection in chapter III.3.

Two other sorts of concepts, however, are not essential to all languages: 'derivational' concepts, which express modification of a basic concept, but still have a rather lexical content (e.g. plurality or diminutiveness, and others of the categories characterized as 'inherent' in the discussion of inflection in chapter III.3); and 'concrete relational' concepts, which function primarily in grammatical structure rather than contributing to word meaning directly. These may have some basis in semantic properties (e.g. gender systems); they are mostly of the sort we will characterize in chapter III.3 as 'agreement properties'.

Languages fall into four types for Sapir, according to whether they allow the expression of (a) neither of these latter concepts, (b) only derivational concepts, (c) only concrete relational concepts, or (d) both. In chapter III.5 below, we will see that properties other than those treated by Sapir as typologically relevant – basic and pure relational, as well as derivational and concrete relational – show considerable diversity across the languages of the world in the way conceptual or semantic material is grouped together into a single word.

In addition to the criterion of 'concept type', Sapir also suggests an independent dimension of morphological 'technique'. Again, four possibilities are suggested: *isolation*, which identifies the word with the formative; *agglutination*, which involves simple juxtaposition of formatives; *fusion*, which involves multiple formatives without clear boundaries between them; and *symbolism*, involving internal modifications such as Ablaut, consonant change, and suppletion. A third independent dimension, that of 'degree of synthesis', distinguishes analytic, synthetic, and polysynthetic types along a more nearly continuous scale of degree of complexity.

This framework is both more flexible and more comprehensive than its predecessors, and so constitutes a major improvement over them. Nonetheless, there is a disquieting lack of evidence for any typological significance to the classification: nothing appears to follow from a language's place in it. While it is perhaps possible to apply the system consistently to a wide variety of languages, it is not clear what else can be predicted from (say) the observation that a given language expresses concrete relational concepts but not derivational ones. It may be that correlations of this sort exist but have simply not been noted; but the temptation is to conclude that the mechanisms of word formation are, in principle, independent of other aspects of linguistic structure. For the field worker, this suggests that in the domain of word formation no possibility can be completely excluded on independent grounds. One should also recall that languages need not be internally uniform in their word formation (as the variety of word types in English can show us), and thus different areas of their vocabularies may show quite different typologies.

## 1.3 *A classification of word formation types*

It may be impossible to assign a systematic and comprehensive classification to entire languages, but it will always be useful to identify particular word formation processes. We can illustrate this by discussing one particular rule of word formation in English. A large number of English words are formed with the suffix *-able* (*-ible*), as in *breakable, movable, inflatable*, etc. Aside from their phonetic resemblance, these obviously share a certain element of meaning. It is also clear that they are related to the words *break, move*, and *inflate*, respectively. The words to which *-able* words are related are typically transitive verbs: intransitive verbs such as *die, go*, and *exist* do not have corresponding forms *dieable, *goable, or *existable, but virtually any transitive verb (including new coinages, like *finalize*) can be the basis of such a formation (e.g. *finalizable*).

In several respects, this process is typical of all word formation processes. First of all, it does not create new words of arbitrary form out of whole cloth: it produces words with the general shape of a base followed by the phonological sequence /-əbl̩/, all of them adjectives. These are related to a particular set of other words: the bases of transitive verbs. We can thus characterize the two classes of forms that are related by the process in question: adjectives ending in /-əbl̩/ and transitive verbs with the same base.

In addition, we can identify systematic relations in meaning and in syntax between the two classes of words connected by the word formation rule. If 'V' is the meaning of a transitive verb, the related adjective in *-able* means roughly 'able to be V'd'. The subject of the *-able* adjective, furthermore, corresponds to the *object* of the corresponding transitive verb.

It is important to be clear about the character of this formulation. We have established that there is a systematic connection in sound, meaning, and syntax between two classes of words. We cannot extend this observation, however, to make one class depend *entirely* on the other (as would be implied if we derived the one from the other in a definite direction exclusively by means of the rule). This is because one class may not always have a correspondent in the other; or one or the other of a pair of otherwise related words may have some extra idiosyncrasies that are not predicted by the statement of the word formation process.

In this particular case, it is not possible to illustrate the general point by showing transitive verbs that do not have a corresponding *-able* adjective, since it appears that *-able* formation is completely productive with transitive verbs (except, interestingly, for those that also do not undergo passivization: thus, *John resembles his father*, but not *John's father is resembled by him*; and there is no adjective *resemblable). Other word formation processes are more limited, however: thus, the process that relates adjectives like *black, sad, soft*, etc. to the verbs *blacken, sadden, soften*, etc. cannot relate *lilac, bad, hot* to *\*lilacen, \*badden, \*hotten*.

In a number of cases, on the other hand, adjectives in *-able* do not correspond directly to transitive verbs. In some cases, the base from which an *-able* adjective is formed is not identical with the simple verb. In forms like *navigable, demonstrable, formulable*, etc. the base consists of the related verb (*navigate, demonstrate, formulate*) minus the final suffix *-ate*. From this, we can conclude that the phonological relation established by a word formation rule may not consist simply of the addition of an affix to a base, but entail the deletion of some other affix as well.

In some forms, the base containing *-ate* does not exist as a separate word, but does serve as the foundation of other derivations: cf. *applicable*, related to *apply*, not *\*applicate*; but also *application, applicative*, etc. From this, we can see that items appearing as the base of one class related by a word formation rule may appear in special, partially idiosyncratic combining forms. In other cases, there is no corresponding verb at all sharing the base of the *-able* form: cf. *eligible, possible, credible*, and others. Nonetheless, all of these forms can be seen as involving the word formation process associated with the suffix *-able/-ible*, since they are of the appropriate form and have appropriate meanings.

Still other cases pose something more of a problem, however, since their bases are apparently not appropriate in terms of the statement of the process above. These include a very small number of formations apparently based on intransitive verbs: cf. *perishable, workable*. There is also a larger, but still limited, class of formations based on non-verbs: cf. *palatable, objectionable, peaceable*, etc. These formations are apparently not particularly productive, and their form and meaning provide only a tenuous indication that the process of *-able* formation is relevant to their structure. In fact, a preferable analysis would probably be to recognize a second, distinct *-able* rule: one which relates nouns to adjectives. The meanings of these are somewhat more difficult to specify than is the case for the deverbal *-able* forms discussed above: roughly, they mean 'characterized by (noun)'. In a few cases, we can find a homophonous noun and verb either of which can be the basis of a (distinct) *-able* form: thus, *fashionable* can mean either 'characterized by being in fashion' (in which case it is denominal), or 'capable of being fashioned' (in which case it is related to the transitive verb *fashion*). We conclude, then, that a single affix (or perhaps other phonological relation, such as Ablaut or reduplication, etc.) may characterize more than one rule of word formation in a given language.

Unlike inflectional forms, -*able* words are not simply dependent members of a paradigm: they are 'autonomous' lexical items. First, their meanings are not entirely predictable from those of their base. Thus, *drinkable, readable*, and a few others mean not simply 'able to be drunk, read, etc.' but 'good to drink, read, etc.' The simpler, 'more basic' meanings are carried by forms built on bases that do not occur as independent words (*potable, legible*). This factor, taken together with the existence of forms with partially idiosyncratic combining forms for their bases, and forms built unproductively on bases other than transitive verbs, shows that the -*able* rule functions to describe a class of words in the lexicon, and not simply as a mechanism for the production of new words.

The -*able* rule just discussed is a stem modification process. The stem that serves as its input is usually an independently occurring transitive verb, but it may be a stem obtained by deleting a final suffix -*ate* (as in *irritable*), one which takes a special form in such combinations (as in *applicable*), one which does not appear independently at all (as in *edible*), or one which is used independently as an intransitive verb (as in *perishable*). In addition, there appears to be another word formation rule which adds -*able* to a small set of nouns (as in *personable*). The modification that is performed in each case is a simple one: the addition of the suffix -*able*. We can similarly identify any word formation process in formal terms by specifying the class of stems affected and the modification performed. At the same time, we associate the formal process with a functional relation. This latter can be similarly identified by the syntactic and semantic relationships between the word and its input stem.

The -*able* rule is rather straightforward in one sense: for the great majority of adjectives in -*able*, a single formal process is uniquely associated with a single functional relationship. As we have suggested, another distinct process of -*able* formation may also exist, establishing a different functional relationship (between nouns and adjectives); but this latter is much less productive, and its semantic properties are closely connected with those of the more productive deverbal -*able* rule. We can compare this situation with that of other word formation rules in English. The formal process of -*er* suffixation, for instance, applies to verbs to create nouns in -*er*. There are at least two distinct semantic functions associated with this suffix: some of the nouns created represent agents ('one who Vs'), like *hunter, trespasser, actor*, etc.; while others represent instruments ('thing with which one Vs'), like *cleaver, computer, typewriter*. Some are ambiguous between the two senses: a *driver* may be one who drives, or a kind of golf club; a *sleeper* may be a person who sleeps or a place (a sofa or a railroad car) where one can sleep, etc. Here one formal process is associated with two distinct functions.

The opposite state of affairs is also easy to find in English. The single functional relationship between verbs and their action nominals is associated with a wealth of different formal processes, as in *act/action, laugh/laughter, synthesize/synthesis*, and many others (these and other nominalization patterns will be discussed in chapter III.7 below). We can conclude, then, that the unitary word formation processes of a language cannot be identified uniquely *either* by their formal aspect *or* by the functional relation they establish. Since we cannot expect a one to one association between these two sides of word formation processes, we must specify both in order to define a particular rule.

We can now ask how the properties of word formation processes such as the two *-able* rules are related to those that have formed the basis of traditional typologies, and (more interestingly, perhaps) to differences among languages of which field workers should be aware.

When we consider the traditional systems of classification, we see that they focus almost exclusively in the *outputs* of word formation processes. 'Isolating', 'agglutinating', 'flectional', and similar identifications refer to the formal structure of the words related by such processes, but not to the nature of the relationship. In part, this results almost necessarily from the attempt to classify whole languages on these grounds. Individual word formation rules within a single language show a great deal of diversity in terms of input classes, semantic, and syntactic structural relations; while the number of formally distinct sorts of structure they can produce is much more limited.

In sections 2 and 3 below, we will discuss differences in the operation of word formation processes, touching (we hope) on most of the varieties of word formation field workers can expect to encounter. We will emphasize a basic difference among rules in terms of their inputs: we will distinguish between rules of *stem modification*, which can be seen as relating a single base to a form which is altered in some systematic way (by addition or deletion of affixes, internal modification, etc.), and rules of *compounding*, which relate a set of two (or more) independent bases to a form in which they are combined in some way (perhaps with addition of further material, or with concomitant modifications). Section 2 below will deal with stem modification and section 3 with compounding. Before moving on to these matters, however, we must discuss one further issue in the characterization of individual word formation processes which cuts across all types: the notion of 'productivity'.

**1.4 *The productivity of word formation rules***

Word formation processes occupy an intermediate status between the full generality of syntactic principles, on the one hand, and the completely individual, arbitrary listing of the lexical properties of particular words on the other. Word formation rules describe the internal structure of a potentially open ended class of lexical items; but the availability of any particular member of such a class is subject to a good deal of idiosyncrasy.

We find some instances in which every potential form described by a very general word formation rule is clearly a word of the language: the formation of -*ing* nominalizations in English is such an example, since this form exists for every verb. There are other processes which, while quite widespread, have some limitations: the formation of nominalizations in -(*at*)*ion* in English applies to a great many verbs, but not to all (cf. the impossibility of *arrivation*, *existation*, etc.). Other processes are quite limited and idiosyncratic, like that which produces de-adjectival nominalizations such as *long/length*, *wide/width*, etc.; while other formations are so fossilized in the lexicon of the language that they are probably not even passively recognized as 'word formation' any more by most speakers, such as the formative common (etymologically) to *father*, *mother*, *brother*, *sister*, *daughter*. The property involved seems to be best characterized as a more or less continuous scale of 'degree of productivity', rather than as a strictly categorical opposition between productive and non-productive rules. 'Productivity' itself, however, is not a single dimension.

*1.4.1 Productivity as a quantitative notion*

Perhaps the simplest sense of productivity refers to the absolute number of forms included in the scope of a given word formation process. By this standard, a process instantiated in, say, ten forms is always more productive than one instantiated in five, regardless of other factors. Few authors would seriously defend the linguistic significance of such a purely numerical criterion; but nevertheless, the evidence offered for characterizing particular processes as 'unproductive' often consists simply of showing that they describe very few forms in the language. On this basis, if the lexicon of a language happened to contain more nouns than verbs, it would follow that nominal inflection was more 'productive' than verbal inflection. This is clearly not the desired conclusion, at least in the general case.

A more significant notion of productivity might be the extent to which a morphological process applies to the forms that constitute its input range. Let us compare two word formation processes on this basis, taking first the formation of French ordinal numbers. Aside from the fact that the ordinal corresponding to *un* 'one' is *premier* 'first', ordinals are formed quite regularly by the addition of the suffix *-ième*: *deuxième* 'second', *huitième* 'eighth', *vingt-et-unième* 'twenty-first', etc. Clearly, however, the process only applies to numbers.

By comparison, consider English nouns ending in *-ist*. These refer to skilled practitioners: performers on particular musical instruments (e.g. *violin/violinist*, *cello/cellist*), creators of artistic objects (e.g. *art/artist*, *symphony/symphonist*), practitioners of artistic styles (e.g. *romantic/romanticist*, *cubist*, *impressionist*), experts in medical and academic fields (e.g. *slavic/slav(ic)ist*, *topology/topologist*, *anesthetic/anesthetist*). The names of the instruments, art objects, styles, and fields are the stems to which the suffix *-ist* is added. This process operates in a large number of forms; however, there are also a large number of forms naming things of which one can be a skilled practitioner but from which nouns in *-ist* cannot be formed: *drummist*, *piccol(o)ist*, *musical-sawist*, *statuist*, *oper(a)ist*, *baroquist*, *calculusist*, *surger(y)ist*, etc. There are also nouns such as *dentist*, *cubist*, and a few others which carry the sense of 'skilled practitioner', but where the stem (*dent-*) does not occur independently, or (*cube*) not with the appropriate meaning.

It is somewhat difficult to compare these two processes on the basis of sheer numbers of forms described. Since the range of numerals is in principle unlimited, we might say that French ordinal formation is too; but there are problems of distinctness involved (is *mille-neuf-cent-cinquante-deuxième* '1952nd' really a distinct formation from *cinquante-deuxième* '52nd'? or even from *deuxième* 'second'?), and in any event the number of ordinal numbers that could be considered part of the active lexicon of a speaker of French is surely subject to some limits in fact, if not in principle. It is thus not at all clear that there are more (distinct) ordinal numbers in the lexicon of French than there are nouns in *-ist* in the lexicon of English.

It is, however, quite clear that there is a sense in which ordinal formation in French is more productive than *-ist* formation in English: given *any* French number (except *un* 'one'), there is a corresponding ordinal formed by the addition of *-ième*. Given a domain in which one can be a 'skilled practitioner', however, there may or may not be such a noun in *-ist*. Instead, there may be some other formation (e.g. *drummer*, *sculptor*, *musician*), or compound (e.g. *piccolo-player*, *song-writer*), or a phrase (*romance linguist*, *baroque composer*). Quite independently of the numbers involved, then, English *-ist* formation is the less productive of the two processes, because it is applicable to a more limited subset of the forms in its *potential* domain.

In assessing the portion of its potential domain which a rule of word formation operates over, there is another factor which must also be taken into account. Often, two or more formally distinct processes coexist in the same language with similar or identical functions, and these processes apply to complementary sets of forms. English action nominalizations (cf. chapter III.7 below) provide a convenient example. A great many verbs have action nominals in -(*at*)*ion* (e.g. *derive/derivation*, *elect/election*), but not all do: from *arrive*, for example, we cannot form *arrivation*. This does indeed constitute a limitation on the process of adding -(*at*)*ion*, but not in the same sense in which the process of -*ist* noun formation is limited. This is because, for those forms to which -(*at*)*ion* cannot be added, some other nominalization process is available. In the case of *arrive*, the form is *arrival*. Some of the other nominalization formations are completely isolated (e.g. *laughter*), but together they provide an action nominal for virtually every verb in the language. Compare this situation with, for example, the formation of English instrument nouns in -*er* (e.g. *opener*, *lighter*, *accelerator*). From *eat* (*spaghetti*), one cannot form (*spaghetti-*)*eater* 'implement with which one eats spaghetti', and furthermore, no other word formation rule exists to fill this gap. Action nominal formation rules can be regarded as of limited productivity, then, but the limitation is of a different sort from that applying to the creation of instrument nouns or -*ist* nouns.

It often appears that in cases like that of English action nouns, a principle of complementarity is at work. The absence of a form *arrivation*, for example, is due (at least in part) to the existence of an alternative form (*arrival*) that fills the same function. When a process is otherwise quite productive within its domain, apparent limitations on its productivity often have the character of being due to the existence of alternative formations, rather than simple restrictions on the scope of the process.

A complementary point is due to the fact that words often become specialized or changed over their history, thus coming to diverge significantly from their original (productively formed) sense. When this happens, it may nonetheless be the case that the existence of the original (formally regular) word precludes the development of a formally similar but functionally regular word despite no longer being connected in meaning with its original function. A number of examples of this sort can be found in Modern Hebrew (cf. Horvath 1979). Given the formal regularity of word formation in this language (cf. the discussion of Semitic word formation below in section 2.2), the range of forms related to a given root is quite predictable, and many of these have expected regular meanings associated with them. From the root of *macaʔ* 'find', for example, we would expect to be able to construct a form (the 'hitpaʔel' form) *hitmaceʔ* meaning 'find each other, oneself' (parallel to the formation of *hitraʔeh* 'see each other, meet' from *raʔah* 'see'). This form, with this meaning, does not exist, however. We might at first ascribe this to simple lexical idiosyncrasy: some verbs simply do not form a 'hitpaʔel' derivative (e.g. there is no form *hitšaʔel* derived from *šaʔal* 'ask'). In this case, however, this is not the correct explanation; for the form *hitmaceʔ* does in fact exist. Instead of having reflexive or reciprocal meaning, however, it is lexicalized in the sense 'find one's way around'. By occupying the formal 'slot' of the 'hitpaʔel' form of *macaʔ*, this (semi-isolated) form blocks the creation of another word which would be both functionally and formally completely regular.

### 1.4.2 *Productivity and the 'activity' of word formation rules*
In addition to the notion of productivity that derives from the extent to which a process applies to everything in its domain, there is another which we can distinguish. Compare the processes discussed above (action nominalization, *-ist* noun and *-er* instrument noun formation in English; ordinal formation in French; etc.) with the English process which produces verbs from nouns by voicing a final fricative consonant (e.g. *life/live, cloth/clothe, house/hou*[z]*e*). There are quite a few such pairs in English, but the set is quite strictly limited, and cannot be extended. Given a new noun ending in a voiceless fricative, it is quite impossible to make from it a corresponding verb. From *path*, for example, we cannot create *\*pathe* 'provide with a path, make a path'. Similarly, from a verb ending in a voiced fricative we cannot (back-) form a noun by devoicing this sound: from *sneeze*, for example, we cannot infer a noun *\*sneese* denoting a product or act of sneezing.

By contrast, any new number in French can be made into an ordinal. Indeed, some years ago the number *googol* 'ten to the one hundredth power' was formed in English; as a borrowing in French (spelled *gougole*), this can serve as the basis of an ordinal form *gougolième*. English *-ist* forms cannot be applied automatically to new or borrowed words, but a large number of such forms have in fact entered the language recently based on newly created stems (e.g. *dadaist*) or borrowings (e.g. *Maoist*). It is not quite clear whether one who performs electronic music on a Moog synthesizer can appropriately be called a *moogist*, but it is certainly not out of the question.

A notion of productivity might thus be based on the possibility of applying the process in question to *new* forms, new in the sense of new for the process (but already in the language, e.g. *path*), or new in the sense of newly added to the language (created *de novo*, e.g. *dada*, or borrowed, e.g. *Mao*). The question then arises whether this kind of productivity ('sense 2') correlates directly with productivity in the previous sense, the extent to which the possible scope of a process is actually instantiated in the lexicon ('sense 1').

It is of course quite difficult to quantify productivity in the sense of applicability to new forms. If we treat it as an all or nothing property, we cannot equate it with complete productivity in sense 1, since we have already seen that the formation of *-ist* nouns in English is limited in sense 1, but applicable (at least to some extent) to new formations. A clearer demonstration of the independence of these two notions would be provided by a process applicable *only* to new formations. In Fula, for example, one of the noun classes which function centrally in the inflectional system is characterized by a $\phi$ class marker in the singular, and *-de* in the plural. This class consists almost exclusively of borrowed words, though some native forms have found their way into it by reinterpretation of their (original) class markers as part of their stem. Here, then, is an example of a word formation process which is largely unattested in the native lexicon, but abundantly productive in its applicability to newly borrowed items.

Probably, then, we want to keep the notions 'applicable to all or most of its potential domain' and 'applicable to new items when these are introduced into the language' apart. The latter kind of productivity (sense 2) is probably related to what we might call the 'active' vs. 'passive' character of word formation processes. This is the extent to which the process in question functions as a living part of the language and determines the shape of new words, or simply allows for the recognition of the structure of existing lexical items. It appears, that is, that some processes of word formation are more or less actively involved in creating forms (including those that have been created before), while others have more of the character of patterns, providing keys to the analysis of forms, but not serving as the basis for the creation of others.

Inflectional processes, of course, are the most typical of 'active' word formation mechanisms. The active character of such processes is often revealed in historical change. When an inflectional process is altered, the resulting change extends directly to all words more or less *en bloc*. If each such form were an independent entity, however, we would expect each to have a separate history and for a change affecting one item to have no necessary effect on others. Inflectional systems would then show more chaos as a result of their history than is usually the case. For example, in Old Icelandic (essentially, the ancestor of the modern Scandinavian languages), case and number were represented together in a single formative (e.g. -a 'genitive plural'), as is the case in Modern Icelandic. In the course of the development of modern Danish, Swedish, and Norwegian, however, the case system has been largely lost except for the retention of the old ending -s in the general function 'genitive' (originally, 'genitive singular' for some but not all classes of nouns). Case and number are now represented separately: in Danish *bøgers* 'of books', the ending -er (together with the umlaut of the stem vowel) represents the plural (of *bog* 'book'), while the final -s represents the genitive (compare this with Old Icelandic *boka*). The change may well have affected some forms before others, but the separation of case and number quickly became reasonably uniform. This suggests that it was not simply individual forms that changed, but the word formation process itself. In that case, the forms should be looked at as being continually under the active control of the word formation process, rather than existing independently of one another.

We can compare this situation with the strong verbs of English (the 'irregular' ones, e.g. *sing, sang, sung; catch, caught*). When we study their history in Middle and Modern English, we find a chaos of individual developments and partial analogies of one to another. The absence of uniform, overall change suggests that already in Early English the patterns of strong verb inflection had ceased to be 'active' parts of the grammar, but instead were passively controlled patterns for the recognition of relations in the lexicon.

This difference between active and passive word formation may be a difficult one to determine from the synchronic facts of a language. For example, what appears to be the same process may well be 'active' in some domains, but 'passive' in others. The formation of English -able adjectives from transitive verbs (e.g. *pronounceable, electable*) is quite productive (in either sense), and there is no reason not to take this to be an actively controlled process in the language. In other domains, however (e.g. intransitives such as *perishable* and non-verbs such as *comfortable*), the range of forms is quite limited, and undoubtedly more 'passive' in character.

We may see both an 'active' and a 'passive' pattern with the same stem and essentially the same morphological process. In Early English, a great many words had plurals in -en, as opposed to the case today. The rules of plural formation changed over time, however, generalizing the ending /z/ with very few -en relics. *Children* and *oxen* are the only direct examples (*oxen* surviving in part because it has always served as the standard example of an -en plural in grammar books!). In the case of the pair *brother/brethren*, however, the change was more complex. In addition to its productive sense of 'plural of brother', *brethren* had also acquired a more idiosyncratic sense of 'group of men (and perhaps women) sharing a strong moral bond'; and here the relation to *brother* was unproductive, more derivational than inflectional. Accordingly, when the active process of plural formation changed, this resulted in a new plural *brothers* for *brother*, but the (now derivationally) related *brethren* was unaffected. Of course, the field worker frequently does not have access to such historical information; but it is there that one finds explanations for many curiosities in the area of productivity.

We have now surveyed a variety of the dimensions on which word formation processes can be classified. These included the formal nature of the change produced; the syntactic or semantic domain of the forms the rule applies to; the syntactic and semantic relations between the 'inputs' and the 'outputs' of the process; and the degree of productivity (in at least two senses) of the process. There are other points to be made in each of these areas, to provide a complete account of word formation. For example, we must also treat 'productivity' in the sense of the extent to which a process is semantically 'compositional' (that is, the degree to which the meaning of the base suffices, together with regular principles of the language, to predict the meaning of a derived form). A process such as *-able* formation in English is almost completely compositional in this sense, with a few exceptions (such as the special meaning of *readable*, etc. as 'good to read', not simply 'able to be read'). On the other hand, it has been pointed out by Zimmer (1971) that virtually any relation between two nouns that could be focused on could be the basis of the meaning of a noun–noun compound in English. This process is thus much less compositional, since knowledge of the meanings of the bases alone is not sufficient to predict the meaning of the compound as a whole.

Equipped with this range of distinctions among word formation processes, then, we can now proceed in the sections that follow to illustrate a variety of systems, bearing in mind the importance of concentrating attention on individual rules rather than attempting to generalize across an entire language.

## 2.0 Stem modification processes

We distinguished above between processes that take a single stem as input and modify it in some way (e.g. by adding an affix), and processes that take two (or more) independent stems and combine them according to some pattern. In this section, we survey some of the range of processes of the former sort.

As we noted in section 1.3, a word formation process is identified by specifying both the formal change involved and the functional relationship between the two classes involved. With respect to the former parameter, we find the same grammatical processes in (derivational) word formation as those employed in inflectional morphology: affixation (addition of prefixes, suffixes, or infixes), internal change (of vowels, consonants, or suprasegmentals), reduplication, and suppletion. In addition to these, we should also recognize the possibility of 'zero derivation', where no formal change at all is required in the stem (as in the derivation of action nominals such as *murder, love, change* etc. from the homophonous verbs). Of course, some inflectional categories are marked by no modification to the stem whatsoever (e.g. the accusative form of most masculine and neuter nouns in Germanic languages, such as Icelandic *hatt* 'hat (acc. sg.)', opposed to the nominative singular form *hattur* which involves an overt suffix), and we might add this possibility to those surveyed in chapter III.3 below.

The categories of classical word formation typology can be viewed in terms of these different sorts of stem modification and their interaction with the phonology of the language. An isolating language, of course, is one which has no (or, at most, very few) stem modification processes. Agglutination results from the (nearly) exclusive use of processes of affixation combined with a phonology which does not subsequently obscure the borders between formatives. Sapir's category of fusional processes can be reduced to the phonological effects that result from mutual interaction of (fundamentally separable) affixes. In Bahasa Indonesia, for example, one can identify a prefix with various functions whose shape can be given as /meN-/. If this prefix were merely added to stems, with no further consequences, we would have a simple example of agglutination. However, when this prefix is added to verbs beginning with a voiceless stop, the prefix-final nasal element and this stem-initial stop coalesce, yielding a nasal consonant homorganic with the original stop (e.g. from *kapur* 'lime', the prefix in question yields *me[ŋ]apur* 'to whitewash'; from *tepi* 'side', it yields *menepi* 'to move aside', etc.). Here the reciprocal phonological effect obscures the boundary between stem and prefix, yielding a process of the sort Sapir would characterize as fusional. Sapir's other process type, symbolism, corresponds directly to the use of internal modifications such as vowel, consonant, or suprasegmental change.

The classical category of (*in*)*flectional* languages does not correspond unitarily to a single process type in these terms, but rather to the range of processes associated with both the fusional and symbolic types in Sapir's scheme, together with the possibility that a number of distinct categories could be involved in determining the shape of a single formative. In chapter III.3 it will be demonstrated that formatives and categories do not always stand in a one to one relationship (as implied by the traditional notion of the 'morpheme' as a unity of form and meaning). Where the morphological system of a language involves a substantial number of many to one or one to many associations between formatives and categories of meaning or inflection, it is likely to be called 'inflectional' in traditional terms. This type is thus not a unitary one, but rather corresponds to a variety of ways in which words may not display a direct one to one correspondence between easily segmented formatives and the component categories that make up their content.

We consider below some aspects of the morphological structure of two languages in which stem modification processes play a significant role. These two languages are close to being polar opposites with respect to one dimension we might wish to isolate for such processes: the extent to which word formation rules take as their input stems which are already the result of other word formation rules. In Kwakw'ala, word formation is the result of a large (indeed, potentially open ended) set of stem modification processes which take essentially any stem, whether simple or of arbitrary complexity, as their input. The other case described here is the system characteristic of Semitic languages such as Arabic or Hebrew. Word formation here is primarily the result of a limited set of processes, all of which operate on forms of essentially the same, 'basic', character.

We should emphasize that these two cases do not represent some limited set of language types: our premise is that it is individual word formation processes, not languages, that are usefully discussed in terms of types. While the languages chosen for illustration are relatively homogeneous in their morphological systems, this situation is by no means general in language, and we stress that the basis of our choice is the desire to present interesting sorts of rules, rather than to contrast distinct language types.

## 2.1 *Derivational processes in Kwakw'ala*

We first sketch some of the general properties of the language; examples will then be given to make these points more concrete.

Kwakw'ala morphology is based almost exclusively on suffixing. Prefixes are entirely absent, and the only instances of internal modification are a set of rules of reduplication (some including root vowel lengthening as a special case). Reduplication serves independently in several distinct processes of plural formation, and also serves to create special stem forms that are required by certain suffixes. Provided their meanings are compatible, the class of stems to which an affix can be added is usually quite free. In general, each suffix takes as the 'scope' of its semantic and syntactic material the stem consisting of all the material which precedes it. As a result, the relative order of suffixes can reflect semantic differences, though in practice the order does not vary greatly. Suffixes are not in general sensitive to the complexity of the stem to which they are added, though some impose a requirement that the stem contain (or sometimes end in) a suffix from a particular designated set. From the freedom with which suffixes can be added, it follows that there can be a sort of recursion, and that there is in principle no limit to the complexity of certain sorts of formation. Some suffixes seem remarkably free in their combining possibilities; for example, it is unusual from an English point of view (but not in Kwakw'ala) that suffixes indicating time relations (future, distant past, recent past, etc.) are applicable to nouns as well as to verbs.

Kwakw'ala is one of the classic examples of the 'polysynthetic' language type. This means in practice that words can display a great deal of internal structure, and that some affixes have a content corresponding to that of independent words in other languages (and in Kwakw'ala as well, as we will see). Affixes can in fact be identified whose meanings and functions are similar to members of all major word classes. Nonetheless, these affixes do not simply represent clitic forms of independent words (at least from the synchronic point of view; and there is little or no evidence from the history of the language that bears on this question).

Among several hundred suffixes, virtually all are totally dissimilar in form from corresponding free forms. This dissimilarity is reinforced by significant differences in function between affixes and any particular word of the language. In some cases, there is no (non-complex) word that corresponds in meaning to a given suffix. There is a small class of 'dummy' stems which do not contribute to the meaning of complex words formally based on them; these serve simply as bases to which semantically rich suffixes may be added. The commonest of these is /aẋ-/ (glossed as 'do' when unsuffixed): to this can be added suffixes such as /-exsd-/ 'want to ...' giving *aẋ'exsd* 'want', /-'sta-/ 'water' giving (with the further element /-la/ 'continuous aspect') *aẋstala* 'to be in water', etc.

Each of the morphological elements of the language has its own properties in the class of stems it applies to, its possibilities of appearance, its effect on stems, etc. Morphological elements do not in general fall into classes parallel to the classes of independent words (cf. chapter I.I). We present affixes below in terms of rough classes arranged for expository convenience but with little formal justification. Such classes as do have formal significance, such as the set of locative suffixes, do not correspond to word classes in the vocabulary as a whole. If the morphological elements were simply reduced forms of full words, we might expect some class of words to correspond *as a class* to a class of suffixes: to find, for example, that (nearly) every noun had a correspondent within a formally distinguishable set of suffixes. But this is not the case. In this respect, Kwakw'ala can be contrasted with a language whose word formation is based on the compounding of independent stems, as will be discussed below in section 3.

Once the set of possible suffixes has been identified, the morphological structure of words is quite transparent. With a few exceptions, the roots which serve as the bases of all formations are monosyllabic. In terms of its effect on the final consonant of the preceding stem, each suffix can be classed as either 'neutral', 'hardening (roughly, glottalizing)', or 'softening (roughly, voicing)'. We assume the effects of these processes below without explicitly identifying them. Aside from these effects, and a limited amount of cluster simplification, there is very little phonology to obscure the boundaries between formatives. In addition, there is a rather close correspondence between individual affixes and distinct morphological functions. While there are a few cases of multiple affixes with (roughly) the same function, and vice versa, in general the language presents the kind of structure represented by the ideal agglutinating type, and the classical notion of the 'morpheme'.

To illustrate some of the morphological possibilities, we will summarize below the major kinds of suffixes by semantic types.

We can identify first a group of suffixes which is of central significance in the language, one corresponding to notions of *location*. These suffixes fill virtually all of the functions usually performed by prepositions or postpositions in other languages. Suffixes added to the stem /la-/ 'go' create the difference between *laxso* 'go through something', *la'i-* 'go into something', *laqa* 'go past something', and many others. Some such suffixed formations take objects directly: thus, *dəχʷsəq'a-χa gʷaxλawi* 'to jump over the stick' consists of the stem /dəχʷ-/ and the suffix /-səq'a/ over', followed by the direct object marking determiner /χa/ and the object noun /gʷaxλawi/'stick'. Other suffixed forms take their objects as part of a prepositional phrase. The preposition in these cases has no independent semantic content: it is uniformly the same element /la-/ (historically identical with the verb 'go', and replaced when its object is first person by /gax-/, historically identical with the verb 'come') followed by an object marking determiner. From the stem *λ'əpa* 'climb' can be formed both *λ'əpusto* 'climb up' and *λ'əpaχa* 'climb down'; both require their object to appear preceded by *laxa* (/la-/ plus object determiner): cf. *ƛ'əpusto laxa ƛo's* 'climb (up) the tree' vs. *ƛ'əpaxa laxa ƛo's* 'climb down the tree'.

Besides general directional and locational notions, these suffixes express a large number of concrete locations: 'into the water', 'onto a flat object', 'through a round opening in the side of an object', etc. They express features of the landscape ('into the woods', 'at the mouth of a river', 'on a rock') or of everyday life ('in a canoe', 'on the fire', 'in front of the house'). A particularly common set of suffixes is /-iɫ/ '(on the floor) in the house', /-s/ 'on the ground', and /-is/ 'on the beach', which occur as further specification with many other locational elements (e.g. *dzəlkʷa* 'run', *dzəlxʷsi'stala* 'run around in circles', *dzəlxʷsi'stəliɫəla* 'run around in circles in the house', *dzəlxʷsi'stəlisəla* 'run around in circles on the beach', etc.). Not all locations are directly represented by suffixes, of course: specific places like 'to the left of the big tree', 'outside the window', etc. are still represented outside of the verb word. The object need not be more specific than the type whose sense is conveyed by verb suffixes, however, in order to call for external expression: it need only be one for which no particular suffix exists. Thus, in (1) below, the main verb *axaltso* means 'to put in a hollow place', but as there is no suffix specifically referring to holes in the ground, the external specification is needed as well:

(1)   Axalts'oxda 'wats'e xa   xaq  laxa      xʷəp'əs
      put in-DET   dog   DET bone PREP DET hole in ground
      'The dog buried the bone in the hole'

The content of suffixes thus does not serve to replace or 'incorporate' an external locational or directional phrase, but only to render the meaning of the verbal form more specific in this respect.

A particularly interesting set of locational suffixes refers to parts of the body. Most major body parts (e.g. 'head', 'arm', 'tooth', etc.) have corresponding suffixes, which can be attached either to nouns or to verbs (as in, for example, both *dəiɫbənd* 'wipe someone's nose' and *kʷawiɫpa* 'hole in the nose', which contain the same suffix /-iɫpa/ 'nose'). Again, while many body parts are represented by suffixes, this is not true for all named parts of the body: in (2) below, an external phrase is necessary because there is no suffix that corresponds exactly to *qoma* 'thumb'.

(2)   Ləxtsan-ənƛa-sən    qoma
      hit on hand-1SG-my thumb
      'I hit my thumb (with a hammer)'

Although the meaning of the verb specifies (through the lexical suffix /-tsana/) that the object hit was (part of) the hand, the more precise specification appears as the object of the complex word form: here, *-sən qoma*.

One group of suffixes is limited in applicability in that they attach almost exclusively to numeral stems. They correspond in use to the classifier elements commonly found in languages such as Chinese. As in such languages, when a numeral modifies a noun (as in 'five sticks'), a classifier element must be used which is determined in part by properties of the noun modified. In Kwakw'ala, these are suffixes on the numeral word. Thus, *ma'ł* 'two' is the form used in counting, but *ma'lukʷ* is used to count people, *ma'łəxsa* to count flat objects, *ma'łəx̌a* to count dishes, etc. Thus, we have *ma'lukʷ bəgʷanəm* 'two men', *m'łəxsa map* 'two blankets', *ma'łəx̌a ha'mats'i* 'two plates'. There are roughly a dozen of these classifiers for general counting, plus a few for measures of length ('finger-width', 'fathom') and time ('days', 'times', as in *ma'łp'əna* 'twice'). In a few cases, these have developed special meanings: thus, *ma'łsgəm* is literally 'two round objects', but more commonly 'two dollars'. The number 'ten' in counting is *la'stu*, but when suffixed with a classifier, *nəqa-* (e.g. *nəqasgəm* 'ten dollars'). These classifier suffixes do not correspond to any independently occurring words.

Other suffixes determine the syntactic class of words. Intransitive verbs generally do not require a suffix, but many transitive verbs end in *-a* (e.g. *'amx̌* 'watertight', *'amx̌a* 'to make watertight'). After certain (mostly locative) suffixes, transitive verbs end in *-(n)d* (e.g. *kʷ'əmdədzud* 'suck on (a flat surface)', related to *kʷ'əmta* 'suck').

A large class of suffixes forms nouns from other stems. As one might expect, the range of notions expressed here is vast. A few examples include: 'instrument for (verb)ing' (e.g. *ts'usa* 'dig wild alfalfa roots', *ts'uyayu* 'stick for digging wild alfalfa roots'), 'thing which could be (verb)ed (e.g. *t'osa* 'cut a slice from something', *t'it'osəma* 'something sliceable'), 'reason for (verb)ing' (e.g. *la* 'go', *lagił* 'reason for going'), 'expert at (verb)ing' (e.g. *q'ək'a* 'bite,' *q'ək'enuxʷ* 'good trapper'), 'something that has been (verb)ed' (e.g. *kʷ'əpa* 'cut', *kʷ'əkʷ'əpsala* 'cut up into little pieces', from which can be further derived *kʷ'əkʷ'əpsa'akʷ* 'stuff that has been cut up into little pieces'), 'residue, remains of' (e.g. *gawiqanəm* 'small clams', *gagəwixmut* 'clamshells'). The meanings of many of these suffixes can be paraphrased by expressions with independent nouns. Not all nouns correspond to suffixes, however, and there is no resemblance in form between noun roots and suffixes even where there is a resemblance in function.

Such noun forming suffixes are quite parallel to elements found in many languages: consider English *-er* 'one who (verb)s' or 'instrument with which one (verb)s', for example. Kwakw'ala also has a set of suffixes corresponding to *verbs*, however, some of which are more unusual. Though many languages could provide parallels for some members of this class (e.g. *-amas* 'cause', as in *ɬə'lamas* 'kill', from *ɬə'l* 'be dead'; or *-(g)ila* 'make', as in *gukʷila* 'build a house', from *gukʷ* 'house'), others are less common. Examples include: *-p'ala* 'smells like', as in *gexʷp'ala* 'smells like deer', from the same root as *gewas* 'deer'; *-alisəm* 'die of (verb)ing', as in *qʷ'ayalisəm* 'die of crying', from *qʷ'asa* 'cry'; *-g* 'eat (noun)', as in *gəgewasg* 'eat deer', from *gewas* 'deer'; *-wətəla* 'carry along in the hand', as in *ləxʼwətəla* 'going along carrying a basket', from *ləxe* 'basket'; *-a'mala* 'quarrel about', as in *supa'mala* 'quarrel about an axe', from *supa* 'chop', and many others.

What is special about these verb-like affixes is not only the large number of concrete meanings they express, but also the central role they play in expressing meanings. In most languages, adverbs and quantifiers are subordinate to main verbs. In Kwakw'ala, however, main verb meanings are often expressed by suffixes added on to adverb stems. The suffix *-qənu*, for example, means 'be attacked, snuck up on': it appears in formations such as *aɬaqənud* 'to sneak up on (someone) from behind' (cf. *aɬi* 'backside, behind') and *yəxqənu* 'be attacked, get sick, quickly' (cf. *yəxa* 'be quick'). *-mola* 'walk together' appears in *q'e'mola* 'many walk together' (cf. the stem *q'əy-* 'many') and *'wi'lamola* 'all walk together' (cf. *'wi'la* 'all'); *-dzəqʷa* 'speak' appears in *'wi'ldzəqʷa* 'all spoke' (cf. again *'wi'la* 'all') and *'et'ədzəqʷa* 'to speak again' (cf. *'et'id* 'to do again'), etc. In these cases, there are independent verbs expressing the same meanings as the verb-like suffixes, but in other cases only suffixes are available to express a given meaning (cf. the verb *ax'exsd* 'want' already cited, from the semantically empty stem /ax-/ and the suffix *-exsd* 'want'; the latter also appears in forms such as *q'aq'oɬa'exsd* 'want to learn', from *q'aq'oɬa* '(try to) learn'). This central role played by suffixes with 'verbal' content is basic to the character of 'polysynthetic' languages.

In addition to being noun-like and verb-like, suffixes may also correspond to what in other languages can be adjectives (e.g. *-bidu'* 'small', *-dzi* 'large', *-kas'u* 'beautiful', *-o'ɬ* 'ugly', and a few others) and adverbs (e.g. *-ak* 'easily', *-uɬ* 'completely', *-χɬe* 'very'). It is not easy to draw the line between these and suffixes representing a class of sentence modifiers. The latter include markers for the source of information (e.g. 'from hearsay, it is said', 'evidently, it appears', 'in a dream') and for the degree of the speaker's confidence in his assertion (e.g. 'perhaps', 'probably', 'certainly', 'it seems').

Another rather interesting group of suffixes function as conjunctions. That coordinating elements should appear as suffixes (e.g. 'and so', 'but') is not particularly unusual (cf. Latin -*que* 'and', a clitic appearing in the position of a suffix), nor are subordinating conjunctions unusual as suffixes on the subordinate verb. Kwakw'ala has two suffixes, however, that function somewhat differently: -*to'yi* 'to do while (verb)-ing' and -*dzək*ʷ 'to do before (verb)ing'. These appear as suffixes on the *matrix* verb, marking the fact that a later verb is subordinated as in (3):

(3)     Q'aq'alalo's-to'yə-x̣os xʷənukʷə-xs ha'mixsilaex
        watch-while doing-her child-COMP    cooking
        'She's watching her child while she cooks'

In this sentence, the matrix verb ('watch') is converted by the addition of -*to'yə* into a verb taking a sentential complement (here, -*x̣s ha'mixsilaex* 'cooking') in addition to its normal arguments (here, -*x̣os xʷənukʷ* 'her (own) child').

We see thus that affixation processes in Kwakw'ala can supply elements corresponding to all major word classes. Other affixes correspond to what in many languages are inflectional categories: temporal (remote past, recent past, future, and recently-completed), aspectual (momentaneous or inchoative, continuative, occasional, habitual, and repetitive), voice (two distinct passive forms, depending on which of two categories of verbal object corresponds to the subject of the derived form), and modality (hypothetical, potential, optative, and exhortative). To these, one can also add the three distinct plural formations (simple plural, distributive, and iterative or repetitive). As in many languages, it is hard to find secure criteria for classifying these elements as derivational or inflectional: we take it to be significant for the derivational status of at least the temporal, aspectual, and plural groups that they are (a) optional, and present only where necessary for emphasis or disambiguation; and (b) equally applicable to words of any syntactic function or word class (thus, *xʷak*ʷ*əna* 'canoe' has a future form *xʷak*ʷ*ənaƛ* 'canoe that will be, that will come into existence', and a recent past form *xʷak*ʷ*ənaxdi* 'canoe that has been destroyed'). These forms involve the same suffixes as those appearing with verbs to mark the same categories, and this is general across all members of these classes.

We have seen how remarkably uniform these word formation processes are in formal terms, since they are confined almost entirely to suffixation. We should note, however, that there is not the same uniformity in the semantic and syntactic relations between the basic stem and derived words. In general, a suffix modifies the meaning of just the stem material to which it is added, but this is not always the case: the suffix -wəł, for example, has an effect on the sense of a *following* locative suffix, reversing the direction it implies (e.g. *aχts'ud* 'put into' vs. *aχ'wəłts'ud* 'take out of'). In this case, we could perhaps consider the combination /-wəł-ts'u-/ as a unit meaning 'out of', but the productive nature of the relationship (all other locative suffixes implying direction have reversed forms with /-wəł-/) suggests we have to do with a separate unit here. We might, however, treat this as an *in*fix, added to a stem ending in a locative suffix and positioned before this latter. A similar analysis could be given for the suffix -əm, which specifies that the things whose location is specified by a *following* locative suffix are plural: thus, *aχaχud* 'put down' vs. *aχəməχud* 'put several down.' Again, we could say that -əm is infixed into a stem ending in a locative suffix, and placed immediately before this.

Even when the 'scope' of a suffix is clearly a part of the meaning of the preceding stem, different suffixes may choose different parts of this meaning. The suffix -enuxʷ, for instance, means 'good at (verb)ing'. With an intransitive verb, it is clear that it is the subject of the verb who is described as 'good at' whatever it describes (e.g. *gəlqa* 'swim', *gəlq'enuxʷ* 'good swimmer'). With a transitive verb, however, it is at least logically possible that it could be either the subject or the object that is described: thus, *məχa* means 'punch, strike with fist', and one might think that a *mə'nenuxʷ* might be either one who is good at punching, or one who is good at getting punched (either very resistant to injury, or perhaps prone to excite hostility, for example). In fact, it describes only the former, and means 'good puncher'; and in general, the suffix -enuxʷ always describes one who is good at, or prone to performing some action – as its *agent*, not its patient.

This behavior can be contrasted with that of the locative suffixes, for example. The intransitive verb *kʷə'lił* 'lie down in the house' involves the suffix -*ił* '(on the floor) in the house', which obviously describes the position of the subject in this example. The transitive verb *aχ'alił* 'put (on the floor) in the house' involves the same suffix; here it describes the position of the object rather than the subject. Indeed, with transitive verbs it is only the object that can be described by a locative suffix. The verb *łaƛa'lə'amasa*, for example, means 'try to kill', and we might expect that by adding the suffix -*ił* (followed by a 1sg. subject marker and the object-marking determiner), we could produce a sentence such as (4):

(4)   *łaƛalə'amadz-ił-ənλa-χoχda        qaqadinuxʷ
       try to kill-in house-1SG-these(OBJ) flies
       'I'm in the house trying to kill these flies'

The sentence is ungrammatical, however, because -*ił* cannot describe the location of the *subject* of such a transitive verb, and apparently flies are not the sort of thing that can be appropriately described as located '(on the floor) in the house'. Quite a number of Kwakw'ala suffixes are similar in that they make reference to the subject of an intransitive, or the object of a transitive verb. In chapter III.2 following, we will see that these are just the positions typically occupied by the central semantic category *figure* or *patient*, and it is in fact quite common in most languages for derivational material to affect or refer to this part of the meaning of the stem to which they apply.

There is some evidence for the view that the semantic category is relevant here, rather than the syntactic combination of intransitive subject/transitive object. Consider formations involving the suffix -(*g*)*il* 'make', for example (e.g. *k'ikʷila* 'make a totem pole', from *k'ikʷ* 'totem pole'). These are formally intransitive verbs, and do not take objects. If locative suffixes described intransitive subjects or transitive objects as a strictly syntactic category, it ought to be possible to add -*ił* 'in the house' to them to describe the location of the subject. In fact, however, \**k'ikʷililłuxʷ* 'he is making a totem pole in the house' is not well formed. This is because the figure or patient of the action described is not 'he', but rather the totem pole, and the latter is not represented by an independent constituent in syntactic structure (though it plays its expected role in the semantic structure of the utterance). The appropriate generalization would thus seem to be both semantic and syntactic: -*ił* 'in the house' (and the other suffixes of the same class) locate the figure or patient of a verb stem, provided that this semantic category corresponds to some independent external syntactic argument of the verb.

There is at least one suffix that displays yet another sort of behavior. Plurality of second or third person human participants may be marked by the suffix -*xda'xʷ*. This generally refers to the subject or to a possessor (e.g. *dənx'idəxda'xʷ* 'they sing', with an intransitive verb, or, with a transitive verb, *ƛəlx'idəxda'xʷ* 'they carry (it)', or, in a possessive construction [where *sis* marks third person possessor without regard to number, and plurality is shown by suffix on 'friend'], *sis 'nəmuxʷda'xʷi* 'their friend'. When a transitive verb has human subject and object, however, the suffix may express plurality of either (e.g. *hamx'idəxda'xoƛ* can be either 'he eats you (pl.)' or 'they eat you (sg. or pl.)').

In the survey of Kwakw'ala derivational categories given above, we hope to have provided some idea of the properties related to the traditional label 'polysynthetic'. Much of what is unusual about such a language resides in the range of functions that can be filled by derivational formations. Many of these correspond to syntactic functions in languages of more familiar type. It is not only their content that is of interest, however, but also their relative freedom. In general, their occurrence is limited only by semantic or lexical factors, rather than the sort of principle which is often represented as a set of (arbitrary) position classes in many other languages. This gives rise to the possibility that alternate orders can exist, corresponding to distinct meanings. Consider the suffixes *-amas* 'cause' and *-exsd* 'want', for example. From the verb *ne'nakᵂ* 'go home', we can form *ne'nakᵂ'exsd* 'want to go home'. From this, in turn, we can form *ne'nakᵂ'exsdamas* 'cause to want to go home', as in (5):

(5)     Ne'nakᵂ'exsdamas-ux̣ᵂ          John gaxən
        cause to want to go home-he John PREP(ISG)
        'John made me want to go home'

On the other hand, from *q'aq'oƛa* 'learn', we can make *q'aq'oƛamas* 'cause to learn, teach', and from this can be formed in turn *q'aq'oƛa-madzexsd* 'want to teach', as in (6):

(6)     Q'aq'oƛamadzexsd-ux̣ᵂ     John gaxən          q-ən gukᵂile
        want to cause to learn-he John PREP(ISG)     that-I build house
        'John wants to teach me to build a house'

Note that in (5) and (6), the same suffixes appear on the verbs, but in opposite orders corresponding to distinct meanings ('cause to want' in (5) vs. 'want to cause' in (6)). With this sort of capability, there is obviously a sort of recursive capacity built into the system of Kwakw'ala word formation, such that one could (in principle) make up new forms of arbitrary complexity ('want to cause to want to cause to ...'). The extent to which this is exploited in the language today appears to be limited, however: only in the formal style characteristic of traditional storytelling does one find much productive use of very complicated formations.

Of course, as with any lexical system, some Kwakw'ala suffixation is subject to variation in the extent to which particular affixes can be used to create new forms. The limitations are not due to the formal nature of the system, but rather to the (often arbitrary) contents of the lexicon. Some suffixes can be freely added to virtually any semantically compatible stem (e.g. the locatives; *-agawi'* 'extreme, -er [used to form comparatives]'; *-(g)il* 'make'; etc.). In other cases, more than one suffix is available with the same meaning, and the choice is largely arbitrary or lexical in nature. For example, both *-əm* and *-ayu* form instrument nouns, but the choice between them is arbitrary: one says, for example, *k'əmλayu* 'adze' from *k'əmλa* 'to adze', but *sələm* 'drill', from *səla* 'to drill'.

Other suffixes can be used with some, but not other stems with which their meaning would seem to be compatible; and there is often no other, comparable morphological formation to fill the gap. The suffix *-anuma* means 'to come to (verb)', as in *sixʷanuma* 'to come to paddle', but only applies to a fairly limited class of stems (e.g. *\*qətanuma* 'to come to troutfish', from *qəta* 'fish for trout' does not exist, though it would appear to be semantically, syntactically, and morphologically well formed). Some are really quite limited in productivity: for example, a formative *-mp* appears only in a few kinship terms (such as *ump* 'father', *'abəmp* 'mother', and *ginp* [from /gis-mp/] 'wife's sister'). Further, in many cases a derived formation has acquired a special meaning, with the result that it is sometimes no longer available to express its most 'literal' interpretation. This issue was treated above in section 1.4, in connection with the general problem of the productivity of word formation processes.

Languages like Kwakw'ala are characterized by an essentially open ended set of word formation processes, and a rather close (though by no means perfect) relation between the formal effects of word formation and the functions it serves. We now turn briefly to a language type in which the word formation system contrasts strongly with this state of affairs.

## 2.2 *Derivation in Classical Arabic*
The Semitic languages, particularly Arabic (in its various dialects) and Hebrew, are well known as representatives of a very different morphological type, that of '(in)flectional' languages. The term (in)flectional here refers to all of word formation, including derivational as well as inflectional morphology. We will ignore here any of the variations introduced by inflectional morphology in the sense of chapter III.3 below. In principle, in these languages there is a narrowly limited and formally very regular set of patterns, into each of which any one of a large set of roots can be shaped. The relations among these patterns thus serve as stem formation rules, but the resulting system is of quite a different character from that of languages like English or Kwakw'ala.

We can consider as an example the form of verbal derivation in Classical Arabic. Each verbal stem is based on a root, whose formal distinctness from other roots is based on its consonants. Thus, *katab* 'write' *qatal* 'kill', *ḥasun* 'be good, beautiful' can each be identified by the sequence of consonants that make them up, abstracting away from the vowels and the syllabic structure. The sequence *k-t-b* thus appears in words related to writing, *q-t-l* in words relating to killing, and *ḥ-s-n* in words related to goodness or beauty. Most roots in Classical Arabic (and its near relatives) have three consonants, though some have more and a few only two. We will describe the patterns of the great majority of words, referring to the root by three consonants $c_1$-$c_2$-$c_3$.

In addition to the 'basic' verb form of Classical Arabic, there are some fourteen derived verbal patterns. Of these, the number with enough actual forms to have practical significance is at most ten. All verbs have the same formal relation between the 'base' and the 'derivatives'. This formal regularity, however, is not matched by a comparable functional uniformity. Some patterns carry a number of possible meanings, with frequent idiosyncrasies for particular verbs. Further, the range of meanings covered by some forms overlaps with that carried by others. Despite the theoretical possibility of fifteen distinct forms for each root, roots typically only appear in three or four forms; further derived forms may be created anew, but these often have only a tenuous status. This sort of situation is entirely consistent with the listing of forms in the lexicon: only those items appear that are part of the language (as opposed to others, formally well formed but not in fact part of the lexical stock); and entries in the lexicon, being autonomous lexical items, are free to undergo the sort of drift in meaning that leads to apparent chaos in the relation between form and function.

To illustrate this situation, we take the (linguist's typical) Classical Arabic root, that of *katab* 'write'. The third derivative (in the classical grammatical scheme) has the form $c_1āc_2ac_3$: thus, the third derivative of *katab* is *kātab*, with the sense 'write to (someone)'. This and many other third derivatives can be generally glossed as 'directing an action or quality toward someone': cf. *xāsan* 'treat harshly', from *xasun* 'be harsh', *ḥāsan* 'treat kindly', from *ḥasun* 'be good'. Other third derivative forms, however, have the sense 'try to do something': cf. *xāda9* 'try to deceive', from *xada9* 'deceive' [the symbol /9/ here and below denotes a voiced pharyngeal fricative]; *qātal* 'fight with and try to kill', from *qatal* 'kill'. Still others are hard to classify, and represent individual specializations of meaning: e.g. *fāxar* 'compete with (someone) for praise', from *faxar* 'praise'.

In addition to its third derivative form, *katab* has other derivatives. The fourth derivative, for example, has the shape ʔac$_1$c$_2$ac$_3$, yielding (for *katab*) the form ʔaktab 'dictate'. Many fourth derivative forms, like ʔaktab, can be glossed as 'causative', but not all: from *kaḏab* 'lie', for example, the fourth derivative ʔakḏab can mean either 'cause to lie' or 'call or prove someone a liar'. Other fourth derivatives display other idiosyncratic meanings.

The sixth derivative has the form $tac_1āc_2ac_3$ which (again, from *katab*) yields *takātab* 'correspond'. Other sixth derivatives also express reciprocal action (e.g. *taqātal* 'fight with each other', from *qatal* 'kill'), but some others express pretending or simulation: *tašāġal* 'pretend to be busy', from *šaġal* 'occupy'. The eighth derivative has the form $c_1tac_2ac_3$, giving *ktatab* 'be registered' from *katab*. These forms often have reflexive sense. Sometimes, however, they are reciprocal: cf. *qtatal* 'fight with each other'. The tenth derivative has the shape $stac_1c_2ac_3$, giving *staktab* 'ask someone to write' from *katab*. Other tenth derivatives, again, have rather different meanings: cf. *staḥsan* 'consider good, admire' from *ḥasun* 'be good, beautiful', or *staʕlam* 'seek information' from *ʕalim* 'know'.

In some instances, the basic verb form may not exist, because the root is a noun. When verbal derivatives are formed from the consonants of a noun, the meaning is likely to be even more idiosyncratic. From *sāḥil* 'coast' we have the third derivative *sāḥal* 'make for the coast'; from *ʕayn* 'eye', *ʕāyan* 'see with one's eyes'; from *safar* '(a) journey' we can form *sāfar* 'travel', etc. None of these has anything obvious to do with the 'central' meanings of third derivative forms ('direct an action or quality toward someone', or 'pretend to do something'). Other forms derived from nouns, however, may show greater regularity: thus, many fourth derivatives are causative, as in *ʔamṭar* 'produce rain', from *maṭar* 'rain'; *ʔaqfar* 'become desert', from *qafr* 'desert'. Similarly, the tenth derivative form *stamṭar* 'ask for rain' is parallel in sense to *staktab* 'ask someone to write'. By contrast, *šarraq* 'go east', a second derivative (pattern: $c_1ac_2c_2ac_3$) from *šarq* 'east' has no particular similarity to *qattal* 'massacre', an intensive form from *qatal* 'kill'.

This system of verbal derivation is not limited to Classical Arabic, of course. Hebrew verbs for example appear in seven distinct 'binyanim', or 'constructions', exactly parallel to the Classical Arabic types. In this case, two of the patterns are completely productive and semantically regular: the so-called 'puʔal' ($c_1uc_2ac_3$) and 'hufʔal' ($huc_1c_2ac_3$) forms always represent passive correspondents of other derivatives (the 'piʔel' pattern, $c_1ic_2ec_3$, and the 'hifʔil' pattern, $hic_1c_2ic_3$, respectively). They can thus be disregarded here, and thought of as properly part of the inflectional rather than the derivational system (voice is after all a typically inflectional category, when represented by a productive marker). In the remaining five forms, we find the usual semi-predictability combined with considerable idiosyncrasy. Each root appears in a particular selection of the five lexically possible root shapes, and even though the number of forms is considerably less than in Classical Arabic, it appears that there is no single root in the language which appears in all five (or seven) 'binyanim'.

A similar sort of 'root and pattern' system functions in nominal derivation. Classical Arabic shows about thirty-five distinct patterns in nouns, and in addition a set of prefixes and suffixes (though not many of these). The situation is thus more complex than in the verb, but not different in principle: each pattern has a certain 'core' of meanings, such as $c_1uc_2ayc_3$ for diminuitives (e.g. *kulayb* 'little dog', from *kalb* 'dog'), $c_1uc_2\bar{a}c_3$ for diseases (e.g. *suɣāl* 'cough'), $c_1\bar{a}c_2ic_3$ for agents (e.g. *kātib* 'writer'), etc. Nonetheless, there is a far from perfect correlation between formal types and functional classes. Again also, a single root may appear in several forms, but not in all, and the range of forms that actually occur is only partly predictable from the meaning of the root, since it is partly a lexical idiosyncrasy.

Altogether, such a system is quite different from one based more directly on affixation, as in Kwakw'ala. For one thing, the limited (though substantial) number of formally distinct processes available in, for example, Classical Arabic verbal derivation means that the correlation between forms and functions cannot be as close as in an affixing system where distinct affixes can usually be created without limit to represent distinct functions. Given the limited number of patterns available, a single derivational pattern may have several uses – partly out of necessity, and partly as a result of individual changes in meaning of lexical items. The other side of this coin is the fact that more than one pattern may come to serve the same function: fourth derivative forms such as *ʔaktab* 'dictate' are frequently causative in function, but the same is true of second derivative forms ($c_1ac_2c_2ac_3$) like *ɣallam* 'teach' from *ɣalim* 'know'; and we have already seen that both the sixth derivative *taqātal* and the eighth derivative *qtatal* of *qatal* 'kill' have the reciprocal sense of 'fight with one another'. Thus, the connection between forms and functions in such a system is in principle a many to many relation.

The formal character of Semitic word formation processes has other consequences, as well. Since each pattern is a unitary whole, and provides a complete framework of vowels, affixes, and syllable structure within which the consonants of a root appear, it follows that such processes cannot be cumulative. Once a root has been put into a given pattern, the only way to put it into another pattern is to replace the entire structure – thus destroying any reflection of the 'first stage' in a derivation. Derived forms thus cannot be the basis of further derivatives. In Kwakw'ala, it is always possible to add more suffixes to already suffixed forms. This possibility is what leads to the semi-recursive word formation systems of polysynthetic languages. In the Semitic system, virtually all of the functional connections between a derivative and the basic stem must be associated with a one step relation. Of course, the

Semitic languages also employ a limited amount of affixation, and these affixes can be added to derived forms, but they are primarily inflectional in their use. The degree of cumulative derivation found in these languages is extremely low.

The aspect of the Semitic word and pattern system that gives rise to the traditional view of these languages as (in)flectional is the difficulty of dividing the word into coherent and non-overlapping pieces. Since words are formed by inserting the root consonants into a discontinuous pattern, it is not possible to segment a form into a part representing the root and another part representing the derivational function. For example, it is not possible to segment Arabic *gallam* 'teach' into two non-overlapping formatives meaning 'know' and 'cause': the two are inextricably bound up with one another in the overall structure of the word. Contrast this with the Kwakw'ala form *q'aq'oƛ'amas* 'teach', where *q'aq'oƛ'a* means '(try to) learn' and *-(a)mas* means 'cause'. (In)flectional languages differ from agglutinating (and polysynthetic) ones precisely in this 'fusional' character of their word formation systems, developed perhaps more highly in the Semitic languages than anywhere else.

The more common kind of morphological fusion, found in languages all over the world, is even more opaque than what we have just discussed above. In Semitic, it is possible to isolate in a given word a set of consonants corresponding to the root, and a set of vowels (plus syllable structure, plus perhaps some affixal material) corresponding to the derivational category. Though these overlap in actual words, and thus resist analysis in terms of a string of discrete formatives, it is nonetheless possible to abstract the relative contributions of the two from a given form. In inflection, however, we often find instances in which several categories coalesce in a single formative in a way that resists any such analysis. Icelandic, for example, marks nouns for both case and number; but any given ending in the system conflates the two: from the noun *steinn* 'stone', for example, we have genitive singular *steins*, dative singular *steini*, genitive plural *steina*, and dative plural *steinum*. Clearly, we cannot take these endings apart into a portion that indicates 'genitive' or 'dative' and a portion that indicates 'plural'.

We might ask whether this kind of fusional formation (which is quite common in the marking of inflectional categories) is to be found in derivation as well. The answer, however, is likely to be a matter of definition. By their very nature, derivational categories do not have the sort of compulsory applicability to all forms of a given word class that inflectional ones do, and thus do not provide the same sort of support for analyzing forms as 'necessarily' reflecting several categories in a single form (similar to the inflectional paradigms of nouns and verbs). In fact, if we find a form which appears to bear a derivational relationship to some other form, but in which there is no overt formal resemblance to be abstracted from the pair (as when we say, for example, that in Old Irish the form *gal* 'fight' serves as verbal noun corresponding to *fichid* '(he) fights'), we are likely to describe this state of affairs not as fusional derivation, but rather as suppletion.

We have discussed above two properties of Semitic word derivation, the limitations on cumulation and on segmentability, and the many to many character of the relation between forms and functions. The word and pattern derivational system of Semitic contributes to the second of these as well as the first. There are, after all, only a limited number of canonical patterns for words that are logically possible: certainly fewer than the number of affixes that could be created out of a language's phonetic resources. It is also possible, however, for a language to limit the number of its word formation processes even when they are affixal. Most of the languages of the Philippines, for example, make use of a small, closed set of affixes for verbal derivational functions. To a limited extent, these can be cumulated, since affixation can always lend itself to derivative-based derivation; but the limited number of affixes employed (combined with the fact that affixes do not have unique functional interpretations) contributes to the character of a system resembling the Semitic one in its many to many relation between forms and functions, and lack of recursion. Ilocano, for instance, displays in large part a word and pattern system like that of Classical Arabic, but based on 'patterns' consisting of selections from a limited set of affixes, rather than the kind of vowel plus syllable structure skeletons for word forms characteristic of Semitic.

This discussion has contrasted two very different types of language, not to imply a discrete categorization (as is explicit in the traditional classificatory schemes), but to illustrate the range of processes found in languages. It is word formation processes, not languages, that can usefully be distinguished in type. A language may well make predominant use of a single process type (as is indeed true of both languages discussed above). More generally, though, we find a mixture of processes. English is an excellent example: in addition to a great many processes of affixation (some of which are potentially applicable to arbitrarily complex derived forms), we also find a certain amount of 'word and pattern' derivation in the Ablaut system (e.g. the relation between *song* and *sing*). A mutually exclusive categorization of languages on the basis of their morphology is inevitably either trivializing, procrustean, or impossible.

## 3.0 Compounding processes

To stem modification processes such as those discussed above, we oppose processes of compounding: word formation based on the combination of two or more members of (potentially) open lexical classes. Often the two items that are brought together in a compound also appear as independent words in the language, as in English *truck-driver*, *skeet-shoot* (clay pigeon shoot), *open-door* (*policy*). In some cases, only one of the two appears as an independent word: the classic example of this situation is the name of berries in English, such as *raspberry*, *huckleberry*, *loganberry*, *cranberry*. In some cases, both members of a compound are elements that only occur combined with others: e.g. *chipmunk*, *mushroom*, *somersault*. Frequently the sense of an element in a compound seems to have nothing to do with the sense of a (formally similar) element that appears elsewhere: *broadcast*, *black-smith*, *hot dog*, *strawberry*. We will consider such formations to be compounds (as opposed to stem modifications) even when one (or both) of the elements involved does not occur freely, so long as they form a part of a structural pattern based on open ended word classes. That is, where a word formation pattern involves two or more such members of open classes, it will be treated as compounding; where it involves only one (together, perhaps, with an element drawn from a circumscribed list, not parallel with any independently motivated part of speech class in the language), we will treat it as an instance of stem modification (including, perhaps, the addition of an affix).

The line between compounding and stem modification is not always easy to draw (do we call *telegraph*, *telephone*, *phonograph*, *dictaphone*, etc. compounds, prefixes plus stems, or stems plus suffixes?), but this is not a matter of major importance since the division is primarily a matter of convenience. More significant, however, is the distinction between compounds and phrases: since the former are the result of word formation processes, while the latter result from syntactic operations, we might expect them to display interestingly different properties. On the other hand, since both are instances of the combination of independent elements into larger units whose form and meaning are (at least in part) based on those of the items combined, we might also expect them to show interesting similarities. Much of the discussion below will focus on this issue, exploring the ways in which compounds do and do not reflect the properties of phrasal constructions.

One difference between compounds and phrases follows from their definitions. Since compounds are lexical items, formed by rules of word formation, they are *words*, while phrases are not. It is noted below (in chapter III.3 of this volume and elsewhere) that there are a variety of potential definitions for the notion 'word', and that these sometimes fail to converge on the same class of linguistic items in a given language. Nonetheless, many languages provide more or less reliable criteria for distinguishing words from phrases that can be of use in identifying compounds. In English, for instance, compounds are stressed on the first of two (independently stressable) elements (e.g. *hót dog* 'frankfurter'), while phrases are stressed on the last such element (e.g. *hot dóg* 'dog that is hot').

Other languages provide other criteria which may be useful for the same purpose. In the Wu dialects of Chinese, for example, compounds differ from phrases with respect to the phonological rules of tone sandhi. Another kind of phonological mark for words is manifested by stress in Mandarin Chinese. Contrastive stress can only fall on the stress center of a 'word', including compounds. The compounds *bái-guǒ* 'gingko' and *qīng-guǒ* 'olive' are both based on the noun *guǒ* 'fruit', and both have stress on this second element. If the two are contrasted, in a sentence such as 'I told you to buy gingkos; how come you bought olives instead?' (cf. Chao 1968:385), the contrastive stress falls on the stress centers of the two compounds, and thus in both cases on *guǒ*, rather than on the parts of the compounds that are actually different (here, *bái* vs. *qīng*). When the same structures are taken as phrases, however, contrastive stress is free to fall on the words in which they differ (since each, being a word, has an independent stress center). The unity of compounds is thus demonstrated by the fact that, like any other single words, they present only a single possible location for contrastive stress.

Aside from phonological criteria, elements of morphology can also provide indications of compound status. A language with genitive inflection for noun modifiers in phrases may well not show such inflection in compounds (cf. English *dúck-egg*, a compound, vs. *duck's égg*, a phrase). In Mandarin, there is a particle *de* which marks modifiers in many phrases: the presence of this particle identifies a construction as phrasal, and thus as non-compound (the opposite is not quite true, as *de* is lost after certain modifiers even in phrases).

In studying compounding processes, we find questions of the same general sort as those associated with other word formation rules. Compounding processes can differ with respect to the class(es) of the elements compounded, and the structures that result. Some of these structures may be characterized by additional elements, not directly associated with any of the compound items but rather with the compound structure itself. In German, for example, one of several elements (*-e*, *-en*, or *-(e s)*) is often inserted between members of a compound.

Though these to some extent resemble original (genitive) case endings on the first element, from a synchronic point of view they cannot be identified with these, and must be treated as purely markers of compounding. In *Bischoffskonferenz* 'bishop-s-conference:conference of bishops', the element -s could only be a genitive *singular* marker if it were a case ending, and this is inappropriate to the sense of the compound. In *Schwanenhals* 'swan-en-neck:swan's neck', the element -en could not be the genitive ending, since the genitive of 'swan' is *Schwans* (cf. *Hals des Schwans* 'neck of the swan', a phrasal equivalent). These elements are motivated only by the word formation pattern itself, in which they serve as a sort of morphological 'glue' rather than as independently meaningful elements.

The comparison of compounding with the formation of phrases involves several different kinds of structural questions. Aside from phonological and morphological idiosyncrasies such as those surveyed above, we must also ask about the ways in which the stems related in a compound structure differ in arrangement from the same stems in a related phrase. For example, English has relatively fixed word order, with verbs preceding their objects in phrases; but there are also object plus verb constructions such as *sight-see*, *housekeep*, etc. that we can thus identify as compounds (despite the existence of other compounds, like *spoil-sport* and *pickpocket*, with verb plus object order). In these cases, the compound status is confirmed by the initial stress.

Compounds are commonly paraphraseable (at least approximately) by phrases, and the comparison of the two may reveal systematic aspects of compound formation. This is especially true with respect to the other major aspect of compounds: the relation of their interpretations to that of their component stems. The interpretation of phrases is in general quite 'compositional': given the interpretation of the words that make up a phrase, there is generally a principle of interpretation according to which the interpretation of the whole is a determinate function of the interpretations of the parts. Many compound types have interpretations that are quite parallel to those of phrases, and may be said to utilize the same principles of interpretation (verb–object interpretation of many verb plus noun or noun plus verb compounds in English, for example). Other compounds, however, involve special interpretive principles that are not paralleled by any principle applicable to phrases. We will see an example of this below in the treatment of Mandarin 'coordinate' compounds.

In addition, since compounds are words (and thus lexical items), they may (once formed) be subject to shift, specialization, generalization, and other change of meaning like other words. As a result, even though there may be a general principle of interpretation applicable to compounds of a given structural type, many actual forms may have meanings that are only vaguely or metaphorically related to that which is predicted. An example is Mandarin *yún-yǔ* 'cloud-rain:sexual intercourse', where the connection between the literal and lexicalized senses is hard to find. Examples of such lexicalized compounds abound in languages with relatively productive compounding processes; but this does not impair the importance of general interpretive principles for the expression of important or 'central' aspects of their formation. The point at issue is similar to one that could be made for phrases: the existence of idioms (such as 'kick the bucket [=die]') shows that phrases, too, may become separated in their interpretation from their compositional foundation. The phenomenon appears to be much more widespread with compounds, however, as we would expect from the intrinsically lexical nature of word formation.

We will illustrate some of these possibilities with the compounding system of Mandarin Chinese, a language which employs compounding virtually to the exclusion of other word formation processes. We will then consider briefly another, more restricted sort of compounding found in a number of languages, usually described as the 'incorporation' of nouns into a verbal stem.

## 3.1 *Mandarin Chinese compounds*

A number of factors combine to make Mandarin a particularly fertile field for the study of compounds. Stem modification plays little role, aside from a very small number of derivational affixes (nominal suffixes *-tou*, *-zi*, *-r*; *-men* for a few animate plurals; the prefix *dì-* for forming ordinal numbers; and a small set of aspect markers for verbs). Further, the comparatively limited inventory of possible syllables combined with the rather strict monosyllabism of formatives leads to a situation in which compounding is the major device by which the lexical stock of the language is formed and augmented. As any student of the language can attest, fixing the meaning of individual formatives (even where this is possible in isolation) is only a small part of the task of acquiring a working vocabulary. Most of the lexicon, in fact, consists of combinations of formatives produced by compounding. We depart from standard Pinyin orthography in the use of hyphens to show the articulation of compounds.

As we will see below, several classes of compounds in Mandarin are structurally quite similar to syntactically created phrases. Sometimes the same sequence of formatives, in fact, may correspond either to a phrase or to a compound: e.g. *dǎ* 'strike' plus *shǒu* 'hand' may be either a verb phrase ('strike the hand') or a compound word ('hired rioter, thug'). In such cases it is necessary to have some basis for classifying a given expression in one or the other way.

The fundamental way in which phrases differ from compounds, of course, is that the latter are (by definition) syntactically unitary words, and therefore members of a lexical part of speech category, while the former are not. Thus, *dǎ-shou* 'thug' appears in the syntactic positions occupied by other nouns, with modifiers and other elements exactly like those that would be found with any other noun (whether simple, like *shǒu* 'hand', or compound). The phrase *dǎ shǒu* 'strike the hand', however, is a verb phrase, and consequently appears in structures of that sort rather than as a member of a basic lexical category.

Unfortunately, while this characterization of the difference between phrases and compounds is the essential one in principle, it provides little help in many particular cases for deciding on the analysis of a particular structure. This is because phrases may often be made up of a single word (for instance, *lái* 'come' is a lexical verb, but it may also be the only word in a well formed verb phrase); and also because phrases may contain other phrases as members (thus, the fact that *silkworm* can appear preceded by a determiner and a numeral, as in *those three silkworms*, does not suffice to establish its status as a compound word, since *fat worm*, a phrase rather than a compound, can appear in exactly the same structure). Thus, it would be desirable to have other criteria to appeal to at least in order to motivate a central core of cases which constitute the basis of an analysis.

One property of compounds to which appeal is often made is the fact that they are often semantically non-compositional. Many compounds, that is, have a meaning which cannot be derived from the meanings of their parts alone, together with general principles of the language. The fact that *dǎ-shou* as a compound means 'thug' is an arbitrary, idiosyncratic fact to be listed in the lexicon just as the fact that *shǒu* means 'hand'; while the fact that the same sequence of formatives, taken as a phrase, means 'to strike the hand' is derivable from the meanings of *dǎ* and *shǒu*, together with the general principles for interpreting verb plus object phrases. This factor of degree of lexicalized meaning is often suggestive of the unitary nature of a compound, but cannot be taken as absolute: on the one hand, there are compounds (such as *jī-dàn* 'chicken-egg:chicken's egg') whose meaning is entirely compositional; and, on the other, there are phrases with idiomatic sense (such as *yòng shuǐ* 'use water: urinate') which are not compositional. Thus, while the degree of compositionality of compounds is generally much lower than that of phrases, this cannot be taken as defining the difference.

In some instances, even completely compositional constructions may be shown clearly to be compounds by the principles which are relevant to their interpretation. Thus, while the principles for interpreting many classes of compounds are parallel to those applying to similar phrases, there are some instances in which an interpretive principle is applicable *only* to compounds. We will see an instance of this in the discussion of 'coordinate' compounds below.

In some languages, there are reasonably reliable phonological factors which can be employed to make the distinction, as we have noted above. In Mandarin, there is no single property of the phonology of compounds which is as general as, say, the different stress patterns of compounds and phrases in English; but there are some which are useful in particular cases. Most syllables (except for the small class of affixes referred to above) in Mandarin have an associated tone, and correspondingly, the capacity to take stress. In many compounds, however, the second element of the construction loses its tone, and thereby its stress. This is the case, for example, with *dǎ-shou* 'thug' (whose toneless second element *shou* is identical with *shǒu* 'hand'). Wherever the second of a sequence of formatives has no tone, and therefore no stress, we can be sure that we have to do with a compound rather than a phrase. The reverse is not true, however, since many compounds do not lose the tone of their second element (such as *tiān xià* 'under-heaven:the world').

Somewhat more reliable is the fact that compounds, like other words, have only one possible stress *center*: that is, there is only position in which main or contrastive stress may fall. We have already noted above that, as a result of the fact that the last stress within a given constituent is the main stress in Mandarin, only the final (stressed) formative of a compound can take contrastive stress regardless of which part of the compound is actually being contrasted.

Yet another feature of compounds which is useful in their identification is the fact that in general, pauses are only possible in (natural) speech between words. Since compounds are (from this point of view) unitary words, it is not in general possible to pause or insert parenthetical material, etc., between their component elements. Of course, in actual speech we do not generally pause between every pair of words: clearly it is the *potential* for pause, rather than its necessary appearance which we appeal to here.

There is not, it appears, any single feature which is to be found in all and only compounds in Mandarin; and which therefore would assure their correct classification in every instance. Nevertheless, there are a number of properties of compounds which are applicable to enough instances to establish the general classes to be discussed below; and other structurally parallel types can then be treated as members of these same classes in so far as their integration into the language appears to be parallel to that of members of lexical categories, rather than of phrases.

In classifying compounds, we can refer either to their formal structure or to the semantic relations between their components. The formal structure can be characterized in terms of (a) the elements which are compounded; (b) the manner in which they are joined; and (c) the category of the resulting compound. Thus, *fēi-jī* 'fly-machine:airplane' is composed of a verb followed by a noun; the entire compound is a noun. We can thus characterize its structure by the formula $[v\text{-}n]_N$. Similarly, *kāi-guān* 'open-close:switch' has the structure $[v\text{-}v]_N$. All of the Mandarin compounds with which we will be concerned below are composed of elements from the major parts of speech (N[oun], v[erb], Adj[ective], and Adv[erb]), and all belong to one of these categories themselves, so such formulas give a satisfactory characterization of the structures involved.

A distinction which is frequently made in the treatment of compounds can be described in terms of such formulas. A *fēi-jī* 'airplane' is in fact a kind of *jī* 'machine': the entire compound has a function similar to that of one of its parts. Such a compound is often called *endocentric,* and *jī* is said to be its center. A *kāi-guān* 'switch', however, is not similar in syntactic function to either of its components: it is thus *exocentric* and has no center. We can go further, and consider *yì-si* 'idea-thought: meaning' as a compound with the structure $[n\text{-}n]_N$ which is endocentric, and in which both components are 'centers'. We will not, however, have much to say about the difference between endocentric and exocentric compounds (though we will occasionally refer to the 'center' of a compound), since it is not clear that this distinction corresponds to anything of typological interest. Rather than focusing on this structural characteristic, we will instead divide compounds into various types on the basis of the special principles of interpretation they require (e.g. 'verb–object' compounds, 'modifier–modified' compounds, etc.). Some interesting principles for the overall organization of the word formation system appear to emerge from this treatment.

### 3.1.1 *Modifier–modified compounds*

A large number of Mandarin compounds are of the type *gāng-bǐ* 'steel-pen:(fountain) pen', in which the first element of the compound serves as a modifier of the second. The sense of 'modifier' here is a familiar one, with modifiers serving to limit or make more specific the reference of the element they modify. Thus, in *gāng-bǐ*, the modifier *gāng* 'steel' serves to delimit, out of all the things called *bǐ* 'pen', those that are fountain pens (made of steel) – as opposed to *máo-bǐ* 'hair-pen:writing brush', *qiān-bǐ* 'lead-pen:pencil', etc.

In structural terms, we can identify the following types of modifier–modified compounds: (1) Compounds that function as nouns. (a) [N-N]$_N$, e.g. *niú-ròu* 'cow-meat:beef'; (b) [Adj-N]$_N$, e.g. *xiāng-liào* 'fragrant-material:spice'; (c) [V-N]$_N$, e.g. *fēi-chuán* 'fly-boat:dirigible'. (2) Compounds which function as verbs. (a) [N-V]$_V$, e.g. *yóu-zhá* 'oil-fry:deep fry', (b) [Adv-V]$_V$, e.g. *hú-shuō* 'randomly-talk:talk non-sense'. Some apparently adjectival stems appear as the first members of such compounds: e.g. *dà-pǎo* 'big-run:run with great strides'. In such cases, however, Chao (1968:403ff) argues that the adjective is func-tionally an adverb, by showing that only those adjective stems which can occupy adverb positions independently in the sentence can appear in this position in compounds. We thus do not recognize a distinct class of [Adj-V]$_V$ compounds. (3) Compounds that function as adjectives. (a) [N-Adj]$_{Adj}$, e.g. *xuě-bái* 'snow-white:very white'; (b) [V-Adj]$_{Adj}$, e.g. *gǔn-rè* 'boil-hot:very hot'; (c) [Adv-Adj]$_{Adj}$, e.g. *xiāng-jìn* 'mutually-near:near'.

An interesting property of these modifier-modified types in Mandarin is that they all have phrasal counterparts. That is, each of the types of modifier element that appear in these compounds is also a type of modifier which appears in phrases, with heads of the same type as that of the modified element in the corresponding compound. Furthermore, since modifiers precede their heads in Mandarin phrasal constructions, the syntactic structures of phrases and compounds are quite parallel. The modifier–modified relation, for example, characterizes phrases such as *xiě de zì* 'write (particle) character:written character(s)', as well as the phrases above, and each type of modifier that appears in a compound of the type [X-N]$_N$ also appears as a prenominal phrasal modifier.

Further, and perhaps even more strikingly, all of the particular semantic variations of the modifier-modified relation in noun com-pounds are paralleled by noun phrase constructions: whole modifying part (as 'dog-tail' vs. 'dog's tail'), material modifying thing (as 'lead-pencil' vs. 'gold jewelry'), action modifying goal (as 'smoke-fish' vs. 'written words'), and so on. Chao (1968:281ff) documents some twenty-one different senses of the relation, and provides both compound and phrasal examples for most.

Turning to the compounds that function as verbs and as adjectives, we find much the same thing: again, the adverbial modifiers of verbs typically precede them within phrases, as do the adverbial modifiers of adjectives. Compounds with the structures [Adv-V]$_V$ and [Adv-Adj]$_{Adj}$

are thus interpretable by the same principles as those involved in the parallel phrases, with the modifier element within the compound appearing before the head. Most [N-Adj]$_{Adj}$ compounds have a comparative interpretation ('as *Adj* as N'), and these too have a phrasal analog:

(7)    Tā yǒu Lâo Sān cōng-ming ma? .
       he as (name) clever    PCL
       'Is he as clever as Lao San?'

In such a structure, the term of comparison precedes the adjective denoting the dimension of comparison, just as in *tiān-dà* 'sky-big:very big'. We can thus conclude that, for modifier–modified compounds of all types, the principles governing both structure and interpretation are quite parallel to those that control phrases.

### 3.1.2 *Verb–object compounds*

Another substantial class of compounds have the internal structure [V-N], but cannot be interpreted as modifier–modified compounds with the N as center: e.g. *xiū-xíng* 'cultivate-conduct:become a Buddhist'. Most of these function as intransitive verbs, and their interpretation is (structurally) straightforward: N is interpreted as the object of V (which in such compounds is always transitive). Again, the parallel with phrasal structures is clear. In Mandarin, objects follow their verbs (unless displaced for reasons of emphasis, topicality, or the like). Even the tendency in Mandarin for postverbal objects to be indefinite in reference is paralleled by the impossibility of interpreting the N of such a [V-N] compound as definite.

    [V-N] compounds with verb–object interpretation may also serve as nouns: e.g. *dǒng-shì* 'supervise-affairs:member of the board', *wā-ěr* 'dig-ear:earpick'. It is again easy to find a phrasal type which has parallel structure and interpretation. In fact, in Mandarin, noun phrases containing a relative clause modifying the head have the clause preceding the noun; the shared noun in the relative clause (which may play virtually any role within it) is omitted, and the particle *de* appears between the clause and the head:

(8)    zuó-tian lái   de rén
       yesterday come PCL man
       'the man who came yesterday'

When the head of such a construction is indefinite (corresponding to an English construction like 'the *one*, *thing*, etc. that came yesterday'), it is not overtly represented in Mandarin: thus, *zuó-tian lái de*, by itself, means 'the (one) who came yesterday'. Accordingly, a compound like *dŏng shì* 'member of the board' can be regarded as analogous in structure and interpretation to a phrase like '(one who) supervises affairs'; the only difference being that the particle *de* which marks phrasal constructions is not present in the compound. All of these [v-n]$_N$ compounds thus have a straightforward interpretation as [v-n] *de* n', where n' is an indefinite head. The principle involved is again one which is closely parallel to one involved in interpreting (structurally similar) phrasal examples.

In the case of both classes of compounds surveyed thus far, we have seen that the structures are nearly identical to those of syntactic phrases, and furthermore, the interpretation of the compounds follows from independently necessary principles for the interpretation of the corresponding phrases. It is apparent that this is a relevant aspect of compounding processes in general: within a given language, we may find principles that join two (or more) stems into a larger unit both within the lexicon (as rules of compound formation) and within the syntax (as rules of phrase structure). It is important to inquire about the extent to which the structural and interpretive principles governing these two construction types are (and are not) similar to one another.

### 3.1.3 *Subject–predicate compounds*

Another class of compounds shares some but not all of the characteristics of the two just discussed. These are structures which are internally [n-v], as in (a) [n-v]$_N$, e.g. *tiān-liáng* 'day-brightens:dawn'; (b) [v-n]$_V$, e.g. *zuĭ-shuō* 'mouth-speak:promise with the mouth only'; (c) [n-v]$_{Adj}$, e.g. *tóu-téng* 'head-hurt:have a headache'. In these cases, we can identify a central part of the meaning of the compound by taking the n to be the subject of the v. Since subjects in Mandarin typically precede their verbs, we again have a structure in which the interpretation of compounds is generalized from that of phrases.

In this instance, however, it is not clear that the parallel is as close as in the previous cases. Though of course the language displays sentential complements, a sentential structure does not generally function in a way parallel to a noun, verb, or adjective; and, of course, sentences have a rather different sort of interpretation (as expressing a proposition) than do members of these classes. While the independent rule of subject–predicate interpretation (which applies to sentences) thus gives a portion of the meanings of the compounds, it appears that some additional principle(s) must be at work here in order to yield interpretations for the compounds that will be appropriate to their roles in the sentence. Whether it is possible to state such a principle in a general fashion we leave undetermined: our point here is that whatever principle is involved, it is one which is restricted in that it applies only to compounds and not to phrases.

### 3.1.4 Coordinate compounds

The existence of principles of interpretation that are specific to compounds can be illustrated by consideration of a different group of Mandarin word structures. These are compounds consisting of two (or more) members of the same lexical class: [N-N], [V-V], [Adj-Adj], and [Adv-Adv]. Any of these may function as a member of the same class as its members, or as a member of other classes, as illustrated below. [N-N]$_N$: *chē-mǎ* 'vehicle-horse:traffic'; [N-N]$_{Adj}$: *jiāng-hú* 'rivers-lakes:adventuresome'; [V-V]$_N$: *hū-xi* 'expire-inspire:breath (also breathe)'; [V-V]$_V$: *yī-kào* 'follow-lean on:rely on'; [V-V]$_{Adj}$: *yǒng-* 'skip-leap:enthusiastic'; [Adj-Adj]$_N$: *dà-xiǎo* 'big-small:size'; [Adj-Adj]$_{Adj}$: *qí-guài* 'novel-weird:strange'; and [Adv-Adv]$_{Adv}$: *héng-shù* 'horizontal-vertical:anyway'.

In all of these cases we have to do with compounds in which neither element can be identified exclusively as the center, and they are typically described as 'coordinate' compounds. Now coordination in Mandarin is typically the result of simply juxtaposing phrases with parallel structure, as in (9):

(9)   a. Tā-men mài juō-zi yǐ-zi
      3-PL    sell table  chair
      'They sell tables and chairs'

   b. Shā rén  fàng huǒ dou yǒu zuì
      kill man  set  fire both have crime
      'Murder and arson are both criminal'

The compounds considered above could thus be regarded as having a structure appropriate for interpretation as coordinate. The problem is that this would not yield an appropriate interpretation: coordinated phrases are interpreted as a logical conjunction ('A and B') or disjunction ('A or B'), rather than being assigned a unitary meaning of the type which characterizes coordinate compounds.

We can classify the compounds in question into three semantic types: (a) compounds of synonyms (e.g. *yì-si* 'idea-thought:meaning'; *huó-dòng* 'lively-moving:active'; *fēn-sàn* 'divide-scatter:disperse'), (b) compounds of antonyms (e.g. *cháng-duǎn* 'long-short:length'; *ruǎn-yìng* 'soft-hard:degree of hardness'), and (c) 'parallel' compounds, involving grammatically similar but not synonymous elements (e.g. *shān-shuǐ* 'mountain-water:landscape'; *fù-mû* 'father-mother:parents'; *rè-nào* 'hot-noisy:full of life'). While these three appear to present quite diverse logical types, the meanings of all three sorts follow from the same basic principle: the interpretation of a coordinate compound is found (more or less) as the sum of what the elements of the compound have in common. Thus, both 'lively' and 'moving' denote modes of activity; the meaning of *huá-dòng* is simply 'active'. Both 'long' and 'short' are measures of length; thus, *cháng-duǎn* denotes length in general, unspecified as long or short. Similarly, both 'mountains' and 'water' are part of a landscape, and it is here that they are found together; thus, *shān-shuǐ* denotes a 'landscape'. Larger coordinate compounds are also found, and in these the operation of the interpretive principle just sketched is even clearer (e.g. *jī-yā-yú-ròu* 'chicken-duck-fish-meat:animal foodstuffs'; *tǐng-tái-lóu-gé* 'pavilions-terraces-upper stories-raised alcoves:elaborate architecture').

The interest of the principle just suggested, for our purposes, lies in the fact that it is apparently applicable precisely to coordinate compounds, and not to genuinely phrasal structures. In this respect, coordinate compounds (which are in fact extremely common in the language, to some extent for historical reasons) differ from other compound types to which the interpretive principles applicable to phrases apply as well.

### 3.1.5 *Resultative verb compounds*

One final group of Mandarin compounds will serve to illustrate another type. This is the group of 'resultative verb' compounds, which are structurally [v-v]$_V$ (e.g. *guān-jǐn* 'shut-tight:shut tight'; *xiě-cuò* 'write-wrong: write incorrectly'; *zuò-wán* 'do-finish: finish'). The bulk of these compounds (indeed, virtually all) involve intransitive verbs as their second members. A few apparent exceptions (e.g. *kàn-jiàn* 'look at-perceive:see') may be explicable in terms of the general possibility for Mandarin transitive verbs to appear as intransitives with 'passive' interpretations. The meanings of these compounds are generally that the second verb describes the state of the object (or of the subject, if the first verb is intransitive) after the completion of the action described by the first verb. There are a few exceptions: thus, in *tā hē-zuì le jiǔ lue* 'He got drunk on the liquor', the resultative verb compound *hē-zuì* 'drink-drunk:drink so as to become intoxicated' involves a second element that describes the state of the subject, rather than the object of the first verb after the action.

Both the structures and the interpretations of resultative [v-v]$_V$ compounds are comparable to those of phrasal constructions, but there are two special word formation processes applicable (only) to these compounds. From nearly any resultative [v-v]$_V$ item, we can also form a compound with the structure [v-*de*-v]$_V$, with the meaning 'can (do whatever the original compound means)', and one with the form [v-*bu*-v]$_V$ meaning 'cannot (do whatever the original compound means)'. These patterns do not have a parallel in phrasal constructions, and they are so important as a source of 'potential' meaning that single-element verbs are often made into 'dummy' compounds by the addition of a second element with little or no independent meaning, just so that the two word formation rules that create structures with potential interpretation can apply. A common second element in such constructions is *lái* 'come', as in *zuò-bu-lái* 'do-PCL-come: cannot do'; this is perhaps related to the fact (cf. Chao 1968:454) that *lái* also serves as a pro-verb in elliptical constructions such as 'You don't know how to repair it; let me *do it*'. Another common verb in these compounds is *liăo* 'finish', as in *chī-de-liăo* 'eat-PCL-finish:can eat', which can mean either 'can finish eating', where *liăo* is interpreted literally as 'finish', or simply 'be able to eat' (as in 'I can't eat this: it has too much sand in it'), where the second element is simply a dummy.

This further class of compounds involves a distinctive rule of (potential or negative-potential) interpretation. The structures themselves also illustrate the point that compounds may involve the insertion of extra formatives as construction markers: a sort of 'morphological glue' that binds and identifies a class of distinctive compound structures.

Before leaving this survey of compound structures in Mandarin, there is another general point to be made. Nearly all examples above have involved simple combinations of two monosyllabic stems. Compounds can be much more complex than this, however. Consider *jūn-shì-wěi-yuán-huì* 'army-affair-delegate-member-group:military affairs committee'. This has the structure [[N-N]$_N$-[[N-N]$_N$-N]$_N$]$_N$ where all of the intermediate stages are [N-N]$_N$ compounds of the modifier–modified type. Since compounds are formed from lexical elements, and are themselves lexical, they can enter into the formation of further compounds in a recursive fashion. Of course, a language might restrict the degree of recursion allowed as a special condition on the input class affected by the compounding rule (perhaps by allowing only simple formatives to be compounded). Quite commonly, however, compounding displays a degree of recursive structure which is richer than that found in stem modification processes in most languages.

### 3.2 *Noun incorporation*

In the early years of the twentieth century, North American languages attracted a considerable amount of attention on account of a construction in which the objects of transitive verbs (and sometimes the subjects of intransitives and certain obliques as well) were 'incorporated' into the main verb of the sentence. In Nahuatl (cf. Merlan 1976), for example, one finds both sentences below with similar meanings:

(10)     a. Ni-k-qua in-nakatl
            I-it-eat   ART-meat
            'I am eating (the) meat'

         b. Ni-naka-qua
            I-meat-eat
            'I eat meat; I am a meat eater'

More recently, it has been observed that such constructions are by no means confined to North America: Turkish, Malagasy, Fijian, Chuckchee, and the Munda language So:ra are but a few of the languages outside of North America that have been analyzed as displaying 'noun incorporation'.

Sapir described the essential features of the construction in 1911. At first glance, one might well be tempted to treat incorporated noun objects as similar to the stems in Kwakw'ala constructions such as *gəgewasgən* 'I am eating deer', from *gewas* 'deer'. One might analyze the main verb here, that is, simply as *-g* 'eat', and treat the object noun 'deer' as incorporated into it in a fashion similar to that in the Nahuatl example in (10b). Sapir points out some significant differences between the two cases, however. The Kwakw'ala suffix *-g* 'eat' bears no resemblance (either synchronically or etymologically) to the independent stems (*ha'm-* or *qəs-*) that mean 'eat', whereas in the Nahuatl case the verb stem is the same whether or not the object is 'incorporated'. Nahuatl object stems may have slightly different phonological forms in incorporated and unincorporated constructions (e.g. *naka-* vs. *nakatl* in (10) above), but their basic identity is clear. Furthermore, though Sapir did not emphasize this fact, the classes of nouns and of verbs that can appear in 'incorporation' constructions are typically open ended; while in a system like that of Kwakw'ala, one of these classes (the lexical suffixes, here taken as filling a role similar to that of verbs) is limited even within a coherent semantic domain. That is, there is a limited, specific number of idiosyncratic elements which appear only in such structures, as opposed to the Nahuatl case in which an independent lexical category ('verbs') is involved.

Other candidates for 'incorporation' status in Kwakw'ala might be the set of body-part locative suffixes discussed in section 2.1; here of course the suffixes are taken as analogous to the incorporated nouns, rather than to the verbs. Once again, however, the construction shows a similar limitation: while body-part suffixes can appear on any verb, there is a fixed, limited number of available suffixes. Again, the construction does not show the open endedness characteristic of true 'incorporation' constructions. Sapir and Boas went so far as to assert that the two processes ('lexical suffixes', like those of Kwakw'ala, and incorporation) cannot coexist in the same language, though Hagège (1977) has argued that at least one language (Sliammon, or Mainland Comox, a Coast Salish language) displays both independently.

The 'incorporated' noun most often fills the role of transitive object, as in (10b), but it may also represent an intransitive subject: cf. Modern Nahuatl *tla-se-weci* 'INDEF-snow-fall: it is snowing' (Merlan 1976:183). Instrument nouns may also be incorporated in Nahuatl: cf. *ki-kočillo-tete?ki* 'he/it-knife-cut:he cut it with a knife'. Other oblique functions are rare.

Much recent discussion of this construction (e.g. Rigsby 1975; Woodbury 1975; and also, for lexical suffixes, Saunders and Davis 1975) assumes that it is the result of syntactic rules, much like passive constructions (cf. chapter 1.5). If so, it would be a rule of quite an unusual type, since it would apply to incorporate only intransitive subjects or transitive objects (just those elements which are marked as 'absolutive' in an ergative language; cf. chapter III.3 below), but not transitive subjects, which are not known to be incorporated in any language. Sapir had already pointed out in his 1911 paper, however, the sort of process 'noun incorporation' really is: a species of word formation, and specifically, a type of compound formation.

The properties of noun incorporation constructions are fairly straightforward in this light. The 'incorporated noun' in such compounds is the figure or patient of the action represented by the verb, a notion we have already seen plays a role in word formation. A further semantic constraint is that incorporation is limited to non-animates in many languages (e.g. in those of the Iroquoian and Caddoan families). Such semantic constraints are more common in lexical than in syntactic structure. Furthermore, it is apparently restricted even in what objects 'incorporate' with what verbs: in Iroquoian, 'plant corn' does not incorporate. Such idiosyncratic factors are again a common correlate of the lexical status of a principle.

In many languages, the noun of noun–verb (or verb–noun) compounds can be interpreted only as 'generic' or indefinite. An English *beer-drinker*, for instance, is not one who is drinking some particular beer here and now, but one who has a general propensity to drink beer. The compounded noun must usually be without modifiers, articles, deictic elements, etc. Precisely these restrictions apply to noun incorporation constructions, such as that in (10b). Merlan (1976) shows that in Nahuatl, incorporation also serves in discourse as a variety of anaphora. Significantly, however, the type of anaphora involved seems similar to that of English 'I'll take the long straw and you get the short *one*', rather than 'I'll take the long straw so you don't get *it*'. This sort of indefinite, identity of sense function rather than identity of reference is consistent with the generally non-specific role of noun elements in compounds.

Anyone who would still maintain that noun incorporation represents a straightforward syntactic process by which, for example, the object of the verb is moved into the verb word must also deal with facts such as those in (11), from Onondaga (cf. Woodbury 1975):

(11)     a. Tony waʔhatshɛniʔ neʔ ohnyúhsaʔ
             Tony he found it     the large globular vegetable
             'Tony found the squash/pumpkin/melon/etc.'

         b. Tony waʔhahnyuhsatshé:niʔ
             Tony found(vegetable)
             'Tony found a squash/pumpkin/melon/etc.'

         c. Tony waʔhahnyuhsatshɛniʔ ohnyuhsowá:nɛ
             Tony found(vegetable)     it vegetable big(melon)
             'Tony found a melon'

Sentences (11a) and (11b) show that the object of the verb 'find' may appear incorporated into the verb. In (11c), however, we see that although the incorporated noun may well specify the character of the 'patient' (here, that it is one of a class of large vegetables and fruits), it does not *represent* or *replace* that object (here, specifically, a melon, as opposed to other sorts of *hnyuhsaʔ*).

We can conclude, then, that there are good reasons to ascribe the special character of 'noun incorporation' to a rule of word formation, rather than to the syntax. More specifically, given the (grammatically) open ended character of the class of verbs and nouns that are typically involved in this construction, together with both general and idiosyncratic limitations on its productivity, we can agree with Sapir that the process is a case of compound formation.

## 4 Conclusion

The sections above have surveyed a variety of processes by which languages fill out and expand their lexicons. We distinguish (largely for expository convenience, though the distinction can be defended as a principled one) between the inflectional processes by which languages mark fully productive categories that are of relevance to the rules of the syntax, and derivational processes that serve to produce members of basic lexical classes. Within the latter, we distinguished between processes that take a single lexical stem as input and relate it to some systematically different form ('stem modification') and processes that take two or more stems and combine them. In both domains, it is necessary in order to characterize a word formation process to describe (a) the class of input stems it affects; (b) the structure of the resulting form; and (c) the syntactic and semantic relations between the rule's inputs and its outputs. In addition, the character of the rule as an active process, yielding new formations, or a passive one, serving simply to analyze existing word forms in the lexicon, may be relevant. Finally, in relation to compounding processes, the similarities and differences between these and the principles of phrase structure and semantic interpretation for phrases described by the syntax may be of importance.

Throughout this chapter, we have emphasized the fact that derivational morphology is a domain in which languages generally do not show a consistent typology of the sort sought by nineteenth-century writers on language. Instead, the parameters of interest and importance are relevant in a local sense, to particular word formation processes rather than to whole languages. While many languages indeed do have a preponderance of processes of a single general cast, this is by no means a general feature of natural languages, and the field worker must be prepared (as with everything in the domain of the lexicon) to proceed with one piece at a time.

# 2 Lexicalization patterns: semantic structure in lexical forms

LEONARD TALMY

## 0.0 Introduction[1]

This chapter addresses the systematic relations in language between meaning and surface expression. Our approach to this has several aspects. First, we assume we can isolate elements separately within the domain of meaning and within the domain of surface expression. These are semantic elements like 'Motion', 'Path', 'Figure', 'Ground', 'Manner', and 'Cause', and surface elements like 'verb', 'adposition', 'subordinate clause', and what we will characterize as 'satellite'. Second, we examine which semantic elements are expressed by which surface elements. This relationship is largely not one-to-one. A combination of semantic elements can be expressed by a single surface element, or a single semantic element by a combination of surface elements. Or again, semantic elements of different types can be expressed by the same type of surface element, as well as the same type by several different ones. We find here a range of typological patterns and universal principles.

We do not look at every case of semantic-to-surface association, but only at ones that constitute a pervasive pattern, either within a language or across languages. Our particular concern is to understand how such patterns compare across languages. That is, for a particular semantic domain, we ask if languages exhibit a wide variety of patterns, a comparatively small number of patterns (a typology), or a single pattern (a universal). We will be interested primarily in the last two cases, as well as in the case where a pattern appears in no languages (universal exclusion). Our approach can be summarized as in this procedural outline:

(1)     ('entities' = elements, relations, and structures: both particular cases and categories of these)

  a. Determine various semantic entities in a language.
  b. Determine various surface entities in the language.

c. Observe which (a) entities are expressed by which (b) entities – in what combinations and with what interrelations – noting any patterns.

d. Compare findings of this sort across languages, noting any patterns.

This outline sketches the broad project of exploring meaning–surface relations. But our present undertaking is narrower in several ways. First, there are two directions for exploring meaning–surface relations, both of them fruitful. One direction is to hold a particular semantic entity constant and observe the surface entities in which it can appear. For example, one could observe that the semantic element 'negative' shows up in English as a verb-complex adverb (will *not* go), as an adjective (*no* money), as an adjectival derivational affix (*un*kind), and as a verbal incorporated feature (*doubt*); in Atsugewi as a verb requiring an infinitive complement (*mit*[h]*i:p* 'to not'); and in some languages as a verbal inflection. The other direction is to hold constant a selected surface entity, and to observe which semantic entities are variously expressed in it. The present chapter explores in only this second direction.

Within this limitation, we narrow our concerns still further. One can examine surface entities of different morpheme count for the meanings that appear in them. At the small end of the scale are the 'zero' forms. Thus, by one interpretation, there is a missing verbal expression in English constructions like *I feel like [having] a milk shake* and *I hope for [there to be] peace*, or in German ones like *Wo wollen Sie denn hin [gehen/fahren/ . . .]?* 'Where do you want to go?'. One might conclude that such missing verbal meanings come from a small set, with members like 'have', 'be', and 'go'.[2] Alternatively, one could investigate the meanings that are expressed by surface complexes. A comparatively lengthy construction might encode a single semantic element. Consider the approximate semantic equivalence of the construction *be of interest to* and the simple verb *interest*, or of *carry out an investigation into* and *investigate*. However, this chapter looks only at the middle size levels – single morphemes and, to a lesser extent, words (composed of root and derivational morphemes).

In particular, we will investigate one type of open-class element, the verb root, the topic of section 1, and one type of closed-class element, the 'satellite', defined and treated in section 2. These two surface types are vehicles for a connected set of semantic categories. Our aim in these sections is to set forth a class of substantial meaning-in-form language patterns, and to describe the typological and universal principles that they embody. The conclusion in section 3 compares the advantages of the approach adopted here and extends this to the issue of informational foregrounding and backgrounding. And, finally, the Appendix in section 4 tabulates and augments the meaning-form relations described in the text.[3]

### 0.1 *Characteristics of lexicalization*

We outline now some general characteristics of lexicalization, as part of this chapter's theoretical context. A meaning can be considered associated with surface forms mainly by three processes: lexicalization, deletion (or zero), and interpretation. We can contrast these three in an example where no one process clearly applies best. Consider the phrase *what pressure* (as in *What pressure was exerted?*), which asks 'what *degree of* pressure' – unlike the more usual *what color*, which asks for a particular identity among alternatives. We could account for the 'degree' meaning by lexicalization: *pressure* here differs from the usual usage by incorporating an additional meaning component: $pressure_2 = $ *degree of pressure*$_1$ (or, alternatively, there is a special *what* here: $what_2 = what_1$ *degree of*). Or we could assume that some constituent like *degree of* has been deleted from the middle of the phrase (or that a zero form with the meaning 'degree of' now resides there). Or else, we could rely on a process of semantic interpretation, based on present context and general knowledge, to provide us with the 'degree' meaning.[4]

In general, we assume here that lexicalization is involved where a particular meaning component is found to be in regular association with a particular morpheme. The study of lexicalization, however, must also include the case where a *set* of meaning components, bearing particular relations to each other, is in association with a morpheme, making up the whole of the morpheme's meaning. In the clearest case, one morpheme's semantic makeup is equivalent to that of a set of other morphemes in a syntactic construction, where each of these has one of the original morpheme's meaning components. A familiar example here is the approximate semantic equivalence between *kill* and *make die*. However, such clear cases are only occasional: it would be unwise to base an approach to lexicalization on semantic equivalences solely between *extant* morphemes. What if English had no word *die*? We would still want to be able to say that *kill* incorporates the meaning component 'cause' (as we would for the verb (to) *poison* 'kill by poison', which in fact lacks a non-causative counterpart for 'die by poison'). To this end, we can establish a new notion, that of a morpheme's *usage*: a particular selection of its semantic and syntactic properties. We can then point to usage equivalences between morphemes, even ones with different core meanings, and even across different languages. To consider one example, there is a usage equivalence between *kill* and *make appear*. *Kill* includes in its meaning the notion 'Agent acting on Patient' ('causative') and, syntactically, takes an Agent subject and Patient object; this usage is equivalent to that of *make*, which incorporates the notion 'Agent-to-Patient relation', in construction with *appear*, which incorporates the notion 'Patient acting alone' ('non-causative') and takes a Patient subject. Such relationships can be represented, for cases involving both lexical (L) and grammatical (G) morphemes, as:

(2)       usage of        =        usage of
          $L_2$              $L_1$ in construction with G
          (e.g. $L_2 = kill$, $L_1 = appear$, and $G = make$)

We can say here that $L_2$ incorporates the meaning of G and that $L_1$ either does not incorporate it or incorporates a meaning complementary to it. In the special case where a single morpheme can function equally as $L_1$ or $L_2$, we can say that it has a *range* of usages. For example, there is a usage equivalence between $break_2$ and $make\ break_1$, as seen in *I broke the vase* and *I made the vase break*, so that *break* can be said to have a usage-range covering both the causative and the non-causative. An equivalent way of characterizing such a usage-range is as in (3). As an example of this, the causative/non-causative usage-range of *break* equals the causative usage of *kill* plus the non-causative usage of *appear*.

(3)       usage-range of        =        usage of        +        usage of
          $L_3$                          $L_2$                     $L_1$
          where $L_2$ and $L_1$ are related as in (2)

One terminological note: we will refer to the meaning-in-form relation with three terms. They are 'lexicalization' from McCawley (e.g. 1968); 'incorporation' as used by Gruber (1965); and 'conflation', a term that was coined for this purpose by the author (Talmy 1972) and that has now gained general currency. These terms have different emphases and connotations that will become clear as they are used below, but all refer to the representation of meanings in surface forms.

## 0.2 Sketch of a motion event

A number of the patterns looked at below are part of a single larger system for the expression of motion and location. We will here provide a sketch of this system. A fuller analysis appears in Talmy (1975).

To begin with, we treat a situation containing movement or the maintenance of a stationary location alike as a 'motion event'. The basic motion event consists of one object (the 'Figure') moving or located with respect to another object (the reference-object or 'Ground'). It is analyzed as having four components: besides 'Figure' and 'Ground', there are 'Path' and 'Motion'. The 'Path' (with a capital P) is the course followed or site occupied by the Figure object with respect to the Ground object. 'Motion' (with a capital M) refers to the presence *per se* in the event of motion or location (only these two motion states are structurally distinguished by language). We will represent motion by the form 'move' and location by 'be$_L$' (a mnemonic for 'be located').[5] In addition to these internal components a Motion event can have a 'Manner' or a 'Cause', which we analyze as constituting a distinct external event. All these semantic entities can be seen in the following sentences:

| (4) | | Manner: | Cause: |
|---|---|---|---|
| | motion: | The pencil rolled off the table | The pencil blew off the table |
| | location: | The pencil lay on the table | The pencil stuck on (to) the table (after I glued it) |

In all four sentences, *the pencil* functions as the Figure and *the table* as the Ground. *Off* and *on* express Paths (respectively, a path and a site). The verbs in the top sentences express motion, while those in the bottom ones express location. In addition to these states of Motion, a Manner is expressed in *rolled* and *lay*, while a Cause is expressed in *blew* and *stuck*.

The terms 'Figure' and 'Ground' are taken from Gestalt psychology but we give them a distinct semantic interpretation here: the Figure is a moving or *conceptually* mov*able* object whose path or site is at issue; the Ground is a reference-frame, or a reference-point stationary within a reference-frame, with respect to which the Figure's path or site is characterized.[6]

### 1.0 The verb

In this study of the verb, we look mainly at the verb root alone. This is because the main concern here is with the kinds of lexicalization that involve a single morpheme, and because in this way we are able to compare lexicalization patterns across languages with very different word structure. For example, the verb root in Chinese generally stands alone as an entire word, whereas in Atsugewi it is surrounded by many affixes that all together make up a polysynthetic verbal word. But these two languages are on a par with respect to their verb roots.

Presented first are three lexicalization types for verb roots that together constitute an apparently exhaustive typology. Any language uses only one of these types for the verb in its most characteristic expression of Motion. Here, 'characteristic' means that: (i) It is *colloquial* in style, rather than literary, stilted, etc. (ii) It is *frequent* in occurrence in speech, rather than only occasional. (iii) It is *pervasive*, rather than limited, that is, a wide range of semantic notions are expressed in this type.

### 1.1 *Motion + Manner/Cause*

In a motion-sentence pattern characteristic of one group of languages, the verb expresses at once both the fact of Motion and either its manner or its cause. A language of this type has a whole series of verbs in common use that express *motion* occurring in various manners or by various causes. There may also be a series of verbs expressing *location* with various manners or causes, but they are apparently always much fewer. The semantic-to-surface relationship here can be represented as follows:

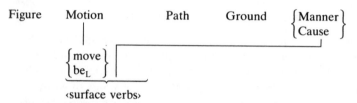

Figure 2.1  Manner or Cause conflated in the Motion verb

Language families that seem to be of this type are Chinese and apparently all branches of Indo-European except (post-Latin) Romance. English is a perfect example of the type:

(5)    English expressions of Motion with conflated Manner or Cause

**be$_L$ + Manner**

a.  The lamp *stood/lay/leaned* on the table

b.  The rope *hung* across the canyon from two hooks.

**move + Manner**

non-agentive

c.  The rock *slid/rolled/bounced* down the hill

d.  The gate *swung/creaked* shut on its rusty hinges

e.  The smoke *swirled/squeezed* through the opening

agentive

f.  I *slid/rolled/bounced* the keg into the storeroom

g.  I *twisted/popped* the cork out of the bottle

self-agentive

h.  I *ran/limped/jumped/stumbled/rushed/groped* my way down the stairs

i.  She *wore* a green dress to the party

**move + Cause**
non-agentive

j.  The napkin *blew* off the table

k.  The bone *pulled* loose from its socket

agentive

l.  I *pushed/threw/kicked* the keg into the storeroom

m.  I *blew/flicked* the ant off my plate

n.  I *chopped/sawed* the tree down to the ground at the base

o.  I *knocked/pounded/hammered* the nail into the board with a mallet[7]

To a speaker of a language like English, such sentences may seem so straightforward that they offer little to ponder. How else might such propositions be colloquially expressed? But in fact there are languages with very different patterns of expression. Even a language as seemingly kindred as Spanish *can express virtually none* of the above sentences in the way that English does, as is demonstrated below.

Some indication can be given of the type of conflation pattern involved here by paraphrases that represent the separate semantic components individually – i.e., that 'unpack' the sentences. The Manner or Cause notions conflated in the verbs are then best represented by separate subordinate clauses, as in the following:

(6)   Unconflated paraphrases of English Motion expressions

**be$_L$ + Manner**
a′.  (The lamp lay on the table =)
    The lamp was-located on the table, lying there

b′.  (The rope hung across the canyon from two hooks =)
    The rope was-located [extended] across the canyon, hanging from two hooks

**move + Manner**
non-agentive

c′.  (The rock rolled down the hill =)
    The rock moved down the hill, rolling [the while]

d'. (The gate swung shut on its rusty hinges =)
The gate moved shut [= shut], swinging on its rusty hinges [the while]

agentive

f'. (I bounced the keg into the storeroom =)
I moved the keg into the storeroom, bouncing it [the while]

self-agentive

h'. (I ran down the stairs =)
I went down the stairs, running [the while]

i'. (She wore a green dress to the party =)
She went to the party, wearing a green dress [the while]

**move + Cause**
non-agentive

j'. (The napkin blew off the table =)
The napkin moved off the table, from [the wind] blowing on it

agentive

l'. (I kicked the keg into the storeroom =)
I moved the keg into the storeroom, by kicking it

n'. (I chopped the tree down to the ground at the base =)
I moved the tree down to the ground, by chopping on it at the base[8]

Paraphrase pairs like these reveal a further fact about English: it has a system of *lexicalization doublets*. In many cases, a single verb form can be used either with or without an incorporated idea of motion. For example, in its basic usage the verb *float* refers to the buoyancy relation between an object and a medium, and in this sense it is equivalent to *be afloat*, as in:

(7)    The craft floated/was afloat on a cushion of air

Given the subscript '1' to mark this usage, the verb can also appear in a subordinate clause, next to a main clause referring to motion:

(8)    The craft moved into the hangar, floating$_1$ on a cushion of air

But the same verb form has a second usage that includes the idea of motion together with that of buoyancy. The verb in this usage – here marked with the subscript '2' – can appear in a one-clause sentence that is virtually equivalent to the preceding two-clause sentence:

(9)    The craft floated$_2$ into the hangar on a cushion of air

We can represent the relationship between the two meanings of *float* in this way:

(10)    The craft moved [floating₁ (the while)] into the hangar on a
        floated₂                                cushion of air

The final occurrence here of phrases of two different kinds – the directional *into the hangar* and the locative *on a cushion of air* – support the interpretation that this verb conflates two otherwise separate concepts, one of motion and one of locative relationship: each component of the verb is, at least semantically, 'in construction with' a different one of the two final phrases.

The same pair of usages can be seen in an agentive verb such as *kick*. In its basic usage, this verb refers to an agent's impacting his/her foot into some object, but entails nothing about that object's moving. This is obvious when that object is understood in fact to be fixed in place:

(11)    I kicked₁ the wall with my left foot

Again, this verb can be used in a subordinate clause alongside an independent reference to motion, as in (12a). Again, it has a second usage that incorporates this reference to motion, as in (12b). And again, this latter two-in-one form can link up with a corresponding pair of final phrases, also seen in (12b):

(12)    a. I moved the ball across the field, by kicking₁ it with my left foot

        b. I kicked₂ the ball across the field with my left foot

The relation between the two usages here, corresponding to that shown in (10), can be represented as: $kick_2 = {}_A move [by\ kicking_1]$ – where the subscript '$_A$' indicates the agentive (i.e., 'cause to move').[9]

We can further support the idea that these verbs each represent two distinct lexicalizations by showing verbs that have only the one or the other. *Lie* as in *The pen lay on the plank* is semantically much like *float₁* in referring to the support relation between one object and another (rather than buoyancy the relationship here is one of linear object in contact along its length with a firm surface). But it cannot also be used in a motion-incorporating sense like *float₂*: *The pen lay down the incline* – i.e., moved down the incline while in lengthwise contact with it. Conversely, *drift* and *glide* only express motion through space, in the way that *float₂* does. They cannot also be used in a non-motion sense: *The canoe glided on that spot of the lake for an hour.*

Comparably, *throw* is semantically much like $kick_2$ in referring to a distinct motion event caused by a prior body action: *I threw the ball across the field with my left hand.* But it has no usage parallel to $kick_1$ referring to the body action alone – i.e., to swinging an object around with one's arm without releasing it into a separate path. By contrast *swing* itself is generally restricted to this latter sense, parallel to $kick_1$, and cannot be used in a sentence like *\*I swung the ball across the field with my left arm* to express consequent motion through space.

All these forms fit – and can further illustrate – the lexicalization formulas of (2) and (3). When plugged into (2), the forms immediately above exhibit not only usage equivalence but also semantic equivalence. Thus, the usage and meaning of *throw* ($L_2$) is the same as that of *swing* ($L_1$) when this form is in construction with the largely grammatical sequence (G) *cause to move by . . .-ing* ('throw' = 'cause to move by swinging'). And as for *kick*, this form is seen to possess a range of usages because it can be plugged into *both* sides of formula (2): $kick_2$ = *cause to move by kicking*$_1$; or, equivalently by formula (3), *kick* ($L_3$) has usages equaling the usage of *throw* ($L_2$) taken together with the usage of *swing* ($L_1$).[10]

In the languages that have it, the conflation pattern being described here normally applies far beyond the expression of simple Motion. It extends as well to Motion compounded with mental-event notions (13A), to Motion compounded with other specific material in recurrent semantic complexes (13B), to embeddings involving more than one Motion event (13C), and to metaphoric extensions of Motion (13D). Below, small caps indicate a posited 'deep' or 'midlevel' morpheme, one that represents a basic semantic element or a specified semantic complex. As an underlying main clause verb, it conflates with an element (usually the verb) from the accompanying subordinate clause. Again, virtually none of these additional forms can be expressed as such in languages like Spanish.

(13)    **Extensions of the Motion conflation pattern in English**
(F = Figure, G = Ground, A = Agent, (to) AGENT = (to) cause agentively, $_A$MOVE = agentively cause to MOVE, small caps = a deep or midlevel morpheme)

A. conflation involving Motion compounded with mental-event notions

a.    GO: [A] AGENT himself [i.e., his whole body, = F] to MOVE

   She WENT to the party, wearing a green dress.
   ⇒ She wore a green dress to the party.

   Similarly: I read comics all the way to New York.

b. GET: [A₁] INDUCE [A₂] to GO

I GOT him out of his hiding place, by luring/scaring him
⇒ I lured/scared him out of his hiding place.

Similarly: I talked him down ⸤ f the ledge.
I prodded the cattle ⸤nto the pen.

c. URGE: [A₁] AIM to INDUCE [A₂] to GO

I URGED him away from the building, by waving at him.
⇒ I waved him away from the building.

Similarly: I beckoned him toward me.

B. conflation involving Motion in other recurrent semantic complexes

d. GIVE: [A₁] ₐMOVE [F] into the GRASP of [A₂]

I GAVE him another beer, sliding it
⇒ I slid him another beer.

e. PLACE: [A] ₐMOVE [F TO G] with limb motion but without body translocation

I PLACED the painting down on the table, it lying there.
⇒ I laid the painting down on the table.

Similarly: I stood/leaned/hung the painting on the chair/against the door/on the wall.

f. COVER: [F] BE_L all-over [G]

Paint COVERED the rug, BEING in streaks/dots
⇒ Paint streaked/dotted the rug.

C. double conflation: example of a lexical triplet

g. Could you GIVE me the flour,

having first ₐMOVED it down off that shelf,
having first reached₁ to it with your free hand?

⇒ Could you GIVE me the flour,
having first reached₂ it down off that shelf with your free hand?

⇒ Could you reach₃ me the flour down off that shelf with your free hand?

D. conflation involving metaphoric extensions of Motion non-agentive

h. 'MOVE': [F] MOVE metaphorically (i.e., change state)

He 'MOVED' to death, from choking on a bone.
(⇒ He died from choking on a bone. —or:)
⇒ He choked to death on a bone.

i. BECOME: 'MOVE' in the environment: __Adjective

The shirt BECAME dry, from flapping in the wind.
($\Rightarrow$ The shirt dried from flapping in the wind. —or:)
$\Rightarrow$ The shirt flapped dry in the wind.

Similarly: The tinman rusted stiff.
The coat has worn thin in spots.
The twig froze stuck to the window.

j. FORM: [F] 'MOVE' into EXISTENCE (cf. the phrase *come into existence*)

A hole FORMED in the table, from a cigarette burning it.
$\Rightarrow$ A hole burned in the table from a cigarette.

agentive

k. '$_A$MOVE': [A] AGENT [F] to 'MOVE'
I '$_A$MOVED' him to death, by choking him.
($\Rightarrow$ I killed him by choking him. —or:)
$\Rightarrow$ I choked him to death.

Similarly: I rocked/sang the baby to sleep.

l. $_A$BECOME = MAKE$_1$: '$_A$MOVE' in the environment:__Adjective
I MADE$_1$ the fence blue, by painting it.
$\Rightarrow$ I painted the fence blue.

m. $_A$FORM = MAKE$_2$: [A] AGENT [F] to 'MOVE' into EXISTENCE (cf. the phrase *bring into existence*)

I MADE$_2$ a cake out of fresh ingredients, by baking them.
$\Rightarrow$ I baked a cake out of fresh ingredients.

Similarly: I knitted a sweater out of spun wool.
I hacked a path through the jungle.

Mandarin Chinese is the same type of language as English. It conflates Manner or Cause with Motion in its verbs. But the parallel goes further. It also has the same double usage for a single verb form:

(14)  a. Wǒ yòng    zuó jiǎo tī$_1$  le  yī  xià    qíang
      I    use(-ing) left foot kick PERF one stroke wall
      'I kicked the wall with my left foot'

      b. Wǒ yòng    zuó jiǎo bǎ qiú tī$_2$  guò  le  cāo-chǎng
      I    use(-ing) left foot OBJ ball kick across PERF field
      'I kicked the ball across the field with my left foot'

## 1.2 *Motion + Path*

In the second typological pattern for the expression of Motion, the verb root at once expresses both the fact of Motion and the Path. If Manner or Cause is expressed in the same sentence, it must be as an independent, usually adverbial or gerundive type constituent. In many languages – for example Spanish – such a constituent can be stylistically awkward, so that information about Manner or Cause is often either established in the surrounding discourse or omitted altogether. In any case, it is not indicated by the verb root itself. Rather, languages of this type have a whole series of surface verbs that express motion along various paths.[11] This conflation pattern can be represented schematically as in Figure 2.2.

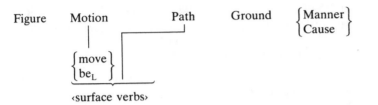

Figure 2.2 Path conflated in the Motion verb

Language families that seem to be of this type are Semitic, Polynesian, and Romance. Spanish is a perfect example of the type. We draw on it for illustration, first with non-agentive sentences, and point out how pervasive the system is here:

(15)   Spanish expressions of Motion (non-agentive) with conflation of Path

   a.  La botella *entró*   a la  cueva (flotando)
       the bottle  moved-in to the cave  (floating)
       'The bottle floated into the cave'

   b.  La botella *salió*   de  la  cueva (flotando)
       the bottle  moved-out from the cave  (floating)
       'The bottle floated out of the cave'

   c.  La botella *pasó*   por la  piedra (flotando)
       the bottle  moved-by past the rock  (floating)
       'The bottle floated past the rock'

   d.  La botella *pasó*        por  el  tubo (flotando)
       the bottle  moved-through through the pipe (floating)
       'The bottle floated through the pipe'

   e.  El globo *subió*    por   la  chimenea (flotando)
       the balloon moved-up through the chimney  (floating)
       'The balloon floated up the chimney'

f. El globo *bajó*        por    la  chimenea (flotando)
   the balloon moved-down through the chimney  (floating)
   'The balloon floated down the chimney'

g. La botella *se fué*        de   la   orilla (flotando)
   the bottle  moved-away from the bank (floating)
   'The bottle floated away from the bank'

h. La botella *volvió*        a  la   orilla (flotando)
   the bottle  moved-back to the bank (floating)
   'The bottle floated back to the bank'

i. La botella le    *dió vuelta*    a la  isla   (flotando)
   the bottle  to-it   gave turn     to the island (floating)
              (= 'moved-around')
   'The bottle floated around the island'

j. La botella *cruzó*        el  canal (flotando)
   the bottle  moved-across the canal (floating)
   'The bottle floated across the canal'

k. La botella *iba*        por  el  canal (flotando)
   the bottle  moved-along along the canal (floating)
   'The bottle floated along the canal'

l. La botella *andaba*        por   el  canal (flotando)
   the bottle  moved-about about the canal (floating)
   'The bottle floated around the canal'

m. Las dos botellas *se juntaron*        (flotando)
   the two bottles  moved-together (floating)
   'The two bottles floated together'

n. Las dos botellas *se separaron* (flotando)
   the two bottles  moved-apart (floating)
   'The two bottles floated apart'

In its agentive forms as well, Spanish shows the same pattern of conflating Path in the verb. Again, Manner or Cause, if present, is expressed in an independent constituent. We can see this for Manner:

(16)    Spanish expressions of Motion (agentive) with conflation of Path

a. *Metí*        el  barril a la  bodega    rodandolo
   I ₐmoved in the keg   to the storeroom rolling it
   'I rolled the keg into the storeroom'

b. *Saqué*        el  corcho de   la  botella retorciendolo
   I ₐmoved out the cork   from the bottle  twisting it

(or:  *Retorcí* el corcho y  lo saqué        de  la botella)
      I twisted the cork  and it  I <sub>A</sub>moved out from the bottle
      'I twisted the cork out of the bottle'

And we can see it for Cause:

c. *Tumbé* el  árbol serruchandolo // a hachazos / con
   I felled the tree  sawing it       by ax chops  with
   una hacha
   an  ax
   'I sawed // chopped the tree down'

d. *Quité*        el  papel del      paquete cortandolo
   I <sub>A</sub>moved off the paper from the package cutting it
   'I cut the wrapper off the package'

Among such agentive forms, those that refer to the placement or removal of a Figure object – the 'putting' verbs – together comprise a subsystem that, again, involves different verb forms for the separate indication of distinctions of Path, as seen in Table 2.1.

Table 2.1. *Spanish 'putting' verbs, differing according to distinctions of Path (A = Agent, F = Figure object, G = Ground object)*

| | |
|---|---|
| A poner F en G | A put F onto G |
| A meter F a G | A put F into G |
| A subir F a G | A put F up (on)to G |
| A juntar F$_1$ & F$_2$ | A put F$_1$ & F$_2$ together |
| A quitar F de G | A take F off G |
| A sacar F de G | A take F out of G |
| A bajar F de G | A take F down from G |
| A separar F$_1$ & F$_2$ | A take F$_1$ & F$_2$ apart |

Notice that English does use different verb forms here, *put* and *take*, in a way that at first suggests the Spanish type of Path incorporation. But an alternative view is that these are simply suppletive forms of a single more general and non-directional 'putting' notion, where the specific form that is to appear at the surface is determined completely by the particular Path particle and/or preposition present. This single 'putting' notion involves an Agent moving a Figure with respect to a particular location by the action of some body part(s) without the whole body moving through space (and, hence, is distinct from the 'carrying' notion of *carry/take/bring*). In expressing this notion, English uses *put* in conjunction with a 'to'-type preposition (*I put the dish into/onto the stove*), *take* with a 'from'-type preposition except when *up* is present (*I took the dish off/out of the stove), pick* with a 'from'-type preposition in the presence of *up* (*I picked the dish up off the chair*), and *move* with an 'along'-type preposition (*I moved the dish further down the ledge*). As further evidence of their purely formal character, these distinctions of verb form are effaced when there is Manner conflation. Thus, beside a different-verb pair of sentences such as *I put the cork into/took the cork out of the bottle* is the same-verb pair *I twisted the cork into/out of the bottle*, where the Manner verb *twist* supplants both *put* and *take*. Comparably, beside *I put the hay up onto/took the hay down off the platform* is *I forked the hay up onto/down off the platform*. Thus, it can be seen that any Path information borne by the English 'putting' verbs is less than and no different from that expressed by the particles and prepositions occurring in the same sentence and, accordingly, they can be readily supplanted under the Manner conflation typical of English. On the other hand, the Spanish 'putting' verbs express the bulk of Path distinctions – the only prepositions used with this subsystem are *a, de,* and *en* – and so are central, unsupplanted fixtures in the Spanish sentence, as is typical for *that* language.

English does have a certain number of verbs that genuinely incorporate Path, as in the Spanish conflation type, for example: *enter, exit, pass, rise, descend, return, circle, cross, separate, join.* And these verbs even call for a Spanish-type pattern for the rest of the sentence. Thus, Manner must be expressed in a separate constituent as in *The rock passed by our tent (in its slide/in sliding)* by contrast with the usual English pattern in *The rock slid past our tent.* But these verbs (and the sentence pattern they call for) are not the most characteristic of English. In fact, the majority (here all except *rise*) are not original English forms but rather borrowings from Romance, where they are the native type.

## 1.3 *Motion + Figure*

In the third major typological pattern for the expression of Motion, the verb expresses the fact of Motion together with the Figure. Languages with this as their characteristic pattern have a whole series of surface verbs that express various kinds of objects or materials as moving or located. This conflation type can be represented schematically as in Figure 2.3.

This pattern can first be illustrated close to home, for English does have a few forms that conform to it. Thus, the non-agentive verb (to) *rain* refers to rain moving, and the agentive verb (to) *spit* refers to causing spit to move, as seen in (17).

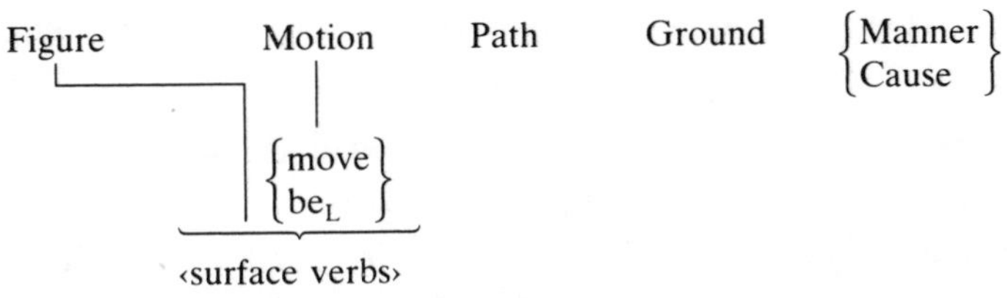


Figure 2.3 The Figure conflated in the Motion verb

(17) a. It *rained* in through the bedroom window [non-agentive]
b. I *spat* into the cuspidor [agentive]

But in the languages for which this pattern is characteristic, there are scores of Motion + Figure verbs with the most colloquial and extensive of usages. Atsugewi, a Hokan language of northern California, is an example *par excellence* of this type. The following verb roots are just a sampling:

(18) Atsugewi verb roots of Motion with conflated Figure

-lup- 'for a small shiny spherical object (e.g. a round candy, an eyeball, a hailstone) to move/be-located'

-t̓- 'for a smallish planar object that can be functionally affixed (e.g. a stamp, a clothing patch, a button, a shingle, a cradle's sunshade) to move/be-located'

-caq- 'for a slimy lumpish object (e.g. a toad, a cow dropping) to move/be-located'

-swal- 'for a limp linear object suspended by one end (e.g. a shirt on a clothesline, a hanging dead rabbit, a flaccid penis) to move/be-located'

-qput- 'for loose dry dirt to move/be-located'

-st̓aq̓- 'for runny icky material (e.g. mud, manure, rotten tomatoes, guts, chewed gum) to move/be-located'

These verb roots can also have an agentive meaning. For example, *-st̓aq̓-* has the further meaning option: '(for an Agent) to move runny icky material'. Thus, such verb roots typically function equally in the expression of events of location, of non-agentive motion, and of agentive motion. Each of these usages is now exemplified with *-st̓aq̓-*, here in referring to guts (an instance of 'runny icky material'). Each example gives both the morphophonemic and the phonetic form (the superscript vowel represents a special morphophoneme of this language):

(19)    Atsugewi expressions of Motion with conflated Figure

    a.  locative suffix:      -ik· 'on the ground'
    instrumental prefix: uh- 'from "gravity" (an object's own weight) acting on it'
    inflectional affix-set: '- w- -ᵃ '3d person subject (factual mood)'
    /'-w-uh-staq̓-ik·-ᵃ/ ⇒ [ẇostaq̓ík·a]
    Literal: 'Runny icky material is located on the ground from its own weight acting on it'
    Instantiated: 'Guts are lying on the ground'

    b.  directional suffix:      -ict 'into liquid'
    instrumental prefix: ca- 'from the wind blowing on the Figure'
    inflectional affix-set: '- w- -ᵃ '3d person subject (factual mood)'
    /'-w-ca-staq̓-ict-ᵃ/ ⇒ [c̓wastaq̓íncta]
    Literal: 'Runny icky material moved into liquid from the wind blowing on it'
    Instantiated: 'The guts blew into the creek'

    c.  directional suffix:      -cis 'into fire'
    instrumental prefix: cu- 'from a linear object, moving axially, acting on the Figure'
    inflectional affix-set: s- '- w- -ᵃ 'I – subject, 3d person object (factual mood)'
    /s-'-w-cu-staq̓-cis-ᵃ/ ⇒ [sc̓ustáq̓cʰa]
    Literal: 'I caused it that runny icky material move into fire by acting on it with a linear object moving axially'
    Instantiated: 'I prodded the guts into the fire with a stick'

## 1.4 Manner/Cause, Path, and Figure in a typology for Motion verbs

The three basic conflation patterns for Motion verbs that languages exhibit, in an apparently exhaustive typology, is summarized in Table 2.2. Subcategorization of these three types, based on where the remaining components of a Motion event are expressed in a sentence, is treated later.

Because it is apparently exhaustive, this typology raises questions about the non-occurring combinatory possibilities. It can be seen that one Motion-event component, the Ground, does not by itself conflate

Table 2.2. *The three typological categories for Motion verbs*

| Language/language family | The particular components of a Motion event characteristically represented in the verb root |
|---|---|
| Romance<br>Semitic<br>Polynesian<br>Nez Perce<br>Caddo | Path + fact-of-Motion |
| Indo-European (all?) except Romance<br>Chinese | Manner/Cause + fact-of-Motion |
| Atsugewi (and apparently most<br>   northern Hokan)<br>Navajo | Figure + fact-of-Motion |

with the Motion verb to form any language's core system for expressing Motion. Conflations of this sort may not even form any minor systems. Sporadic instances of such a conflation do occur, however, and can provide an idea of what a larger system might be like. The verb root *-plane* in the (American) English verbs *emplane* and *deplane* can be taken to mean 'move with respect to an airplane', that is, to specify a particular Ground object plus the fact of Motion, without any indication of Path. It is the separate prefixal morphemes here that specify particular Paths. What a full system of this sort would have to contain is the provision for expressing many further Paths, say, as in *circumplane*, 'move around an airplane', and *transplane*, 'move through an airplane', as well as many further verb roots that participated in such formations, say, (*to*) *house* 'move with respect to a house', and (*to*) *liquid*, 'move with respect to liquid'. But such systems are not to be found. It is not clear why the Ground component should be so disfavored. One might first speculate that, in discourse, the Ground object of a situation is the most unvarying component and therefore the one least needing specification. But on further consideration, the Figure would seem to be even more constant, yet it forms the basis for a major typological system. One might next speculate that the Ground object is the component least salient or accessible to identification. But there seems nothing more obscure about airplanes, houses and liquids (to pick some likely Ground objects) than, say, about notions of Path, which do form the basis for a major typological system.

Explanation may next be sought in a concept of hierarchy: the different conflation types seem to be ranked'in their prevalence among the world's languages, with conflation of Path as the most extensively represented, of Manner/Cause next, and of Figure least so. It may therefore be the case that Ground conflation is also a possibility, but one so unlikely that it has not yet been instantiated in any language (that has come to attention). However, while great disparity of prevalence for the different conflation types would be most significant if proved by further investigation, it would then itself require explanation, so that the present mystery would only have moved down a level.

There are further combinatorial possibilities to be considered. Among these: *two* components of a Motion event conflating with fact-of-Motion in the verb root. Minor systems of such conflation do exist. For example, the Ground *and* Path together are conflated with Motion in a minor system of agentive verbs in English, with forms like *shelve* 'cause-to-move onto a shelf' (*I shelved the books*) and *box* 'cause-to-move into a box' (*I boxed the apples*). (The particular Paths occurring in this system appear to be virtually limited to the contact-forming 'into/onto' type; exceptional, thus, is *quarry* 'cause-to-move out of a quarry', as in *We quarried the granite*, and the verb *mine* with a similar sense, *We mined the bauxite*.) Another minor system of agentive verbs in English conflates the Figure and Path together with Motion: *powder* 'cause facial powder to move onto' (*She powdered her nose*), *scale* 'cause the scales to move off of' (*I scaled the fish*).

Conflation systems of this multi-component sort apparently never form a language's major system for expressing Motion. The reason for such a prohibition seems straightforward for systems observing finer semantic distinctions: these would entail an enormous lexicon. There would have to be a distinct lexical verb for each fine-grained semantic combination – for example, beside *box* meaning 'put into a box', there would have to be, say, a verb *foo* 'take out of a box', a verb *baz* 'move around a box', etc., and further verbs for the myriad of Ground objects other than a box. Such a system would be infeasible for language, whose organization relies less on large numbers of distinct elements and more on combinatorial devices that operate with a smaller set of elements. However, one can imagine another kind of multi-component conflational system, one with fairly broad-band references and hence fewer total elements, acting as a kind of classificatory system, that contained verbs with meanings like 'move to a round object', 'move from a round object', 'move through/past a round object', 'move to a linear object', 'move from a linear object', etc. A system such as this would indeed be feasible for language, yet also seems prohibited, and an explanation here, too, must be awaited.

**1.5 *Aspect***

'Aspect' can be characterized as the 'pattern of distribution of action through time'. The term 'action' as used here applies to a static condition – the continuance of a location or state – as well as to motion or change. In Figure 2.4 are some of the aspect-types lexicalized in verb roots, with both non-agentive and agentive English verbs exemplifying each.

| a. one-way non-resettable | b. one-way resettable | c. full-cycle | d. multiplex | e. steady-state | f. gradient |
|---|---|---|---|---|---|

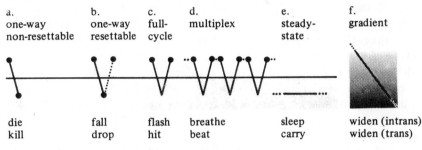

| die | fall | flash | breathe | sleep | widen (intrans) |
| kill | drop | hit | beat | carry | widen (trans) |

Figure 2.4  Aspectual meanings lexicalized in verb roots

Various grammatical tests demonstrate the distinctness of these types and of the verb roots incorporating them. The resettable type of a one-way verb is distinguished from the non-resettable type by its compatibility with iterative expressions, as in *He fell 3 times*; the non-resettable verbs cannot occur here: *\*He died 3 times*. This same one-way form is distinguished from a full-cycle form by its ability to appear in sentences like *He fell and then got up*, which the latter cannot do: *\*The beacon flashed and then went off*. A gradient verb can appear with adverbs of augmentation, as in *The river progressively widened*, unlike a steady-state verb: *\*She progressively slept*. And so on.

Sometimes all that distinguishes two verb forms which otherwise have the same core meaning is a difference in incorporated aspect. In certain sectors of their usage, this is the case with *learn*, which (for many speakers, though not for all) incorporates a completive aspect, and *study*, which is steady-state. The semantically comparable verb *teach* has a lexicalization range covering both of these aspect-types:

(20)   *completive aspect*                    *steady-state aspect*
   We learned/\*studied French          We \*learned/studied French
   in 3 years                                    for 2 years
   She taught us French in 3            She taught us French for 2
   years                                          years

Lexicalized aspect figures in the analysis of a language in several ways. First, aspect generally seems to be part of the intrinsic meaning of verb roots.[12] It is doubtful that any verb root can have a meaning wholly neutral to aspect – even in languages where the root is always surrounded by aspect-specifying inflections.

Second, a verb root's intrinsic aspect determines how it interacts with grammatical elements that also have aspectual meaning. Many of the latter appear only with verb roots of a particular aspect-type, operating on them to yield a different aspect-type as a resultant. For example, in English the grammatical form *keep -ing* operates on a one-cycle verb of the (c) type to yield a multiplex aspectual meaning of the (d) type. This shift takes place for *flash* in *The beacon kept flashing*. Similarly, we can make the reverse change from the (d) type to the (c) type with the abstract grammatical form $V_{dummy}$ *a* [__ + Deriv]$_N$ – that is, by using a construction that has the verb root in a derived nominal form. This is what happens to the verb root *breathe* (with an inherent multiplex meaning) in the sentence *She took a breath* (with a 'once only' meaning).[13]

Third, different languages have different patterns of aspect incorporation in their verbs. For example, we will see in Section 1.7 how verbs referring to states are lexicalized in some languages with the (b) 'one-way' aspect-type – with the sense of entering into the states – while for the same states other languages will use the (e) 'steady-state' aspect-type. And fourth, aspect incorporation can correlate with surrounding factors. For example, it seems generally that a language with a ready inflection indicating 'multiplexity' has few verb roots like English *beat*, *wag*, *flap*, *breathe* with inherent multiplex aspect. Rather, the verb roots by themselves refer to one cycle's worth of the action, and take the inflection to signal multiplexity. One language apparently like this is Hopi (Whorf 1956), and another is American Sign Language (Elissa Newport, personal communication).

### 1.6 *Causation*

By one analysis, there are quite a few distinct types of causation lexicalized in verbs (see Talmy 1976a). The number is appreciably greater than the usually recognized two-way distinction between 'non-causative' and 'causative'. Some verbs incorporate only one causation type while others demonstrate a range of incorporations. A number of such types are listed below, in order of increasing complexity or deviation from the basic (except for the interposed type of (21g)). All but two of these types can be illustrated with the verb *break*; other verbs are given to illustrate types (h) and (i). Most of these types are here named for the kind of element that acts as the verbal subject.[14]

(21) Different types of causative meaning incorporated in the verb root

    a. The vase broke — autonomous event (not causative)

    b. The vase broke from a ball's rolling into it — resulting-event causation

    c. A ball's rolling into it broke the vase — causing-event causation

    d. A ball broke the vase (in rolling into it) — instrument causation

    e. I broke the vase in rolling a ball into it — author causation (i.e. with result unintended)

    f. I broke the vase by rolling a ball into it — agent causation (i.e. with result intended)

    g. I broke my arm when I fell (= My arm broke [on me] when I fell) — undergoer situation (not causative)

    h. I walked to the store — self-agentive causation

    i. I sent him to the store — inductive causation (caused agency)

The autonomous (a) type presents an event as occurring in and of itself, without implying that there is a cause (such causes as there may be fall outside of attention).[15] In the (b) 'resulting-event causation' type, on the other hand, this main event has resulted from another event (expressed in a subordinate clause or a nominalization) and would not otherwise have occurred. English verbs that incorporate both these causation types but no others are *die, fall, drift, disappear, sleep.*

While the (b) type focuses on the main event as *resulting* from another event, the (c) 'causing-event' type focuses on the latter (now the subject) as *causing* the main event.[16] And the instrumental (d) type focuses on just that object within the causing event that actually *impinges* on the affected elements of the resulting event.[17] English has very few verbs that incorporate the (c) or (d) types without also incorporating the (e) and (f) types. One example, though, is *erode* as in *The river's rushing along it/The river/?*The scientists eroded that section of land.*

In both author (e) and agent (f) causation, an animate being wills a bodily action that leads (through a variously sized chain of causal events) to the main event referred to.[18] In the author type, the being intends all these events except the final one; in the agent type, the final one, too, is intended. English verbs associated with the author type and only slightly or not at all with the agentive are *spill, drop, knock (down)*, and bimorphemic *mislay*. Strictly agentive verbs are *murder, throw, persecute.*

The undergoer in the (g) type is like an author in that he does not intend the event mentioned. But he also has not intentionally undertaken any actions that culminate in that event. Rather, the event is conceived of as occurring independently of the undergoer, but as affecting his subjective state, usually adversely. Many languages express the undergoer in an oblique constituent, as does Spanish:

(22)    Se me quebró el brazo
        'The arm broke itself [to] me' = 'I broke my arm'
        Se me perdió la pluma
        'The pen lost itself [to] me' = 'I lost my pen'

English does have this construction (with *on*: My arm broke on me). But it also has verbs that allow the undergoer as subject (I *broke* my arm, I *caught* my sweater on a nail, I *developed* a wart in my ear) as well as ones that require it that way, like *lose* and *forget*. We can contrast the agent, author, and undergoer types with the three verbs in *I hid/mislaid/lost my pen somewhere in the kitchen*. These verbs all have a similar core meaning, one involving an object's becoming not findable. But each incorporates a different causation type:

$$
(23) \quad \begin{Bmatrix} \text{to AGENT} \\ \text{to AUTHOR} \\ \text{to UNDERGO} \end{Bmatrix} \begin{matrix} \text{that NP become} \\ \text{not-findable} \end{matrix} \quad \begin{matrix} \text{approx.} \\ = \end{matrix} \begin{Bmatrix} \text{to } hide \\ \text{to } mislay \\ \text{to } lose \end{Bmatrix} \text{NP}
$$

The self-agentive (h) type is like the agentive except that the animate being's bodily action is itself the final and relevant event, not just a precursor. Often, the whole body is moved through space as a Figure. In their usual usage, the English verbs *go, walk, run, jump, trudge, recline, crouch,* etc., incorporate this type. The verb *roll* can incorporate several different causation types, among them the self-agentive, and so permits a contrastive example:

(24)    a. The log rolled across the field
           – autonomous event

b. The boy rolled the log across the field
   – agent causation

c. The boy rolled across the field on purpose
   – self-agentive causation

In the inducive (i) type, something (whether a thing, an event, or another Agent) induces an Agent to intentionally carry out an act.[19] Some English verbs incorporating this type are: *send, drive (off), chase (away), smoke (out), lure, attract, repel, sic . . . on*. The verb *set . . . upon* has a range that permits a contrastive example:

(25)  a. The dogs set upon us       – self-agentive causation

      b. He set the dogs upon us   – inducive causation

                                       (caused agency)

Our method for distinguishing causation types rests on finding verbs that incorporate only one type or that have ranges differing by only one type (or, at least, ranges which overlap in enough different ways). For example, we can try to use each of the verbs *die, kill, murder* in every one of the causative types listed in (21):

(26)  a. He died/*killed/*murdered yesterday (i.e.: 'He underwent death')

      b. He died/*killed/*murdered from a car hitting him

      c. A car's hitting him *died/killed/*murdered him

      d. A car *died/killed/*murdered him (in hitting him)

      e. She unintentionally *died/killed/*murdered him

      f. She *died/killed/murdered him in order to be rid of him

      g. He *died/*killed/*murdered his plants (i.e.: 'His plants died on him')

      h. He *died/*killed/*murdered (i.e.: 'He killed himself by internal will')

      i. She *died/*killed/*murdered him (i.e.: 'She induced him to kill [others]')

From (26) we can derive the summary in Table 2.3 where we see just the acceptable usages. From the different acceptability patterns here, we can establish that the agentive (f) is a type by itself (it alone accommodates *murder*) and that there are at least distinctions between the (a/b) set of types (*die* but not *kill* ranges over these), the (c/d/e) set of types (*kill's* range minus the agentive (f), already isolated), and the (g/h/i) set of types (suiting none of the verbs). We can now seek cases

Table 2.3. *Acceptable types of causative usage:* die, kill *and* murder

|   | die | kill | murder |
|---|---|---|---|
| a | √ | | |
| b | √ | | |
| c | | √ | |
| d | | √ | |
| e | | √ | |
| f | | √ | √ |
| g | | | |
| h | | | |
| i | | | |

that exhibit distinctions within these clusters of types. The (g) type can be separated out by the fact that it alone accommodates the verb *lose* (in its 'not findable' sense), as we could demonstrate with an array of sentences like that above. Besides, (g) has already been distinguished from (h) and (i) in that *break* can incorporate it but not the latter two types. These themselves are distinguished in that only (h) accommodates *trudge* and only (i) accommodates *sic . . . on*. And so on.[20]

We can establish more conclusively that a verb incorporates a particular causation type by using special test frames. For example, here are two sets of frames that can test for author- and agent-type incorporation in English verbs:

(27)　*s: author-causative*　　*s: agent-causative*

　　　s accidentally　　　　s intentionally
　　　s in (+ Cause clause)　s in order that . . .
　　　s . . . too . . .　　　　NP intend to s
　　　may s!　　　　　　　NP$_1$ persuade NP$_2$ to s
　　　　　　　　　　　　　s!

When placed in these frames, the verbs *mislay* and *hide* show complementary acceptability patterns. In this way each verb is shown to incorporate the one but not the other of the two causation types tested for:[21]

(28)　a. I accidentally mislaid/*hid my pen somewhere in the kitchen
　　　　I mislaid/*hid the pen in putting it in some obscure place
　　　　May you mislay/*hide your pen!

b. I intentionally *mislaid/hid my pen somewhere in the kitchen

I *mislaid/hid the pen so that it would never be seen again

I intend to *mislay/hide my pen somewhere in the kitchen

She persuaded me to *mislay/hide the pen

*Mislay/Hide your pen somewhere in the kitchen![22]

Table 2.4. *Lexicalized causation types shifted by grammatical elements*

| | autonomous | | agentive | self-agentive | undergoer | inducive |
|---|---|---|---|---|---|---|
| (a) | v ————→ | | make v | | | |
| (b) | v ——————————————→ | | | make REFL v | | |
| (c) | {v | or | v} ——————————————→ | | have v | |
| (d) | | | v ———→ V REFL | | | |
| (e) | | | {v | or | v} ——————————————→ | have v |

(a)–(e) correspond to (a)–(e) in (29).

Further evidence that verbs have different causative lexicalizations is that they take different grammatical augments to indicate a shift in causation type. Table 2.4 shows a sample from English of such augments and the shifts they mediate. In (29) each shift is illustrated with a verb that is lexicalized solely in the starting-point causative type and is placed with the relevant grammatical shifters in a clause. Accompanying this, for comparison, is a causatively equivalent clause with an unaugmented verb (in italics) lexicalized solely in the causation type at the end of the shift. Thus, (29a) shows *disappear*, which is solely autonomous (*The stone disappeared/*The witch disappeared the stone*), rendered agentive by the augment *make*, and thereby equivalent to the unaugmented *obliterate*, which itself is solely agentive (**The stone obliterated*):[23]

(29)   a. The witch made the stone   (cf. The witch *obliterated* the disappear   stone)

        b. He made himself disappear   (cf. He *scrammed*)

        c. You might have your toy   (cf. You might *lose* your sailboat drift off   toy sailboat)

          You might have your wallet   (cf. You might lose your (get) stolen in the crowd   wallet in the crowd)

        d. She dragged herself to work   (cf. She *trudged* to work)

        e. I had the maid go to the   (cf. I *sent* the maid to the store   store)

          I had my dog attack   (cf. I *sicced* my dog the stranger   on the stranger)

We can observe causative lexicalization patterns at different levels of linguistic organization. At the level of individual lexical items, a verb's particular range of lexicalizations can often be explained on the basis of its core meaning alone. For example, the basic referent of *break* can apply to a person's body-part but not to his whole body (*I broke his arm/*I broke him*) and, accordingly, the verb lacks a self-agentive usage (*I broke*, in the sense 'I broke myself/my body'). Similarly, *erode* resists agentive usage because an agent cannot generally marshal the instrumentalities of erosion. On the other hand, it seems purely arbitrary that *poison* has an agentive but not an autonomous usage (*He poisoned her with toadstools/*She poisoned after eating toadstools*) while *drown* has both (*He drowned her/She drowned*), or that *conceal* has an agentive but not a self-agentive usage (*I concealed her/*She concealed in the bushes*) while *hide* has both (*I hid her/She hid in the bushes*). But motivated or idiosyncratic, all these lexicalization patterns are associated with particular lexical items.

There are also patterns operating at the level of a whole semantic category. For example, virtually all English verbs that refer to death without expressing its cause (in contrast, for example, to *drown*) observe the basic causative/non-causative distinction – i.e., are lexicalized for either the non-causative (21a/b) types or the (21c–e) causative types but not for both. The pattern applies to both simplex and complex expressions:

(30)    *non-causative*                          *causative*

| die | kick off | kill | exterminate |
|-----|----------|------|-------------|
| expire | kick the bucket | slay | off |
| decease | bite the dust | dispatch | waste |
| perish | give up the ghost | murder | knock/bump off |
| croak | meet one's end | liquidate | rub out |
| pass away | breathe one's last | assassinate | do in |
| | | slaughter | do away with |

By contrast, almost all English verbs expressing the material disruption of an object – e.g. *break, crack, snap, burst, bust, smash, shatter, shred, rip, tear* – apply equally in both non-causative and causative cases (*The balloon burst/I burst the balloon*). There are not many more exceptions than *collapse*, lacking an agentive usage (*I collapsed the shed*), and *demolish*, lacking the autonomous usage (*The shed demolished*).

Different languages often exhibit different lexicalization patterns for a particular semantic category. For example, verbs referring to states are mostly lexicalized in the autonomous type in Japanese but are mostly agentive in Spanish. Japanese adds an inflection to its verbs to express the corresponding agentive, while Spanish adds its reflexive clitics (here serving not in a 'reflexive' but in a 'de-agentivizing' function) to express the autonomous. We can illustrate these complementary patterns with the verbs for 'open':

(31)     Japanese: a. Doa ga    aita
                       door SUBJ open(PAST)
                       'The door opened'

               b. Kare wa doa o   aketa
                  he   TOP door OBJ open (CAUS PAST)
                  'He opened the door'

     Spanish:  c. Abrió      la  puerta
                  he opened the door
                  'He opened the door'

               d. La  puerta se   abrió
                  The door   REFL opened
                  'The door opened'

Finally, at the broadest scope, some lexicalization patterns affect the whole lexicon of a language. One example is that in Japanese the causing-event (21c) and instrument (21d) causation types are barely represented at all. Thus, verbs otherwise corresponding to our *kill* and *break* cannot be used (without extreme awkwardness) with the causing event or Instrument as subject. To express these constituents, one must use the (21b) resulting-event causation type instead.

### 1.7 *Interaction of aspect and causation*
Different verb roots incorporate different combinations of aspectual and causative types. One might at first expect a language to have a roughly equal distribution of the combinations over its lexicon and to have grammatical elements for getting from each combination to any other. But we find two limiting factors. First, not all aspect–causative combinations are relevant to every semantic domain. For example, in many languages the semantic domain of 'states' seems to involve only (or mainly) these three aspect–causative types (compare Chafe 1970):

(32)     a. being in a state (stative)
         b. entering into a state (inchoative)
         c. putting into a state (agentive)

Second, even for such a smaller set, the relevant verbs in a language generally are not evenly lexicalized over the different types. For example, for the expression of 'states', there are languages in which the verb roots are preponderantly lexicalized in only the (a) or only the (b) or only the (c) type. In other languages, such verb roots show a small range of lexicalizations, either over the (a/b) types or over the (b/c) types. There are also languages in which the same verb root is used equivalently for all three aspect–causative types. Sometimes a language's roots exhibit different patterns for different categories within the 'states' domain. Wherever the verb roots are restricted in their aspect–causative ranges, there are generally grammatical devices for getting to the remaining types. But because of all these limitations, the number of devices required can be quite small.

We first demonstrate these lexicalization patterns for one category of states, that of 'postures': postures or orientations that are assumed by the human body or by objects treated as comparable to the body.[24] We can use English here to illustrate the pattern of lexicalization largely limited to the 'being-in-a-state' type. This is seen in verbs like *lie, sit, stand, lean, kneel, squat, crouch, bend, bow*, etc.[25] These verbs must generally take on additional elements for the other aspect–causative types to be conveyed. For example, *lie* by itself refers to being in the lying posture. The verb must be augmented by what we call a 'satellite' – yielding the form *lie down* – to signify getting into the posture. And it must be further augmented by an agentive derivation – yielding *lay down* – to refer to putting into the lying posture:[26]

(33)   a. She *lay* there all during the program

       b. She *lay down* there when the program began

       c. He *laid* her *down* there when the program began

Japanese is a language where posture verbs are generally lexicalized in the 'getting into a state' type, with the other types derived therefrom. For example, the basic meaning of *tatu* is 'to stand up' (comparable to the English verb *arise*). When this verb is grammatically augmented by the *-te iru* form, whose meaning can be rendered as 'to be (in the state of) having [Ved]', the resultant meaning is 'to be in a standing posture'. And when the verb is augmented by the agentive or by the inducive suffix, yielding the forms *tateru* and *tataseru*, the resultant meanings are 'to put into a standing posture' a thing or a person, respectively. To illustrate:

(34)   a. Boku wa  tatta
          I    TOP  arose
          'I stood up'

b. Boku wa tatte      ita
   I    TOP having-arisen was
   'I was standing'

c. Hon o    tateta
   book OBJ AGENTed-to-arise
   'I stood the book up'

d. Kodomo o    tataseta
   child     OBJ INDUCEd-to-arise
   'I stood the child up'

Exemplifying the third pattern, Spanish lexicalizes posture notions in the agentive 'putting-into-a-state' type, the other types being derived therefrom. For example, the verb *acostar* is inherently transitive, with the meaning 'to lay (someone) down'. To it must be added the reflexive morpheme, giving *acostarse*, to get the meaning 'to lie down'.[27] And for the steady-state meaning 'to lie', the verb must be suffixed with the past participle ending and put in construction with the verb 'to be': *estar acostado*:[28]

(35)   a. Acosté      el niño          b. Me      acosté
          I laid down the child            myself I laid down
          'I laid the child down'          'I lay down'

       c. Estaba acostado
          I was   laid down
          'I lay (there)'

These typological findings can be represented together in a single schematic matrix, as in Table 2.5. For each class of language, Table 2.5 shows the aspect–causative type of the verb in which postural notions are generally lexicalized, and the patterns by which the other types are derived therefrom.

Table 2.5. *Lexicalization patterns for verbs of posture (v = verb root, SAT = satellite, PP = past participle inflection)*

|            | be in a posture | get into a posture | put into a posture |
|------------|-----------------|--------------------|--------------------|
| English:   | v ——————→ v + SAT ——————→ v + CAUS + SAT |  |  |
| Japanese:  | 'be' + v + PP ←———— v ————→ v + CAUS |  |  |
| Spanish:   | 'be' + v + PP    v + REFL ←———— v |  |  |

Other languages have other means for deriving the non-basic aspect–causative types from the favored one. For example, German is like English in having the stative type as basic for posture notions, as with verbs like *liegen* and *sitzen*. But it does not derive the inchoative 'getting-into-a-state' type directly from this. Rather, it first derives the agentive 'putting-into-a-state' type, with verbal forms like *legen* and *setzen*. And from this, in the manner of Spanish, it uses the reflexive to get back to the inchoative, with forms like *sich legen* and *sich setzen*. Schematically:

(36)    German:    v $\overbrace{\phantom{xxxxx}}$ v + CAUS + REFL $\longleftarrow$ v + CAUS

In the preceding lexicalization patterns, the verb root incorporated only one aspect–causative type. There are further patterns in which the same verb form serves equally for two types, while grammatical augmentation is required for the third. In one pattern of this sort, the 'being-in-a-state' and the 'getting-into-a-state' types are represented by the same lexical form, but an augmented form is used for the 'putting-into-a-state' type. The verb root in a pattern like this may be thought to capture a factor common to the two types it represents, namely, the involvement of only a single participant (note that the unrepresented 'putting-into-a-state' type, requiring an agent, involves two participants). By one analysis, modern literary Arabic exemplifies this pattern for posture notions (but see below for an alternative interpretation), as in the following root referring to 'sleeping' or 'lying':

(37)    a. *Nām-a*         ṭ-ṭifl-u        ᶜalā
           $\begin{Bmatrix} \text{was-lying} \\ \text{lay-down} \end{Bmatrix}$ he    the-child-NOM $\begin{Bmatrix} \text{on} \\ \text{onto} \end{Bmatrix}$ s-sarīr the-bed
           'The child was lying on the bed'/'The child lay down onto the bed'

        b. *Anam-tu*    ṭ-ṭifl-a        ᶜalā    s-sarīr
           laid-down-I the-child-ACC on(to) the-bed
           'I laid the child down onto the bed'

In another pattern, the same verb root is used to express both the inchoative 'entering-into-a-state' and the agentive 'putting-into-a-state' types, while a different formulation is required for the stative 'being-in-a-state' type. The common factor captured by the verb with two usages in this pattern would seem to be 'change of state'. In familiar languages, there are no apparent instances of this as the predominant pattern for verbs expressing postures. But if we switch here to another category of states, that of 'conditions' (further treated below), the pattern can be exemplified by English. Here, for instance, the verb *freeze* lexicalizes the condition of 'frozenness' together with either the agentive or the inchoative type. For the stative type, however, the grammatical form '*be* + past-participle-inflection' must be added, yielding *be frozen*:

(38)    a. The water *was frozen*
        b. The water *froze*
        c. I *froze* the water

The remaining possible two-way pattern – where the verb root would be used for both the stative and the agentive types, but not the inchoative – does not appear to have any realization. One reason for such a lack may be that these two types do not share a factor that is common to them but absent from the inchoative.

These two-way cases bring us to the pattern where the same verb root is used, without any grammatical augmentation, for all three aspect–causative types. This pattern seems to be the one English posture verbs are moving toward in a process of change going on now,[29] and we can see the pattern fully for several individual verbs of other 'state' categories. One clear example is *hide*, a 'position' verb:[30]

(39 )   a. He *hid* in the attic for an hour
            – being in a position
        b. He *hid* in the attic when the sheriff arrived
            – getting into a position
        c. I *hid* him in the attic when the sheriff arrived
            – putting into a position

We can point to one further lexicalization pattern. Here, the verb root is always accompanied by morphemes with their own aspect–causative meanings, making it difficult to determine whether the verb root itself incorporates any aspect–causative type of its own. Perhaps it does not, and the conclusion to be drawn is that such a verb root refers solely to a particular state, abstracted away from all notions of aspect and causation, and that it requires augmentation for *every* aspect–causative indication. Such augmenting morphemes can exhibit some of the same patterns of incorporation as seen above. In some cases, there would be distinct morphemes for each of the aspect–causative types. In other cases, a single set of elements would serve for some pair of aspect–causative types, with another set for the third. This latter pattern can be exemplified by Atsugewi. Here, a verb root referring to posture is always surrounded by aspect–causation indicating affixes. And among these, generally, one set serves for both the 'getting-into-a-state' and the 'putting-into-a-state' meanings, while a different set is required for 'being-in-a-state'. This is illustrated in (40).

(40)  a. verb root              -it^u-        'for a linear object to be in
                                              // move into/out of/while
                                              in a lying posture'
        directional suffix:    -mič        'down onto the ground'
        inflectional affix-set: s- '- w- -ª 'I – subject, 3d person object
                                              (factual mood)'
        /s-'-w-it^u-mič-ª/ ⇒ [swit^hmíc]
        'I lay down onto the ground'/'I laid it down onto the ground'

     b. verb root:             -it^u-       as for (a) above
        locative suffix:       -ak·         'on the ground'
        inflectional affix-set: s- '- w- -ª 'I – subject, 3d person object
                                              (factual mood)'
        /s-'-w-it^u-ak·-ª/ ⇒ [swit·ák·a]
        'I was lying on the ground'

Arabic forms like those cited earlier have an alternative analysis that
places them at this point of the exposition. The verb root can be taken to
be a consonantal form that – like the Atsugewi root – names the state
alone and always takes different interposed vowel sequences as grammatical augmentations. These grammatical elements, then, follow a
pattern complementary to that of Atsugewi: one vowel sequence
handles both the stative and the inchoative, while another one handles
the agentive.

### 1.7.1 *Consistency of patterns within a language*

Lexicalization patterns for aspect–causative types exhibit different degrees of pervasiveness in a language, first in the degree to which a
pattern predominates *within* a semantic category. For example, posture
notions in English are largely consistent in their stative lexicalization,
with perhaps only inchoative *arise* falling outside this pattern. By
contrast, posture notions in Latin show up in verbs of a variety of
lexicalization types. Each type of verb employs different means to yield
other aspect–causative meanings (e.g. stative *sedere* 'to sit' takes a
prefixal satellite to yield the inchoative *considere* 'to sit down', while
agentive *inclinare* 'to lean (something) against' takes the reflexive to
yield the inchoative *se inclinare* 'to lean (oneself) against'):

(41)

| stative | | inchoative | | agentive | |
|---------|---|-----------|---|----------|---|
| stare | 'stand' | surgere | 'stand up' | ponere | 'lay, set' |
| sedere | 'sit' | | | locare | 'set, lay' |
| iacere | 'lie' | | | inflectere | 'bow, bend' |
| cubare | 'lie' | | | inclinare | 'lean' |

Table 2.6. *Lexicalization patterns for Latin verbs of condition* (v = *verb root*, PP = *past participle inflection*)

|  | be in a condition | enter into a condition | put into a condition |
|---|---|---|---|
| Independent: | v ⟶ | v + INCHOATIVE | v + CAUS |
| Dependent: | 'be' + v + PP | v + MEDIOPASSIVE ⟵ | v |
| *Examples:* |  |  |  |
| Independent: | patere<br>'to be open' | patescere<br>'to open (intr.)' | patefacere<br>'to open (tr.)' |
| Dependent: | fractus esse<br>'to be broken' | frangi<br>'to break (intr.)' | frangere<br>'to break (tr.)' |

Second, a pattern in a language that predominates within one category of a semantic domain may or may not do so *across* the categories. As already seen, English is inconsistent here because its posture verbs are generally lexicalized in the stative, while its condition verbs have the two aspect–causative meanings other than stative.

Latin also exhibits different patterns across categories. To show this, we first point out that what has so far been considered the single category of 'conditions' is better understood as comprising two separate categories. One of these is 'independent conditions': conditions that objects are conceived of as occurring in naturally. The other category is that of 'dependent conditions': conditions conceived of as not original for objects, ones that objects must be brought into by external forces. In many languages, independent conditions are frequently lexicalized in adjectives. In Latin they are, too, but they also frequently appear in verbs. Here they are generally lexicalized in the 'being-in-a-state' type, with the other types derived therefrom. Dependent conditions, on the other hand, are generally lexicalized in verbs in the agentive, and these follow the Spanish pattern for derivation (except that instead of the reflexive, the mediopassive inflections are used). A schematic representation is given in Table 2.6.

The other languages we have looked at in this section show greater consistency across categories. They have the same lexicalization patterns for their verbs of condition as they do for their verbs of posture. We illustrate this extension of the patterns first for Japanese (42a) and Spanish (42b). Compare (34) and (35) with the following:

(42)
a. Japanese

| Mizu ga | *kootte ita* | Mizu ga | *kootta* | Mizu o | *koorasita* |
|---|---|---|---|---|---|
| water SUBJ | frozen be (PAST) | water SUBJ | freeze (PAST) | water OBJ | freeze (CAUSE PAST) |
| 'The water was frozen' | | 'The water froze' | | 'I froze the water' | |

b. Spanish

| El agua *estaba helada* | El agua *se* *heló* | *Helé* el agua |
|---|---|---|
| the water was frozen | the water REFL froze | I froze the water |
| 'The water was frozen' | 'The water froze' | 'I froze the water' |

Comparably, Arabic verbs referring to conditions are lexicalized like posture verbs, with the stative and the inchoative using the same form. Compare (37) with the following:

(43)    ᶜAmiy-a          ṭ-ṭifl-u      Aᶜmay-tu      ṭ-ṭifl-a

{ was blind / became blind } -he the-boy-NOM made blind-I the-boy-ACC

'The boy was/became blind'      'I blinded the boy'

### 1.7.2 *Other aspect–causative types*

There are aspect–causative types other than the three listed in (32) that might seem quite relevant to notions of states. These would involve the transition from being in a state to not being in that state. Such a transition could apply to both the non-agentive and the agentive:

(44)    b'. exiting from a state    c'. removing from a state

However, such types of 'state-departure' seem to be under a universal constraint excluding them from at least one type of lexicalization: a verb root can refer to both state-location and state-entry, but it cannot refer to one of these and also to state-departure. Thus, the Arabic verb form for 'be/become blind' cannot also mean 'cease being blind', and the English *He hid* can refer to 'being in hiding' or 'going into hiding', but not also to 'coming out of hiding'. Beyond such lexicalization ranges, the exclusion of state-departure from lexicalization is total if it is assumed that even singly lexicalized change-of-state verb roots (e.g. *die*) always refer to entry into a new state ('death') rather than departure from an old state ('life').

In addition, state-departure – though not excluded from them – seems quite under-represented among grammatical devices that interact with verb roots. For example, English *hide* cannot be used with departure-indicating satellites or prepositions, either in the postposed location:

(45)    a. *He hid out of the attic = He came out of the attic, where he had been hiding

        b. *I hid him out of the attic = I got him out of the attic, where he had been hiding or prefixally:[31]

(46)  a. *He unhid from the attic

　　　b. *I unhid him from the attic

Comparably, adjectives of condition have ready adjunct verbs or verb-forming affixes to express state-location and state-entry but, in English and many other languages, not state-departure:[32]

(47)  be-in-a-state:
　　　　*be* sick

　　　enter-into-a-state:　　　　　exit-from-a-state:
　　　　*get* sick　　　　　　　　　　*lose* sick
　　　　sick*en*　　　　　　　　　　　*de*sick

　　　put-into-a-state:　　　　　　remove-from-a-state:
　　　　*make* (someone) sick　　　　*break* (someone) sick
　　　　sick*en* (someone)　　　　　　*de*sick (someone)

American Sign Language is similarly constrained. Thus, its signs for conditions (like 'sick') can generally be executed with a number of distinct movement patterns indicating different aspects ('be sick', 'be sick for a long time', 'stay sick', 'become sick', 'become thoroughly sick', 'repeatedly become sick', 'be prone to becoming sick', etc.), but state-departure is not among these (*'cease being sick'). The idea must be expressed with a combination of two signs ('be sick' + 'finish').

It is not clear why there should be this avoidance of expressing state-departure. But in any case, among grammatical elements it is only a tendency, not an absolute. In Atsugewi, verb roots referring to postures and positions (and apparently also conditions) regularly take grammatical elements that indicate state-departure, at least in the agentive. We exemplify this with the verb root used previously in (40):

(48)  verb root:　　　　　　-it^u-　　　'for a linear object to be in //
　　　　　　　　　　　　　　　　　　　　move into/out of/ while in a
　　　　　　　　　　　　　　　　　　　　lying posture'
　　　directional suffix:　　-ic̓　　　　'up off something'
　　　inflectional affix-set:  s- '- w- -ᵃ  'I – subject, 3d person object'
　　　　/s-'-w-it^u-ic̓-ᵃ/ ⇒ [sw̓it·úc̓]
　　　'I picked it up off the ground, where it had been lying'

## 1.8 *Personation*

For actions of certain types, approximately the same actional content is manifested whether one or two participants are involved. For example, whether John shaves himself or shaves me, the action still involves one hand moving one razor over one face. The only relevant difference here is whether the hand and the face belong to the same body. The distinction here is not one of different causation types. For the latter, an increase in participants brings along with it an increment in actional content, as in going from the autonomous *The snow melted* to the agentive *John melted the snow*. Involved here, rather, is a new parameter, one that we will call 'personation', pertaining to the role-structure that is ascribed to an action. An action complex of certain kinds can be taken to manifest either locally, in the body and movements of a single actor (the *monadic* personation type), or distributively, with an actor's body acting on that of a further participant (the *dyadic* personation type).

A verb root can be lexicalized for just one personation type (either one), taking grammatical augmentation to express the opposite type, or it can range over both types. Languages exhibit different patterns, with a bias toward one or another type of lexicalization. Consider, for example, the category of actions involving the use of hands or handled materials on a body. French, for one language, apparently must lexicalize such actions in the dyadic personation type, as actions performed on a *different* person's body. For the case of action on an actor's *own* body, grammatical derivation must be employed – here, the reflexive:

(49)    a. Je raserai    Jean
           I   will-shave John
           'I will shave John'

        b. Je *me*     raserai
           I   myself will-shave
           'I will shave'

English, too, has many verbs with this personation-type, for example:

(50)    a. I cut/bandaged/tickled John

        b. I cut/bandaged/tickled$\left\{ {\text{myself} \atop *\text{-}\phi} \right\}$

But there is a sizable group of English verbs whose simplest form can – in addition to indicating different-person reference – also express the Agent acting on his own body, thus incorporating the monadic personation type as well:

(51)    a. I shaved         f. I scratched (too hard)/Don't scratch!

        b. I washed         g. I buttoned up

        c. I soaped up      h. I dressed

        d. I bathed         i. I undressed

        e. I showered       j. I changed

As discussed in note 4, there is no reason to assume that these verbs incorporate any *reflexive* meaning in conjunction with some 'basically' other-directed sense. It is quite possible to regard these verbs simply as expressing actions that manifest directly in the actor's own person. In having such a group of forms, English distinguishes itself from French, which must use the reflexive with all the corresponding verb forms:

(52)   a.  se raser              f.  se gratter
       b.  se laver              g.  se boutonner
       c.  se savonner           h.  s'habiller
       d.  se baigner            i.  se déshabiller
       e.  . . . (prendre une douche)   j.  . . . (changer de vêtements)

As already noted, English verbs of the type in (51) generally can also express the dyadic personation type (e.g. *I shaved him*), and so cover the range of lexicalization types. But Atsugewi has a group of verbs like those in (51) that refer only to the monadic type. To express the dyadic type, these verbs must add an inflectional element – usually the benefactive suffix *-iray*. With this set of forms, Atsugewi behaves in a way quite complementary to that of French. One example:

(53)   a.  instrumental prefix +
           verb root:            -cu-spaĺ-      'comb the hair'
           inflectional affix-set:  s- '- w- -ᵃ   'I – subject'
             /s-'-w-cu-spaĺ-ᵃ/ ⇒ [sćuspáĺ]
           'I combed my hair'

       b.  instrumental prefix +
           verb root:            -cu-spaĺ-      'comb the hair'
           benefactive suffix:    -iray          'for another'
           inflectional affix-set:  m- w- -isahk  'I – subject, thee – object'
             /m-w-cu-spaĺ-iray-isahk/ ⇒ [mcuspáĺᵊré·sahki]
           'I combed your hair'

American Sign Language appears to lexicalize exclusively in the monadic personation type for referring to a certain class of actions, those that in any way involve the torso. Signs for such actions intrinsically represent them as a person would perform them on himself. These signs must be augmented by additional gestures (such as a shift in body direction) in order to indicate that the actions are performed on someone else. For example, a woman signer can assert that she had put on earrings by (among other gestures) bringing her two hands toward her ears. However, to assert that she had put the earrings on her mother (who has been 'set up' at a certain point of nearby space), she cannot simply move her hands outward toward where her mother's ears would be. Rather, she only begins by moving her hands outward, but then shifts her body direction slightly and adopts a distinct facial expression – indicating that her torso is now representing that of her mother – and curves her hands back around, moving them again to her own ears. That is, an additional gestural complex is necessary to indicate that the referent action is to be understood as other-directed.[33]

## I.9 *Valence*

### I.9.I *General considerations*

In conceptualizing an event that involves several different entities in distinct roles, one is able to direct greater attention to some one of these entities than to the others or, perhaps, to adopt its actual perspective point. A secondary degree of attention or perspective-taking, further, can be accorded to some second entity. Such cognitive forms of focusing in are indicated linguistically by a variety of devices. One device is to make the focused element the grammatical subject – or, for assigning secondary focus to an additional element, to make that the direct object. (Within the scope of our description, it will suffice to adopt simple notions of the grammatical relations 'subject' and 'direct object', and to associate these with the case markings 'nominative' and 'accusative' in the languages that have these.) Now, a lexical verb that refers to a multi-roled event can have built-in constraints on its freedom to assign focus. It can be limited to taking only a particular one of the element types as subject (or direct object), and so lexicalizes focus on that element type. In other instances, a single verb can accommodate different element types in the focus position, and so has a range of lexicalizations. Such focusing properties are here called the 'valence' of a verb. Traditionally, the term valence has been used to refer (either solely or additionally) to the *number* of distinct element types occurring in association with a verb. In this chapter, the issue of element number arises only in the treatment of causation and personation. Valence here is used just for the particular surface case assignment(s) that a verb exhibits, given a fixed number of certain types of elements in association with it.

The notion of incorporated valence can be effectively demonstrated where there are two verbs whose subject limitations together equal the range of subject possibilities of a third verb. This is the case with *emanate* and *emit* on the one hand and *radiate* on the other. All three of these verbs refer to roughly the same event, an event having both a Figure element and a Ground element. But *emanate* requires the Figure as subject, while *emit* requires the Ground as subject – as contrasted

Table 2.7. *Valence properties for selected English verbs*

(i) *Valence properties for emanate, emit, and radiate*

| *Figure as subject* | *Ground as subject* |
|---|---|
| Light emanates from the sun | *The sun emanates light |
| *Light emits from the sun | The sun emits light |
| Light radiates from the sun | The sun radiates light |

(ii) *Valence properties for steal, rob and rip off*

| *Figure as direct object* | *Ground as direct object* |
|---|---|
| I stole his money from him | *I stole him of his money |
| *I robbed his money from him | I robbed him of his money |
| I ripped his money off from him | I ripped him off (? of his money) |

(iii) *Valence patterns with the Figure exhibiting a 'to'-type Path* (F = Figure, G = Ground, A = Agent)

| | *non-agentive* | *agentive* |
|---|---|---|
| *basic order* | Perfume (F) suffused through the room (G) | I(A) suffused perfume (F) through the room (G) |
| *inverted order* | The room (G) suffused with perfume (F) | I (A) suffused the room (G) with perfume (F) |

(iv) *Valence patterns with the Figure exhibiting a 'from'-type Path*

| | *non-agentive* | *agentive* |
|---|---|---|
| *basic order* | The blood (F) drained from his veins (G) | I (A) drained the blood (F) from his veins (G) |
| *inverted order* | His veins (G) drained of their blood (F) | I (A) drained his veins (G) of their blood (F) |

(The word *slowly* can be inserted in the preceding sentences for smoother reading.)

with *radiate*, which accommodates either. Thus, *emanate* incorporates focus on the Figure (the radiation) and *emit* does this for the Ground (the radiator), while *radiate* can incorporate either focus.

We can demonstrate a similar relationship with an agentive example. *Steal, rob,* and *rip off* all refer to the same event and take nominals for the Agent, Figure, and Ground roles.[34] All give the Agent primary focus as subject. But for secondary focus as direct object, *steal* selects the Figure (the possessions) while *rob* selects the Ground (the possessor). *Rip off* accommodates either.

Some verbs – *suffuse* and *drain* are examples – can accommodate their nominals in either the basic Figure-before-Ground order or the inverted Ground-before-Figure order in both the non-agentive and the agentive. Under inversion, the Figure acquires one of two 'demotion particles' – *of* when it exhibits an underlying 'from'-type Path, as with *drain*, and *with* for other Path types, as with *suffuse* (some languages use different cases for this). Thus, the full array of these two verbs' forms in effect constitutes a paradigm against which other verbs, more limited in one respect or another, can be compared. See Table 2.7 for the valence properties of all the preceding English verbs.[35]

In the same way as with aspect and causation, a language can have grammatical devices for use with a verb of one valence type in order to express a different type. German has this arrangement for cases of the secondary focus sort. Its prefix *be-* can indicate a shift in secondary focus from the Figure onto the Ground:

(54)    a. Ich raubte ihm       seine   Tasche
           I   stole   him(DAT) his(ACC) wallet
           'I stole his wallet from him' (Figure as direct object)

        b. Ich *be*raubte  ihn        seiner   Tasche
           I   SHIFT-stole him(ACC) his(GEN) wallet
           'I robbed him of his wallet' (Ground as direct object)[36]

Where a language, as here, has a grammatical device for getting to a particular valence type, it might tend to have relatively few verb roots lexicalized in that type. In fact German appears to have fewer verb roots like our *rob* and *pelt*, roots that intrinsically take the Ground as direct object, using instead its complexes of Figure-taking root plus valence-shifter, like *be-raub(en)* and *be-werf(en)*. The two languages contrast in a similar way in what can be called verbs of giving, this time as to how they indicate focus on (and, hence, the point of view of) the giver or the receiver. Both languages do have cases where the distinction is indicated by distinct verb roots of complementary valence type:

(55)    give                          teach
        get (in the sense of 'receive')  learn

        geben                         lehren
        kriegen                       lernen

But in other cases, English has two verb roots where German has only one, one lexicalized with focus on the receiver. A prefix *ver-* reverses the perspective to the giver's point of view:

(56)    sell       bequeath      lend
        buy        inherit       borrow

        *ver*kaufen *ver*erben   *ver*leihen *ver*borgen
        kaufen     erben         leihen      borgen

This is illustrated in (57).

(57)    a. Ich kaufte das Haus  von  ihm
           I   bought the house from him
           'I bought the house from him'

        b. Er *ver*kaufte      mir     das Haus
           he bought(REVERSE) me(DAT) the house
           'He sold me the house'

Table 2.8. *Derivational patterns for affect verbs focused on the Stimulus or the Experiencer*

| *Stimulus as subject* | ⇒ | *Experiencer as subject* |
|---|---|---|
| It frightens me | | I am frightened of it |
| It pleases me | | I am pleased with it |
| It interests me | | I am interested in it |
| *Experience as subject* | ⇒ | *Stimulus as subject* |
| I fear it | | It is fearful to me |
| I like it | | It is likeable to me |
| I loathe it | | It is loathsome to me |

### 1.9.2 *Valence in verbs of affect*

Consider verbs of affect with respect to valence. These verbs generally require either the Stimulus or the Experiencer of an affective event as the subject. Accordingly, they incorporate focus on either the qualities of the Stimulus or the state of the Experiencer. Compare this lexicalization difference in *frighten* and *fear*, which refer to roughly the same affective situation:

(58)　　a. That frightens me　– Stimulus as subject

　　　　b. I fear that　　　　– Experiencer as subject[37]

For verbs lexicalized in either valence type, there are grammatical, or grammatical–derivational, means for getting to the opposite type. Thus, a verb with a Stimulus subject can generally be placed in the construction 'be – V + PP – Prep' (not a passive: the preposition can be other words than *by*) to bring the Experiencer into subject position. And a verb with an Experiencer subject can often figure in the construction 'be – V + Adj – to', which places the Stimulus as subject. See Table 2.8.

While possibly all languages have some verbs of each valence type, they differ as to which type predominates. In this respect, English seems to favor lexicalizing the Stimulus as subject.[38] While some of its most colloquial verbs (*like, want*) have the Experiencer as subject, the bulk of its vocabulary items for affect focus on the Stimulus, as we see in Table 2.9.[39]

By contrast with English, Atsugewi roots appear to have Experiencer subjects almost exclusively. Virtually every affect-expressing verb (as well as adjective in construction with 'be') elicited in fieldwork was lexicalized with an Experiencer subject. To express a Stimulus subject, these forms took the suffix -*ahẃ*. For one example see Table 2.10.[40]

It may be that the boundaries of the 'affect' category here are too encompassive or misdrawn for good comparative assessments. There

Table 2.9. *Affect verbs in English*

*Stimulus as subject*

| | | | | | |
|---|---|---|---|---|---|
| please | key up | astonish | annoy | incense | worry |
| satisfy | turn on | awe | bother | infuriate | concern |
| gratify | interest | wow | irk | outrage | trouble |
| comfort | engage | confuse | bug | miff | distress |
| soothe | captivate | puzzle | vex | put out | upset |
| calm | intrigue | perplex | pique | disgruntle | disturb |
| charm | fascinate | mystify | peeve | frustrate | disconcert |
| amuse | beguile | baffle | nettle | chagrin | unsettle |
| cheer | entrance | bewilder | irritate | embarrass | shake up |
| tickle | bewitch | boggle | provoke | abash | discombobulate |
| delight | tantalize | stupefy | gall | cow | frighten |
| thrill | matter to | dumbfound | aggravate | shame | scare |
| transport | bore | flabbergast | grate on | humiliate | alarm |
| move | surprise | shock | piss off | disgust | grieve |
| stir | startle | dismay | exasperate | gross out | hurt |
| arouse | amaze | appal | anger | revolt | pain |
| excite | astound | horrify | rile | | torment |

*Experiencer as subject*

| | | | | | |
|---|---|---|---|---|---|
| like | marvel over | want | lust for | abhor | worry about |
| enjoy | wonder at | feel like | crave | deplore | grieve over |
| care for | trust | desire | need | anger over | sorrow over |
| groove on | respect | prefer | covet | fume over | regret |
| fancy | esteem | wish for | envy | seethe over | rue |
| relish | admire | hope for | dislike | gloat over | hurt from |
| love | appreciate | hanker after | resent | distrust | ache from |
| adore | value | hunger for | hate | fear | suffer from |
| delight in | prize | thirst for | detest | dread | bear |
| thrill to | cherish | long for | despise | | stand |
| exult over | revere | yearn for | loathe | | tolerate |

Table 2.10. *Derivation of Experiencer-subject verb roots to Stimulus-subject in Atsugewi*

*Experiencer as subject*

| | | |
|---|---|---|
| verb root: | -lay- | 'to consider as good' |
| instrumental prefix: | sa- | 'by vision' |
| derivational suffix: | -im | (no specific meaning: occurs here idiomatically) |
| inflectional affix-set: | s- '- w- -ᵃ | 'I – subject, 3d person object' |

/s-'-w-sa-lay-im-ᵃ/ ⇒ [swsal·ayíw]
'I find it beautiful'

*Derived to: Stimulus as subject*

| | | |
|---|---|---|
| verb root: | -lay- | 'to consider as good' |
| instrumental prefix: | sa- | 'by vision' |
| valence-shifting suffix: | -ahw | 'from Stimulus to Experiencer' |
| inflectional affix-set: | '- w- -ᵃ | '3d person subject' |

/'-w-sa-lay-ahw-ᵃ/ ⇒ [wsal·ayáhwa]
'It is beautiful'

Table 2.11. *'Cognitive' verbs in English*

| Stimulus as subject | | Experiencer as subject | | | | |
|---|---|---|---|---|---|---|
| strike | occur to | know | think | consider | remember | learn |
| seem to | dawn on | realize | feel | suspect | forget | discover |
| remind . . . of | | believe | doubt | imagine | wonder about | find out |

may be smaller categories following more 'natural' divisions that reveal more about semantic organization. For example, a 'desiderative' category might well be separated out by itself: *all* the English verbs of 'wanting' listed in Table 2.9 have Experiencer subjects, and this arrangement might be universal. Thus, although colloquial expressions with the opposite valence occur in other languages:

(59)　　a. Yiddish:
　　　　　　Mir　vilt　zix　esn
　　　　　　me-IO wants REFL to eat

　　　　b. Samoan:
　　　　　　'Ua sau　('iate a'u) le　fia　'ia
　　　　　　ASP come (to　me) the want (to) eat
　　　　　　'A desire for eating has come on me (I feel like eating)'

they are derived constructions based on verb roots with *Experiencer* subjects. (However, Kaluli of New Guinea may possibly be a language in which all mental verbs – including those of 'wanting' and 'knowing' – put the Experiencer in the surface case that identifies it as the affected argument (Bambi Schieffelin, personal communication).) Perhaps, too, one should separate out an 'assessment' category for notions like 'esteem', 'value', 'prize'; in Table 2.9 the English verbs for these notions again all require Experiencer subjects. We had already separated out a 'cognitive' category for the more intellective mental processes. Verbs of this category were excluded from the affect list above, and again English seems to favor Experiencer as subject for them, as shown in Table 2.11.

　　A single semantic–cognitive principle might account for all these correlations between category of mental event and lexicalization tendency: subjecthood, perhaps because of its frequent association with agency, may tend to confer upon any semantic category expressed in it some initiatory or instigative characteristics. Accordingly, with Stimulus as subject, an external object or event (the stimulus) may be felt to act on an Experiencer so as to engender within him/her a particular mental event. Conversely, with Experiencer as subject, the mental event may be felt to arise autonomously and to direct itself outward toward a selected object. For example, a mental event of 'wanting' might be psychologically experienced across cultures as a self-originating event, and so, by this principle, have a preponderant tendency across languages to correlate with Experiencer subjecthood.

## 2.0 Satellites

Here we will examine the representation of certain semantic categories by a type of surface constituent that has not been generally recognized as such in the linguistic literature, one that we term a 'satellite'. Present in many if not all languages, satellites are certain immediate constituents of a verb root other than inflections, auxiliaries, or nominal arguments.[41] They relate to the verb root as periphery (or modifiers) to a head. A verb root together with its satellites forms a constituent in its own right, the 'verb complex', also not generally recognized. It is this constituent as a whole that relates to such other constituents as an inflectional affix-set, an auxiliary, or a direct object noun phrase. In some cases, elements that are encountered acting as satellites to a verb root otherwise belong to particular recognizable grammatical categories; therefore, it seems better to consider the satellite role not as a grammatical category in its own right but as a new kind of grammatical relation.

The satellite is easily illustrated in English. It can take the form of either a free word or an affix (satellites are marked here by the symbol ◄ that, in effect, 'points' from the satellite to its head, the verb root):

(60)     satellite:     verb complex:     example sentence:
         ◄over          start ◄over        The record started over
         ◄mis-          fire ◄mis-         The engine misfired

As many as four such satellites can appear together in a verb complex:

(61)     Come ◄right ◄back ◄down ◄out from up in there!
         (said, for example, by a parent to a child in a treehouse)

The term traditionally applied to the above element in English is 'verb particle' (see Fraser 1976). The term 'satellite' has been introduced in order to capture the commonality between such particles and comparable forms in other languages. Within Indo-European, such forms include the 'separable' and 'inseparable' prefixes of German and the verb prefixes of Latin and Russian as shown in Table 2.12.

Another kind of satellite is the second element of a verb compound in Chinese, called by some the 'resultative complement'. Another example is any non-head word in the lengthy verbal sequences typical of

Table 2.12. *Satellites as verb prefixes in German, Latin, and Russian*

|  | a. German | |
|---|---|---|
|  | *'separable' prefix* | *'inseparable' prefix* |
| satellite: | ◄entzwei | ◄zer- |
| verb complex: | brechen ◄entzwei (entzweibrechen) | brechen ◄zer- (zerbrechen) |
| ex. sentence: | Der Tisch brach entzwei | Der Tisch zerbrach |
|  | 'The table broke in two' | 'The table broke to pieces' |
|  | b. Latin: | c. Russian: |
|  | *prefixes* | |
| satellite: | ◄in- | ◄v- |
| verb complex: | volare ◄in- (involare) | letet' ◄v- (vletet') |
| ex. sentence: | Avis involavit | Ptica vletela |
|  | 'The bird flew in' | 'The bird flew in' |

Tibeto-Burman languages. In the case of Lahu, Matisoff (1973) has called any such word a 'versatile verb'. A third example is any of the non-inflectional affixes on the verb root in the Atsugewi 'polysynthetic verb'.[42] We now examine a range of types of semantic material that appear in satellites.

### 2.1 *Path*

The satellites in English are mostly involved in the expression of Path. Generally, the Path is expressed fully by the combination of a satellite and a preposition, as in (62a). But usually the satellite can also appear alone, as in (62b). The ellipsis of the prepositional phrase here generally requires that its nominal be either a deictic or an anaphoric pronoun (i.e., that the Ground object be uniquely identifiable by the hearer):[43]

(62)  a. I ran *out of* the house
      b. (After rifling through the house,) I ran *out* [i.e., . . . of it]

Some symbolism here can help represent the semantic and grammatical situation. The symbol > is placed after a preposition, in effect pointing toward its nominal head. Thus this symbol together with ◄ enclose the full surface expression (the satellite plus preposition) that specifies Path, as illustrated in (63a). For a still finer representation, parentheses are used to mark off the portion that can be optionally omitted, and F and G indicate the locations of the nominals that function as Figure and Ground, as shown in (63b):

(63)  a. ◄out of>
      b. F . . . ◄out (of> G)

English has quite a few Path satellites. Some are presented in the sentences below, here without any final Ground-containing phrase:

(64)     Path satellites in English

| | | |
|---|---|---|
| I ran *in* | It flew *up* | He ran *along* |
| I ran *out* | It flew *down* | He ran *around* |
| I got *on* | I went *above* | He ran *past/by* |
| I got *off* | I went *below* | He ran *away* |
| She came *over*$_1$ | He ran *through* | He ran *back* |
| It toppled *over*$_2$ | He ran *across* | She came *forth* |
| | | They rolled *apart* |
| | | They slammed *together* |

In addition, English has a number of Path satellites that would not be generally recognized as such, i.e., as being in the same semantic category as those of (64):

(65)     More Path satellites in English

| | | | |
|---|---|---|---|
| F . . . ◄loose | (from> G) | The bone pulled loose (from its socket) |
| F . . . ◄free | (from> G) | The coin melted free (from the ice) |
| F . . . ◄clear | (of> G) | She swam clear (of the oncoming ship) |
| F . . . ◄stuck | (to> G) | The twig froze stuck (to the window) |
| F . . . ◄fast | (to> G) | The glaze baked fast (to the clay) |
| F . . . ◄un- | (from> G) | The bolt must have unscrewed (from the plate) |
| F . . . ◄over- | $\emptyset$> G | The eaves of the roof overhung the garden |
| F . . . ◄under-$\emptyset$> G | | Gold leaf underlay the enamel |
| G . . . ◄full | (of> F) | The tub quickly poured full (of hot water) |

The languages in most branches of Indo-European have Path systems that are homologous with the one just seen for English. That is, they also use a satellite and a preposition, with the prepositional phrase generally omissible. This is illustrated here for Russian (see Talmy 1975 for an extensive treatment of such forms in this language):

(66)     Path expressions in Russian

| | | | | | | |
|---|---|---|---|---|---|---|
| ◄v- | v + ACC> | 'into' | ◄pere- | čerez + ACC> | 'across' |
| ◄vy- | iz + GEN> | 'out of' | ◄pod- | pod + ACC> | '(to) under' |
| ◄na- | na + ACC> | 'onto' | ◄pod- | k + DAT> | 'up to' |
| ◄s- | s + GEN> | 'off of' | ◄pri- | k + DAT> | 'into-arrival-at' |
| | | | ◄do- | do + GEN> | 'all the way to' |

(67)    a.  Ya vbežal (v    dom)
            I   in ran  (into house(ACC))
            I ran in (-to the house)

        b.  Ya vybežal (iz     doma)
            I   out ran  (out of house(GEN))
            I ran out (of the house)

We want to emphasize for all these Path examples that satellites should be well distinguished from prepositions. No confusion can occur in most Indo-European languages, where the two forms have quite distinct positional and grammatical characteristics. For example, in Latin, Classical Greek, and Russian (cf. (66) and (67)), the satellite is bound prefixally to the verb while the preposition accompanies the noun (wherever it turns up in the sentence) and governs its case. Even where a satellite and a preposition with the same phonetic shape are both used together in a sentence to express a particular Path notion – as often happens in Latin, Greek, and Russian (again, see (66) and (67)) – the two occurrences are still formally distinct. However, a problem arises for English which, perhaps alone among Indo-European languages, has come to regularly position satellite and preposition next to each other in a sentence. For some of these juxtapositions, a kind of merged form has developed, while for others – especially where two occurrences of the same shape might be expected – one of the forms has dropped (we treat this next). Nevertheless, there are still ways in which the two kinds of forms – satellites and prepositions – distinguish themselves. First, it is only a preposition that will disappear when the Ground nominal is omitted: a satellite remains. Next, the two classes of forms do not have identical memberships: there are forms with only one function or the other. For example, *together, apart,* and *forth* are satellites that never act as prepositions, while *from, at,* and *toward* are prepositions that never act as satellites. Furthermore, forms serving in both functions often have different senses in each. Thus, *to* as a preposition ('I went to the store') is different from *to* as a satellite ('I came to'), and satellite *over* in its sense of 'rotation around a horizontal axis' ('It fell/toppled/turned/flipped over') does not have a close semantic counterpart in prepositional *over* with its 'above' or 'covering' senses ('over the treetop', 'over the wall').

We look more closely now at the special feature of the English Path system; it is worth going into because the same feature will appear again in the Mandarin system that we treat next. English has a number of forms like *past* that behave like ordinary satellites when there is no final

nominal, as in (68a), but appear without any preposition when there *is* a
final nominal, as in (68b):

(68)     a. (I saw him on the corner but) I just drove *past*
         b. I drove *past* him

A form like that in (68b) has properties of both a satellite and a
preposition. It receives the heavy stress of a satellite (a preposition
receives light stress, as in 'I went to him'). But like a preposition it is
always positioned before the nominal (an ordinary satellite may follow a
direct object noun, and must follow a pronoun, as in 'I drove him in').
The different English accentual and positional types can be contrasted
thus:

(69)     a. I went tŏ him            – with a preposition alone
         b. I followed him ín       – with a satellite alone
         c. I went ín tŏ him (where he sat)– with both a satellite and a
                                             preposition
         d. I went pást him         – with a satellite-preposition

Because of its special behavior, a form like *past* might be considered a
coalesced version of a satellite plus a preposition – a satellite-preposition (first treated in Talmy 1972) – as suggested symbolically in (70a).
Or, as is assumed here, it can be considered a real satellite that happens
to be coupled with a zero preposition, as suggested in (70b):

(70)     a. ◀past>     b. F. . . ◀past ($\emptyset$ > G)

Mandarin Chinese has Path satellites and constructions that are
entirely homologous with those of English. A number of these satellites
are listed here (they variously may, cannot, or must be further followed
by the satellite for 'hither' or for 'thither'):

(71)   ◀qù     'thither'                        ◀guò    'across/past'
       ◀lái    'hither'                         ◀qǐ     'up off'
       ◀shàng  'up'                             ◀diào   'off (He ran *off*)'
       ◀xià    'down'                           ◀zǒu    'away'
       ◀jìn    'in'                             ◀huí    'back'
       ◀chū    'out'                            ◀lǒng   'together'
       ◀dào    'all the way (to)'               ◀kāi    'apart/free'
       ◀dǎo    'atopple (i.e., pivotally over)' ◀sàn    'ascatter'

These satellites participate in Path expressions of either the coalesced or the uncoalesced type. The only apparent difference from English is an order distinction: the object of the coalesced form follows the verb complex, whereas the prepositional phrase of the uncoalesced form precedes it (as is general with prepositional phrases of any kind). Some satellites can participate in both constructions. One of these is the satellite meaning 'past', which we see here in two different sentences that receive the same translation in English:

(72)　　F. . . ◀guò (-∅> G -biān) (coalescence of satellite and
　　　　　　　　past　　　　　side　preposition)
　　　　Píng-zi piāo guò shí-tóu páng-biān
　　　　bottle　float past rock('s)　　side
　　　　'The bottle floated past the rock'

(73)　　F. . . ◀guò (cóng> G -biān) (the uncoalesced form with both
　　　　　　　　past from　　side　a satellite and a preposition)
　　　　Píng-zi cóng shí-tóu páng-biān piāo guò
　　　　bottle　from rock('s)　　side float past
　　　　'The bottle floated past the rock'

## 2.2 *Path + Ground*

In a conflation pattern distinct from the preceding one, a satellite can express at once both a particular Path and the kind of object acting as Ground for the Path. Satellites of this sort seem to be rare in the languages of the world. However, they constitute a major type in certain Amerindian languages. English does have a few examples, which can serve to introduce the type. One is the form *home* in its use as a satellite, where it has the meaning 'to his/her/. . . home'. Another is the form *shut*, also in its satellite use, where it means 'to (a position) across an opening'. These forms are here illustrated in sentences, optionally followed by prepositional phrases that amplify the meanings already present in the satellites:

(74)　　a. She drove *home* (to her cottage in the suburbs)

　　　　b. The gate swung *shut* (across the entryway)

Atsugewi is one language which has such satellites as a major system.[44] It has some fifty forms of this sort. We can illustrate the system by listing the fourteen or so separate satellites that together are roughly equivalent to the English use of *into* with different particular nominals.

(A '+' here indicates that the satellite must be followed by one of -*im*/-*ik*·, 'hither'/'thither'):

(75)     Path + Ground satellites in Atsugewi

-ict          'into a liquid'
-cis          'into a fire'
-isp -u· +    'into an aggregate' (e.g. bushes, a crowd, a rib-cage)
-wam          'down into a gravitic container' (e.g. a basket, a
              cupped hand, a pocket, a lake basin)
-wamm         'into an areal enclosure' (e.g. a corral, a field, the
              area occupied by a pool of water)
-ipsnᵘ +      '(horizontally) into a volume enclosure' (e.g. a
              house, an oven, a crevice, a deer's stomach)
-tip -u· +    'down into a (large) volume enclosure in the ground'
              (e.g. a cellar, a deer-trapping pit)
-ikn +        'over-the-rim into a volume enclosure' (e.g. a
              gopher hole, a mouth)
-ikc          'into a passageway so as to cause blockage' (e.g. in
              choking, shutting, walling off)
-iksᵘ +       'into a corner' (e.g. a room corner, the wall–floor
              edge)
-mik·         'into the face/eye (or onto the head) of someone'
-mic          'down into (or onto) the ground'
-cisᵘ +       'down into (or onto) an object above the ground'
              (e.g. the top of a tree stump)
-iks          'horizontally into (or onto) an object above the
              ground' (e.g. the side of a tree trunk)

Instances of the use of this satellite system can be seen in the Atsugewi examples appearing earlier, (19a, b, c), (40a, b), and (48); two further examples are given in (76).

(76)     a. verb root:              -staq-      'for runny icky material to
                                                move/be located'
              directional suffix:   -ipsnᵘ      'into a volume enclosure'
              deictic suffix:       -ik·        'hither'
              instrumental prefix:  ma-         'from a person's foot/feet
                                                acting on (the Figure)'
              inflectional affix-set: '- w- -ᵃ  '3d person subject (factual
                                                mood)'

     /'-w-ma-staq-ipsnᵘ-ik·-ᵃ/ ⇒ [ma·staqípsnuk·a]
     Literal: 'He caused it that runny icky material move hither
     into a volume enclosure by acting on it with his feet'
     Instantiated: 'He tracked up the house (coming in with
     muddy feet)'

b. verb root:                    -lup-        'for a small shiny spherical
                                              object to move/be located'

directional suffix:    -mik·      'into the face/eye(s) of
                                  someone'

instrumental prefix:  phu-        'from the mouth – working
                                  egressively – acting on (the
                                  Figure)'

inflectional affix-set: m- w- -ᵃ  'thou – subject, 3d person
                                  object (factual mood)'

/m-w-phu-lup-mik·-ᵃ/ ⇒ [mphol·úpʰmik·a]

Literal: 'You caused it that a small shiny spherical object
move into his face by acting on it with your mouth working
egressively'

Instantiated: 'You spat your candy-ball into his face'

### 2.3 *Patient: (Figure/) Ground*

Another type of satellite is one that indicates the Patient of an event
being referred to. Though apparently rare otherwise, such satellites do
constitute a major system in some Amerindian languages, those known
as 'noun-incorporating'. These languages include an affixal form of the
satellite within their polysynthetic verb. Caddo is a case in point. Here,
the satellite gives a typically more generic identification of the Patient.
The sentence may also contain an independent nominal that gives a
typically more specific identification of the same Patient, but the
satellite must be present in any case. Here first are some non-motion
examples, with (77a) showing the Patient as subject in a non-agentive
sentence, and (b) and (c) showing it as direct object in agentive
sentences:

(77)   a. Ɂíniku? hák-*nisah*-ni-káh-sa? ⇒ [Ɂíniku? háhnisánkáhsa?]
          church PROG-house-burn-PROG
          Literally: 'The church is house-burning
                     (i.e., building-burning)'
          Loosely: 'The church is burning'

       b. cú·cu? *kan*-yi-da?k-ah  ⇒ [cú·cu? kannida?kah]
          milk    liquid-find-PAST
          Literally: 'He liquid-found the milk'
          Loosely: 'He found the milk'

       c. widiš *dá?n*-yi-da?k-ah  ⇒ [widiš dânnida?kah]
          salt    powder-find-PAST
          Literally: 'He powder found the salt'
          Loosely: 'He found the salt'

Without the independent noun, the last example would work in this way:

(78)    dáʔn-yi-daʔk-ah 'He powder-found it'/'He found it 'something powdery)'

In Caddo's general pattern for expressing Motion, the verb root indicates fact-of-Motion together with Path, in the manner of Spanish. The incorporated noun can under limited conditions – it is not yet clear what these are – indicate the Figure, as in this locative example:

(79)    yak-čah-yih        nisah-ya-ʔah ⇒ [dahčahih tisáyʔah]
        woods edge-LOC house-be-TNS
        Literally: 'At woods edge it-house-is'
        Loosely:  'The house is at the edge of the woods'

Usually, the incorporated noun indicates the Ground:

(80)    a. wá·kas na-yawat-yá-ynik-ah ⇒ [wá·kas táywacáynikah]
           cattle   PL-water-enter-PAST
           Literally: 'Cattle water-entered'
           Loosely:  'The cattle went into the water'

        b. nisah-nt-káy-watak-ah            ⇒ [tisánčáywakkah]
           house-penetrate/traverse-PAST
           Literally: 'He-house-traversed'
           Loosely:  'He went through the house'

## 2.4 Manner

Another uncommon satellite type is one expressing Manner. An extensive system of such satellites is found in Nez Perce, another polysynthetic language of North America (see Aoki 1970). In Motion sentences, the verb root in this language is like that of Spanish: it expresses Motion + Path. But at the same time, a prefix adjoining the root specifies the particular Manner in which the Motion is executed. An example of this arrangement is given in (81).

(81)    /hi-quqú·-láhsa-e/ ⇒ [hiqqoláhsaya]
        3d person-galloping-go up-PAST
        Literally: 'He/she ascended galloping'
        Loosely:  'He galloped uphill'

We list here a selection of Nez Perce Manner prefixes. Note that not just locomotive manners are expressed, but also ones of affect ('in anger') and activity ('on the warpath'):

(82)   Nez Perce Manner prefixes

| | |
|---|---|
| ʔipsqi- | 'walking' |
| wilé·- | 'running' |
| wat- | 'wading' |
| siwi- | 'swimming-on-surface' |
| tukʷe- | 'swimming-within-liquid' |
| we·ʔ- | 'flying' |
| tu·ke- | 'using a cane' |
| ceptukte- | 'crawling' |
| tukweme | '(snake) slithering' |
| wu·l- | '(animal) walking/(human) riding (animal at a walk)' |
| ququ·- | '(animal) galloping/(haman) galloping (on animal)' |
| tiqe- | '(heavier object) floating-by-updraft/wafting/gliding' |
| ʔiyé·- | '(lighter object) floating-by-buoyancy' |
| wis- | 'travelling with one's belongings' |
| kipi- | 'tracking' |
| tiwek- | 'pursuing (someone: OBJ)' |
| cú·- | '(plurality) in single file' |
| til- | 'on the warpath/to fight' |
| qisim- | 'in anger' |

Assuming that polysynthetic forms arise through boundary and sound changes among concatenated words, one can imagine how a Nez Perce-type system could have developed from a Spanish type. Originally independent words referring to Manner came regularly to stand next to the verb and then became affixal (and in most cases also lost their usage elsewhere in the sentence). Indeed, one can imagine how Spanish might evolve in the direction of Nez Perce. The preferred position for Manner-expressing gerunds in Spanish is already one adjacent to the verb, as in:

(83)   Entró      corriendo/volando/nadando/ . . . a la   cueva
       he entered running    flying   swimming     to the cave

One could imagine the few changes that would be necessary to take this into the Nez Perce system.

### 2.5 *Cause*
A kind of satellite found in a number of languages, at least in the Americas, has traditionally been described as expressing 'Instrument'. However, these forms seem more to express the whole of a Cause event.

This is because, at least in the familiar cases, not only the *kind* of instrumental object that is involved is indicated, but also the *way* in which this object has acted on a Patient (to cause an effect). That is, a satellite of this sort is equivalent to a whole subordinate clause expressing causation in English. In particular, a satellite occurring in a non-agentive verb complex is equivalent to a *from*-clause, as in (to take an actual example in translation): 'The sack burst *from a long thin object poking endwise into it*'. And the same satellite occurring in an agentive verb complex is equivalent to a *by*-clause, as in 'I burst the sack *by poking a long thin object endwise into it*'.

Perhaps the greatest elaboration of this satellite type occurs in the Hokan languages of northern California, with Atsugewi having some two dozen forms (see Talmy 1972:84–195, 407–67). Here, most verb roots must take one or another of the Cause satellites, so that there is obligatory indication of the cause of the action expressed by the verb root (some verb roots cannot take these satellites, but they are in the minority). The full set of these satellites subdivides the semantic domain of possible causes fairly exhaustively. That is, any perceived or conceived causal condition will likely be covered by one or another of the satellites. The majority of the Atsugewi Cause satellites, those in commonest use, are listed below. They are grouped here according to the kind of instrumentality that they specify. As in other Hokan languages, they appear as short prefixes immediately preceding the verb root:

(84)     Atsugewi Cause satellites (P = the Patient, E = the Experiencer)

*natural forces*

◄ca-     'from the wind blowing on P'

◄cu-     'from flowing liquid acting on P' (e.g. a river on a bank)

◄ka-     'from the rain acting on P'

◄ra-     'from a substance exerting steady pressure on P' (e.g. gas in the stomach)

◄uh-     'from the weight of a substance bearing down on P' (e.g. snow on a limb)
        'from "gravity" (the tendency of things to fall) acting on P'

◄miw-    'from heat/fire acting on P'

*objects in action*

◄cu-     'from a linear object acting axially on P' (as in poking, prodding, pool-cueing, piercing, propping)

◀uh-  'from a linear object acting circumpivotally (swinging) on P' (as in pounding, chopping, batting)

◀ra-  a. 'from a linear object acting obliquely on P' (as in digging, sewing, poling, leaning)
b. 'from a linear/planar object acting laterally along the surface of P' (as in raking, sweeping, scraping, plowing, whittling, smoothing, vising)

◀ta-  'from a linear object acting within a liquid P' (as in stirring, paddling)

◀ka-  'from a linear object moving rotationally into P' (as in boring)

◀mi-  'from a knife cutting into P'

◀ru-  'from a (flexible) linear object pulling on or inward upon P' (as in dragging, suspending; girding, binding)

*body parts in action*

◀tu-  'from the hand(s) – moving centripetally – acting on P' (as in choking, pinching)

◀ci-  'from the hand(s) moving manipulatively – acting on P'

◀ma-  'from the foot/feet acting on P'

◀ti-  'from the buttocks acting on P'

◀wi-  'from the teeth acting on P'

◀pri-  'from the mouth – working ingressively – acting on P' (as in sucking, swallowing)

◀phu-  'from the mouth – working egressively – acting on P' (as in spitting, blowing)

◀pu-  'from the lips acting on P'

◀hi-  'from any other body part (e.g. head, shoulder) or the whole body acting on P'

*sensations*

◀sa-  'from the visual aspect of an object acting on E'

◀ka-  'from the auditory aspect of an object acting on E'

◀tu-  'from the feel of an object acting on E'

◀pri-  'from the taste/smell of an object acting on E'

Instances of these satellites in use in a verb have appeared in examples (19a, b, and c) and (76a and b), to which the reader is referred.

## 2.6 *Motion-related satellites extending the motion typology*

Table 2.2 (section 1.4) showed the three major categories into which languages fall in their treatment of Motion. The typology was based on which element of a Motion event is characteristically expressed in the

Table 2.13. *Typology of motion verbs and their satellites*

| Language/language family | The particular components of a motion event characteristically represented in the: | |
| --- | --- | --- |
| | Verb root | Satellite |
| Romance<br>Semitic<br>Polynesian | Motion + Path | } ∅ |
| Nez Perce | | }Manner |
| Caddo | | }(Figure/)Ground [Patient] |
| Indo-European (all?)<br>  except Romance<br>Chinese | Motion + {Cause / Manner} | Path |
| Atsugewi (most northern<br>  Hokan) | Motion + Figure | a.  Path + Ground<br>b.  Cause |

verb root (with 'fact of Motion', which always appears there). For each such language type, the next issue is where the remaining elements of the motion event are located. The satellite is the most diagnostic surface element to look at after the verb, and so we can make a revealing subcategorization by seeing which motion elements characteristically appear in the satellites that accompany the verbs; see Table 2.13.

**2.7 Aspect**
Many languages have satellites that express aspect. Frequently, these satellites do not indicate purely 'the distribution pattern of action through time' (as aspect was characterized earlier). This purer form is mixed with, or shades off into, indications of manner, quantity, intention, and other factors. Accordingly, a liberal interpretation is given to aspect in the examples below. In this way, we can present together many of the forms that seem to be treated by a language as belonging to the same group. The demonstration can begin with English. Though this language is not usually thought of as expressing aspect in its satellites (as, say, Russian is), it is in fact a fully adequate example:

(85)    English aspect satellites (V = to do the action of the verb)
    ◄re-/◄over    'V again/anew'
        When it got to the end, the record automatically restarted/started over from the beginning

◄on          'continue Ving without stopping'
             We talked/worked on into the night
                    'resume where one had left off in Ving'
             She stopped at the gas station first, and then she drove on from
             there
                    'go ahead and V against opposition'
             He was asked to stay on the other side of the door but,
             adamant, he barged on in
◄away        'continue Ving (with dedication/abandon)'
             They worked away on their papers
             They gossiped away about all their neighbors
                    'feel free to embark on and continue Ving'
             'Would you like me to read you some of my poetry?' 'Read
             away!'
◄along       'proceed in the process of Ving'
             We were talking along about our work when the door suddenly
             burst open
◄off         'V all in sequence/progressively'
             I read/checked off the names on the list
             All the koalas in this area have died off
◄up          'V all the way into a different (a non-integral/
                    denatured) state'
             The log burned up in 2 hours
                (cp. The log burned for 1 hour before I put it out)
             The dog chewed the mat up in 20 minutes
                (cp. The dog chewed on the mat for 10 minutes before I took
                it away)
◄back        'V in reciprocation for being Ved'
             He had teased her, so she teased him back

Other languages have forms comparable to those of English, though
often with different, or more varied meanings. Russian is a case in point.
In addition to several forms like those in the English list, Russian has (at
least) the following (some of the examples are from Wolkonsky and
Poltoratzky, 1961):

(86)    Russian aspect satellites
◄po-         'V for a while'
             Ya pogul'al   'I strolled about for a while'
             Xočets'a poletat' na samolete
             'I'd like to fly for a while on a plane (i.e., take a short flight)'
◄pere-       'V every now and then'
             Perepada'ut doždi   'Rains fall (It rains) every now and then'

Table 2.14. *Atsugewi aspect satellites' meanings*

| V's action is related to: | |
| --- | --- |
| the general temporal flow | an ongoing locomotory event |
| almost V | go and V |
| still V | go Ving along |
| V repeatedly | come Ving along |
| V again/back, reV | V in passing |
| start Ving | V going along with someone |
| finish Ving | V coming along with someone |
| V as a norm | V in following along after someone |
| V awhile/stay awhile and V | V in going to meet someone |
| V in a hurry/hurry up and V | |
| V a little bit/spottily/cutely | |

◄za-　　　'start Ving'
　　Kapli dožd′a zapadali odna za drugoy
　　'Drops of rain began to fall one after another'
◄raz- ◄-s′a  'burst out Ving'
　　Ona rasplakalas′  'She burst out crying'
◄pro-/◄pere-/ . . .   'complete the process of Ving'
　　Pivo perebrodilo  'The beer has finished fermenting'
◄po-/ . . .  'V as one complete act'
　　On yeyo poceloval  'He kissed her' (vs.: was kissing, kept
　　kissing, used to kiss)
◄na- ◄-s′a   'V to satiation'
　　On nayels′a  'He ate his fill'
◄s-　　　'V and de-V as one complete cycle' [only with motion
　　　　verbs]
　　Ya sletal v odin mig na počtu
　　Lit.: 'I there-and-back-flew in one moment to post-office'
　　'I got to the post office and back in no time'

Within its affixal verb complex, Atsugewi has certain locations for a
group of aspect-related satellites. These are semantically of two kinds,
indicating what can be called 'primary' and 'secondary' aspectual
notions. The primary kind indicate how the action of the verb root is
distributed with respect to the general flow of time. The secondary kind
indicate how the action is distributed with respect to another ongoing
event, namely one of moving along. In translation, these forms can be
represented as in Table 2.14.

To illustrate the second satellite type:

(87)   verb root:                    acp-              'for   contained   solid
                                                       material   to   move/be-
                                                       located'

       secondary aspect suffix: -ikc                  'to a position blocking
                                                       passage',   hence:   'in
                                                       going to meet (and give
                                                       to) someone approach-

       inflectional affix-set:    s- '- w- -ᵃ         ing' 'I – sbj (3d person –
                                                       object) [factual]'

       independent noun:          taki·               'acorns'
       nominal marker:            c
              /s-'-w-acp-ikc-ᵃ c taki·/ ⇒ [swacpíkʰca c taʔkí·]

Literally: 'I caused it that contained solid material – namely,
acorns – move, in going to meet (and give it to) someone
approaching'

Loosely: 'I carried out the basket full of acorns to meet him
with, as he approached'[45]


### 2.8 *Valence*

In section 1.9 we saw satellites (German *be-* and *ver-*, Atsugewi *-ahw̓*)
involved solely with valence: they signaled shifts for the incorporated
valence requirements of verb roots. There are also satellites that
basically refer to other notions, such as Path, but themselves incorporate valence requirements. When these are used with verbs that have no
competing requirements, it is they that determine the grammatical
relations of the surrounding nominals. We look at this situation now.

Consider these Path satellites (or satellite + preposition combinations) referring to surfaces:

(88)   a.  Water poured *onto* the table
              – 'to a point on the surface of'

       b.  Water poured *all over* the table
              – 'to all points on the surface of'

These satellites require the Ground nominal as prepositional object
and (in these non-agentive sentences) the Figure nominal as subject.
The same holds for the satellite that refers to interiors in the following
case:

(89)   a.  Water poured *into* the tub
              – 'to a point/some points of the inside of'

However, English has no form comparable to *all over* for interiors:

(89)    b. *Water poured all into/? the tub
        – 'to all points of the inside of'

A new locution must be resorted to. This locution, moreover, differs from the others in that it has the reverse valence requirements: the Figure as prepositional object and the Ground (in non-agentive sentences) as subject:

(90)    The tub poured *full of* water

By the opposite token, the satellite for surfaces does not allow this reverse valence arrangement:

(91)    *The table poured all over with/of water

This same pattern applies as well to agentive sentences, except that what was the subject nominal is now the direct object:

(92)    'surfaces'                          'interiors'
        a. I poured water onto            d. I poured water into the tub
           the table
        b. I poured water all over        e. *I poured water all into
           the table                          the tub
        c. *I poured the table all        f. I poured the tub full
           over with/of water                of water

Using the earlier notation, the valence requirements of these satellites can be represented thus:

(93)    a. F . . . ◄on (-to> G)      c. F . . . ◄in (-to> G)
        b. F . . . ◄all-over ($\emptyset$> G)   d. G . . . ◄full (-of> F)

With the concept of a precedence hierarchy among grammatical relations that places subject and direct object above prepositional object, we can say that in English the notion of a 'filled surface' expressed in a satellite requires the basic Figure-above-Ground, or F–G, precedence, while the notion of a 'filled interior' requires the reverse Ground-above-Figure, or G–F, precedence.

In many languages, certain notions expressed in satellites require one or the other of these same precedences. For example, in Russian, the notion 'into' can only be in the basic F–G precedence:

(94)    a. Ya v-lil       vodu       v stakan
           I  in-poured   water(ACC) in glass(ACC)
           'I poured water into the glass'

b. *Ya v-lil        stakan     vodoy
  I   in-poured glass(ACC) water(INSTR)
  *'I poured the glass in with water'

By contrast, the notion 'all round' (i.e. 'to all points of the surrounding surface of') requires the reversed G–F precedence:

(95)   a. *Ya ob-lil            vodu        na/? sabaku
        I   circum-poured water(ACC) on   dog(ACC)
        *'I poured water all round the dog'

     b. Ya ob-lil            sabaku    vodoy
        I   circum-poured dog(ACC) water(INSTR)
        'I poured the dog round with water'

Accordingly, these satellites can be represented notationally as:

(96)   a. F . . . ◀v- (v + ACC> G)   b. G . . . ◀ob- ($\emptyset$ + INSTR> F)

Outside Indo-European, Atsugewi exhibits similar cases of Path satellites requiring either basic F–G or reversed G–F precedence. Two such satellites, respectively, are ◀-*cis* 'into a fire' and ◀-*mik·* 'into someone's face' (represented below as *afire* and *aface*):

(97)   a. /ac$^h$    $\emptyset$-s-'-i:-$^a$        s-'-w-ra-p̓-cis-$^a$ c ahẃ-i?/
        water OBJ-TOPICALIZER INFL-pour-afire NP fire-to
          ⇒[ʔác$^h$·i se· sẃlap$^h$l̓íc$^h$·a c ʔahwí?]
        'I poured afire water-ACC (F) campfire to (G)'
        'I threw water over the campfire'

     b. /ac$^h$-aʔ      t-s-'-i:-$^a$              s-'-w-ra-p̓-mik·-$^a$
        water-with NONOBJ-TOPICALIZER INFL-pour-aface
        c aẃtih/
        NP man
          ⇒[ʔac$^h$·áʔ c$^h$e· sẃlap$^h$l̓ím·ik· a c ʔáẃte]
        'I poured aface man-ACC (G) water with (F)'
        'I threw water into the man's face' ('I threw the man aface with water')

In some cases, a Path satellite can be used with either valence precedence. English *through* works this way in usages like:

(98)   (*it* = 'my sword')

     a. I (A) ran it (F) *through* him (G)

     b. I (A) ran him (G) *through* with it(F)

In other cases, there are two satellites, with the same meaning and sometimes with similar forms, that act as a complementary pair in handling either valence precedence. The Yiddish forms for 'into', *arayn* and *ayn*, work this way (cf. Talmy 1982):

(99)     a. Ix hob   arayn-geštoxn a dorn (F) in      ferd (G)
            I   have  in(FG)-stuck    a thorn   in the horse
            'I stuck a thorn into the horse'

         b. Ix hob   ayn-geštoxn dos ferd (G) mit   a dorn (F)
            I   have  in(GF)-stuck  the horse    with a thorn
            'I stuck the horse (in) with a thorn'

Certain Russian Path satellites are involved in a further interesting valence distinction. They require the Ground as *direct object* when the Path is bounded and is completed 'in' a quantity of time. For the corresponding unbounded Path that lasts 'for' a quantity of time, there is no Path satellite at all but rather a Path preposition that takes the Ground as *prepositional object*:

(100)    a. (i) Satelit         obletel      zeml'u      (v 3 časa)
                satellite(NOM) circum-flew earth(ACC) in 3 hours
                'The satellite flew around the earth in 3 hours' – i.e.,
                made one complete circuit
            (ii) Satelit         letel        vokrug zemli       (3 dn'a)
                 satellite(NOM) flew-along around earth(GEN) for 3 days
                 'The satellite flew around the earth for 3 days'

         b. (i) On probežal   (vs'u) ulicu         (v 30 minut)
                he length ran all    street(ACC)  in 30 minutes
                'He ran the length of the (whole) street in 30 minutes'
            (ii) On bežal      po     ulice        (20 minut)
                 he  ran along along street(DAT) for 20 minutes
                 'He ran along the street for 20 minutes'

         c. (i) On perebežal ulicu        (v 5 sekund)
                he cross ran   street(ACC)  in 5 seconds
                'He ran across the street in 5 seconds'
            (ii) On bežal      čerez ulicu        (2 sekundy)  i
                 he ran along across street(ACC)  for 2 seconds and
                 potom ostanovils'a
                 then    stopped
                 'He ran across the street for 2 seconds and then stopped'

The question of universality must be asked with regard to satellite valence distinctions like those we have seen. For example, in Indo-

European languages, satellites expressing a 'full interior' seem without exception to require reversed G–F precedence, and satellites expressing bounded Paths largely tend to require the Ground as direct object. Are these and comparable patterns language-particular, family-wide, or universal?

### 3.0 Conclusion

The principal result of this chapter has been the demonstration that semantic elements and surface elements relate to each other in specific patterns, both typological and universal. The particular contributions of our approach have included the following:

First, the chapter has demonstrated the existence and nature of certain semantic categories ('Motion event', 'Figure', 'Ground', 'Path', 'precursor', 'personation', etc.) as well as syntactic categories ('verb complex', 'satellite', and 'satellite-preposition').

Second, most previous typological and universal work has treated languages' lexical elements as atomic givens, without involving the semantic components that comprise them. Accordingly, such studies have been limited to treating the properties that such whole forms can manifest, in particular, word order, grammatical relations, and case roles. On the other hand, most work on semantic decomposition has not involved crosslinguistic comparison. The present study has united both concerns. It has determined certain semantic components that comprise morphemes and assessed the crosslinguistic differences and commonalities that these exhibit in their patterns of surface occurrence. Thus, instead of words' order and role, this study has determined semantic components' surface presence, site (their 'host' constituent or grammatical relation), and combination within a site.

Third, our tracing of surface occurrence patterns has extended beyond treating a single semantic component at a time, to treating a concurrent set of components (as with those comprising a motion event and its circumstance). Thus, the issue for us has not just taken the form: semantic component 'a' shows up in surface constituent 'x' in language '1' and in constituent 'y' in language '2'. Rather, it has also taken the form: with semantic component 'a' showing up in constituent 'x' in language '1', the syntagmatically related components 'b' and 'c' show up there in constituents 'y' and 'z', whereas language '2' exhibits a different surface arrangement of the same full component set. That is, this study has been concerned with whole-system properties of semantic-surface relations.

The present method of componential crosslinguistic comparison permits observations not otherwise feasible. The following section, 3.1, demonstrates this for the issue of information's 'salience'. Former studies of salience have been limited to considering only whole lexical items and, hence, only their relative order and syntactic roles – and, appropriate to these alone, have arrived at such notions as topic, comment, focus, old and new information for comparison across languages. The present method can, in addition, compare the fore-grounding or backgrounding of incorporated semantic components according to the type of surface site in which they show up. It can then compare the systemic consequences of each language's selection of such incorporations.

Following this, the Appendix tabularizes and sketches the semantic-surface relations described earlier, and augments these with a number of additional categories, to provide a one-glance sense of the relationships that have been uncovered as well as to furnish an expanded ground for further research.


### 3.1 *The backgrounding of meaning in the verb complex*

A theoretical perspective that encompasses both sections 1 and 2 pertains to *salience*: the degree to which a component of meaning, due to its type of linguistic representation, emerges into the foreground of attention or, on the contrary, forms part of the semantic background where it attracts little direct attention. In this regard, there appears to be a universal principle. Other things being equal (such as a consti-tuent's degree of stress or its position in the sentence), a semantic element is backgrounded by expression in the main verb root or in any closed-class element (including a satellite – hence, anywhere in the verb complex). Elsewhere it is foregrounded. For example, the two sentences in (101) are virtually equivalent in the total information that they convey, but they differ in that the fact of transit by air is pivotal in (101a) in its nominal (-adverbial) occurrence, whereas it is an incidental piece of background information in (101b) where it is conflated within a verb.

(101)     a.  Last year I went to Hawaii by plane

          b.  Last year I flew to Hawaii

Languages can be quite comparable in the informational content that they convey. However, a way that languages genuinely differ is in the amount and the types of information that can be expressed in a backgrounded way. English and Spanish can be contrasted in this regard. English, with its particular verb-conflation pattern and its multiple satellite capability, can convey in a backgrounded fashion the

Manner or Cause of an event and up to three components of a Path complex, as in (102).

(102)   The man ran back down into the cellar

In this rather ordinary sentence, English has both packed in and backgrounded the information that the man's trip to the cellar was accomplished at a run (*ran*), that he had already been in the cellar once recently so that this was a return trip (*back*), that his trip began at a point higher than the cellar so that he had to descend (*down*), and that the cellar formed an enclosure that his trip originated outside of (*in-*). Spanish, by contrast, with its different verb-conflation pattern and almost no productive satellites, can background only one of the four English components, using its main verb for the purpose; any other expressed component is forced into the foreground in a gerundive or prepositional phrase. The present example, actually, goes beyond the issue of how much can be expressed in the background, to that of how much can be expressed at all in a single sentence, even in the foreground, without being unacceptably awkward. Here, it turns out, Spanish can comfortably express either the Manner alone, as in (103a), or one of the Path notions together with a gerundively expressed Manner, as in (103b, c, and d). For acceptable style, any further components must either be omitted and left for possible inference, or established elsewhere in the discourse:

(103)   Spanish sentences closest to information-packed English sentence of (102)

   a. El  hombre corrió a-l    sótano
      the man     ran   to-the cellar
      'The man ran to the cellar'

   b. El  hombre volvió     a-l    sótano corriendo
      the man    went back to-the cellar  running
      'The man returned to the cellar at a run'

   c. El  hombre bajó       a-l    sótano corriendo
      the man    went down to-the cellar  running
      'The man descended to the cellar at a run'

   d. El  hombre entró    a-l    sótano corriendo
      the man    went in to-the cellar  running
      'The man entered the cellar at a run'

Notice that although the contrast just described was at the level of a general pattern difference between two languages, the same contrast can be observed at the level of individual morphemes, as between such similarly patterned languages as Russian and English. For example, Russian has a Path satellite + preposition complex, ◀pri- k + DAT > 'into arrival at', that characterizes the Ground as an intended destination. English lacks this and, to render it, must resort to the Spanish pattern of expression using a Path-incorporating verb (*arrive*), with a similar attendant awkwardness in expressing further components of meaning, as seen in (104b). (Shown in (104a) for contrast are sentences exhibiting the usual Russian–English parallelism):

(104)  a. Russian: On pod-bežal k  vorotam
               he  up to-ran  to gate(DAT)
      English: He ran up to the gate

    b. Russian: On pri-bežal      k  vorotam
               he  into arrival-ran  to gate(DAT)
      English: He arrived at the gate at a run

At the general pattern level again, we can extend the contrast between languages as to the quantity and types of information they background, for as English is to Spanish, so Atsugewi is to English. While this Amerindian language can, like English, backgroundedly indicate Cause and Path in its verb complex, it can do so as well (as we have seen) for Figure and Ground. Take for example the polysynthetic form in (19b), here approximately represented with its morphemes glossed and separated by dashes:

(105)  (it) – from-wind-blowing –icky-matter-moved –
      [Cause . . . . . . . . . .]  [Figure . . .]
    into-liquid      – Factual
    Path + Ground

We can try to match English sentences to this form in either of two ways. To achieve informational equivalence, the English sentence must include full independent noun phrases to express the additional two components that it cannot background. These NPS can be either accurate indicators of the Atsugewi referents, as in (106a), or, to equal the original form in colloquialness, they can provide more specific indications that would be pertinent to a particular referent situation, as in (106b). Either way, the mere use of such NPS draws attention to their contents:

(106)  a. Some icky matter blew into some liquid

    b. The guts blew into the creek

If, on the other hand, the English sentence is to achieve equivalence to the Atsugewi form in *backgroundedness* of information, then it must drop the full NPs or change them to pronouns, as in:

(107)    It blew in

Such equivalence in backgrounding, however, is only gained by the forfeiture of information, for the original Atsugewi form additionally indicates that the 'it' is an icky one and the entry is a liquid one.[46]

## Appendix: Compendium of meaning–form associations

This chapter's research into meaning–form associations is only a beginning. Among other endeavors, it calls for a thorough cross-linguistic determination of which semantic categories are represented with what frequencies by which surface constituents. The fine-toothed cataloguing thus called for is initiated here in a more modest format in Table 2.15 and its annotations. Incorporated there are the semantic-surface occurrence patterns presented in the text. But these are augmented so as to include a number of additional semantic categories and one additional verb-complex constituent beyond the verb root and satellite, namely, verbal inflections.

While the table's indications are based only on the author's linguistic experience and must be amplified by a thorough cross-language survey, such a survey might nevertheless lead to quite few major upsets. For if a language comes to attention with a semantic-surface association formerly thought non-existent, that association will likely be rare. If the table's discrete plus/minus indications are then simply converted to frequency indications, these will exhibit roughly the same pattern as before.

Given such a pattern, the major issue to be addressed next, of course, is whether the pattern shows any regularities and, if so, what factors might explain them. The data at hand here suggests only partial regularities and, in fact, there are exceptions to every explanatory factor considered. (See Bybee (1980, 1985) for work on related issues.) However, answers may emerge in the future as more pieces come into place:

—with the inspection of more languages
—with a more principled determination of which surface forms are to be considered satellites and how these are to be distinguished from (say) inflections
—with the inclusion of the remaining verb-complex constituents such as adverbial particles and auxiliaries (some of Table 2.15's semantic categories that are not represented in the

root, satellite, or inflections, e.g. 'hedging' and 'spatial location', *are* in fact represented in other verb-complex constituents)

—and with the consideration of further semantic categories and the remaining sentence constituents.

Table 2.15. *Which semantic categories are expressed by which verb-complex elements*

| semantic categories | expressed within the verb-complex by: | | |
|---|---|---|---|
| | (a) verb root | (b) satellite | (c) inflections |
| A. main event | | | |
| 1. main action/state | + | [+/−] | − |
| B. subordinate event | | | |
| 2. Cause | +(M) | + | [+] |
| 3. Manner | +(M) | + | − |
| 4. Purpose | + | (+) | − |
| 5. Result | − | [−/+] | − |
| C. components of a Motion event | | | |
| 6. Figure | +(M) | + | [−] |
| 7. Path (and Direction, no. 25) | +(M) | + | − |
| 8. Ground alone | (+) | + | [−] |
| 7 + 8. Path + Ground | +(M) | + | − |
| D. essential qualities of the event (and of its participants) | | | |
| 9. *hedging | − | [−] | − |
| 10. Xdegree of realization | [−] | (+) | − |
| 11. polarity | + | + | + |
| 12. phase | + | + | [+] |
| 13. aspect | + | + | + |
| 14. Xrate | [−] | [+] | − |
| 15. causativity | + | + | + |
| 16. personation | + | + | [+] |
| 17. number in an actor | + | [+] | + |
| 18. distribution of an actor | + | + | [−] |
| 19. *symmetry/*color . . . of an actor | − | − | − |
| E. incidental qualities of the event or its participants | | | |
| 20. *relation to comparable events | − | − | − |
| 21. Xtemporal setting | [+] | (+) | − |
| 22. *spatial setting | − | [−] | − |
| 23. Xstatus of the actors | (+) | − | − |
| 24. gender/class of an actor | [−] | + | + |
| F. relations of the referent event or its participants to the speech event or its participants | | | |
| 25. Direction (deictic) | +(M) | + | − |
| 26. *spatial location (deictic) | [−] | [−] | [−] |
| 27. tense | − | [−] | + |

## Table 2.15 (*contd*)

| | | | |
|---|---|---|---|
| 28. person | – | [+] | + |
| – relations to the speaker's cognitive state (namely, to the speaker's –) | | | |
| 29. valence/voice (– attention) | + | + | + |
| 30. factivity/evidence (– knowledge) | (+)/+ | + | + |
| 31. attitude (– attitude) | + | + | – |
| 32. mood (– intent) | – | + | + |
| – relations to the speaker–hearer interaction | | | |
| 33. speech-act type | (+) | + | + |
| G. qualities of the speech event | | | |
| 34. status of the interlocutors | [+] | + | + |
| H. factors pertaining neither to the referent event nor to the speech event | | | |
| 35. *speaker's state of mind, *yesterday's weather, . . . | – | – | – |

*Symbols used in Table 2.15*

+      This semantic category shows up in this surface constituent either in many languages or with great elaboration in at least a few languages.

(+)      This category shows up in this constituent in only a few languages, and there with little elaboration.

–      This category does not show up in this constituent in any languages known to the author, and may well never do so.

+/–      This category shows up in this constituent in one capacity or by one interpretation, but not another, as explained in the annotations which follow.

[ ]      There is some question about this assignment of + or –, as explained in the annotations which follow.

x      This category has only slight representation in the verb-complex constituents treated here.

*      This category is possibly never expressed in the verb-complex constituents treated here.

(M)      This category can alone join with the 'Motion' category in the verb root and there form an elaborated system for the expression of Motion events. (The category may also be able to show up in the verb root in other capacities.)

## Brief descriptions and illustrations of semantic categories

(Here, (a), (b), (c) refer to the categories' occurrence in verb roots, satellites, or inflections, respectively.)

1. *Main action/state*. (a) This semantic category – which includes motion and locatedness – is the one most identified with the verb root. It is joined there by the other categories given a '+' in column (a). Thus, in *kill*, agent causativity (no. 15) joins the main action of 'dying' and, in *lie*, a Manner notion (no. 3), 'with a horizontal supported posture', joins the main state of 'being located'. (b) But there may be an exception to the preceding. By the interpretation favored here for the resultative construction in Indo-European and Chinese languages, the satellite presents its expression of a resulting event as the main action or state, while the verb root, generally expressing a cause, presents this as a

subordinate event. Thus, we consider English *melt/rust/rot away* to be best interpreted as meaning 'disappear [= ◄*away*] by melting / rusting / rotting' and German *er-kämpfen/-streiken* as meaning 'obtain [= ◄*er-*] (e.g. territory, wages) by battling/striking'. The alternative interpretation would consider the Result expressed by the satellite as the subordinate event and the verb's Cause as the main one, with the reading of (say) *rust away* then taken to be 'rust with the result of disappearing'. (c) This category is not indicated by inflections.

2. *Cause.* This category refers to the qualitatively different kinds of causing events such as can be expressed by an English subordinate *from*- or *by*-clause. It is distinguished from causativity (no. 15), which corresponds to a superordinate clause of the type 'NP CAUSES S'. (a) Cause is regularly incorporated in the verb roots of European languages expressing either motion or other action. Thus, English *blow* in *The napkin blew off the table* means 'move from (due to) the air blowing on [it]'. (b) Atsugewi has some two dozen prefixal satellites expressing cause, for example *ca-* 'from the wind blowing on [it]'. (c) Causing-event types are generally not expressed in inflections. However, by one analysis, the distinct agentive and inducive inflections of some languages (e.g. Japanese) do indicate different causing events of the types: '[the Agent CAUSES S] by acting physically' vs. '. . . by inducing another Agent (to act physically)'.

3. *Manner.* Manner refers to a subsidiary action or state that a Patient manifests concurrently with its main action or state. (a) It is regularly incorporated in most Indo-European languages' verbs of Motion (as well as other kinds of action), as in English *float* in *The balloon floated into the church*, which means 'move, floating in the process'. (b) Nez Perce has over two dozen prefixal satellites indicating Manner, for example *ʔiyé·-* 'floating in the process'. (c) Manner is not indicated inflectionally.

4. *Purpose.* A purpose event is one that an agent intends to have occur in consequence of his undertaking a main event. (a) Purpose seems universally excluded from incorporation in Motion verb systems. Thus, there is no *I stored the keg into the pantry*, with *store* meaning 'move in order to store'. Purpose *is* incorporated in other type verbs, for example in *wash* 'apply liquid to, in order to clean' and in *hunt* (*I hunted deer*) 'search for, etc., in order to capture'. (b) Purpose is expressed in 'benefactive' satellites (for example the Atsugewi suffix *-iray*), which have the meaning 'in order to benefit/give [it] to [the actor named by the direct object nominal]'. (c) Purpose is not expressed inflectionally.

5. *Result*. A causing event (no. 2) always has a resulting event paired with it because the two are conceived in terms of a single larger causal interaction. (a) When both events are expressed together in a verb root, as they can be, the question here is, which event is the main one and which subordinate? Thus, in *I kicked the ball along the path*, does *kick* mean 'move by booting' with the Result as main event and Cause as subordinate, or instead 'boot with the result of moving', with the reverse ascriptions? We favor the former interpretation (the same as in no. 2). Thus, it may be that Result never incorporates in a verb root as a subordinate event (hence the '−' in the table in the (a) column), but only as a main one. (b) In the resultative construction, Result *is* expressed in the satellite, in many languages with numerous distinctions. However, by the interpretation favored here and already discussed in no. 1(b), it appears there not as a subordinate event but as the main one. Our conclusion is that *all* incorporation of Result, whether in verb root or satellite, is as main event. (c) Result is not expressed inflectionally.

6. *Figure*. The Figure is the salient moving or stationary object in a motion event. (a) It is systematically incorporated in Atsugewi's motion verb roots, for example in *-t'-* 'for a smallish planar object (shingle, button, stamp, etc.) to move/be-located'. The occasional English examples include *rain* (*It rained in through the window*) 'for rain(drops) to fall'. (b) A set of Atsugewi prefixes, overlapping with the causal set, indicates Figures. A set of Caddo prefixes indicates Patient, which sometimes coincides with a Motion event's Figure. (c) Inflections do not represent the Figure *qua* Figure, but they can indicate properties of subject and object – grammatical roles in which the Figure often occurs.

7. *Path*. This category refers to the variety of paths followed, or sites occupied, by the Figure object. (a) It is a regular component in the Motion-verb systems of many language families, for example Polynesian, Semitic, and Romance, as in forms like Spanish *entrar* 'move in', *salir* 'move out', *subir* 'move up', *bajar* 'move down', *pasar* 'move past/through'. (b) Path is the main category expressed by the satellites of most Indo-European languages outside of Romance, as in English with forms like *in, out, up, down, past, through*. (c) Path is not indicated inflectionally.

8. *Ground*. The Ground is the reference-object in a Motion event, with respect to which the Figure's path/site is reckoned. (a) It does not appear alone with the move/be-located component in any language's major Motion verb-root system, but only in occasional forms, like English (*de-/em-*)*plane*, or in combination with additional components

(see following section 7 + 8). (b) A set of Atsugewi prefixes, overlapping with that for Causes, indicates various body-part Grounds – for example 'finger' or 'buttocks' as used with a verb root meaning 'get a splinter'. A set of Caddo prefixes indicates Patient, which often coincides with a Motion event's Ground. (c) Inflections do not represent a Ground object *per se* but only in so far as it serves as a grammatical subject or object.

7 + 8. *Path + Ground.* The combination of Path and Ground is privileged in that it occurs more than other Motion-component combinations (except for those with the 'move' component itself) and certainly more than the Ground alone. (a) Many languages have a series of verb roots in which this combination joins with 'move', for example English *berth* (*The ship berthed*) 'move into a berth' or causative *box* (*I boxed the apples*) 'cause-to-move into a box'. (b) Atsugewi has a major system of suffixal satellites that express some two-score instances of this combination, for example -*ic't* 'into a liquid'. English has a few examples, such as *aloft* 'into the air', *apart* (*They moved apart*) 'away from each other', and *home* (*I drove home*) 'to one's home'. (c) Inflections do not represent this combination.

9. *Hedging.* Among other functions, hedges qualify the categoriality of a linguistic element's referent. They are mostly indicated around verbs by adverbs or special expressions, like those in *He sort of danced/He danced after a fashion*. (a,b,c) However common they may be in that form, they are not incorporated in verb roots nor expressed by satellites or inflections – unless one considers as hedgers such diminutivizing satellites as Atsugewi -*inkiy*, which changes 'to rain' to 'to drizzle' or Yiddish *unter-*, which in *unter-ganvenen* changes 'to steal' to 'to pilfer a bit every now and then'.

10. *Degree of realization.* This category divides a referent action or state – almost anywhere along its semantic continuum – into a more central core of essential aspects and a periphery of commonly associated aspects, and indicates that only one or the other of these is realized. Languages regularly indicate this with adverbs or particles near the verb, for example English *almost* and (*just*) *barely*. Thus, *I almost ate it* can suggest lifting an item to the mouth and perhaps even inserting and chewing it, but excludes at least the essential aspect of swallowing it. Conversely, *I just barely ate it* suggests getting an item down the gullet, but without the usually attendant gusto in chewing and tasting. (a) It is doubtful that a genuine sense of 'almost' or 'barely' is ever really incorporated in a verb root. But perhaps coming close are forms like

*falter* and *teeter* as in *He teetered on the cliff edge*, which suggests 'almost falling'. (b) Atsugewi has a suffixal satellite *-iwt* which indicates 'almost' in all the customary senses. It is the only such form known to the author. (c) This category is apparently not indicated inflectionally.

11. *Polarity*. Polarity is the positive or negative status of an event's existence. (a) Verb roots can incorporate polarity of two kinds, either that pertaining to the root's own referent action/state – for example English *hit* vs. *miss* (= not hit) *the target* – or that pertaining to a complement clause's action/state. In the latter type, incorporated polarity even has some of the same syntactic consequences as independent polarity elements (like *not*), for example in requiring either *some* or *any*:

I managed to/ordered him to/suspect I'll   – see someone/*anyone
I failed to/forbade him to/doubt I'll   – see anyone/*someone

(b) Cheyenne indicates the negative with a prefix *sáa-* in its poly-affixal verb (Dan Alford, personal communication). (c) Some Amerindian and Asian languages are reported to incorporate positive and negative in two distinct sets of inflections that otherwise indicate tense, mood, person, etc.

12. *Phase*. Distinguished from aspect because of its different behavior, the category of 'phase' refers to changes in the status of an event's existence. The member notions are 'starting' and 'stopping', for use with any type of event, and 'initiating' and 'finishing', for events that are intrinsically bounded. To exemplify the two types, *I stopped reading the book* refers to a change from reading to not reading at any point in the book, while *I finished reading the book* refers to reading *all* of the book, and only then not reading. (a) Phase notions can be incorporated in verb roots or collocations, as in *strike up* 'initiate the playing of [a tune]' – and, by one interpretation, also in *reach* (e.g. *reach the border*) 'finish going toward', *shut up* 'stop talking', and *halt* 'stop moving'. Strikingly, 'stopping' is expressed only in verbs like these or as a complement-taking verb (*stop* in *stop eating*) – not as an auxiliary, satellite, or inflection. (b) Phase notions other than 'stopping' are expressed by satellites, for example 'finishing' by German *fertig-*, as in *fertig-bauen/-essen* 'finish building/eating' (or, more literally, 'build/eat to completion'); 'initiating' by German *an-*, as in *an-spielen* 'open play (e.g. at cards)' or *an-schneiden* 'make the opening cut in'; and 'starting' in the specific sense of 'bursting out' by Yiddish *c̷e-* (+ *zix*), as in *c̷e-laxn zix* 'burst out laughing'. (c) Depending on the interpretation, phase either is or is not expressed in inflections. Thus, a preterite inflection

seems to indicate stopping or finishing in conjunction with an unbounded or bounded event, as in *She slept/She dressed*, but may be better
interpreted as being basically a tense/aspect indicator, 'wholly occurring
before now', that merely *implies* cessation. There is also inflectional
indication of 'entry into a state' – i.e. 'becoming' – but it is not clear
whether or not this should be classed together with 'starting'.

13. *Aspect.* Aspect is the pattern of distribution through time of an
action or state. (a) It is regularly incorporated in verb roots, for example
in English *hit*, which can refer to a single impact, as against *beat*, which
indicates an iteration. (b) It also appears frequently in satellites, as in
the Russian prefixal system for indicating perfective/imperfective distinctions. (c) It appears regularly in inflections as well, as in the Spanish
conjugational forms indicating the preterite and imperfect.

14. *Rate.* Rate refers to whether an action or motion takes place
faster or slower relative to some norm. (a) Though some verb roots
obviously indicate different rates of speed – for example English *trudge,
walk, run* or *nibble, eat, bolt* (one's food) – languages seem to include
them haphazardly and in conjunction with further semantic differences,
rather than base a genuine system of lexical distinctions on rate alone.
(b) Satellites generally appear not to indicate rate, with some potential
exceptions: an Atsugewi suffix *-iskur* – which has the same form as an
independent verb 'to hurry' and, with a verb root, was in elicitation
always translated as 'hurry up and V' – might actually or additionally
there mean 'V quickly'. Dyirbal (Dixon 1972) has a suffix *-nbal/-galiy*
said to mean 'quickly' but only as part of a semantic range that also
includes 'repeatedly', 'start' and 'do a bit more'. We have heard one
report that Yana may have had affixes with precisely the meanings
'quickly' and 'slowly'. (c) Rate is not indicated inflectionally.

15. *Causativity.* With the notions in this category, an event is
conceived either as occurring by itself or as resulting from another
event, where this latter event is either initiated by an agent or not, and
such an agent is either volitional or not. (a) Causative notions are
regularly incorporated in verb roots. Thus, English *die* indicates only an
event of death itself, while *murder* indicates that a volitional agent has
initiated an action that has caused the event. (b) As an example for
satellites, the Yiddish prefix *far-* can be combined with a comparative
adjective in a verb formation meaning 'to cause to become . . .', as in
*far-beser-n* 'to improve (transitive)' (from *beser* 'better'). If the reflexive
*zix* can be considered a satellite, then it too is an example, for it changes
a causative form into a non-causative: *farbesern zix* 'to improve

(intransitive)'. (c) In Japanese, separate inflections indicate agent causation, inducive causation, and decausitivization.

16. *Personation*. Personation refers to the configuration of participants that an action is conceived to be associated with. (a) Different languages' verb roots tend to incorporate different personation types. Thus, typical for French, the verb for 'comb the hair', *peign*, intrinsically refers to one's doing the action to another (dyadic). The corresponding Atsugewi verb, *cu-spal*, refers to one's manifesting the action in oneself (monadic). (b) Satellites can reverse a root's personation type. The Atsugewi benefactive suffix makes the 'comb' very dyadic, and the French reflective – considered here as a satellite – converts its verb to monadic. (c) Inflections otherwise involved with causativity may also serve in switching personation types

17. *Number in an actor*. This is the numerosity of the participants – from one to many – behaving as any single argument of an event. It is listed under category "D" as an essential aspect of an event because such numerosity affects how the event is manifested. (a) Many Amerindian languages have distinct roots for an action manifested by different numbers of Patients. Thus, the Southwest Pomo verb roots -*w*/-*ʔda*/-*pʰil* mean, respectively, 'for one/two or three/several together . . . to go'. It is a possible universal that the Patient is the only semantic role characterized for number in the verb root. (b) It is not clear whether satellites indicate number. The closest case I know is an Atsugewi dual clitic, -*hiy*. (c) Inflections in many languages indicate the number of the subject nominal and sometimes also of the direct object nominal. Interestingly, inflectional indications of number seem always to be linked to a particular *syntactic* role, such as subject or object, while those in the verb root correlate instead with a *semantic* role, the Patient.

18. *Distribution of an actor*. This refers to the arrangement of multiple Patients – whether they form an aggregate or a linear distribution in space and/or time (in the latter case correlating with aspect). (a) Different distributions are incorporated systematically in certain Southwest Pomo roots: -*pʰil*/-*hayom* 'for several together/separately to go', *hsa*/*ʔkoy* 'act on objects as a group/one after another'. (b) The Atsugewi suffix -*ayw* indicates 'one after another' for multiple Patients. Though less freely usable, the English satellite *off* can do the same: *read off*/*check off* (items on a list), (animals) *die off*. (c) There is some indeterminacy as to whether a type of affix like Atsugewi's -*ayw* might not be better considered inflectional. Other than this, though, inflections seem not to indicate distribution.

19. *Symmetry, color of an actor.* There are many characteristics of an event's participants that are not marked anywhere in the verb complex, even though they seem as reasonable (from an a priori perspective) as the qualities that *are* marked. Thus, while an argument's numerosity and distribution can be marked, there will be no marking for its color or whether it has a symmetrical arrangement, even though these very qualities are important in other cognitive systems, such as visual perception.

20. *Relation to comparable events.* Many adverbial or particle forms indicate whether an action or state has occurred alone, or in addition to, or in place of another one of a comparable category, like the forms in English *He only danced/ also danced/ even danced/ danced instead.* These notions, however, seem never to be expressed as satellites or inflections, or incorporated in the verb root.

21. *Temporal setting.* This category locates an event within a particular time period, especially a cyclic one. (a) There may be small systems of verb roots differing principally as to temporal locale. Thus, English *to breakfast, brunch, lunch, sup/dine* could be interpreted as meaning 'to eat in the morning/late morning/midday/evening'. (b) Yandruwanhdha verbs optionally take the suffixal satellites *-thalka* 'in the morning', *-nhina* 'by day', or *-yukarra* 'at night' (Bernard Comrie, public presentation). It is possible that only the day's cycle is ever thus represented and not, say, that of the month or year. (c) Inflections appear not to indicate this category.

22. *Spatial setting.* This category would indicate something about the physical setting in which an event takes place, perhaps with contrastive notions like 'indoors/out of doors', 'in the water/on land/in the air', 'next to something/in an open space'. But such notions do not seem to be marked in our three verb-complex elements. One possible exception is Klamath's locative suffixes, though these seem really more to indicate Ground than setting, i.e., to indicate something more like *She hit him in the nose* than *She hit him in the kitchen.* The satellites in English *eat in/eat out* (suggested by Martin Schwartz) are perhaps a real, if very limited, exception.

23. *Status of the actors.* This refers to either absolute or relative social characteristics of animate participants in an event. (a) Japanese verbs of giving differ according to the relative social rank of the giver and the receiver, and so incorporate status. (b, c) Actors' status does not seem to appear in satellites or inflections.

24. *Gender/class of an actor.* This refers to category memberships based on sex or other characteristics, and associated either with an event's actors themselves or with the nouns that refer to them. (a) It appears that no verb roots are lexicalized specifically for use with nouns of a particular *grammatical* gender or class. Thus, for example, Spanish could not have two different verbs for 'to fall', one for use with feminine-noun subjects and the other with masculines. While there do exist verb roots associated with nouns of a particular *semantic* gender (or various other properties), for example roots referring to pregnancy, the association seems less one of systematic categorial distinctions involving selectional features or the like than a matter of individual pragmatic applicability; thus, if a man were in fact to become pregnant, one could simply proceed to say 'The man is pregnant'. (b) The grammatical class of the subject and at times also the direct object noun is marked by affixal satellites in Bantu languages. (c) The subject's grammatical gender is indicated in the inflections in all Hebrew tenses and in the Russian past tense forms, for example in *P'os layal/Sabaka layala* 'The hound barked/The dog barked'.

25. *Direction* (deictic). This refers to whether the Figure in a Motion event is moving toward or away from the speaker. (a) It is found incorporated in verb roots, for example English *come/go* and *bring/take*. (b) It is frequently marked by satellites, for example the pair in Atsugewi, *-ik·/-im*, and in Mandarin, ... *lái/* ... *qù.* (c) It is not marked inflectionally.

26. *Spatial location* (deictic). This category would characterize the location of an event's occurrence with respect to the speaker or hearer (e.g. near or away from one or the other, in or out of their range of vision). It is readily indicated by adverbs or particles, such as English *here* and *there.* But it appears not to occur otherwise in the verb complex. As possible exceptions: we have heard a report that some Northwest Coast Amerindian languages have distinct verb roots meaning 'to be here' and 'to be there', And the evidential satellites or inflections for visual versus other-sensory information, in Wintu as well as other languages, might be used for inferences about spatial deixis.

27. *Tense.* Like the preceding category, but for time instead of space, tense characterizes the temporal location of an event with respect to the moment of the speaker–hearer interaction. (a) By our interpretation, tense is not incorporated in verb roots. A possible candidate such as English *went* is considered not as a conflation of semantic 'go' + 'past' but as a suppletive form standing in the place of the morphemes *go* and

-ed. The reason is that *went* can only appear in environments where other verb roots are followed by -ed. If *went* genuinely incorporated a past sense, one might expect its use as well in expressions like *I am wenting* = 'I was going', or *I will went* = 'I will have gone'. (b, c) Tense is marked by affixes and particles (as well as auxiliaries) in many languages. It is not clear that any of these should be taken as satellites; the affixes among them would normally be taken to be inflections.

28. *Person.* Person refers to the relation between an actor in a referent event and a participant in the speech event (i.e., the speaker or hearer). Thus, in English, if an actor is the same individual as the speaker, the form *I* is used; if the same as the hearer, *you*; and if neither, *he/she/it* or a full nominal is used. (a) No verb roots appear to be specific to a particular person. Distinct forms like English *am/is* invite the same objection as was raised for *went* above. Japanese verbs of giving, sometimes suggested as incorporating person, seem rather to basically indicate relative status, which in turn has certain canonic associations with personal arrangements. (Note that some *noun* roots do incorporate person, for example the distinct Kikuyu nouns for 'my father', 'your father' and 'his father'.) (b) If clitics like Spanish *me/te* can be construed as satellites, then this part of speech can be given a plus for person. (c) Person is notably indicated by inflections.

29. *Valence/voice.* This category refers to the particular distribution of attention and perspective point that the speaker assigns to the different actors in an event, when this factor correlates with the surface cases (grammatical relations) of the nouns referring to the actors. The two traditional terms for this category differ only in that 'voice' refers to the assignment when it is marked by inflections or auxiliaries and 'valence' otherwise. (a) The category is often incorporated in verb roots, for example English *sell* and *buy*, which place the main perspective point at the giver and the receiver, respectively, for the same event. (b) The German satellite *ver-* redirects the main perspective onto the giver in an exchange, as in *ver-kaufen* 'sell' (vs. *kaufen* 'buy'). (c) The category is frequently marked by inflections, as in Latin *emere* 'to buy' and *emi* 'to be bought'.

30. *Factivity/evidence.* This category distinguishes the speaker's belief in, versus ignorance of, an event's truth. The two traditional terms, factivity and evidence, differ only as to whether this category is indicated in the verb root itself or outside it. (a) Only rarely, it seems, does a verb root indicate a speaker's state of knowledge as to its own referent event. One example might be English *be*, indicating speaker's certainty of a copular attribution, and *seem*, indicating uncertainty, as in

*She was/seemed sad.* But many verbs indicate state of knowledge pertaining to a *complement* event, as in *Jan (i) realized/(ii) concluded that she'd won:* (i) the speaker believes the winning to be factual, (ii) the speaker is noncommittal about its actuality. (b) Wintu has a set of 'evidential' suffixes, probably to be taken as satellites, that indicate whether the speaker knows for sure or infers an event, as well as the evidence by which he arrived at his knowledge or supposition (Harvey Pitkin and Alice Schlichter, conference presentation). (c) In Atsugewi, there are two distinct inflectional sets for the 'factual' and the 'inferential'.

31. *Attitude.* The category here is the speaker's attitude toward the referent event. (a) Attitude is incorporated in verb roots. For example, the verbs in *They raided/marauded the village* refer to roughly the same objective event, but *maraud* additionally indicates the speaker's attitude of disapproval toward the event. The negative attitudinal content of *traipse*, as compared (say) with *walk*, is evident from the leadingness of this question by a trial attorney: *Did you confirm that Miss Burnett was traipsing around the restaurant?* (b) The Atsugewi suffixal satellite *-inkiy* indicates the speaker's 'cute' regard for the event. For example, with a root 'flap', it could be used to speak of baby ducklings moving their wings about. (c) Attitude seems not to be indicated inflectionally.

32. *Mood.* Mood refers to a speaker's feelings or intentions with respect to the actualization of an event. It includes a neutral regard, a wish for (something unrealizable), a hope for (something realizable), a desire to (realize something), and an attempt at (realizing something). (a) It appears that no verb roots have an intrinsic mood to them. It might at first be thought that a verb like *want*, as in *She wants to go*, is desiderative, but it really only refers to the *actor's* desire, not to that of the speaker, whose mood toward this event is here neutral. (b,c) Many languages have affixes – whether taken as satellites or inflections – that indicate mood under terms like indicative, subjunctive, optative, desiderative, conative.

33. *Speech-act type.* This category indicates the speaker's intentions with respect to the hearer in referring to an event. (a) The vast majority of verb roots are neutral with respect to speech-event type. But a few verbs do incorporate a particular type, for example the Halkomelem roots meaning 'to be where' and 'to go whither' are solely interrogative, and mainly imperative are English *beware*, the collocation *be advised* (which does accommodate modals, but only with an imperative sense: *You should/*can be advised that . . .*), and perhaps forms like *whoa,*

*giddiyap, scat.* (b,c) The category is often marked by satellites and inflections. For example, Atsugewi has distinct inflectional paradigms for these speech-act types: declarative (I tell you that . . .), interrogative (I ask you whether . . .), imperative (I direct you to . . .), admonitive (I caution you lest . . .).

34. *Status of the interlocutors.* Status is the same here as in no. 23 but refers to the participants of the speech event rather than to the actors of a referent event. (a) The Japanese verbs of giving do not really fit here; they basically indicate the actors' status, and it is only incidental if some of the actors turn out to be participants in a speech event. However, some of Samoan's distinct status-level verbs (e.g. those for eating) may well have usages sensitive solely to who it is that is speaking and being addressed. (b) Satellites and clitics are used by a number of languages to indicate the absolute or relative gender (men's and women's speech) and status of the interlocutors. (c) Inflections for second person in many European languages distinguish degrees of formality that are partly based on relative status.

35. *Speaker's state of mind, . . .* It seems that no markers or incorporations indicate notions unrelated to either the referent event or the speech event. If they existed, one might encounter cases like *The chair broke-ka* meaning 'The chair broke and I'm currently bored' or 'The chair broke and it was raining yesterday'.

NOTES

1 Grateful acknowledgement is here extended to several people for their native-speaker help with languages cited in this chapter: to Selina LaMarr for Atsugewi (the language of the author's fieldwork studies), to Mauricio Mixco and Carmen Silva for Spanish, to Matt Shibatani and to Yoshio and Naomi Miyake for Japanese, to Tedi Kompanetz for French, to Vicky Shu and Teresa Chen for Mandarin, to Luise Hathaway and Ariel Bloch for German, to Esther Talmy and Simon Karlinsky for Russian, and to Ted Suppala for American Sign Language.

   In addition, thanks go to several people for data from their work on other languages: to Wallace Chafe for Caddo, to Haruo Aoki for Nez Perce, to Robert Oswalt for Southwest Pomo, to Donna Gerdts for Halkomelem, to Ariel Bloch for Arabic, to Bradd Shore for Samoan, and to Elissa Newport and Ursula Bellugi-Klima for American Sign Language – as well as to several others whose personal communications are cited in the text. The author has supplied the Yiddish forms, while the Latin data are from dictionaries. Special thanks go to Tim Shopen for his invaluable editorial work with earlier drafts for this chapter. And thanks as well to Melissa Bowerman, Dan

Slobin, Johanna Nichols, Joan Bybee, and Eric Pederson for fruitful discussions.

2 A zero form in a language can represent a meaning not expressed by any actual lexical item. For example, no German verb has the general 'go' meaning of the zero form cited (*gehen* implies walking, so that one could not ask *Wo wollen Sie denn hingehen?* of a swimmer).

3 For a further theoretical discussion, exploring questions like: What deeper properties of language can account for why the patterns are as they are?, or What still broader phenomena do the observed patterns fit into? see Talmy (1976b, 1978c, 1983, in preparation).

4 Apart from these three processes, an analyst can sometimes invoke what we might term *semantic resegmentation*. Consider the case of *shave* as used in (f):

(a) I cut John      (c) I cut myself      (e) *I cut
(b) I shaved John   (d) I shaved myself   (f) I shaved

We could believe here that a reflexive meaning component is lexicalized in the verb, deleted from the sentence, or to be inferred by pragmatics. However, we need to assume that a reflexive meaning is present only if we consider this usage to be derived from that in (b)/(d). We could, alternatively, conclude that the (f) usage is itself basic and refers directly to a particular action pattern involving a single person, with no reflexive meaning at all.

5 These forms express universal semantic elements and should not be identified with the English surface verbs used to represent them (they are written in capitals as MOVE and BE$_L$ in other works by the author to underscore this distinction).

6 These notions of Figure and Ground have several advantages over Fillmore's (e.g. 1977) system of cases. The comparison is set forth in detail in Talmy (1978a), but some major differences can be indicated here. The notion of 'Ground' captures what is common – namely, a function as reference-object – to all of Fillmore's separate cases 'Location', 'Source', 'Goal', and 'Path', which otherwise have nothing to indicate their commonality (as against, say, 'Instrument', 'Patient', and 'Agent'). Further, Fillmore's system has nothing to indicate the commonality of its Source, Goal, and Path cases as against Location, a distinction captured in our system by the move/be-located opposition within the Motion component. Moreover, the Fillmorian cases' incorporation of path notions (together with reference-object function) opens the door to adding a new case for every newly recognized path notion, with possibly adverse consequences for universality claims. Our system, by abstracting away all notions of path into a separate 'Path' component, allows for the representation of semantic complexes with both universal and language-particular portions.

7 The assessment of whether it is Manner or Cause that is conflated in the verb is based on whether the verb's basic reference is to what the Figure does or to what the Agent or Instrument does. For example, in 'I rolled the keg . . .', *rolled* basically refers to what the keg did and so expresses Manner, whereas

in 'I pushed the keg . . .', *pushed* refers to what I did, and so gives the Cause of the event.

8 There appear to be constraints, some of them apparently universal, on the kinds of subordinate-clause material that can systematically conflate with Motion. For example, while English readily conflates the Manner or the Cause into a main Motion event, as demonstrated in (6), it cannot do so for the Purpose. Thus, beside the complex sentence with subordinate Purpose clause in (ia), there exists no conflated analog like (ib):

(i)     a.   I moved the keg into the pantry, in order to store it

        b.   *I stored the keg into the pantry

In English, then, a non-main event is allowed to conflate with a main Motion event if its time of occurrence is before or during that Motion event, but not after it. This restriction may well be universal.

Under language-particular constraint, on the other hand, is another type of non-main event, 'precursor', which expresses an action already undergone by the Figure object that is currently in Motion. Thus, Atsugewi does regularly exhibit forms analogous to (iib) with meanings like that in (iia):

(ii)    a.   I moved (put) the blanket into the basket, having first folded it

        b.   I folded the blanket into the basket

In English the sentence in (iib) would have to be interpreted as expressing concurrent Manner: folding the blanket *in the process of* placing it in. However, English does minimally exhibit the precursor pattern with sentences like *Reach/Get me the salt*, meaning 'Give me the salt, having first reached to/gotten it', or to the extent that speakers accept sentences like *He scooped up some jelly beans into my bag* in the sense of 'He put into my bag some jelly beans that he had scooped up/having first scooped them up'.

Aside from any systematic conflation with Motion that they may or may not exhibit, certain types of non-main events do otherwise show up conflated in main verbs. Purpose, for example, *is* conflated in the non-motion-system English verbs *wash* and *rinse*. These verbs, beyond referring to certain actions involving the use of liquid, indicate that such actions are undertaken *in order to* remove dirt or soap. Evidence for such an incorporation is that the verbs are virtually unable to appear in contexts that pragmatically conflict with the Purpose:

(iii)   a.   I washed/rinsed the shirt in tap water

        b.   *I washed/rinsed the shirt in dirty ink

whereas otherwise comparable verbs like *soak* and *flush*, which seem not to express any Purpose beyond the performance of the main action, *can* appear there:

(iv)   I soaked the shirt in dirty ink/I flushed dirty ink through the shirt

Further, Cause and Manner can be conflated as well in verbs that do not participate in the Motion system. For example, the English verb *clench* expresses (in one area of its usage) the curling together of the fingers of a hand specifically caused by internal (neuromotor) activity. No other cause can be compatibly expressed in conjunction with this verb:

(v)  a. My hand clenched into a fist from a muscle spasm/*from the wind blowing on it

  b. I/*He clenched my hand into a fist

By contrast, *curl up* expresses a main action similar to that of *clench*, but it incorporates no restrictions as to the cause of the action:

(vi)  a. My hand curled up into a fist from a muscle spasm/from the wind blowing on it

  b. I/He curled my hand up into a fist

9 The systematic relations of the kind shown here are discussed with greater detail and rigor in Talmy (1975). But one point from that discussion can be brought in here. A distinction must be made between translational motion and contained motion. In the former, an object's basic location shifts from one point to another in space. In the latter, the object keeps its same basic, or 'average', location. This latter case usually involves rotation, oscillation, expansion/contraction, or 'contained wander'. This distinction in types of motion underlies the analysis shown in (6) for *roll* and *bounce*. Both these verbs in their non-translational sense refer to motion, but only to contained motion, as seen in (a) and (b).

  (a) The log rolled over and over in the water

  (b) The ball bounced up and down on the pavement square

These verbs, like *float* in the sense of 'be afloat', can then take on the additional meaning of translational motion through space.

10 The usage relationships posited here are accorded some psychological reality by data on children's errors. Bowerman (1981) documents a stage in English acquisition where children become 'aware' of motion conflation in verbs and then overextend the pattern. Thus, verbs that in adult English, idiosyncratically, cannot be used with an incorporated motion meaning become so used by children:

  (a) Don't hug me off my chair (= by hugging move me off)

  (b) When you get to her [a doll], you catch her off (on a merry-go-round with a doll, wants a friend standing nearby to remove the doll on the next spin around)

  (c) I'll jump that down (about to jump onto a mat floating atop the tub water and force it down to the bottom)

Further support comes from historical changes in word meaning, which exhibit similar extensions beyond previous category boundaries. Thus, in their traditional use the verbs *hold* and *carry* formed a near perfect suppletive pair, differing only in that *carry* additionally incorporated a Motion event while *hold* did not:

| without motion | with motion |
|---|---|
| I held the box as I lay on the bed | *I held the box to my neighbor's house |
| *I carried the box as I lay on the bed | I carried the box to my neighbor's house |

Currently, though, *carry* in some contexts (those where motion just has occurred or is about to occur) can also be used in a locative sense: *I stood in front of the door carrying the box*. (While the children's examples extended non-motion verbs to motion usages, this case has gone in the opposite direction.)

11 This regular conflation of motion with path in these languages seems rarely to extend to any regular conflation of location with site – i.e., to any basic system of distinct verb roots expressing 'be-in', 'be-on', 'be-under', etc. Such a system has recently been reported (Donna Gerdts, personal communication) for Halkomelem, a Salish language of Canada. But generally, these languages instead use some single form, roughly expressing 'be-at', in conjunction with a series of adpositions – much like English when no Manner has conflated with *be*, as in *The pen was* (rather than *lay*) *in/on/under the box*.

Though rarely forming a core system, the verbal expression of location + site is clearly under no prohibitory constraint. English, for one, has a number of incidental instances of such conflation, for example *surround* ('be around'), *top* ('be atop'), *flank* ('be beside'), *adjoin, span, line, fill* – as in *A ditch surrounded the field, A cherry topped the dessert, Clothing filled the hamper*. It is just that such verbs seldom constitute the colloquial system for locative expression.

12 This is not to imply that a verb root always has exactly one basic aspect. A verb root can show a certain range of aspects, each manifesting in a different context. Thus, English *kneel* is one-way in *She knelt when the bell rang* and is steady-state in *She knelt there for a minute*.

13 These two grammatical forms – 'keep -ing' and '$V_{dummy} a [\_ + Deriv]_N$' – may be thought to trigger certain cognitive processes. Respectively, these are 'multiplexing' and 'unit-excerpting'. Such processes are discussed in Talmy (1978c).

14 Other linguistic treatments (e.g. McCawley 1968) represent their incorporated causative element by the capitalized form 'CAUSE'. Since more distinctions are recognized here, more representational forms would be needed (and are in fact used in the author's other writings):

a. . . . broke . . .          = . . . broke . . .
b. . . . RESULTed-to-break . . .    = . . . $_R$broke . . .
c. . . . EVENTed-to-break . . .    = . . . $_E$broke . . .

d. . . . INSTRUMENTed-to-break . . .= . . . $_I$broke . . .

e. . . . AUTHORed-to-break . . .  = . . . $_{Au}$broke . . .

f. . . . AGENTed-to-break . . .  = . . . $_A$broke . . .

g. . . . UNDERWENT-to-break . . .= . . . $_U$broke . . .

The causing event can be expressed not only by a full clause, as in the text examples, but also by a verb-derived nominal, as in (b) below, or by what can be termed an 'action noun', as in (c). A standard noun as in (d), however, will not do:

The window cracked –

(a)  from a ball's sailing into it        – nominalized clause

(b)  from the pressure/bump of a branch
     against it        – verb-derived nominal

(c)  from the wind/a fire/the rain        – action noun

(d)  *from a ball        – standard noun

The clause-like behavior of action nouns can be attributed to their being in fact conflations of full clauses. Thus, the examples in (c) might be considered to have internal semantic structures equivalent to the following clauses:

wind    'air's blowing [on the Figure]'
rain    'rainwater's falling [on the Figure]'
fire    'flames acting [on the Figure]'

Such semantic conflation, taking place in the noun, exemplifies lexicalization in a grammatical category other than those, the verb root and the satellite, addressed in this chapter. (For further examples, involving conflation in subordinating and coordinating conjunctions and in certain adverb classes, see Talmy 1978b).

15 It is not only intransitive sentences that can be autonomous. For example, *An acorn hit the plate* is autonomous. The requirement, rather, is that the sentence must not express a cause (as does *An acorn broke the plate*).

16 Arguments are given in Talmy (1976a, 1978b) why the resulting-event (b) form should be considered semantically more basic than the causing-event (c) form.

17 This impinging object is the Figure within the causing event, but it is the Instrument with respect to the overall cause–effect situation. That is, for this author 'Instrument' is not a basic notion as it is, say, for Fillmore (1975). It is a derived notion, to be characterized in terms of other, more basic notions: the Instrument of a cause–effect sequence is the Figure of the causing event.

18 The act of will is the first link in the causal chain. Through internal (neuromotor) activity, it brings about the movement of the body. Note that such bodily motion, even when not referred to, is a necessary link for a final physical event. Thus, while *Abe burnt the leaves* only mentions Abe as the

initiator and the leaves' burning as the final event, we must infer not only that fire was the immediate Instrument but also that Abe (due to his will) acted physically to marshal it.

19 To describe this more analytically: something acts on a sentient entity, causing within it the intention to carry out an act. The intention in turn leads to its actually carrying out the act, in the usual manner of agency. Thus, the entity is caused to act as an Agent (so that another good term for the 'inducive' is 'caused agency').

The act that is referred to in most inducive verbs is a self-agentive one, and in particular one of 'going', e.g. *smoke* (*out*) 'by applying smoke, induce to go (out)' (atypically, *sic*/*set* . . . *on* refer to an agentive act of 'attacking'). Because most self-agentive verbs are intransitive like most autonomous verbs (the other verb types require a direct object), an inducive construction relates to a self-agentive one in much the same way that an agentive construction relates to an autonomous one:

(a) inducive:                            (b) self-agentive:
    They sent the drunk out of the bar.     The drunk went out of the bar

(c) agentive:                         (d) autonomous:
    They threw the drunk out of the     The drunk sailed out of the bar
    bar

There seems to be a corresponding kind of semantic 'drift': we tend to understand a self-agentive event as occurring in and of itself, and to take the inducer of an inducive event as directly bringing about the final event without the intermediary volition of the actor.

20 It is, however, quite possible that no verbs distinguish between the (c) and (d) causation types, even cross-linguistically, so that these would have to be merged. The (a) and (b) types are distinguished perhaps only in the stative, as in English by the verbs *be* and *stay*:

(a) The pen was on the incline (autonomous situation)

(b) The pen *was/stayed on the incline from a lever pressing against it (resulting-event causation)

21 We can avoid the problem with *mislay* – that it is bi-morphemic, with a prefix explicitly expressing unintentionality – by using the verb *spill* in a pair with *pour*. This same pair would also allow illustration of the 'S . . . too . . .' frame, which *mislay*/*hide* do not easily fit: *I spilled/*poured the milk by opening the spout too wide.*

22 The same test frames employed here can also be used with verbs like *break*, that can incorporate any of a range of causative types, to select out one particular causative reading. For example, *break* is interpretable only as an author type verb in (a) and only as an agent type in (b):

(a) I broke the window by pressing against it *too* hard

(b) I broke the window *in order* to let the gas escape

23 Verbs that range over two lexicalization types can be used either with or without a grammatical augment for the *same* meaning. We see this for *hide* over the agentive and self-agentive types, and for *set . . . upon* over the self-agentive and inducive types:

(a) She hid herself behind the bushes = She hid behind the bushes

(b) He had his dogs set upon (i.e. fall upon) us = He set his dogs upon us

24 For these, the three aspect–causative types we have noted for verbs of state have the following particular manifestation: (a) a body or object is in a posture non-causatively, or else an animate being self-agentively maintains its body in the posture; (b) a body or object comes into a posture non-causatively, or else an animate being self-agentively gets its body into the posture; (c) an agent puts a body other than its own, or some other object, into a posture.

25 The stative usage of the last two verbs here may not be immediately obvious. It can be seen in the following:

(a) She bent over the rare flower for a full minute

(b) He bowed before his queen for a long minute

26 The pattern we are concerned with here held better in older forms of English. Thus, the idea of agent derivation for the verb is quite questionable for modern English. But enough of the pattern remains to serve as illustration and to represent languages that do have such forms clearly. Among these latter are apparently many Uto-Aztecan languages (Wick Miller, personal communication) and Halkomelem.

27 This use of the reflexive is a special grammatical device, not a semantically motivated one, because there is no way to construe the normal meaning of the reflexive in this context. Normally, the reflexive entails that exactly what one would do to another, one does to oneself. In the present case, what one does to another is to place one's arms around his/her body, lift, and set down. But that is clearly not what one does with oneself. The movement is accomplished, rather, by internal – i.e., neuromuscular – activity.

28 This suffix in Spanish generally incorporates a passive meaning (unlike the otherwise comparable Japanese *-te*, which has no voice characteristics). However, the present construction, as in *estaba acostado* – which might be taken literally as 'I was laid-down' – will generally be understood with a non-passive reading, as in the sentence gloss 'I lay (there)'.

29 As noted earlier, it is somewhat forced for modern English to interpret posture verbs as pure statives, with augmentation required for the other aspect–causative types. For one thing, marking of an agentive–non-agentive distinction has all but disappeared colloquially, with forms like *lay* or *sit* serving for both meanings. For another, the satellite can often appear in

stative usages as well. Thus, the combination of verb + satellite can to a large degree be used equally for all three aspect–causative types:

(a) He laid down/stood up all during the show

(b) He laid down/stood up when the show began

(c) She laid him down/stood him up on the bed

Nevertheless, a distinction in the use of forms does still hold to this extent: the satellite seems somewhat awkward in some stative expressions, for example in *He laid (?down) there for hours.* And the verb without satellite is somewhat awkward in colloquial speech for the agentive usage: *?She laid/stood the child on the bed.*

30 The postures category is mostly non-relational. One can largely determine a body's configuration by observing it alone. But the 'positions' category is relational. It involves the position assumed by one object with respect to another (especially where the latter provides support). Some position notions that are frequently found lexicalized in verbs across languages are: 'lie on', 'stand on', 'lean against', 'hang from', 'stick into', 'stick out of', 'stick/adhere to', 'float on (surface)', 'float/be suspended in (medium)', 'be lodged in', '(clothes) be on', 'hide/be hidden (from view) + Loc'. The postures and positions categories may have no clear boundary between them or may overlap. But these heuristic classes, in some version, do seem to be treated differently in many languages.

31 English does have a few instances where a lexical item, unlike *hide*, can participate in expressions for all three state relations, including state-departure:

(a) She *stood* there speaking

(b) She *stood up* to speak

(c) She *stood down* when she had finished speaking

32 To be sure, English has *un-* and *de-/dis-* for use with some position and condition verbs (*unload, decentralize*). But their use is limited, and it is also largely secondary in that the forms indicate *reversal* of state-entry rather than state-departure directly. (Thus, *central* must first add *-ize* indicating state-entry before it can add *de-*; there is no *\*decentral.*)

The distinct treatment that languages accord state-departure as against state-location and state-entry often shows up as well in their adpositional systems expressing Path. For example, the same morpheme expresses 'at' and 'to' but a different one expresses 'from' in French *à/à/de*, Japanese *ni/ni/kara* (though *e* is also used for the 'to' meaning), and Atsugewi *-i?/-i?/-uk·a*. English exhibits this pattern in some of its prepositional and relative–interrogative forms:

(a) She was *behind* the barn        *Where* was she?

(b) She went *behind* the barn        *Where* did she go?

(c) She came *from behind* the barn        *Where* did she come *from*?

33 Note that actions lacking physical contact can also be lexicalized with different personations. For example, the English verb *get* ('go and bring back') is basically monadic but can add a benefactive expression for the dyadic. On the other hand, the roughly equivalent *serve* ('bring to someone') is basically dyadic but can add a reflexive for the monadic type (the reflexive here signals only this change in personation type, for it lacks the literal interpretation it has in *I shaved John/I shaved myself*):

|  monadic | dyadic |
|---|---|
| I got some dessert from the kitchen$\Rightarrow$ | I got some dessert from the kitchen for Sue |
| I served myself some dessert from$\Leftarrow$ the kitchen | I served Sue some dessert from the kitchen |

34 For this section, the earlier limitation to single-morpheme verbs has been relaxed. Considered here, thus, are a lexical complex like *rip off* and, later, a morphemically complex verb like *frighten*. This is feasible because valence properties can inhere in morphemic complexes of this sort as well as in single roots.

35 Actually, this paradigm is abridged from a still larger one (see Talmy 1972:301–375) that distinguishes three Figure-Ground precedence relations: the basic format with Figure above Ground in the case hierarchy, that with Figure demotion alone, and that with Figure demoted and Ground promoted. Perhaps no single verb exhibits all the forms, but a pair of verbs can serve to illustrate (cp. Fillmore (1977), Hook (1983)):

| non-agentive | agentive |
|---|---|
| basic precedence | |
| The bees swarmed in the garden. | I pounded my shoe on the table. |
| with Figure demoted | |
| It swarmed with bees in the garden. | I pounded with my shoe on the table. |
| and with Ground promoted | |
| The garden swarmed with bees. | I pounded the table with my shoe. |

Note that the *with* appearing here as a demotion particle and still marking the Figure becomes the *with* that marks the Instrument when a sentence of the present sort is embedded in a causative matrix (cf. note 17). Thus, the sentence in (a) can be embedded as in (b) to yield (c):

  (a) I kicked the ball (G) with my left foot (F)
      [<I kicked my left foot (F) into the ball (G)]
  (b) I $_A$MOVEd the ball ($F_2$) across the field ($G_2$)
      by kicking it ($G_1$) with my left foot ($F_1$)
  (c) I kicked the ball (F) across the field (G) with my left foot ($F_1 \Rightarrow$ I)

36 The final genitive expression here would now be only literary. However, there are other verbs that take a colloquial *mit* phrase containing the Figure:

<blockquote>

(a) Ich warf faule Äpfel auf ihn    Ich *bewarf* ihn *mit faulen Äpfeln*
'I threw rotten apples at him'   'I pelted him with rotten apples'

(b) Ich schenkte ihm das Fahrrad   Ich *beschenkte* ihn *mit dem Fahrrad*
'I "presented" the bicycle to    'I "presented" him with the
   him'                 bicycle'

</blockquote>

37 The two valence types here pertain not only to verbs but also to adjectival and larger constructions that express affect. Thus, the expressions italicized below can be used only with the case-frame surround shown for them:

| Stimulus as subject | Experiencer as subject |
|---|---|
| That *is odd to* me | I *am glad about* that |
| That *is of importance to* me | I *am in fear of* that |
| That *got the goat of me* → got my goat | I *flew off the handle over* that |

38 English used to favor Stimulus–subject even more than it does now, but a number of verbs have shifted their valence type. For example, the affect verbs *rue* and *like* – as well as the sensation verb *hunger* and the cognition verb *think* – used to take the Experiencer as grammatical object but now take it as subject.

39 These lists avoid verbs that refer more to an affect-related action than to the affect itself. For example, *quake* and *rant* – candidates for the Experiencer– subject group – really refer directly to the subject's overt actions, and only imply his/her accompanying affect of fear or anger. Similarly, *harass* and *placate* – potentially Stimulus–subject verbs – refer more to the activities of an external Agent than to the resultant state of irritation or calm in the Experiencer.

40 This arrangement applies as well to verbs of sensation. Thus, 'be cold' is lexicalized from the point of view of the Experiencer feeling the sensation. *-Ahẃ* is added for the perspective of the Stimulus object rendering the sensation:

(a) verb root:           -yi:sḱap-      'feel cold'
    inflectional affix-set:   s- '- w- -ᵃ   'I – subject (3d person-object)'
    /s-'-w-yi:sḱap -ᵃ/ ⇒ [sẃye·sḱápʰ]
    'I am cold (i.e., feel cold)'

(b) verb root:           -yi:sḱap-      'feel cold'
    valence-shifting suffix: -ahẃ      'from Stimulus to Experiencer'
    inflectional affix-set:   '- w- -ᵃ    '3d person-subject'
    /'-w-yi:sḱap-ahẃ-ᵃ/ ⇒ [ẃye·sḱapáhẃa]
    'It is cold (i.e., to the touch)'

41 There is some indeterminacy as to exactly which kinds of constituents found in construction with a verb root merit satellite designation. Clearest are the

forms named next in the text, such as English verb particles, Latin verb prefixes, Chinese resultative complements, and the non-inflectional affixes in the Atsugewi polysynthetic verb. Probably also deserving satellite status are such compound-forming verbal adjuncts as the first element in English (*to*) *test-drive*; on the other hand, free adverbs, even ones related semantically to the verb root rather than (say) to the whole clause, seem less like satellites. Also seeming to merit satellite status are the incorporated nouns in Iroquoian polysynthetic verbs, whereas pronominal clitics as in French seem less to do so and full noun phrases are entirely excluded. What status should be accorded such verb-phrase forms as a negative element or closed-class particles like English *only* and *even* is uncertain. It is not clear whether this indeterminacy is due to the present theory's early stage of development or to a cline-like character for the satellite category.

42 There appears to be a universal tendency toward satellite formation: elements with certain types of meaning tend to leave the locations in a sentence where they logically belong and move into the verb complex. This tendency, whose extreme expression is polysynthesis, is also regularly evident in smaller degrees. Examples in English are the negative and other emphatic modifiers on nouns:

    (a) *Not* Jóan hit him ⇒ Jóan didn'*t* hit him

    (b) *Even* Joan hit him ⇒ Jóan *even* hit him

    (c) Joan gave him *only* one ⇒ Joan *only* gave him óne

43 Not all Path expressions permit omissions of this sort. Such is the case with *up to* in the sense of 'approach' and also with *into* in the sense of 'collision':

    (a) When I saw Joan on the corner, I walked up to her (\*. . . walked up)

    (b) It was too dark to see the tree, so he walked into it (\*. . . walked in)

44 Judging from their distribution, satellites of this type seem to be an areal phenomenon rather than a genetic one. Thus, Atsugewi and Klamath, neighboring but unrelated languages, both have extensive suffixal systems of these satellites. But the Pomo languages, related to Atsugewi and sharing with it the extensive instrumental prefix system (see section 2.5), quite lack Path + Ground satellites.

45 Though this may remove some of Atsugewi's mystique, notice that the German satellite *entgegen-* also has the 'in going to meet' meaning, as in *entgegenlaufen* 'run to meet', while Latin *ob-* parallels Atsugewi *-ikc* still further in having both the 'meeting' and the 'passage-blocking' meanings, as in *occurrere* 'run to meet' and *obstruere* 'build so as to block off'.

46 The Atsugewi polysynthetic verb can background still more: Deixis and four additional nominal roles – Agent, Inducer, Companion, and Beneficiary. However, Deixis is distinguished only as between 'hither' and 'hence', and the nominal roles only as to person and number or, in certain circumstances, merely their presence in the referent situation.

# 3 Inflectional morphology

STEPHEN R. ANDERSON

## 0.0 Introduction: the study of word structure

This chapter, as well as chapter III:1 (dealing with 'Stem formation'),
will be devoted to the study of the internal structure of words. It is an
intuition long familiar from traditional approaches to the study of
language that grammatical description can be divided into two domains:
*syntax*, or the study of the relations among words in a sentence, and
*morphology*, or the study of the formal and semantic composition of the
individual words. This division also implies a sort of parallelism between
the two domains: just as sentences are made up of words, so words are
made up of smaller pieces that can be called *formatives* (a more neutral
term than the traditional *morpheme*: see below, 0.2). But there appear
to be significant differences between the sorts of principles that determine the combination of words on the one hand, and that of formatives
on the other, and this justifies the distinction between syntax and
morphology. Such a distinction rests on the criteria by which we delimit,
in so far as we can in any particular language, the units we will call
words, establishing the boundary between the two domains.

### 0.1 *The notion of 'word'*

When we think about English, it seems obvious that a sentence can
always be broken down into smaller parts: that *The baby is not feeling
well*, for example, consists of no more and no less than six smaller pieces
of *words*. We might suggest that this is simply an illusion, fostered by
the fact that we have learned to write English with spaces in certain
places and not others; but it is clear that these spaces correspond (in
most cases at least) to something real about the organization of the
sentence. Confirmation of this opinion is available from a number of
directions, unfortunately not always mutually reconcilable.

### 0.1.1 *Phonological criteria for the word*

One obvious source of support for word divisions is the fact that it is
usually possible to pause where there is a space (at the boundary

between words, that is) but not (naturally) elsewhere. The pause in *The baby is not – ummh – feeling well* is thus quite different, and much more natural, than if we were to say *The baby is not fee – ummh – ling well*. Furthermore, we can reorganize the word divisions of this sentence, either as 'The baby isn't feeling well' or as 'The baby's not feeling well'. The reorganization corresponds just to a shift in the location of these potential pause locations: a pause was possible between *is* and *not* in the original, but not between *is* and *n't* when we have *isn't*. Since we have not altered the content of the sentence in any other obvious way, it would appear we have changed the structure of the sentence just in terms of word boundaries.

The possibility of pausing thus supplies a certain kind of support for the division of a sentence into words. The divisions allowed (or required) by one language, however, may be quite different from those of another. In some languages, such as Vietnamese, practically every syllable forms a 'word' in this sense; while in a language like (West Greenlandic) Eskimo, a form like *iqalussuarniariartuqqusaagalua-qaagunnuuq* 'It is said that we have admittedly got a strict order to go out fishing sharks' is as indivisible as English *isn't*, though sentences in Eskimo are generally made up of several words (one of which is the form just cited), and pauses between these are perfectly possible.

Defining words in terms of the location of (potential) pauses treats them as units from the point of view of sound structure, and this definition is reinforced in many languages by other processes. In some cases, for instance, the location of the accent is fixed by reference to the boundary between words. In Czech, the accent is always on the initial syllable of the word; in Polish, on the next-to-last; and in Latin on the third from last (antepenultimate) if the next-to-last consists of a short vowel plus at most one consonant, otherwise on the next to last. In a language with this kind of accent ('culminative' as opposed to free or 'distinctive'), we have an additional means of defining word boundaries.

Besides accent, other phonological processes may be sensitive to the difference between word boundaries and other positions. A well-known example of this is the distinction between 'internal' and 'external' sandhi (phonological change) in Sanskrit. Word internally, sequences of vowels are always eliminated by contraction, conversion of diphthongs or mid vowels to vowel-plus-glide sequences, or other changes. At the boundary between words, on the other hand (in 'external' combination), such sequences are allowed to stand, or are even created, as when final *-as* becomes *o*. While there are many instances of similar rules applying both within and across word boundaries, there are also sufficient differences to allow one to identify at least some of the word boundaries on this basis.

Like many other languages, Sanskrit also imposes much more rigid restrictions on the class of sounds that can appear at the end of a word than are applicable in the middle of a word. There are no final clusters of consonants, and the only consonants that can appear at the end of a word are voiceless unaspirated stops. In consequence, we can often determine negatively that a given position must *not* be the end of a word by the appearance of (syllable-final) consonants that could not appear word finally. Another well-known example of this sort is modern Italian, in which only a restricted subset of consonants is possible in final position. While most consonants do appear either singly or as geminates, geminates do not appear in word-initial position. The set of consonants that occur word finally is also quite limited. As a result of those restrictions, when we find a double consonant it is often a sure indication of word-medial position.

While some phonological properties of 'words', such as the limit on consonant clustering at word boundaries, are found in similar form in many languages, many others are peculiar to an individual language and can be arrived at only as a result of a detailed knowledge of the phonology of the language.

### 0.1.2 *Grammatical criteria for the word*

Besides the phonological clues, however, there are often other criteria for determining whether two adjacent elements belong to the same word or not. In general, the composition of words in terms of formatives is much more rigid and restricted than is the combination of words into sentences. Words are often permutable with one another (at least to a limited extent): at the extreme we have 'free word order' languages such as Latin where we can say *puer puellam amat* 'The boys loves the girl', *puellam amat puer*, *amat puer puellam*, or any other permutation of these three words, without changing the meaning of the sentence. Formatives, on the other hand, can virtually never be reordered without change (or loss) of meaning: *amat* can be regarded as made up of *ama-* 'love' and *-t* 'third singular present indicative', but *tama* is totally impossible as a variant of this form. Similarly we can generally insert other words between two words, but not between two formatives that are parts of the same word, and thus *puer ama-puellam-t* is not a permissible variant of our Latin sentence. In some languages the same formatives can appear within a single word in more than one order, but generally with some difference of meaning. In Turkish, for example, formatives that could be represented as /türk/ 'Turk, Turkish', /lEr/

'plural', and /dIr/ 'be' can be combined either as *türklerdir* 'It is the Turks', or as *türktürler* 'They are Turkish'. While subtle, this difference is semantically significant, and not a matter of stylistic or discourse-conditioned variation as in the Latin word-order example quoted above. The units which can thus be permuted or interrupted freely by other 'words' can therefore be taken to establish a syntactic notion of 'word', independently from any phonological criteria.

In some languages, there is still another possible basis for the notion of 'word', which is strictly morphological. In heavily inflecting languages, words belonging to different part-of-speech classes obligatorily include the expression of different categories. Latin nouns, for example, obligatorily express the categories of case and number, while Latin verbs obligatorily indicate tense, mood, voice, and the person and number of their subjects. A 'word' belonging to one of these classes is incomplete if some of the associated categories are unexpressed. In such a language, then, we could define a word in terms of a base together with the expression of the categories appropriate for its part-of-speech class. In Latin *bonōs librōs* 'good books (acc. pl.)', for instance, we could identify two such morphological words: *librōs*, made up of the base *lib(e)r* 'book', a noun, and an ending expressing case (accusative) and number (plural); and *bonōs*, made up of the base *bon-* which is an adjective and an ending expressing case, number, and gender (all required for adjectives). Where formally expressed grammatical categories are associated with particular parts of speech, then, they provide another potential approach to the definition of the word.

### 0.1.3 *Conflicts among criteria*

In most languages, perhaps, these approaches to the word yield the same units: thus, the domain within which 'word-bound' phonological processes and limitations apply is the same as the unit which is manipulated by the syntax (permuted, deleted, etc.), and is made up of a base (perhaps complex in its internal structure, as with compounds and derivational formations) together with formal expression of whatever grammatical categories are relevant for the given part of speech. Phonological, syntactic, and morphological 'words' thus coincide in the most usual case. In many instances, however, this happy congruence of criteria does not obtain, and different definitions result in different word divisions for the same sentence. As a result of this, the 'proper' definition of the word is one of the classic chestnuts of traditional grammar, and a vast amount of literature can be found attempting to reconcile the apparent conflicts among the distinct and equally plausible bases for the notion of 'word'.

A simple example of such a conflict is provided by French. We are accustomed to write a sentence such as *Il les a vus en France* 'He saw them in France' as a sequence of six words (separated by spaces), but this division is at least potentially questionable. One could say that French has a rule of 'culminative' accent, with stress falling on the last (non-schwa) vowel of the word. On this basis, however (and arguably for some other phonological purposes as well), the sentence just cited is made up of only one word, since as normally spoken the sentence has only one stress. We can resolve the difficulty by saying that stress in French is simply not bound to the word, but rather to a larger unit (a 'phonological phrase'); to do so, however, is to recognize that culminative stress is not, in the general case, the basis of the definition of 'word', but rather a property which is frequently associated with a unit of this size.

In fact, French culminative stress is typical of properties that yield a notion of the word in various languages: for any one of these properties, some language can probably be found in which it does not coincide with other potential defining characteristics of words. This suggests that the traditional notion of 'word' conflates a number of different, distinct notions which do not always converge on the same unit. The situation is thus similar to that of the notion of 'subject' in traditional grammar, defined from the point of view of morphological categories (e.g. nominative case), semantic roles (subjects are typically Agents), discourse function (subjects are typically Topics), and sentence-internal syntax (subjects are typically antecedents for reflexive pronouns, the missing nominal elements in complement structures, etc.). As with the criteria for defining the word, these traditional bases for the notion of subject frequently but not always coincide. Nonetheless, we need not give up hope in either case, provided we make it clear in a given instance what sort of 'subject' or 'word' we are talking about.

### 0.1.4 *The problem of clitics*

A problem is posed by so-called *clitic* elements. The form *les* ('them') in *Il les a vus en France* ('He saw them in France') for instance, can correspond to a full phrase (e.g. *les gens dont j'ai parlé* 'the people I spoke of'), and so our intuition is that it 'ought' to be a separate word. Yet in phonological terms, it forms an indissoluble unit with the following *a*. Furthermore, in syntactic terms the sequence *les a* cannot be interrupted by adverbs, the second part of the negative marker *ne pas* (which otherwise comes after the first word of the verbal phrase) or other words, with the exception of other clitic pronouns. Such an element, which does not stand alone but must rather 'lean on' (the meaning of the Greek word from which the name comes) some other form is called a clitic: *pro*clitic if it comes before the element to which it attaches, *en*clitic if it comes after it.

Clitic forms present a particularly severe challenge to a general definition of the word, precisely because they involve a direct conflict of phonological and (some) syntactic criteria with morphological and (other) syntactic properties. On the one hand, the combination of a clitic and its *host* (a term introduced by Zwicky (1977) for the element to which a clitic attaches) displays unitary and often distinctly word-internal phonology; it is generally subject to more rigid ordering restrictions than other elements of sentence structure, and is not interruptable by other words. On the other hand, clitics generally correspond to elements that can also be expressed (sometimes in the same language) by independent words: pronouns, auxiliary verbs, conjunctions, and the like, not simply to be part of the meaning of an independent word. They may also display a number of unique properties, phonological and syntactic, that establish their position as midway between that of independent word forms and simple constituents of morphologically complex words. For a useful and informative survey of the special properties of clitics, the reader is referred to Zwicky (1977).

While the distinction between a clitic and a component of a complex word is a rather subtle one, it is quite essential, and failure to make it can lead to incorrect (or at least misleading) analyses of linguistic structures. An excellent example of this possibility is furnished by the grammar of Nootka-Nitinaht, a group of dialects of the Wakashan family. In a major source of information on this language, Swadesh (1939) characterizes Nootka as having no part-of-speech distinction between noun and verb. In fact, while diligent search reveals some characteristics distinguishing these classes (cf. chapter 1:1), the difference is anything but obvious. Swadesh's claim is not based on negative evidence, however, but rather on the positive assertion that any word in a Nootka sentence can serve as its predicate. He gives examples (some of which are cited in chapter 1.1) to show that in a simple intransitive sentence such as *The man is going*, either the 'verb' *go* or the 'noun' *man* can apparently serve as predicate without undergoing any other obvious change in form. This identity of function, then, and its formal correlates appear to establish a positive case for a single part-of-speech class including 'nouns' and 'verbs', and other words as well which can equally serve as the predicate of a sentence in Swadesh's sense, including adverbs and even prepositions and particles.

Let us examine the correlates of the notion of 'predicate' which

Swadesh appeals to, however. In Nootka sentences, the predicate (in this sense) appears in initial position in the sentence, and is characterized by a set of suffixal elements indicating tense/mood for the sentence and person/number of the subject. Since this is the classic sort of inflection displayed by verbs (see below), there is no immediate reason to doubt Swadesh's analysis. A closer look, however, shows that there is an alternative account. Consider the pair of sentences below in (1), taken from a Nitinaht dialect (parallel in all relevant respects to the Nootka dialect described by Swadesh) described by Klokeid (1976a) and presented in his orthography:

(1)    a. Tl'itcitl-ibt-ʔa      John ʔōyoqw bowatc ʔaq
          shoot-PAST-DECLAR John ACC     deer    ART
          'John shot the deer'

       b. ʔōoqw-obt-ʔa       bowatc ʔaq tl'itcitl John
          ACC-PAST-DECLAR deer     ART shoot   John
          'The deer, John shot (it)'

These two sentences describe the same event, and involve the same words (the difference between *ibt* and *obt* being phonological only), but in (1a) the inflectional elements for tense/mood (as well as, inferentially, person/number where this is overt: in a sentence of the type given in (1), third person singular subject is unmarked) appear on the 'verb', while in (1b) they appear on the preposition marking accusative (object) function. Surely in such a language anything can serve as a 'verb'.

But it is not necessarily accurate to say that *ʔōyoqw* in (1b) has the inflectional material because it is a 'verb' (or more generally, 'predicate'). Rather, this material can be seen to be attached to a particular word (*tl'itcitl* in (1a), *ʔōyoqw* in (1b)) by virtue of its position at the beginning of the clause. When we examine the range of word-order variants of a Nootka-Nitinaht sentence, a somewhat different picture emerges from that presented by Swadesh (according to whom virtually any word of the sentence is equally eligible to serve as 'predicate'). In the most neutral form of a sentence, uninfluenced by particular discourse conditions, the initial word (to which the inflectional material is attached) is the one which from translation equivalence we might expect to be the verb. Where this is distinguishable, this word is a 'verb'. Under appropriate discourse conditions, however, most other constituents of the sentence can appear in initial position by a process of topicalization. When this happens, the inflectional material of the sentence will still be suffixed to the first word, whatever this may be.

Sentence (1a) thus displays a 'basic' pattern, with the verb initial and therefore suffixed with tense and mood affixes. Sentence (1b) differs, in that 'the deer' is Topic, and first. Notice that when the phrase *ʔōyoqw bowatc ʔaq* thus appears initially, the endings do not appear after the whole phrase, but rather after the first word: the accusative-marking preposition. Clearly, then, the appearance of these endings with a given word does not indicate its syntactic function ('predicate'), but rather its position ('first word').

Behavior of this sort is typical of clitic elements. The positions in which they can appear are limited. In some instances they are attached to a host word which is adjacent to the position in sentence structure that they 'come from': thus, articles, for example, most generally attach to the noun phrase they determine. Otherwise, there are certain preferred positions in the sentence, and a language in which a category of clitics is important tends to collect all of these at some such position. French displays the common case of a language that collects clitics (here, the object pronouns and related elements) immediately adjacent to the verb of the clause. Nootka-Nitinaht, on the other hand, illustrates the other common case, in which the clitics attach to one of the boundaries of the clause. This is sometimes the end of the clause, as in many languages with question particles (e.g. Mandarin Chinese *ma* in *Nǐ huì shuō zhōngguo huà ma?* 'You speak Chinese?'). Most commonly, however, it is the beginning. This gives rise to the impression that they are placed in 'second position', but this is perhaps misleading. Recall that *en*clitics must appear after their host: obviously, if they are to be placed at the beginning of their clause, this will position them after the first potential host. This is generally the first word or, in some languages, the first constituent such as a complete noun phrase. In some cases, such as Serbo-Croatian, these two interpretations of 'first potential host' are optional variants. The absence of a corresponding tendency for *pro*clitics to collect at the end of a clause, however, still requires explanation.

In Nootka-Nitinaht, then, we analyze elements such as *ibt-ʔa* (or its phonological variant *obt-ʔa*) in (1) not as inflections on the first word of the clause, but rather as clitic elements which have been 'attracted' to their position after the first word without regard for the function of that element. In consequence, their appearance with a particular item in the clause cannot be regarded as providing evidence for the syntactic function of that item, and Swadesh's principal basis for his assertion that any word can be a 'predicate' in Nootka disappears. This possibility is further supported by the fact that in Nootka-Nitinaht not only clauses contain clitic elements, but noun phrases do also. The article *ʔaq* in the phrase *bowatc ʔaq* 'the deer' is such a noun phrase clitic, for example. We can see this when we add an adjective (such as *ʔix* 'big') or numeral (e.g. *ʔatl* 'two'): we then get *ʔiẋ ʔaq bowatc* 'the big deer' or *ʔatl ʔaq bowatc* 'the two deer'. Clitics representing elements of the entire clause (including a wide variety of tense, mood markers, particles, pronouns, and other items surveyed by Klokeid (1976a)) appear in second position in the clause; clitics representing elements or categories internal to the noun phrase, such as determiners, appear after the first word of the noun phrase, regardless of the position they thus come to occupy in the sentence as a whole. Some further discussion, and a slightly broader perspective can be found in Jacobsen (1979).

Clitics are found in many other languages. Hale (1967) shows, for example, that the Australian language Warlpiri has an auxiliary, made up of tense markers plus certain clitic pronoun forms, which appears either in first or in second position in the clause depending on whether its phonological form (particularly the number of syllables in the base, which marks tense) requires the entire auxiliary to be enclitic or not. Failure to recognize that the elements in question are clitics rather than affixes (with respect to their host), on the other hand, would result in a very confusing picture of the language and its morphology. The description relies essentially on our recognition of the special properties of clitics, and of the problems they pose for the definition of the 'word'.

We will be concerned below with the structure of words in the grammatical, rather than the phonological sense, and accordingly will not in general consider clitics to be part of a single word with their hosts. We thus assume that their special properties can be accounted for by a combination of principles of sentence structure (syntax) and phonology, and that they do not therefore impinge on the domain of morphology (although of course, considered as grammatical words in their own right, they may have a morphological structure which can be studied as with any other word class).

### 0.2  *The structure of words*

A word can, of course, be looked on simply as a stretch of phonological material with an associated meaning, but this is not by itself sufficient to yield an interesting notion of word structure, *per se*. When we consider a word like *mice*, we can see that its meaning is decomposable into two relatively discrete parts: reference to a class of small rodents (the same class referred to by the word *mouse*), and reference to plurality. This sort of decomposability is even more transparent in the case of *rats*: here we can not only find two distinct parts of the meaning, but we can also see that the form of the word is decomposable into *rat* (the same material that forms an independent word) and *-s* (the same material found in words like *books*, and also, we can say on phonological grounds, *pigs* and *horses*). Such a formal analysis is rather more difficult with *mice*: here it is clear that the /m/ at the beginning and the /s/ at the end have to do with a mouse, but the value of the vowel in the middle can be (and has been) the subject of controversy and alternative analyses. The idea of plurality here is associated less directly with a particular piece of phonological material, but part of the make-up of the word is the relation between /aį̯/ (in *mice*) and /au̯/ (in *mouse*). One might represent this relation directly ('/aį̯/ marks the plural, /au̯/ the singular in such a word') or as a substitution ('the plural is formed by replacing /au̯/ with /aį̯/'), but somehow the relation is part of the word's shape and structure.

These simple examples suggest a division of the study of word structure into two domains, corresponding roughly to the analysis of the meaning of the word and the analysis of its form. In the case of a word like *cat*, for example, the 'analysis' required is trivial: there is no reason to say anything more than that there is an association between the sequence /kæt/ and the notion of a cat. When we look at words in general, though, we find that both their meaning and their form are decomposable into smaller parts that recur (at least potentially) in other words. Word structure, then, is concerned with this decomposition and with the principles by which a complex meaning is associated with a complex form.

The relation between *mouse* and *mice* is formally a vowel alternation, and it expresses the meaning 'plural'. A vowel alternation between /aį̯/ and /au̯/ can be used for other purposes (as in the relation between *find* and *found*), and the idea of plurality can be expressed by other means (as by the suffix -*s* in *rats*): the two are logically distinct, and we can follow Boas and other earlier writers in separating the study of *grammatical processes* (such as vowel alternation, suffixation, etc.) from the study of the 'ideas' or *categories* expressed by these grammatical processes.

If cases such as *rats* are typical, however, we might take such a separation to be rather artificial. That is, while we can divide the word formally into two parts (*rat* and -*s*) and semantically into 'rat' and 'plural', there is a one-to-one association between the two divisions: *rat* means 'rat', and -*s* means 'plural'. If words generally have such structure, we will be missing it if we treat grammatical processes separately from the categories they express.

It is, in fact, this intuition that underlies traditional definitions of what is usually taken to be the minimal unit of analysis in word structure: the *morpheme*. The notion of a 'smallest recurrent unit of sound/meaning association' implies that a one-to-one association between the two domains is general. If words are indeed built up out of such morphemes, we ought to reflect this fact in our analysis by treating sound and meaning together in determining word structure. We may well get into arguments about what are the morphemes in *mice*, but the idea that even this form is made up of two parts in each domain is still clear and there is apparently a one-to-one association between the two domains.

The study of languages of the traditional *inflectional* (as opposed to *isolating*, *agglutinative*, etc.) type shows, however, that the notion of the morpheme as it expresses a one-to-one correspondence between aspects of form and aspects of meaning can be an oversimplification. For a simple case, consider an Old English word like *bær* 'he bore'. This form is a third person singular past tense indicative verb: if we alter any of these categories, we get a different word (e.g. *bære* if we change person to second, *bæron* if we change number to plural, *birþ* if we change tense to present, or *bære* if we change mood to subjunctive). By studying other forms of the word, we see that (besides the part which corresponds to the basic meaning of the verb, 'to bear') there are two formal markers by which these categories are indicated: the stem vowel (here short *æ*) and the 'ending' (here *ø*, or phonologically null). But it is obvious that there is no one-to-one correspondence here between the formal markers and the categories they express. In fact, the stem vowel and the ending of *bære* can each be found in some other form of the same verb which differs from this one along any one of the dimensions of person, number, tense, or mood. There is no association between either the stem vowel or the ending and some one of the categories expressed by the form (or some unitary subset of these categories): rather the association is between the entire form *bær* (composed of the stem for 'to bear', together with the stem vowel *æ* and the ending *ø*) and the entire set of categories 'third person singular past indicative'. The association, that is, is not one-to-one but many-to-many, and since the grammatical processes involved in the shape of the word are not unitarily associated with grammatical categories, the analysis of word form in either domain cannot be directly tied to its analysis in the other.

This is not to say, of course, that the study of word structure can neglect the relations between the subparts of the shape of a word and the subparts of its meaning: quite the opposite. The point of this observation is that if a proper account of this relation is to be given, it is necessary to go beyond the simple notion that it is a one-to-one correspondence, as implied by the notion that the 'morpheme' is the minimal unit of analysis, and that it establishes a direct association of form with meaning. Since we wish to accommodate the general case (including languages like Old English, as well as those like Turkish where the notion of a one-to-one correspondence runs into much less trouble), we will therefore avoid talking about morphemes; rather, in the analysis of word structure we will talk about minimal subparts of the phonological content of a form as *formatives*, and elements of the semantic structure of words as *roots* (or *stems*) and *grammatical categories*. In the simplest case a given formative may directly and unequivocally express a single category, but in other instances the relation is more complex.

In dealing with problems of the sort we have just been discussing, an analysis based on the notion of the morpheme usually avoids the issue in the following way. Consider the Latin verb form *scrībō* 'I write', a first person singular present indicative. We might want to say that the ending (here, -ō) is the 'first person singular' morpheme, since we can compare the word with *scrībīs* 'you (sg.) write', which differs in ending and in person/number categories. But when we consider *scrīpsī* 'I wrote', we see that the ending also provides information about tense and mood. If we wish to find a 'first person singular' ending, indeed, we are in trouble, for there is no aspect of this form which is unequivocally associated with all and only first person singular forms. Nonetheless, we can say that -ō in *scrībō* is 'really' the first person singular marker, and that the difference between -ō in *scrībō* and -ī in *scrīpsī* does not express, but is rather 'conditioned by' the difference between present and past indicative.

Clearly, however, we could equally well have decided to say that -ō is 'really' the present indicative marker, and that the difference between -ō and -īs (in *scrībīs*) does not express, but rather is conditioned by the difference between first and second person. The choice between the two analyses is arbitrary, at least in formal terms. When we consider other paradigms in Latin, of course, we see that we get a more coherent analysis if we say that -ō marks first person singular, and that present tense is not directly expressed (except in so far as it conditions the choice of person/number ending), rather than the other way around. But this is to miss the point of the example: the truth is that -ō does not mark just first person singular *or* just present indicative, but rather all at once. The association between form and the categories it expresses is not a simple, one-to-one relation, and the choice of either 'person/number' or 'tense/mood' as the 'meaning' of the ending 'morpheme' is a distortion of the facts. In the general case (often approximated closely in inflecting languages like Latin), the entire (possibly highly complex) form is related to the entire cluster of grammatical categories it marks. There is a continuum in language between this situation and the rather simpler one-to-one correspondence between formal elements and categories (typified by items such as English /-z/ 'plural') which is the basis of the notion of the morpheme. Because we wish to be able to deal with any language that may be encountered in the field, then, we will preserve the division of the morphology of a language into the description of (a) the set of morphological processes found in the language; (b) the set of grammatical categories represented morphologically; and (c) the relation between particular processes (e.g. particular affixes or sound alternations) and particular categories involved in conditioning their application. In fact, having observed that this relation may be complex in principle, we will have little to say about it below, except by inference, and will concentrate our attention on form and categories.

## 0.3 *Subdivisions of the study of word structure*

It is by now quite traditional to distinguish in grammatical description between *inflectional* and *derivational* morphology. The central insight of this opposition is that derivation produces new lexical items (perhaps complete words, perhaps stems) from other lexical material, with the derived items on a par with simple, underived ones as far as their role in grammar is concerned; while inflection on the other hand serves to 'complete' a word by marking its relations within larger structures. Inflection typically marks categories which are applicable (at least potentially) to any item in a given word class, rather than being specific properties of individual lexical items. The 'completive' aspect inflection may (but need not) be shown in its conversion of stems which represent a coherent meaning but cannot occur alone into independent full words of the language, integrated into larger structures.

Though this distinction is quite an intuitive one, it is difficult to provide it with a firm definitional foundation. Derivation cannot be separated from inflection in terms of their formal realization, since none of the grammatical processes of prefixation, vowel change, etc. which appear in grammar are confined to one or the other domain. Similarly, the distinction cannot be made directly in terms of the grammatical categories involved, for a category which is inflectional in one language (in terms of our presystematic intuitions of the difference) may be derivational in another. The categories of diminutive and augmentative forms of nouns, for example, are fully inflectional in Fula (a West Atlantic language): these are marked by noun-class suffixes exactly as the categories of singular and plural, and function in the noun-class agreement system just as these latter do. In German, on the other hand, diminutives are formed by the idiosyncratic addition of suffixes (typically -*chen* or -*lein*). Aside from the fact that diminutives are always grammatically neuter, their formation is unintegrated into the system of inflections, and most grammarians would consider it derivational in character. Certainly diminutive formation in English (by the addition of suffixes such as -*y* and -*let*) is much too limited and 'lexical' to be called inflection by anyone.

If the distinction is a real and significant one, then (as is indeed suggested by the very fact that we can usually agree on the character of specific examples), it must have some other basis. We can probably isolate some general characteristics of one or the other type of process. Thus, any process which involves a shift in word class between the basic and the derived forms (as for instance nominalization) could probably be called derivational, since it is rather far from the notion of inflection as 'completing' a form or integrating it into a larger structure to imagine it changing major lexical categories. Obviously, though, while this criterion is sufficient for a morphological process to be classed as derivational, it is not a necessary one: many derivational processes do not alter lexical category.

Typically, inflectional categories are fully productive within a given lexical class, in the sense that all items of the class, including new formations or borrowings, are potentially subject to them. Thus, verbs generally appear in all person/number/tense/aspect forms, at least potentially; nouns have a plural (where this makes sense semantically) or an accusative case if these categories are marked in the language, etc. Derivation is much more idiosyncratic, at least typically. Thus, while most verbs in English have a nominalized form, the shape and even sense of this may vary considerably (compare *pollution, rehearsal, laughter*, etc.). Some derivational processes may be quite productive and even extend to new forms (as, for example, the derivation of adjectives from verbs by means of the 'past participle' suffix – *closed, inflated, driven*, etc. – though even here the form is not always the same), but most are limited to part of the vocabulary or possibly even to a single word. They are thus quite properly part of the lexicon of the language, while inflection is somehow independent of any particular word, and a property of the grammar itself.

Even here, however, we are not on perfectly firm ground. On the one hand, derivational formations may have virtually complete productivity (as for instance the class of -*ing* nominalizations in English); while on the other, inflectional categories may not extend in fact to all members of a major lexical class. Thus, in Russian there is a group of about 150 verbs which (probably by virtue of their phonological structure) *cannot* be inflected for first person singular subjects in the present tense. We would certainly hesitate to conclude from this that person/number is not an inflectional category in Russian, however. In English we have *pluralia tantum* nouns such as *scissors, spectacles, trousers*, etc. which cannot appear in the singular (formally speaking) except as modifiers: *trouser leg, spectacle case, scissor grinder*, etc. And of course there are many nouns (including all abstract notions such as *inflation*) which cannot appear in the plural, probably by virtue of their semantics (but nonetheless quite generally). We certainly would not conclude from these facts that number is not an inflectional category in English, but this means that we cannot take complete productivity as a defining criterion for the division between derivation and inflection.

We may well ask whether there is any independent way of defining the distinction we have in mind in terms of other notions, and indeed there does not appear to be any fully satisfactory candidate among the host of proposals that have been made in the traditional literature – much as there is no fully adequate general definition of the 'word'. Nonetheless, we will assume here that the limits of derivation in a language can be equated with the limits of its lexicon. Processes that are involved in the internal structure of a word as an independently occurring lexical form – derivation in the broadest sense, including compounding, incorporation, and others – are treated in chapter III:1. Here we will be concerned with inflection, in the intuitive sense suggested above.

We will presume that inflectional categories can be organized into a set of dimensions applicable within a given lexical class (a *paradigm* for members of that class), such that (virtually) any lexical item can be specified for one of a set of opposed categories along each dimension. For instance, nouns in Latin may be specified along a dimension of number (as singular vs. plural), as well as along a dimension of case (as nominative, genitive, etc.). A different set of dimensions applies to verbs, adjectives, and other classes. Sometimes the same dimension may apply to more than one class (as when both nouns and adjectives in Latin are characterized for number and case, with adjectives additionally varying in gender, for which a given noun is invariant). The dimensions, however, are in principle independent of the content of any particular lexical item, and it is this fact (as well as their involvement in the larger relations contracted by words in syntactic structures) that gives them their specifically inflectional character.

Our discussion below will deal with the inflectional aspects of word structure. On the formal side, we will briefly survey the range of grammatical processes that serve in various languages to specify a word's membership in inflectional paradigmatic categories. We will then survey the major lexical classes that serve as the domain of these paradigmatic categorial functions, and consider the range of dimensions characteristic of each of these classes (as presented in chapter 1:1).

## 1.0 Grammatical processes in inflection

Considered individually, the grammatical processes that are utilized in inflection (or elsewhere in morphology) are quite straightforward. As we have noted above, however, it is important to distinguish between grammatical categories and the processes that reflect them, since the formal reflection of a given category may be quite complex. In Chickasaw (Muskogean), for example, a verb is made negative (an inflectional category in this language) by making the following changes in its positive form: (a) the verb is preceded by a prefix (*i*)*k*-; (b) the next to last vowel is laryngealized (or followed by a glottal stop) unless followed by a consonant cluster; (c) the last vowel of the word is replaced by *o*; and (d) active subject affixes are replaced by members of a different set used otherwise for non-agentive relations. Thus, the active positive form *hilhali* 'I'm dancing' corresponds to the negative *akhi'lho* 'I'm not dancing' (where *lh* = voiceless [ɬ], ' = glottal stop [ʔ]). Such a relation is certainly difficult to describe formally as a 'morpheme' of negation, but each of the components is of a well-established type. It is neither the category itself nor the formal devices which reflect it, but only the complexity of their relationship which is at all unusual.

## 1.1 *Separate particles*

We should note at the outset that there is probably no category of inflection which is marked morphologically, as part of a word to which it is applicable, which is not also marked in some (other) language by a separate particle which does not form part of a word with the 'relevant' material to which the category applies. Thus case, number, tense, aspect, and so on are often reflected inflectionally, but sometimes indicated by separate particles (e.g. *ga, o, no* for case in Japanese). Particles of this sort do not have independent lexical content; they are also prime candidates to become clitics. They may well cliticize to a word whose category they reflect. This is the case, for example, with the set of original postpositions in Uralic languages such as Hungarian, which have become clitic on preceding nouns resulting in the developing of a system of a vast number of local 'cases'. This can be seen synchronically in Modern Hungarian, where the integration of some of these 'case endings' into the set is more recent, and less complete, than that of other 'cases'. Since there are many ways in which cliticization may be manifest, there is a resulting continuum between full-fledged independent words, reduced clitics, and affixes. In some cases, the cliticization may result in unusual surface patterns. In Kwakw'ala (or 'Kwakiutl', a Northern Wakashan language), for example, noun phrases are preceded by particles indicating them as subject, object, or instrumental/genitive. These particles, however, cliticize not to the noun phrase itself, but to the *preceding* word:

(2)    Nep'id-i-da    gənanəm-ҳa gukʷsa    t'isəm
       throw-SUBJ-ART child-OBJ    house-INSTR rock
       'The child threw a rock at the house'

In such a case, the appearance is that a word is inflected not for its own grammatical categories, but for those of the following word.

Having observed that grammatical categories can be indicated by separate particles (which may then, as in Kwakw'ala, behave quite independently of their origin), we will ignore this fact below. We will speak of grammatical categories as morphological categories, even though these categories may be manifested in some languages by non-morphological means.

## 1.2 *Affixes*

The simplest and most direct means, perhaps, by which a language can mark a category is by the addition of some affixal material to the stem to which it applies. Affixes appearing before the root are *prefixes*; those coming after the root are *suffixes*; and one coming inside an (otherwise unanalyzable) root, such as the inserted glottal stop in Chickasaw negative verb forms, are *infixes*. Another example of an infix is the marker of past tense in Palauan (Micronesian) *milənga* 'ate' (cf. *mənga* 'eat').

It is quite often the case that the morphology of a language is based predominantly on one or another of the possible types of affix. Languages such as Kwakw'ala or Turkish are almost exclusively suffixing; Navajo (Athabaskan) and Abkhaz (northwest Caucasian) are primarily prefixing. The four languages just cited have highly complex inflectional systems involving the cumulation of many affixes in a single stem but there are probably no languages of this sort whose morphology is based primarily on infixation. While many languages can be classified as prefixing or suffixing, this classification is unlikely to be absolute: even fairly pure examples of one type or the other generally admit at least a very few examples of the opposite sort of affix. The more complex the affixal system, however, the more likely a language is to lean in one direction or the other: a language with ten position classes for both prefixes and suffixes would be likely to pose real difficulties in locating the roots of words. Since the opposition between prefixing languages and suffixing languages does not appear to correlate well with basic word-order type or other aspects of syntactic structure, it is a typological parameter of rather limited utility.

### 1.3 *Stem modifications*

The model of word structure based on a notion of morpheme performs well enough where a grammatical category is marked by an affix, with a one-to-one correspondence between categories and affixes. Difficulties arise, however, when a category is marked not by the presence (vs. absence) of overt phonological material but rather by the opposition between two (or more) parallel forms neither of which can be obtained by subtraction from the other (that is, of A vs. B, rather than of A+B vs. A). It is here that analysts have employed ingenious devices such as subtractive or replacive morphs.

#### 1.3.1 *Alternations in vowels, consonants, stress and tone*

Many languages indicate grammatical categories by a shift of vowel quality and/or quantity. In English, for example, this device marks tense in verbs such as *drink/drank/drunk*. This is in turn a reflex of the system of vocalic Ablaut reconstructed for common Indo-European, by which every root appeared in several related but distinct shapes: a full grade, with the vowel /e/ in a certain position; an *o*-grade, with /o/ in place of /e/, and a zero grade, with no vowel in the corresponding position. Each of these shapes is associated with a rather heterogeneous collection of grammatical categories. In general, some other marker of a given category is present in a form, as well as the 'grade' of the root, but in some cases (e.g. English *drink* vs. *drank*) the vowel grade may be the only indication of a distinction between categories. The replacement of the final vowel of Chickasaw negative forms seen above is another instance of such vowel change; here, of course, there are abundant additional markers of the category as well. Yet another example of the same type is the vowel alternation in German *Haus/Häuser* 'house/houses'. This particular alternation is accompanied in German usually, but not always, by some additional mark of the plural, and it occurs in other categories such as diminutives as well. It is usually given the distinct name *Umlaut* for reasons having to do with its historical origin, but from the point of view of the synchronic morphological system, it is simply another alternation of vowel quality like *Ablaut*, correlated with certain grammatical categories.

Probably the most extensive systems of vowel alternation are found in the Semitic languages. Here the root or 'lexical item' can often be represented simply as a skeleton of consonants (e.g. *k-t-b* 'write'): in an actual form every vowel is correlated with the set of grammatical categories to which the word belongs. Thus, the same root may with one pattern of vocalism (for instance, Egyptian Arabic *kitaab*) represent 'book'; with another (Egyptian *kátab*) 'he wrote', etc. Some affixes may appear with the word as well, but the point is that the entire pattern of vowels in a given word is determined by the complex of categories (derivational as well as inflectional) to which the word belongs.

Grammatical categories marked by vowel alternations (perhaps in combination with other elements) are quite common, but in some languages this purpose is served by consonant alternations as well. In Fula, for example, every root appears in one of three grades (some of which may in some cases be superficially identical): a 'continuant grade', a 'stop grade', and a 'nasal grade' (cf. Anderson 1976 for further information and references on this system). The root /wor-/'man', for example, is the continuant form: the stop grade of this root is /gor-/, and the nasal grade /ngor-/. The difference among the grades consists in an alternation in root-initial consonant, and the choice of a particular grade is determined by grammatical categories. For nouns, for example, each of the approximately two dozen (depending on dialect) noun classes is associated with a particular grade. Membership in a given class is marked both by a suffix and by the grade of the root: thus, the noun 'man' in the singular (non-diminutive, etc.) belongs to a class marked by suffix -*ko* and stop grade (hence, *gorko*), but in the plural to a class marked by suffix -*ɓe* and continuant grade (hence, *worɓe*). In this instance the category is marked not only by consonant alternation but also by overt affixation; but elsewhere in the language the consonant alternation may be the only indication of a grammatical feature. In some instances, number is marked in the verb only by the alternation in initial consonant. The verb stem appears in continuant grade for singular subjects, but in nasal grade when the subject is plural or, in most dialects, when the subject is a postposed pronoun.

Many languages mark grammatical categories with suprasegmental features such as stress and tone. In Spanish verbs, for example, the location of stress is (partly) correlated with tense, and thus *háblo* '(I) speak' is opposed to *habló* '(he) spoke' only in terms of the location of the stress (though in other cases there is some additional overt indication of the tense distinction). A number of West African tone languages (e.g. Tiv, Etung) utilize tone patterns to mark tense/aspect distinctions in a fashion similar to the Semitic use of vowel patterns. Each combination of tense and aspect categories is associated with a particular tone pattern (e.g. 'all high', 'high-low-high', etc.). The segmental material of the verb then indicates the lexical content, together with subject and object markers, etc.: on this segmental skeleton can be imposed any of the possible tone patterns to form a complete inflected verb.

Thus, languages may make use of alternations in any of the various domains of phonological structure (vowels, consonants, stress, tone) to indicate the grammatical category to which a form belongs. Though such processes of 'Ablaut', 'stem modification', 'consonant gradation', 'accent shift', etc. are frequently supplemented by overt inflectional affixes, this is not always the case, and such alternations are an important part of the overall inventory of grammatical processes in the languages of the world. More often than with simple affixes, however, they can be sets of categories, and as a result the field worker who expects to find a unitary 'meaning' for each piece of grammatical material will often find these alternations frustratingly difficult to pin down, or indeed miss their grammatical significance altogether.

### 1.3.2 *Reduplication*

This process which consists in the copying of part (or all) of the affected stem, perhaps modified in some systematic fashion (such as by the insertion of a constant vowel), could be treated either as a special sort of affix or as a type of stem modification. It has sufficiently special properties, however, to justify separate discussion.

Reduplication most typically affects the leftmost portion of the stem. The material copied may consist of (1) the initial consonant (or cluster), perhaps reinforced by a constant vowel; (2) the initial $c_o v$; (3) the entire first syllable; or perhaps (4) the entire root. There may be some additional modifications performed in the process of copying: thus in Kwakw'ala, some types of reduplication insert the segment $/s/$ or $/ɬ/$ between the copy and the original, some impose rigid vowel length or accentual relations between the two, etc. It seems that the copied material is always placed adjacent to the 'template' from which it is made: thus, we do not find instances in which $c_1 v c_2 v c_3$ is copied as $c_3 v c_1 v c_2 v c_3$, etc. Reduplication is not, however, limited to initial material. Chickasaw for example has a process by which the repetitive aspect of verbs is formed as follows: take the penultimate vowel, nasalize it, and place it after the original, separated from it by *h* (thus, *yopi* 'he's swimming', but *yohompi* 'he goes swimming all the time'; *ishi* 'he's taking it', but *ihinshi* 'he keeps on taking it (as, for example, medicine)'). This is surely a type of reduplication, but does not always affect the first syllable: cf. *toksali* 'he's working', but *toksahanli* 'he works all the time' (in fact, the syllable affected is the one that bore the main accent in proto-Choctaw-Chickasaw).

The same language may have several different sorts of reduplication processes, used for different purposes. In Kwakw'ala for example, from the stem of *madálqʷala* 'it is boiling', we can form (a) *mi'madálqʷala* 'many are boiling; (b) *ma'm̥dalqʷala* 'it is boiling all over'; and (c) *madálx̌ʷmadálqʷala* 'it is boiling repeatedly' by various types of copying. In some cases, one type of reduplication can apply to the output of another: thus, from the root of *nuɫá* 'worried' there is a (derivationally related) form *nanú'lu* 'reckless' which illustrates one sort of reduplication, and which undergoes another to yield the plural *nísnanu'lu*.

The phonological properties of reduplication in natural languages are quite engrossing, but this is not the place to explore them: for our purposes the general characterization of the process as a (partial) copying of phonological material is sufficient to distinguish it from simple affixation (which adds constant material) or other sorts of stem modification. What is of interest to us, however, is the fact that unlike other sorts of grammatical processes, reduplication seems always to reflect one of a fairly limited set of categories. Thus, in nouns we typically find reduplication marking plurality or diminutive (or augmentative) forms but not case, gender, or deictic/referential categories; in verbs, we find it marking aspectually distinct forms (such as progressives, imperfects, perfects as representing a state, distributives, iteratives, etc.), plural forms, and such 'moods' as hypothetical, unrealized, etc., but not person, voice or the like, or even tense (where this distinction is uncontaminated by aspectual oppositions). One can speculate on the possibly iconic nature of the process of reduplication (see chapter III:4 for some remarks on this in connection with the marking of aspect), and no doubt there are isolated counterexamples (perhaps with historical explanations, as when an aspectual opposition develops into one of pure tense), but it is still striking that this formal process is much more directly linked with the content of the category it represents than others in morphology.

### 1.3.3 Suppletion

The most extreme form of stem modification is the complete replacement of one form by another, as in the English type *go/went*. This is most frequently encountered in the closed word classes of the grammar: pronouns, the copula, etc. In some languages, however, it is fairly extensive even in the productive classes of the lexicon (as for instance in Georgian, where aspectual oppositions in a number of verbs are indicated by stem suppletion). When this situation arises, it is reasonable to ask whether we are in fact dealing with a single lexical item, whose morphology involves suppletion to mark an inflectional category, or with two (or more) distinct lexical items, each restricted to a single category. A large number of languages in Western North America, for example, display root suppletion based on number: thus, the root for 'one is standing' differs from that for 'several are standing'; and the root for 'pick up one round object' differs from the root for 'pick up several round objects' in languages like Navajo and other Athabaskan-Eyak languages, Tsimshian, the Salish family, and others. In some cases there are even separate forms for duals: in Chickasaw the verb 'be sitting' is *bini'li* in the singular, *chi'ya* in the dual, and *binohma* in the plural. One could plausibly argue, perhaps, that this does not reflect a simple morphological fact, but rather a different perception of the action, according to which the fact of one thing's sitting is simply different in character from the fact of two, or of several things sitting. The situation would be somewhat similar to that in a few verbs in English: an act of massacring, for example, can only be carried out on a group and not on an individual.

In most cases, such speculation on the possible basis of suppletion is rather pointless and circular, but in a few instances it can be confirmed. The Moses-Columbian dialect of Salish (according to Kinkade 1977) contains (at least) twenty-two pairs of roots differing in number as singular versus plural, expressing the expected range of meanings such as sit, stand, lay down a round object, kill, etc. Thus 'one sits' is *ɫáq-lx*, while 'several sit' is *yər-íx*. The fact that these are not simply inflectionally different forms related by suppletion, however, is shown by the fact that each stem can undergo the language's general plural-marking processes. Such a 'pluralized singular' is *ɫəqɫáqlx lx* 'each of several has a place to sit'; a 'pluralized plural' is *yəryəríx* 'people are sitting around and resting'. In fact, the 'plural' stems refer to activities as carried out by a group, as opposed to an individual, so when several perform the action individually, a 'pluralized singular', rather than a 'plural' is called for, and when several groups perform (or undergo) the action, a 'pluralized plural' is required. Indeed, one of the other pairs on Kinkade's list, a singular vs. a plural stem for 'tree' (better, 'be a tree') is directly parallel to English *trees* vs. *forest* or *grove*, which illustrates the distinction involved. Suppletion thus forms the borderline between inflectionally related forms of the same lexical item and distinct lexical items with a great deal of shared semantic material. The field worker should be open to both possibilities.

This completes our discussion of the formal devices employed for the indication of inflectional categories. We turn now to a survey of the grammatical oppositions which make up inflectional systems.

## 2.0 Inflectional categories expressed by grammatical processes

Within the general domain of inflection as sketched in section 0.3 above, we can distinguish three different sorts of categories that may be given formal realization. First, a given inflectional property may be an *inherent* one, in that it reflects a property whose domain is the inflected word itself. This property may be one which contributes to the meaning of the word (and hence, to that of the larger structure within which it appears), like the difference between singular and plural; or it may be a totally arbitrary and meaningless one, such as (usually) membership in a particular inflectional class. For our purposes, the distinctive aspect of inherent categories is that they are not imposed by the structural position occupied by the word and they do not depend on the properties of other words in the structure.

The second class of inflectional properties which we can distinguish is the set of *relational* categories, which reflect the position the word occupies in larger structures. A noun may designate or refer to an entity of a certain sort by virtue of its meaning, and it may be singular or plural on its own account, as it were, but it can only be a subject or an object, etc., by virtue of its position in some syntactic construction. An indicator of such position is the formal reflection of a relational category.

Finally, we can recognize a class of grammatical categories that arise in a word by *agreement* with properties of some other word or phrase. Most languages exhibit particular syntactic connections between words through inflectional agreement: some of the properties of one word, either inherent or relational, are marked also in the other. A common role for agreement processes is to identify the members of a grammatical phrase. Properly speaking, for example, a relational property such as one marking 'subject' does not refer to a single word, but rather to an entire noun phrase. In many languages, such a property is indicated by a single particle located at the beginning of the phrase (as in Kwakw'ala sentences such as the one in (2) above) or at the end of the phrase. In Chickasaw, for instance, subjects are marked by a following particle such as *at*, *ot*, *akot* (with the choice depending on emphasis and discourse factors):

(3)  a. Hattuk at    toksali
        man   SUBJ work
        'The man is working'

     b. Hattuk yamma (a)kot       toksali
        man    that   (EMPH)SUBJ work
        '*That* man's working'

c. Hattuk yamma-n pinsa-li-k akot     toksali
   man    that-OBJ  see-I-SUBJ EMPH-SUBJ work
   'The man I see is working'

Here the particle appears as a clitic on the end of the phrase, regardless
of its internal complexity. In other languages, categories applicable to
an entire phrase are realized on its head, or in some other determinate
position.

Another possibly more common situation however, is for a category
applicable to an entire phrase to be represented on all (or a certain
subclass) of the words of the phrase. Thus, in Finnish, *näiden miesten*
'these men' is a genitive, opposed to *nämä miehet*, a nominative version
of the same phrase: the category of case is realized not only on the head
noun, but on the modifier (here a demonstrative) as well. The fact that
all of the constituents of a phrase show the same category serves to
identity them as part of the same phrase: this is the basic function of
agreement within the phrase. The importance of this is particularly clear
in Warlpiri, where word order is strikingly free. As long as a noun
phrase remains intact, with its parts not separated by any other material,
only its head need be marked for case; but as soon as word order is
varied so as to separate parts of a phrase from one another, they must all
be marked individually:

(4)     a. Ngarrka nyampu-rlu wawirri    pantu-rnu
           man     this-ERG      kangaroo spear-PAST
           'This man speared a kangaroo'

        b. Ngarrka-ngku wawirri    pantu-rnu nyampu-rlu
           man-ERG        kangaroo spear-PAST this-ERG
           'This man speared a kangaroo'

In cases where a category is realized on all (or several) of the parts of
the phrase, we might suggest that it is, in principle, a property of just
one of those parts, independently of the others. We might regard it, that
is, as distributed secondarily to other elements by agreement with the
head. This is clearly not possible in cases displaying more structure,
however. Latin *bonōs librōs*, for example, not only shows accusative
case on the adjective as well as the noun: the adjective is also inflected
as masculine and plural. One could plausibly argue that when 'good
books' is used as an object, or in some other position where the
accusative is called for, 'good' is as much part of the object as 'books',
and hence just as suitable for marking as accusative; but there is nothing
masculine – or indeed plural – about 'good', either inherently or by
virtue of its structural position as a modifying adjective. It is only by

agreement with the head of its phrase, 'books', that it acquires these properties. There are clearly some inflectional categories which arise through agreement in this way, then, rather than inherently or relationally; and we could also assume that in other instances, relational properties are primarily assigned to heads of phrases, and secondarily to other members of a phrase through agreement.

For our purposes in this chapter, the distinction among types of inflectional categories is primarily an expository convenience. For the field worker confronted with an unusual formal distinction, however, it is quite important to bear in mind the various possible origins of such grammatical categories.

## 2.1  *Grammatical categories of nouns*
### 2.1.1  *Inherent categories of nouns*
Probably the most widespread inherent category realized in nouns in the languages of the world is that of *number*. Most languages provide some formal way of marking nouns or noun phrases as singular or plural. As with most categories, this may be done by any of the formal devices of morphology, including (as noted above) reduplication. The formal expression of plurality in the noun may be obligatory (as for most nouns in English); limited to certain categories, such as animates (as with the suffix -*men* in Mandarin) or referentially prominent nouns (as with proximate forms in most Algonquian languages, opposed to referentially less prominent obviative forms); not marked if there is any other overt indication of number (as in Kwakw'ala); optional as in Halkomelem (Salish); or absent (as in Chickasaw).

Some languages make distinctions similar to that of number, but not quite equivalent to the English difference between simple single versus multiple reference. In Tlingit, for example, there is not really a category of plural, but rather of collective: the difference between a singular and a coherent group. The 'plural' of *łingit* 'man' is *łingitq'*, which really refers to a group of men, not simply to multiple men randomly distributed in space. Similarly, the 'plural' of *q'a:t'* 'island', which is *q'a:t'q'i*, really means something like 'archipelago'. In fact, we can make a 'plural' form *yuyai tlanq'* 'the big whale', which refers to a single whale but stresses that it was very large and had many parts to be cut out. Sometimes, as in Old Breton, these collective forms are distinct from and coexist with the more usual sorts of plural.

In some languages, number marking in nouns shows unusual interactions with numerals. Thus, Hungarian, Turkish, and some other languages use the singular when number is overtly indicated by an accompanying numeral. Russian has a special form for nouns, resembling (but not completely identical with) the genitive, used after the numbers 2, 3 and 4. Serbo-Croatian has a special form for nouns and their modifiers under the same circumstances: *ruski film* 'Russian film', *dva, tri, četiri ruska filma* '2, 3, 4 Russian films', and *ruski filmovi* 'Russian films'. Bulgarian and Macedonian have the special form in -*a* for masculine nouns after all numerals above 1, although the plural appears too.

Some languages make more distinctions in the category of number than simply singular versus plural. A significant number of languages, for instance, distinguish also a *dual* form applying to two individuals (e.g. Sanskrit); and at least a few languages also distinguish a *trial* form referring to three individuals (e.g. Marshallese, a Micronesian language). Commonly duals are extended to become *paucals* – referring to a few, more than one, but not so many as would call for a plural. In a system such as that of Marshallese, the dual may refer to 'a few', the trial to more than that, but still a clearly limited number, and the plural to 'lots', depending on the sort of object referred to and the discourse circumstances.

As one might expect, languages do not distinguish duals unless they also have plurals; nor trials without duals. Quite generally, these non-singular forms are made by modifying the singular (by affixation, reduplication, etc.), which represents the base: overt 'singulative' marking taking plural forms as basic is not often found. Singulative affixes may be added to collectives in Breton, though this is apparently a derivational rather than inflectional formation. Similar forms are also found in Welsh. A large set of masculine nouns in Slavic languages, mostly meaning 'man from such-and-such place' add -*in* to the plural to make the singular: thus, Russian *angličane* 'Englishmen', but *angličanin* 'Englishman'. At least in origin, these are also derivational formations; but synchronically they reflect the opposition singular/plural. One might also regard mass nouns (such as *jewelry*) as inherently plurals, from which 'singulatives' are formed syntactically (*a piece of jewelry*), but this is obviously taking us far afield from inflection.

Another common category in nouns is that of *gender*. This consists in a division of the lexicon of a language into a number of different classes for purposes of agreement. The number of classes may range from two (as in French), three (as in Latin), four (as in the Australian language Dyirbal), to as many as twenty or so (in the noun-class languages of West Africa, such as Fula, depending on whether plural, diminutive, etc. classes are counted). The basis for these distinctions is generally at least partially semantic. Particularly common are systems based on sex (masculine, feminine, and neuter) or animacy (with the variant 'human/non-human'), but other dimensions may enter in as well, as with the proliferation of semantically semi-coherent noun classes in Bantu languages, or the 'edible' and 'drinkable' genders (in addition to animate and neuter) of Fijian. Despite the fact that some aspect of meaning can often be found (at least historically) at the base of gender systems, there is almost always at least some element of arbitrariness as well. For instance, the Algonquian languages oppose animate to inanimate nouns as a fundamental grammatical category, but a few items do not fit this distinction: kettles and certain kinds of berries (among other non-animals) are 'animate', but frying pans and other kinds of berries are 'inanimate'. The amount of grammatically arbitrary classification in this system is actually quite small, but in the case of most two or three gender systems in Indo-European languages it affects the great bulk of the lexicon, since the opposition of masculine vs. feminine and/or neuter is extended into the vast areas of vocabulary where natural gender is strictly speaking meaningless.

We should be careful to distinguish gender or noun-class systems from simple differences in inflectional class. Thus Icelandic nouns belong to several different declensional classes ('strong' declension vs. 'weak' declension, '*i*-stems', '*u*-stems', etc.), based on systematically different forms taken by the inflections for case and number. This division partially correlates with, and partially cross-cuts the distinction among masculine, feminine, and neuter genders. Rules of agreement in the language, however, show that gender is a distinct inherent category: adjectives, demonstratives, etc. agree with the head of their noun phrase in gender, but not at all in declensional class. The noun *hestur* 'horse' (acc. *hest*, nom. pl. *hestar*), for example, is a 'strong *a*-stem' masculine noun, while *afi* 'grandfather' (acc. *afa*, nom. pl. *afar*) is a 'weak' masculine noun. Adjectives agree with both of these in the same way, however, since it is only the feature 'masculine' that is relevant: *gamall hestur* 'old horse' (acc. *gamlan hest*, nom. pl. *gamlir hestar*), *gamall afi* 'old grandfather' (acc. *gamlan afa*, nom. pl. *gamlir afar*). A feminine 'strong *a*-stem' noun, like *kerling* 'old woman' (acc. *kerlingu*, nom. pl. *kerlingar*) or 'weak' noun, like *amma* 'grandmother' (acc. *ömmu*, nom. pl. *ömmur*) similarly results in adjectives agreeing for gender, but not for declensional class: *gömul kerling*, *gömul amma* (acc. *gamla kerlingu*, *gamla ömmu*, nom. pl. *gamlar kerlingar*, *gamlar ömmur*).

In some languages noun class ('gender') distinctions are represented overtly in the surface form of the noun itself. Thus, Bantu and other African class languages generally mark nouns with a prefix (and/or suffix) indicative of the class to which they belong; most nouns in

Russian can be identified as masculine, feminine, or neuter by their phonological shape, etc. In many others, however, the situation is closer to that of French or Breton, where there is no clue to the gender of a noun in its surface form. Certain derivational categories may belong systematically to a particular gender, of course, but this association is just as arbitrary in both semantic and phonological terms as any other. The category of gender is an inherent one in nouns, but often not the basis of any grammatical process applying *to* nouns: it is realized overtly only in other areas of inflection, through the operation of agreement. This sort of behavior is not strictly limited to noun class: for instance, some languages (including some in the Mayan family) do not generally mark number in nouns, but indicate plurality primarily through agreement in verbs or elsewhere in the noun phrase. Nonetheless, such indirect reflection of an inherent category is reasonably common for noun-class systems, and rather rarer elsewhere in grammar.

Distinct from gender or noun class, but related to it in some languages, is the category of *diminutives* (and occasionally *augmentatives* as well). It is quite common for a language to have such a formation, of course, but even in cases of such fairly productive affixes as German *-chen/-lein* or Spanish *-ito*, there is little real basis for calling this an inflectional rather than a derivational category. In a few cases, however, the formation of diminutives is so thoroughly integrated into the language's inflectional system that its status is not in doubt. In Fula, for instance, each noun belongs, in its simple singular form, to a particular class. Corresponding to these there are a (rather more limited) set of plural classes. Any noun, however, regardless of its class can be made into a diminutive (providing this is semantically appropriate, of course) simply by inflecting it as a member of one of the two diminutive singular classes (which differ in that one has pejorative connotations – 'puny little . . .') or as a member of the special diminutive plural class. In addition, there is an augmentative singular and an augmentative plural class, giving rise to a paradigm of seven forms for any noun: singular, basic plural, two diminutives, diminutive plural, augmentative, and augmentative plural. This process is (in principle – given semantic limitations) completely productive, and its full integration into the noun-class system, which is the basis of the agreement and concord system of the language, makes its inflectional status clear.

A less striking, but quite clear case is furnished by Halkomelem. In this language, nouns belong to one of two classes as shown through agreement. One of these classes consists of feminine persons and all diminutives (marked formally by a distinctive reduplication pattern), and the other consists of all other nouns. Diminutive formation is completely productive, and its status as an inflectional category is confirmed by its integration into the gender system.

A number of languages display in their nominal inflection one or more categories of a referential or deictic sort. Consider first the difference between definite and indefinite nouns. A language like Danish, in which we can distinguish *hus* 'house' and *huset* 'the house' appears to treat definiteness as an inflectional category, but this is not entirely clear. When a noun is modified, for example, it is no longer 'inflected' as definite: cf. *et lille hus* 'a little house', *det lille hus* 'the little house'. The analysis that suggests itself here is that definite nouns are accompanied by an article which, in the absence of any additional modifiers, becomes a clitic on the noun. In that case, there would be no reason to treat definiteness as an inflectional category in Danish.

In the closely related languages Swedish and Norwegian, however, it appears that definiteness has been reanalyzed as inflectional. The directionality of the development is clear, since Old Norse and Modern Icelandic, which represent the language from which all three developed, are like Danish in this respect. Here the definite ending remains even in the presence of a modifier and a demonstrative, for example Norwegian *hus* 'house', *huset* 'the house', and *det store huset* 'the big house'. The situation is also fairly clear in Basque, where definiteness forms a dimension of the inflectional system, and there is no apparent alternative analysis taking definiteness as marked by a clitic article. Compare *buru* 'head', *burua* 'the head', *bura bat* 'a head'; *buruk* 'head (erg.)'; *buruak* 'the head (erg.)'. The argument here comes from the fact that the formal mark of definiteness precedes the case ending; but it should be noted that in Basque, definiteness is marked at only one point in the noun phrase: *buru handi* '(a) big head', *buru handia* 'the big head'.

It is comparatively common for definiteness to interact with the marking of case in certain syntactic positions. It is often the case that direct objects receive distinctive marking only if they are definite. In languages as diverse as Turkish and Chickasaw, object marking does not apply to indefinite noun phrases. Here, while there is no formal representation of definiteness in isolation, its status as an inflectional category is clear. It would be incorrect to identify the object marker in such a language as *either* an 'accusative' marker (deleted for indefinites) *or* a 'definite' marker (appearing only in object position): rather, this is an example of the fact that grammatical processes do not correspond one-to-one with the categories they reflect. It is the conjunction of categories 'definite' and 'accusative' that is represented.

In some languages, of course, the category of 'definiteness' that may receive inflectional or other formal indication is not the same as that marked in English by the definite article. Some languages have a category of 'specific' noun phrases instead, including expressions for which (as with 'definite' noun phrases) it is presumed that a referent exists, but about which (unlike 'definites') it is not presumed that the identity of this referent is known.

Another variant of such a category is the recognition of a category of proper, as opposed to common nouns. Most languages assign some distinctive properties to proper names, such as the special articles found in Polynesian languages. Such a category may interact with definiteness where both are formally realized.

Yet another category related to those above is the marking of nouns for deictic status. The variety of systems of this sort is surveyed below in chapter III:5. They are generally restricted in their formal realization to a set of demonstrative elements, but in a few cases these distinctions are marked inflectionally on nouns as well. A particularly well-known example (thanks to Boas) is Kwakw'ala: here a noun phrase is not only preceded by a demonstrative element, but its first word is also marked (obligatorily) as belonging to one of six categories. These are based on two dimensions: near me/ near you/ distant (roughly), and visible/invisible. Given the fact that this distinction is marked on the first word of the noun phrase, whatever that is, it may well be that we are dealing with a case of clitics rather than inflection here: there are very few examples of languages in which such a deictic category has clearly inflectional status.

The primary inherent categories of nominal inflection, then, are number, gender, and referentiality/deixis. Other categories are reported for various languages: in Kwakw'ala, for example, the verbal category of tense is said to extend to the inflection of nouns, as in *χən χʷakʷ'əna* 'my canoe', *χən χʷakʷəna* 'my future canoe (as, one I am presently building')', and *χən χʷakʷənxde* 'my past canoe (as, one that sank, or that I sold)'. Marshallese is another language in which tense is said to be a category applicable to nouns. In this and numerous other cases, however, it is difficult to show that we are really dealing with an inflectional category, rather than with a derivational formation made on the analogy of verbal inflection. Tense in this sense does not seem to function in agreement rules, to be part of a network of interlocking inflectional dimensions, or generally to show the sort of productivity and semantic uniformity we expect of inflectional categories.

### 2.1.2 *Relational categories of nouns*

The traditional term 'case' is fundamentally a name for the entire class of relational categories applicable to noun inflection. As the formal reflection of all of the roles played by nouns in larger structures, this is a large and somewhat homogeneous set. We can generally divide case categories into grammatical or *direct* case (marking syntactic functions such as 'subject' and 'object' determined primarily by structural position) and *oblique* cases (marking a range of functions, including but not limited to spatial or local ones, with more independent semantic content and less dependent on structural role). Terminology is not well standardized here: traditional grammarians often use 'oblique' to designate all cases except the 'nominative', though some include the 'accusative' as a direct case as well. In distinguishing between grammatical cases and those with more independent, meaningful content, one might choose to call the two classes 'syntactic' and 'semantic', respectively; but as we will see, the oblique cases often have syntactic functions and the direct cases (in our sense) frequently convey meaning as well as relational information. We thus prefer the more manifestly arbitrary terms 'direct' and 'oblique'. Inevitably, the boundary between the two is somewhat hard to draw; one might also argue that at least some of the oblique cases ought really to be treated as inherent rather than relational categories. We will assume here that case is a uniform notion (at least as the basis for inflectional categories as they affect word formation), but that we can distinguish direct from oblique case functions at least for expository purposes.

2.1.2.1 *Systems of direct cases.* The direct case categories serve to indicate basic grammatical relations such as 'subject', 'object', and 'indirect object'. We might expect, therefore, that the range of possible systems of these cases would follow closely this inventory of functions, but the actual picture presented by the languages of the world is rather more complex than this would suggest.

Confining our attention for the moment to the marking of subject and object, we note at the outset that the transitivity of the verb with which a noun phrase is associated plays an important role. Bearing in mind the problems noted in chapter 1:2 with the notion of 'subject', we can distinguish three major categories of interest: the category of subjects of intransitive verbs ($s_i$), that of subjects of transitive verbs ($s_t$), and that of direct objects of transitive verbs (o). We could imagine that a language might provide distinct categories of inflection for all three of these functions, but such systems occur marginally at best. Motu (a language of New Guinea) is said to mark $s_i$ and $s_t$ with distinct particles, and o with no overt mark at all: this may be the closest we can come to the sort of system we seek, though the particle for $s_t$ (*ese*) is apparently optional. The particle *na* marks $s_i$, but this also is optional in most dialects, and even appears (under conditions that are not understood) with some o noun phrases. Other languages, particularly in Australia, display such a system for a small subcategory of noun phrases (usually pronouns); these cases will be noted below.

In the Australian language Wangkumara (cf. Breen 1976) pronouns display such a three-way distinction among Ergative, Accusative, and Nominative (Absolutive) case forms. Noun stems in this language, furthermore, are followed by reduced clitic forms of these pronouns: thus, the Ergative, Accusative, and Nominative masculine singular pronouns *ṇulu*, *niṇa*, and *ṇia* are added to a stem such as *kaṇa* 'man' to give *kaṇaula*, [*kaniṇa*] (implied but not actually cited in Breen (1976)), and *kaṇia*. These forms, with attached clitics, may not yet constitute a three-way case-marking system for nouns, but if not it may safely be assumed that such a system is in the process of development.

Another logical possibility would be a language that provided a category of $s_i$, and another that marked $s_t$ and o identically. Note that this would be equivalent to marking the noun phrases of a clause for the transitivity of its verb: such a system does not appear to occur anywhere.

When we also ignore the possibility of identical marking for all three functions (equivalent to no distinctive marking for any, and hence not the basis of a possible inflectional category within the range of direct cases), we are left with two possibilities: (i) a category of $s_i$ and $s_t$ opposed to one of o alone; and (ii) a category of $s_i$ and o, opposed to one of $s_t$ alone. Both of these occur, and both are distributed throughout the language families of the world. The first possibility is of course the familiar system of Latin and many other languages, with $s_i$ and $s_t$ belonging to a category usually called the *nominative* and o assigned to the *accusative*. In many languages with such a system, the nominative is the formally unmarked base form of the noun, and the accusative involves the addition of some grammatical process; but in others (e.g. Cushitic, Yuman, Muskogean, and others) it is the nominative that is formally marked as opposed to the accusative.

The other possibility is realized in 'ergative' languages. Here the category containing $s_t$ noun phrases is called the *ergative* case (other names that appear in the literature include relative case, active case, agent case, and others): the category opposed to it, containing $s_i$ and o, is usually called an *absolutive* case. Sometimes this category is called a nominative, but it seems better to reserve that name for a case category opposed to an accusative, as above. In ergative systems the ergative case is apparently always marked formally, and the absolutive is usually the unmarked base form of the noun. Examples of ergative languages include Basque, Eskimo, Tsimshian, Tibetan, Avar (Northeast

Caucasian), virtually all of the languages indigenous to Australia, and a host of others.

When we speak of a language as having an accusative or an ergative case-marking system, we are describing it as belonging to one or the other of the above ideal types. Especially with 'ergative' languages, this can be something of an exaggeration, since these generally display at least some features characteristic of other systems. Most 'ergative' languages are actually 'mixed-ergative' languages, in the sense to be discussed now. There are several different sorts of 'mixed ergative' system, which have distinct motivations and thus should be treated separately.

We should mention first a linguistic type that does not find a natural place in this survey, which treats noun morphology and verb morphology separately. As we will see below (in section 2.2.3), verbal agreement patterns may also be divided into an 'ergative' type and a 'nominative/accusative' type. Frequently, ergative case marking is associated with ergative verb agreement (as for instance in Avar), but in other languages, ergative case marking co-occurs with nominative/accusative verb agreement (this is the situation in the Indo-Iranian Dardic language Shīnā, for example). Apparently there are no instances of languages in which agreement is ergative but case marking nominative/accusative.

We can next note the existence of a number of languages in which ergative case marking is restricted to sentences in which the verb is in a particular tense/aspect category. This is the case, for example, in Georgian, in Hindi and a number of other Indic languages, in Pashto (Iranian), and in the language-isolated Burushaski (all of which are spoken in roughly the same part of the world, though they are not all genetically related). In each case, ergative marking is associated with sentences in perfect tenses (or in tenses that are the modern reflex of a perfect, as in Hindi). The opposite asymmetry does not seem to occur, nor do other tense/aspect conditioned splits. This fact appears to have an interesting explanation in terms of the historical processes that lead to the development of (new) perfects and new imperfects (cf. Anderson 1977a), but it is not necessary to develop that explanation here in order to establish the typological status of the systems that do exist.

Another sort of split-ergative system is particularly common in Australian languages, though instances can be found elsewhere as well. In Dyirbal, for example, we find that while ordinary noun phrases are assigned case on the ergative/absolutive pattern, first and second person pronouns are marked as nominative vs. accusative. Several other related possibilities exist, which can be given a unitary account in terms proposed by Silverstein (1976). He suggests that we can arrange possible participants in an event along a scale like that in (5):

(5)

| 1st person pronoun | 2nd person pronoun | demonstratives & 3rd person pronouns | proper nouns | human | common nouns animate | inanimate |
|---|---|---|---|---|---|---|

$\longleftarrow$ ⎯⎯⎯⎯⎯⎯⎯⎯⎯⎯⎯⎯⎯⎯⎯⎯⎯⎯⎯⎯⎯⎯⎯⎯⎯⎯ $\longrightarrow$

Roughly, the further an item is to the left on this scale, the more likely it is to receive case marking on an accusative pattern, and the further to the right, the more likely to be case-marked by an ergative system. There are several possible dividing points, and in a few languages (such as the Australian language Yidiɲ), a zone of 'overlap' in the middle of the scale actually displays both systems. For demonstratives with human reference, Yidiɲ separates both an accusative (o case) and an ergative ($s_t$ case) from a form limited to $s_i$. There do not, however, appear to be 'split-ergative' systems of this sort in which a middle zone on the scale in (5) is left completely without case marking. Again, it is unnecessary to go into the basis of a scale like (5) to make the point that it characterizes a dimension along which such split-ergative morphological systems can be ranged typologically.

A final type of 'split-ergative' system that has been reported for a number of Mayan languages involves ergative marking in main clauses, but accusative marking (apparently through generalizing the ergative marker to apply to $s_i$ as well as $s_t$) in certain types of subordinate clauses. The opposite situation (with accusative marking in main clauses and ergative marking in subordinate – specifically, relative – clauses) has been suggested for the Australian language Ngarluma, but this may be the result of a misanalysis (cf. Nash 1977). The status (and indeed, the existence) of split-ergative systems based on the opposition of main vs. subordinate clauses is not at all clear.

A final, related sort of phenomenon should be noted here. In some languages which otherwise display nominative/accusative case-marking patterns (e.g. Finnish, Southern Paiute, and the Australian languages Lardil and Ngarluma), direct objects in certain constructions appear not in the accusative, but in the nominative. The constructions in question include imperatives in all of the above languages; in some (e.g. Finnish), impersonal infinitives are included as well (of the type 'It is necessary to kill the bear').

It is rather difficult to maintain that the objects in these constructions are 'really' subjects, and thus appropriately marked as nominative; but fortunately, there is no need to do so. When we consider both of the commonly occurring case systems (accusative and ergative), we can see that they have one thing in common: both provide a formal differentiation of subject and object phrases in transitive clauses, the kind of clause in which both subjects and objects occur. It is clear why systems of the sort we are considering should exist: accusative marking can fail to apply to the objects of transitive verbs precisely in constructions where there is no subject noun phrase. Imperatives in virtually all languages involve the systematic deletion (or at least non-appearance) of a presumed second person subject and the impersonal infinitives relevant here have no subject expressed; thus the appearance of a verb as an imperative (or impersonal infinitive) guarantees that an associated noun phrase will be identified as object, independent of case marking. We are not dealing with a different sort of case-marking system here (much less with an unusual class of subjects), but simply with the failure of accusative marking to apply in a well-defined class of environments in which its operation is not functionally motivated.

Thus far, we have been dealing with case-marking systems in which the choice of inflection is based primarily on grammatical relations (subject and object) and the transitivity of the associated verb. When we consider verbal agreement systems (in many ways closely related to noun inflection) below in section 2.2.3, we will encounter languages in which there is a role played by semantic as well as structural properties of the relation between verbs and their associated noun phrases. In some languages, uses of oblique cases for the subjects of particular verbs can be said to follow semantic principles (these will be discussed in the next section), but it is noteworthy that there are no (direct) case-marking systems that are based fundamentally on semantic principles (rather than on syntactic relations). Even a language like Chickasaw, with a highly 'semanticized' verb-agreement system, marks noun phrases straightforwardly as subjects or as objects.

Before leaving the topic of direct-case systems, we should mention the formal treatment of indirect objects, since these are frequently felt to occupy the status of a third basic grammatical relation. Many languages, of course, mark this function with a preposition (or postposition), along the lines of English *I gave a fish to John*. Others have a distinct case, generally called a *dative*, for this function, as in German *Ich gab dem Mädchen einen Fisch*. Still others present indirect objects as a special instance of the direct object, as in English *I gave the girl a fish*. English, as well as some others languages (e.g. Indonesian) allows for both the first and the third possibility. There are apparently no languages in which the indirect object appears in the same case form as the subject (unless, of course, there is no case-marking at all, in which event all noun phrases have the same inflectional form). It should also be noted that in some languages, the semantic structure of certain verbs is such that what we expect to find as an indirect object is in fact treated as a direct object. In Kwakw'ala, for example, the verb(s) meaning 'give' take as their direct object the Recipient, and express the thing given in an instrumental phrase. There is no reason not to treat this structure as basic: it is simply that acts of giving are expressed in Kwakw'ala with a verb that might be more accurately glossed as 'present', as in 'I presented the girl with a fish'. Field workers exploring the case system of a new language must always be alert to this sort of possibility – the translations given may employ verbs that are subtly different in semantic structure, thus not preserving the grammatical relations of the original English (or other language) sentence.

The final direct case to be considered is the genitive. The most obvious function of the case usually given this name is the expression of possession ('John's dog'), but it generally functions to express a whole range of other relations between nouns. Thus, *John's picture* may be the one he has, the one he took, the one someone else took of him, the one he chose to copy, etc. The genitive really expresses the fact that one noun is subordinate to, and a modifier of, another: this is our motivation for treating it as a direct case function. Sometimes this function is even more general, as in the case of the Mandarin particle *de* which can indicate many sorts of subordination – not just that of noun to noun.

A variant of the construction 'Noun$_{subord}$ + genitive – Noun$_{head}$' is found in some Semitic and Nilotic languages, among (very few) others. Here it is the head Noun which is inflected – put in the so-called 'construct state', or 'appertentive' form to indicate that it is in fact modified. The subordinate noun in the structure then appears in its basic form. This situation can be distinguished from that of possessive inflection on nouns (discussed in section 2.1.3 below), since a 'construct state' form does not indicate the person, number, gender or other features of the subordinate noun, but only that there is one.

Many languages use cases including those just dealt with (especially the dative and genitive) idiosyncratically to mark the objects of certain verbs. This is sometimes associated with a semantic distinction, as in Warlpiri or Maori where the marking of a direct object as dative rather than absolutive (in Warlpiri) or accusative (in Maori) indicates that the action was unsuccessful, or incompletely carried out, or that it affected only a part of the object, etc. It may also be associated with a semantic class, as when all Russian verbs meaning 'control' take their objects in the instrumental case – even new ones, such as *dirižirovat'* 'conduct (an orchestra)'. In other cases, however (as with the verbs in German whose objects are marked dative or genitive, rather than accusative), it is simply a morphological idiosyncrasy of a particular verb, without a coherent semantic basis (so far as we know).

2.1.2.2 *Oblique cases.* Many of the oblique relations borne by nouns to the larger structures in which they appear are expressed commonly by prepositions (or postpositions). Like other members of closed classes, however, these elements (especially postpositions) have a tendency to be de-stressed, and to turn into clitics. As we have already noted above, this is the first step on the road to reinterpretation as an inflectional affix; and thus there is probably no function which is expressed prepositionally in, say, English, which is not expressed somewhere in the world by an oblique 'case'.

We should first note that some of the direct cases can also serve oblique functions. Thus, in Old English, phrases such as 'he went *three miles*', or 'it snowed (for) *a week*' were put in the accusative not because they were direct objects, like other accusatives, but because this was one of the local uses of the same inflectional form. Similarly, German, with a set of four cases and a large number of prepositions, marks noun phrases that are objects of prepositions with the accusative, dative, or genitive depending partly on semantic factors and partly on lexically idiosyncratic grounds.

We simply list here some of the more common case categories recognized by languages, that are not fundamentally 'grammatical' in content.

(i) Many languages recognize an *instrumental* form expressing the means or manner or implement with which something is done. In ergative languages (such as most of those of the Northeast Caucasian family) this is frequently identical with the ergative. In Kwakw'ala, it is the only distinct case form besides the object and subject cases, and serves to express possession as well as instrumentality.

(ii) Some languages (e.g. Finnish) recognize a distinct *partitive* case, whose content is 'some (part) of the (Noun)'. This case is used in Finnish in some ways similar to that of the dative in Maori or Warlpiri for the objects of unsuccessful or incomplete actions mentioned in the previous section. It is also used for the objects of negative verbs, which is surely a related fact. Compare the fact that Russian also marks the objects of negative verbs in a special way (under complex conditions), namely with the genitive rather than the accusative.

(iii) Some languages have a special *comitative* case, indicating accompaniment (e.g. Yidiɲ in Australia).

Other languages recognize many different unusual and quasi-unique categories by case inflections, in ways that do not lend themselves to systematization. Yidiɲ, for example, has not only absolutive, ergative, instrumental, dative, and a set of cases for spatial location, but also a case for the purpose of an action (as 'we set a trap *for fish*') and a case for expressing something the subject is afraid of (as 'the child sat still (for fear of) *the person*'), among others.

We turn now to systems of cases expressing spatial location (and metaphorical extensions of this, as temporal extent, etc.) – usually called *local* cases. Many people, when first told that Uralic languages such as Finnish and Hungarian typically display more than a dozen cases, consider (perhaps recalling their own difficulties with the five cases plus vocative of Latin) that this must be some sort of highly aberrant and unstable situation. The majority of these cases are local in nature, however, and as local case systems go the Uralic situation is quite restrained. Some of the languages of the Caucasus (such as Lezghian, Lak, and others known almost exclusively by reputation to European and North American linguists) have systems with more than thirty local cases alone, in addition to a set of direct cases and other oblique forms, some with grammatical functions. These systems generally show quite interesting degrees of internal organization and coherence, from which the simpler systems of local cases in Europe can often be better understood. The fairly straightforward system of Avar, for example, contains twenty distinct inflectional categories of a local nature (again, in addition to a set of grammatical cases), though for semantic reasons any given noun can appear in at most sixteen of these. The categories can easily be seen to be organized along two dimensions: first, whether reference is being made to location or motion on top of, beside, under, inside a compact object, or among the parts of a dispersed object; and second, whether location at, motion toward, motion away from, or motion by way of (or along a path contacting) the object is referred to. This yields a five-by-four matrix of categories, defining the twenty different cases. We can now see a system with locative, allative, and ablative cases as analogous to (a part of) the second dimension that functions in Avar, with neutralization of the distinctions made along the first dimension; and the opposition among inessive, illative, and elative cases in Finnish as the special case of the second Avar dimension where the first has the value 'inside of' or 'among the parts of' the object.

Sometimes local (and other oblique) cases develop grammatical uses in a particular language. The frequent coincidence of ergative and instrumental cases noted above, for example, is probably sometimes the result of an original instrumental developing a secondary use for the subjects of transitive verbs. Frequently verbs whose subjects are not

'Agents' mark them with some oblique case: commonly the dative, as in earlier English 'me thinks', from *me þynceþ* '(it) seems to me'. Avar has a well-developed situation of this sort: intransitive subjects are marked with the absolutive; subjects of most transitive verbs are marked with the ergative; the verb of possession has its subject in the genitive; the two verbs 'like' and 'love' have their subjects in the dative; and most verbs of perception mark their subjects with the case indicating location at the inside of something ('inside of me sees John').

### 2.1.3 *Agreement categories of the noun*
Rules of agreement in most languages function to copy inherent or relational features from nouns onto other parts of the structure, rather than the other way around, and it is thus quite rare to find a situation in which nouns are marked for some feature to agree with something else. One notable exception, however, is found in possessive structures. Many languages (e.g. Turkish, Finnish, Athabaskan, Muskogean, Mayan, Algonquian, and a great many others) inflect nouns for the person and number categories of a possessor. This inflection is generally highly similar to, if not identical with, the way verbs in the same language are inflected for agreement with their subject (or whatever else they agree with).

There may also be two distinct patterns for possessive inflection, one for 'inalienably' possessed nouns (those that are always possessed, inseparable from their possessors, etc., or some grammaticized extension of this class), and one for 'alienably' possessed nouns. The content of this distinction varies somewhat from language to language: typically close relatives and body parts, etc. are inalienably possessed, but in some languages the class may extend to many other things, such as houses, dogs, and other things that are thought of as inextricably linked with their possessors. In Samoan, the distinction is roughly between things that act on, or determine the identity and place in the world of their 'possessors' (such as relatives, one's house, and many other things), and things that one acts on, or influences. The same noun may be treated either way in some cases, with a difference in meaning: thus, 'my (inalienable) king' is the one who rules over me, but 'my (alienable) king' is the one I help to choose.

It is quite rare for any other agreement category than possession to be manifested inflectionally in nouns. Nouns in the genitive, like other adnominal modifiers, may agree with their heads in categories such as case in some languages (e.g. Dyirbal), but generally do not. There are other sporadic examples of agreement in nouns: in the Australian language Lardil, for instance, nouns in the accusative case have two forms depending on whether their governing verb is a future or a non-future form. One might also regard the split-ergative systems based on tense/aspect, noted above, as manifesting a category of tense/aspect agreement with the verb, intersecting with such relational categories as subject and object to determine the inflectional form of the noun.

## 2.2 *Grammatical categories of verbs*

In most languages, a large part of the complexity of word formation (and inflection in particular) concerns the verb. A complete catalog of the distinctions of meaning that can be indicated formally by verbs in the languages of the world (independent of the lexical meanings of stems) would be extraordinarily long and difficult; beyond the dimensions indicated below, much of what remains displays little cross-linguistic structure of typological interest. We concentrate here on the major parameters of inflectional specification.

### 2.2.1 *Inherent categories of verbs*

Most of the bulk of the 'complete catalog' just referred to would come in this area. Especially in dealing with 'polysynthetic' languages, such as Eskimo or Kwakw'ala, there seems often to be a nearly open-ended list of adverbial, verbal, adjectival, and even nominal modifications to the basic meaning of a verb root that can be indicated by essentially productive processes (generally in the form of affixes). Notions such as the direction in which an action is directed, the instrument with which it is performed, the manner in which it is carried out, the generic type of object on which it is performed, and so on – and on – may all correspond to such productive or semi-productive affixes. In general, these matters seem best treated as lexical derivation rather than as inflection.

A somewhat 'adverbial' category which is sometimes clearly related to inflection, however, is that of evidential markers. Several languages (including Turkish, Bulgarian, Georgian, Hopi, and Kwakw'ala) recognize formally a category of 'reportive' verb forms: verbs describing events for which the speaker cannot vouch personally, since he did not witness them, but has only second-hand knowledge. Kwakw'ala also has a marker for events described from the evidence of a dream, and other languages have a category for events of which the speaker is frankly doubtful. These forms are generally marked by discrete affixes which could well be derivational in character, and so it would be difficult to be sure that they are functionally part of the inflectional system; but at least in the case of Georgian, we can be fairly sure. In this language, reportive verb forms involve a major rearrangement of the tense-marking, agreement, and even case-marking pattern of the language;

they are completely integrated into the morphology of the verb, and are thus at the very heart of the inflectional apparatus.

Another category that is not far from adverbial notions is that of polarity (or negation). Chapter 1.4 surveys the properties of negation in a variety of languages; here we only note that this is indicated directly in verbal inflection in some languages, such as Abkhaz (Northwest Caucasian) and Chickasaw. We have seen above something of the mechanism of Chickasaw negative formation; among other things, the change in the verbal agreement pattern that this involves confirms its status in this language as part of the system of inflectional categories.

We should also note that a variety of modal functions performed in languages like English by auxiliary verbs are filled in others by categories of the verbal system. Abkhaz, for example, has an affix appearing in verbs to mark *potential* ('be able to') forms; Kwakw'ala has affixes to mark *potential* and *obligatory* ('be obliged to') forms, as well as one (which appears together with reduplication marking irrealis) marking *attemptive* ('try to') forms. A similar (but not identical) distinction has been found to be quite fundamental in several languages of the Salish family: here the question of whether the subject (especially of transitive verbs) was fully in control of the action, or whether he simply performed it or brought it about without effectively controlling it determines much of the overall inflectional pattern in languages like Bella Coola, Halkomelem, and Thompson. This parameter may be reflected not only in an overt affix, but in the choice of pronominal affixes indicating agreement.

Perhaps the most important inherent category of verbs which is undeniably inflectional is that of tense and aspect (together with mood). Tense and aspect systems are surveyed in chapter III:4 following and there is thus little to be added here. These categories can be reflected formally in the direct application of grammatical processes of all sorts (affixes, stem modification, reduplication, or suppletion); they may also be reflected less directly, as when tense conditions the form taken by agreement markers (e.g. in Takelma) or even the form of case marking on noun phrases (as observed above).

A distinction which is sometimes made in inflectional systems is that between actions and states. *Active* and *stative* verbs (the latter frequently including many of what are treated as adjectives in English: cf. chapter I:1) may have somewhat different tense and aspect systems, and different patterns of agreement – as well as some direct, overt indicator of the difference. In Ubykh (Northwest Caucasian), for example, there is a set of eight different tenses found with active verbs, but only two (parallel to two of the active tenses, but formed differently) for statives.

Nouns in Ubykh can be inflected as stative verbs and thus used predicatively ('I am a man'), a not uncommon state of affairs.

A final inherent category of verbs is that of conjugation class. Like the category of declension class in nouns, this is generally a more or less arbitrary, formal difference in the way verbs are inflected. In the more archaic Germanic languages, for example, there were typically four distinguishable patterns of inflection for 'weak' verbs (in which tense was indicated primarily by a suffix) and seven or more for 'strong' verbs (where tense was primarily indicated by vowel change in the stem). The partitioning of the lexicon among these classes was largely arbitrary, from the point of view of semantics and other grammatical categories. Furthermore, such a class does not figure elsewhere in the grammar (as in an agreement rule, for instance): it is simply a formal idiosyncrasy of particular verbs that they belong to one or another conjugation. Morphology is a little like that, sometimes.

### 2.2.2 *Relational categories of verbs*
Among the relational categories that receive formal indication on verbs, we can distinguish between those that reflect aspects of the structure of the clause in which the verb appears, and those that are based on the position of that clause in still larger structures.

It is not at all uncommon for the inflectional pattern of a verb to reflect the number and source of the grammatically related (direct case) noun phrases that co-occur with it in its clause. A difference between the inflections of transitive and intransitive verbs has this effect. In Basque, for example, most verbal inflection appears on a small set of auxiliary verbs, and transitive and intransitive verbs take different auxiliaries. In Algonquian, a set of stem formatives distinguish transitive from intransitive verbs, and similar examples can be found in a considerable number of languages.

Somewhat commoner, however, is the overt indication of the fact that a given verb is associated with a different set of noun phrases than its basic sense admits. The Circassian languages, for example, have a marker for verbs normally transitive, but in which an object noun phrase is absent (of the type 'John doesn't smoke'). In Bella Coola (Salish), a formative in the verbal inflectional system reflects the (non-transitive) use of transitive verbs in circumstances where the action rather than its object is of importance (of the type 'John is (doing some) carving'). Such 'detransitivized' forms appear formally marked in a few instances.

Far the most common category of this sort, however, is that of *causative* verbs. The syntax of causative constructions is reviewed in chapter III:6, but we should note that it is extremely common for such uses of basically intransitive verbs in transitive constructions, or of transitive verbs in bi-transitive constructions, to be formally marked in some way. Typically this is by means of an affix (which one might call derivational), but not always. In Bella Coola, for example, causative verbs employ a different set of subject/object agreement markers than do ordinary transitive verbs.

Another aspect of clause structure which a verb may display inflectionally is *voice*, or, more generally, foregrounding constructions (cf. chapters I:5 and I:6). Passives, in which a notional direct object has been 'promoted' to subject status, are one such type. A language may provide for more than one sort of passive, as in Kwakw'ala: here one set of affixes marks the promotion of direct objects to subject status, while another set marks the promotion of instrumentals or other oblique complements (where the direct object retains its original form and structural position).

Not only advancements to subject position may be inflectionally reflected in the verb; a number of languages allow the 'promotion' of oblique noun phrases to direct object status, and reflect this in the verb. Fula, for instance, has (separate and distinct) markers for the promotion of indirect objects, instruments, location phrases, and certain other oblique complement types.

A category similar to voice is that of reflexive and reciprocal forms. When subject and object of a transitive verb coincide in reference, most languages provide a distinctive treatment. Some provide a distinctive affix, replacing the normal object agreement markers (assuming the language has agreement with objects, of course): this is the case in some of the dialects of the Abkhaz-Abaza group in the Northwest Caucasian family, for example. Other languages provide a distinct marker for reflexive forms, but otherwise treat them as if they were structurally intransitive (as in Dyirbal, for instance). Reflexive pronouns in some languages are formed as possessed forms of some specified noun (typically 'head', 'body', 'heart', etc.), and in at least one case, a similar form is given to reflexive *inflection*. In dialects of Abkhaz (other than those referred to above, which simply have a distinct reflexive affix), reflexive forms involve an incorporated noun stem (meaning 'head'), preceded by an agreement marker indicating formally a possessor, in the place of an object agreement prefix.

Reciprocals ('each other') are similarly reflected by distinct inflections, though perhaps less commonly than reflexives. Sometimes, however, the two are treated as the same category, and receive the same marking.

Related to reflexives and reciprocals are other inflectional forms stipulating identity between the participants filling various roles in an event. In many languages, what is called the 'middle voice' falls under this description (in others, such as Icelandic, this refers rather to a set of reflexive forms); the subject is described as performing the action for his own benefit or in his own interest. When an object noun phrase is present with middle-voice verb forms, it is often treated inflectionally as an oblique rather than a direct complement, and the verb has inflectional characteristics of an intransitive (or detransitivized) form.

Another kind of stipulated coreference which may be marked inflectionally is between the direct object (or, more accurately, between the possessor of the direct object) and some other noun phrase. Chinook inflects the verb to indicate whether the direct object is (or becomes) the possession of (a) the indirect object; or (b) the subject. The Georgian verb is inflected for a category called (rather unrevealingly) 'version' in the descriptive literature; this is somewhat similar to the Chinook category, but (as with many things in Georgian) somewhat more complicated. In addition to benefactive and possessive 'version', denoting a relation of the appropriate type between the direct object and either subject or indirect object, Georgian also has a 'superessive' version in sentences like *gelam surati daaxaṭa ḳedels* 'Gela painted a picture on the wall', where the second *a* of the verb form *daaxaṭa* indicates that the direct object (*surati*) is *on* the indirect object (*ḳedels*).

A final sort of indication of coreference in verb forms perhaps belongs better with categories indicating the integration of a clause into larger structures. This is the indication of 'switch reference': the marking of a clause (or its verb) to indicate that its subject is, or is not, coreferential with the subject of another clause (either the next clause in sequence, or the next higher level of embedding). Switch-reference systems are found in a number of American Indian languages (in the Yuman languages and several others of the 'Hokan' stock, for example, and in Muskogean), as well as elsewhere in the world. The languages of New Guinea quite commonly mark verbs differently depending on whether they have the same or different subjects (e.g. Kâte); some of these languages go so far as to mark a clause for agreement not only with its own subject, but in case this is different from the subject of the next clause, for agreement with that too.

The major way in which verbs can be inflected to show the position of their clause in a larger structure is by the differentiation of forms used in main clauses from those used in subordinate clauses of various sorts. In some instances, such a verb form (often called a 'subjunctive') can also appear in main clauses, perhaps with the function of marking an irrealis mood. A number of languages (including Fula) have special sets of verbal forms for use in relative clauses (discussed in chapter II:3). The properties of other subordinate clause types are discussed in chapters II:2 and II:4 and will not be further reviewed here. We should note, though, that in terms of their inflection such clauses range from types with all of the basic categories of main clauses marked, together with some additional element to indicate the subordinate status (as in the Northwest Caucasian languages, in one complement type), through forms similar to main clauses but with a different (and usually reduced) set of tense/aspect distinctions, to forms usually called participles or infinitives, in which most of the verbal categories of main clauses are neutralized. These forms are often treated inflectionally like stems of some other class. Thus, 'participles' may display the agreement properties of adjectives, and be marked for categories like noun class and case in agreement with some overt noun phrase elsewhere in the clause referring to their notional subject or object. Similarly, 'infinitives' may behave like nouns inflectionally; Fula has a special noun class for marking and agreeing with infinitives, and both Basque and Finnish allow a full range of case endings to be added to infinitives to mark a variety of relations between these reduced clausal types and the larger structures in which they appear.

### 2.2.3 *Agreement properties of verbs*

The borderline between genuine inflectional verb agreement and simple attraction of clitic elements to the verb is extremely difficult to draw in many languages. Since there do not appear to be significant differences between the grammatical categories reflected in these two ways, however, the distinction will be ignored below. We divide the discussion of verbal agreement between the questions of (a) the choice of other elements of sentence structure the verb agrees with; and (b) the categories of those elements with which the verb agrees.

The most basic sort of verbal agreement is with a single noun phrase in its clause. There are apparently two major patterns that are attested in language: either the verb agrees with the subject – $s_i$ or $s_t$, depending on transitivity – or it agrees with the noun phrase which is marked as an absolutive, or fills the same role as an absolutive: $s_i$ in intransitive clauses, o in transitive ones. The former, 'accusative' (better, 'nominative') pattern is familiar from languages like Latin, and indeed most of the Indo-European family; while the latter, 'ergative' (better, 'absolutive') agreement is attested only in languages in which ergative case marking applies to noun phrases, such as Avar. There do not seem to be any languages in which agreement takes place only with the accusative (o) or only with the ergative ($s_t$) function.

In other languages, the verb can agree with more than one noun phrase in its clause. One of the dimensions of such multiple agreement is always one of those mentioned in the previous paragraph (i.e., either 'nominative' or 'absolutive'). If the first dimension is absolutive, the other is agreement with the ergative (this is the case in the languages of the Mayan family). Where the first dimension of agreement is nominative, the second is usually with a direct-case indirect object, if one is present, or otherwise with a direct object.

In such two-dimensional agreement systems, the two components may interact to produce unitary, unanalyzable affixes (perhaps including tense and other information as well), as in Eskimo or Bella Coola; or they may be related to two distinct 'slots' in the verb form. This latter situation is particularly clear in some instances. In Georgian, for example, one dimension of agreement is with the subject ($s_i$ or $s_t$, regardless of its case marking). The other dimension is with a direct case benefactive, indirect object, or direct object, when one is present. Now any one of these latter functions can also be presented in an oblique form (in a postpositional phrase), in which case there is no agreement with it. When the direct object is not third person in form (e.g. 'I sent you to him'), any indirect object or benefactive must be in oblique, non-agreeing form. When the direct object is third person, however, this constraint does not hold, and the verb agrees with a direct-case indirect object or benefactive. This is probably because third person object agreement in Georgian is formally unmarked, and thus the verb does not have to 'use up a slot' agreeing with such an object. 'I sent him to you', therefore, is possible with the verb agreeing with both subject and indirect object, although in 'I sent you to him', a third person *in*direct object, even though marked by no change, apparently does count as 'using up' the object agreement slot.

Another clear 'two-slot' system is the Algonquian one. Here the verb agrees with either one or two noun phrases, without regard for their function, but only for their position on a dimension of person categories. A further affix in the verb then expresses the orientation of the action. In Ojibwa, for example, both *nwaːbmaːg* 'I saw them' and *nwaːbmigoːg* 'they saw me' contain the prefix /ne-/ 'first person', the stem /waːbam/ 'see (animate goal)', and the suffix /-ag/ 'third plural'; they differ in that the first form has the element /aː/ 'direct orientation (here, first person acts on third)', while the second has /ego/ 'inverse orientation (here third acts on first)'.

A number of such 'polypersonal' agreement systems are not limited to agreement with two noun phrases in the clause. Chinook, and the languages of the Northwest Caucasian family, are examples of languages in which up to four noun phrases can be represented in the verb. West Circassian (Adyge) *gə-s-ye-we-ye-tə* 'you (*we*) make (*ye*) him (*ye*) give (*tə*) me (*s*) it (zero initial) hither (*gə*)' is such a form, though periphrastic constructions are often employed to avoid having more than three participants indicated in such forms, in causatives of causatives, etc. Often some of the indicators of person in such polypersonal verbal forms are accompanied by overt indicators of grammatical function: 'postpositions' following the affixes, as in Ubykh *a-s-x'a-w-ya-nə-wt°'ạy-awt* 'he (*nə*) will (*awt*) take (*wt°*) it (*a*) away (*ạy*) from (*ya*) you (*w*) for (*x'a*) me (*s*)'.

The agreement systems we have described thus far are based on dimensions that can be defined in terms of grammatical functions such as subject and object. Another kind of system has also been found, however, in languages of the Siouan-Iroquoian-Caddoan and Muskogean families in North America and also in the Northeast Caucasian language Bats. In such a system (called 'active' as opposed to ergative or accusative) the subjects of (most) transitive verbs have one set of agreement affixes, and the objects of (most) transitive verbs another. A third set may represent indirect objects. Let us call these three sets the *agent* set, the *goal* set, and the *oblique* set, respectively. When we now turn to intransitive verbs, however, we do not find a single uniform pattern. Roughly, those verbs describing activities agree with their subject by means of the agent set affixes (as Chickasaw *hilha-li* 'I'm dancing'); while most of those describing states, or events not under the control of their subjects show agreement by the goal set (as in Chickasaw *sa-lhpokonna* 'I'm dreaming'). A few may even show agreement by means of the oblique set (as in Chickasaw *am-ilha* 'I'm scared'). Further, some transitives agree with their objects by means of the oblique set, and some may use forms other than agent affixes to agree with their subjects. The choice of agent or goal set may be optional for some intransitives, with the sort of semantic difference we might expect: in Chickasaw, *hotolhko-li* 'I'm coughing (agent set)' says in effect 'that's what I'm doing, that's what's going on, that's the source of the noise you hear', etc., as opposed to *sa-hotolhko* 'I'm coughing (goal set)', which says 'that's what's wrong with me, that's why I'm going to the doctor'. In these systems, agreement is with the direct-case noun phrases in the clause, but a parameter more important than grammatical function is (roughly) the semantic role played by the referent of the noun phrase. To some extent, these languages have all grammaticized the distinction in at least part of the vocabulary (thus,

Chickasaw uses the oblique set with the verb 'be lazy', though generally this is only true with verbs describing emotional states like fear and surprise).

The systems above account for most verbal agreement in the languages of the world, though there are a few unusual examples that do not quite fit into these categories. Thus, in the Northeast Caucasian language Dargwa, agreement is preferentially with the absolutive noun phrase, but if the object is third person and the transitive subject first or second person, the verb agrees with $s_t$ instead of with o. In Basque, there are markers for 'agreement' with the honorific status of the person addressed, even though no second person participant appears in the clause. This includes agreement with the gender of a person familiarly addressed – the only place gender appears in the entire language! Other languages, such as Japanese and Korean, show quite extensive agreement with the honorific status of various participants. In Blackfoot and in Breton, agreement only takes place with noun phrases that are not overtly present in the clause (by reason of anaphoric processes) – otherwise the verb is third person singular regardless of the noun phrase itself (NB in Breton there is another construction for indefinite or unspecified agent, a category that will be mentioned for this language below). And in Wichita (a Caddoan language), agreement is primarily of the 'active' sort discussed above for Chickasaw, but where a third person noun phrase is possessed by first or second person, agreement may be with the possessor: thus one says, literally, 'my horse *am* running'. But however interesting such cases may be, they are definitely marginal by comparison with the vast number of 'well-behaved' agreement systems.

When we turn to the categories that are manifested in agreement, there are few surprises: verbal agreement is usually in terms of *person* and *number*. The category of person seems universally to distinguish speaker (first person), addressee (second person), and non-participant (third person). Some languages distinguish, in the forms for plural first person, between *inclusive* (speaker + addressee, plus perhaps others) and *exclusive* (speaker + others, excluding addressee) forms. Within the 'non-participant' category, a 'fourth person' may be distinguished: this may be one that is referentially less distinct, or less central to the discourse at this point (as in Algonquian and in Navajo); or one that is explicitly unspecified, an impersonal agent like French *on* or German *man*; or a sort of reflexive, a noun phrase coreferential with the subject of some higher verb (as in Eskimo).

The category of number as reflected in verbs is of course the same as that described above for nouns: verb agreement, too, may distinguish singular from non-singular and, if so, may also distinguish plural from dual, and even trial. Person and number agreement generally follow the same pattern, if a language has both. One kind of exception concerns the sort of stem suppletion for number discussed above in section 1.3.3. Where a verb displays different stems depending on number, it is virtually always the number of s or o that is relevant (i.e., of a potential absolutive); this is true regardless of whether the language has any other 'ergative' morphological properties, and even of whether it has independent marking for the person/number of its subject. This gives reason to believe that this suppletion is fundamentally different from normal inflectional verb agreement (cf. the remarks of section 1.3.3).

In some languages, the verb may agree with the gender or noun class of relevant noun phrases, instead of or in addition to their person/number categories. Verbs in the Bantu languages, for example, as well as many other African noun-class languages, agree with not only the number but also the noun class of third person participants; first and second person might be considered simply as additional 'genders'. In Avar, agreement in the verb is with the *noun-class* (masculine/feminine/non-rational/plural classes), and not with the *person* of the absolutive. In fact, the verb shows no indication of person whatsoever, but only noun class, which is especially interesting as Avar distinguishes only person and not gender, in non-third person pronouns.

A final category of agreement for verbs is that of definiteness or specificity. Hungarian, for example, has separate endings in transitive verbs depending on whether the object is specific or not (that is whether the object has a specific referent, which is typically the case for definites, and sometimes so for indefinites). It may be noted that this is often the *only* category of the object which is indicated in the Hungarian verb; person and number are not generally expressed. There is, however, a specific suffix *-lak/-lek* (depending on vowel harmony) which is used just in case the subject is first person singular and the object is second person (singular or plural). In other languages with object agreement in person, number, or noun class it is sometimes possible to indicate that the object is indefinite by suppressing object agreement (just as we saw above that object case marking can be used for the same function); in such a system, the definiteness of the object noun phrase is clearly an agreement category in the verb.

## 2.3 *Grammatical categories of adjectives*

Unlike nouns and verbs, adjectives are comparatively poor in inflectional terms. Only a few categories are realized in their morphology (though of course the formal indication of these may be quite difficult and complex: it takes comparatively few inflectional dimensions to produce a heavy burden on the memory of the language-learner, as any student of the classical languages can attest!).

### 2.3.1 *Inherent categories of adjectives*

Aside from the fact that adjectives may manifest differences in declension class without any relation to non-arbitrary features (just as verbs and nouns can), the only genuinely inherent category of their inflection is apparently that of comparison, as in English *big/bigger/biggest*. Some languages (e.g. Irish) also have a category of 'equative' ('as big as') inflection. In morphological terms, it is not at all clear that comparison should be considered an inflectional (rather than derivational) category at all.

### 2.3.2 *Relational categories of adjectives*

Both nouns and verbs appear in a considerable variety of structures; this is not really true for adjectives. They are virtually always either (a) noun modifiers, or (b) predicates. By virtue of this fact, there is little reason to expect them to show relational distinctions, and they generally do not. When used as predicates, they may be given verbal inflections (as when they are treated as stative verbs in the Northwest Caucasian languages), or affixed with a copula of some sort: this constitutes at least implicitly an indication of their relational position.

When used as noun modifiers, there is generally no formal indication of that fact for adjectives (except for the possible operation of agreement). There are a few exceptions to this. First, some languages, such as Tagalog, have an overt marker (here called a 'ligature') that appears between modifier and head in nearly all modification structures. In other languages, when an adjective is used to modify a 'head noun' that is not overtly present (as in '*the rich* are in revolt in California'), there may be some reflection of the fact. For example, in Mandarin the subordinating particle *de* is not normally used with certain short and common adjectives and other modifiers; but when no head is present, the particle must be used after all modifiers. Finally, the overall structure of the noun phrase may have an influence on the pattern of adjective inflection, as in German and related languages, where adjectives are inflected according either to the strong or the weak declension depending on the presence of one of a certain class of determiners. This and other instances of special forms for adjectives with 'definite' noun phrases, as in the Baltic and (other) Slavic languages, could be treated either as a relational category or as a type of agreement.

### 2.3.3 *Agreement categories of adjectives*

Since adjectives are used either as modifiers of a distinct head or as predicates whose subject is uniquely determined, there is no problem in identifying the element with which they agree. Typically, any of the inherent or relational categories of the noun (gender, number and case, most commonly) may also be reflected in adjectives modifying it. Arbitrary declension class properties that cannot be treated as noun classes, of course, are not eligible for agreement in this case (or under other types of agreement). Frequently, the declension of adjectives, since it reflects the same categories as nominal declension, involves the same formal elements (affixes, etc.) as the nouns with which the adjectives agree, but this is not necessary.

### 2.4 *Grammatical categories of adverbs*

Since adverbs typically do not even manifest agreement, they are even simpler in inflectional structure than adjectives.

### 2.4.1 *Inherent categories of adverbs*

Adverbs frequently show close similarities in formation to adjectives, and thus in some languages inflected comparative and superlative forms exist. Other than this, they do not manifest overt inherent categories.

### 2.4.2 *Relational categories of adverbs*

In languages in which adverbs are productively formed from adjectives, the process of their formation could be regarded as reflecting relational information, since adverbs occupy structural positions distinct from those of adjectives. Otherwise, there are no categories of this sort for members of this class.

### 2.4.3 *Agreement categories of adverbs*

In line with their general inflectional poverty, adverbs do not normally manifest agreement: they do not generally agree, for example, in an inherent category such as tense with a verb they modify. In Yidiɲ, adverbs apparently are inflected exactly like verbs, for the same range of categories and in agreement with the verb they modify; but here the parallelism is so close (and so unusual) that one could accordingly question whether Yidiɲ really has a distinct word class of adverbs. Some clear cases of agreement in an adverb class can be cited, however. In Maori, adverbs show agreement in voice (as passive vs. non-passive) with their accompanying verb, though they do not indicate any other verbal category, and are not plausibly considered as simply a subclass of verbs. In Avar, some adverbs (depending on their phonological shape) may show agreement in noun class with the absolute noun phrase of their clause. Recall that this is the same pattern as agreement in Avar verbs, although the adverbs are not marked for other categories, such as tense, which are specified for verbs. If adverbs do show agreement, one would expect it to be of this sort: parallel to the agreement shown by verbs in the same structures.

### 2.5 *Grammatical categories of closed classes*
Most of the closed classes that can be identified in languages are either of the sort that could not be expected to show any sort of inflection (e.g. interjections) or of the sort that are clearly parallel to some open class (e.g. pronouns to nouns, copulas and auxiliaries to verbs), and thus show some variant of the inflection displayed by this corresponding class. There are a few surprises, such as the inflection of prepositions for person and number of their object in Celtic languages (a residue of the combination of prepositions with clitic pronouns). Different sorts of pronouns could be taken as reflecting a set of relational categories, and of course the category of person which is at the basis of pronoun systems is an inherent one for this word class. There are not, however, categories manifested by members of closed classes that have not been surveyed above. Frequently a class with small, closed membership can by virtue of that fact retain historically archaic patterns of inflection. Grammatical categories that are not marked in the corresponding open class in a given language may thus be preserved, such as the accusative in Finnish, found as a distinct case only in pronouns; or the dual in Old Icelandic, found only in pronouns.

## 3 Conclusions

The above survey of inflectional word formation is inevitably somewhat anecdotal and list-like in places, with few coherent patterns being apparent. This is to some extent inherent in the nature of the subject: morphology, like the lexicon, is a finite system in important ways (though both may be arbitrarily expandable in a given language). It can thus tolerate a substantial degree of arbitrariness and idiosyncrasy.

Space has permitted few concrete examples of the morphological categories referred to above; abundant examples of virtually all, however, will be found in other places in this work. The one most important point which the overall weight of such examples supports is that made above in section 0.2: the correspondence between form and category in word formation is not a simple one, and the field worker who expects it to be will find morphology a most intractable study.

# 4 Tense, aspect, and mood*

SANDRA CHUNG and ALAN TIMBERLAKE

## o Introduction

Tense, aspect, and mood are all categories that further specify or characterize the basic predication, which can be referred to as the event. Tense locates the event in time. Aspect characterizes the internal temporal structure of the event. Mood describes the actuality of the event in terms such as possibility, necessity, or desirability.

In order to describe the tense, aspect, and mood systems of different languages, we need to identify and compare uses of morphological categories across languages in terms of a universal descriptive framework. The best candidate for such a framework seems to be one based (at least in part) on a priori distinctions. However, the map between the universal framework and language-particular systems usually turns out to be indirect, so there is no guarantee that it will describe every language-particular system of tense, aspect, and mood simply or elegantly. For example, our framework defines 'past' as anteriority of an event to a reference point on the temporal dimension. In particular languages, it may turn out that the morphological form used to express anterior events will also be used in certain contexts to express other temporal relations; conversely, anterior events may occasionally be expressed by morphological forms used more generally for other temporal relations.

The indirectness of the map has influenced the descriptive strategy adopted below. Our basic goal is to provide a framework for the description of each category. Although this framework is a prioristic, it is not intended to describe every logically possible distinction of tense, aspect, or mood, but rather is oriented around those distinctions that are overtly signaled by the morphology of particular languages, specifically by verbal morphology. For tense and mood we provide illustrations from language-particular systems as we present the framework; for aspect we present the framework first, and then illustrate it with extended sketches of some language-particular systems.

The basic elements of our descriptive framework center around the notion of an event. Intuitively, an event is simply whatever occurs (or could occur) at some time period under some set of conditions. This intuition suggests that an event can be defined in terms of three components: a predicate; an interval of time on which the predicate occurs, which we call the event frame; and a situation or set of conditions under which the predicate occurs, which we call the event world. In the course of our discussion further elements of the framework will be introduced as needed.

## 1.0 Tense

### 1.1 *Framework for tense*

Tense can be described in terms of a temporal dimension that is directional, with a privileged point or interval of time we will call the tense locus. As suggested immediately above, an event occurs on an interval of time, the event frame. Tense locates the event in time by comparing the position of the frame with respect to the tense locus. The two most important considerations in tense systems are the selection of the tense locus, and the nature of the relationship between the tense locus and the event frame.[1]

Although the tense locus can in principle be any point on the temporal dimension, most systems give priority to the tense locus defined by the moment of speech. Typically no further context or adverbial specification is required to use the speech moment as tense locus, but some contextual specification – for example, deictic adverbial phrases of the type 'then', 'at that time', 'when' – is required to establish some other point as the tense locus. Tense systems (or subsystems) in which the speech moment serves as the tense locus are traditionally called absolute tense; systems (or subsystems) in which some other point is the tense locus are called relative tense.

The second factor in tense systems is the relationship between the event frame and the tense locus. The frame can be anterior to the tense locus; it can include the tense locus (be simultaneous with it); or it can be posterior to the tense locus. These distinctions define the three tenses past, present, and future. Further refinements could be introduced. For example, the tense locus can be strictly internal to the frame, or else a boundary point (upper or lower) for the frame. If the tense locus is not simply a point on the temporal dimension, but is itself an event with some duration, there are more possibilities: one event can include the other; they can coincide exactly; or they can overlap partially. Most tense systems, however, can be discussed in terms of the tripartite set of distinctions given above.

Although the relations anterior and posterior are logically symmetrical, the temporal dimension is assumed to have directionality from past to future. This implies an asymmetry in the sense that the past is known or established fact while the future is unknown and potential. This in turn implies a connection between tense and mood, as discussed below.

The distinctions of anterior, simultaneous, and posterior are concerned only with the relationship between the frame and the tense locus. The tense systems of some languages seem in addition to be metrical, in the sense that they measure the distance between the frame and the tense locus in approximate terms.

### 1.2 *Speech moment as tense locus*

One language in which the tripartite tense system is encoded directly in the verbal morphology is Lithuanian (Senn 1966). The past tense is used for events occurring prior to the speech moment, the present is used for events overlapping the speech moment (either actual unique events in progress or else generic events), and the future is used for events subsequent to the speech moment.[2]

(1)    a.  dirb-au
          work-1SG(PAST)
          'I worked/was working'

    b.  dirb-u
          work-1SG(PRES)
          'I work/am working'

    c.  dirb-s-iu
          work-FUT-1SG
          'I will work/will be working'

The direct encoding of three tenses is not particularly common. It is more usual to find only a two-way distinction in tense, either future vs. non-future or past vs. non-past. For example, Takelma distinguishes future from non-future tenses by differences in the stem morphophonemics and personal endings of the verb (Sapir 1912). (One stem, glossed 'REALIS' below, is used for the non-future; another stem, glossed 'IRR' (for 'irrealis') is used for the future and other non-actual moods.) The future is used for future events that are not immediate:

(2)    yaná-t'ē
      go(IRR)-1SG(FUT)
      'I will go'

The non-future is used for events in the past, ongoing events in the present, and future events that are imminent in the present:

(3)   yān-tˤeʔ
      go(REALIS)-1SG(NONFUT)
      'I went/am going/am about to go'

Similarly, Dyirbal (Australian) distinguishes future vs. non-future tenses, with the non-future used for both past and present events; compare *balgaɲ* 'will hit', *baniɲ* 'will come' vs. *balgan* 'hit, is hitting', *baniɲu* 'came, is coming' (Dixon 1972).

Conversely, Yidiɲ (also Australian) distinguishes past vs. non-past tenses (Dixon 1977). The past is used for events before the speech moment, whether in progress (the first clause of (4a)) or completed (the second clause of (4a) and (4b–c)). The non-past is used for present events ((5a)), future events that are imminent in the present (often marked by *-ala* 'now', as in (5b)), or future events ((5c–d)):

(4)   a. Bana: yuŋa:ɲ    gaɲaraŋgu bala baḍa:l
         water cross(PAST) alligator   shin bite(PAST)
         'He was crossing in the water when an alligator bit one shin off'

      b. ŋuŋ:ṛiɲ   miɲa ŋaɲḍi buga:ɲ
         that kind meat we    eat(PAST)
         'We ate that kind of meat'

      c. ŋayu gunḍi:ɲ
         I      return(PAST)
         'I have returned'

(5)   a. Waɲi:ra   mayi bugaŋ?
         what kind fruit eat(NONPAST)
         'What kind of fruit are you eating?'

      b. ŋayu gunḍiŋ-ala
         I      return(NONPAST)-now
         'I'm returning now/I'm about to return now'

      c. Mayi waɲi:ra    garu       ŋaɲḍi bugaŋ?
         fruit what kind by-and-by we    eat(NONPAST)
         'What kind of fruit shall we eat by and by?'

      d. Biri:ɲḍa biṛi gunḍiŋ
         sea       back return(NONPAST)
         'I'll return back by sea'

### 1.3 *Correlations of tense, mood, and aspect*

The different temporal locations of an event – past, present, and future – are inherently correlated with differences in mood and aspect. An event that will occur after the speech moment is non-actual and potential. Hence there is a correlation between future tense and non-actual potential mood and, by implication, between non-future tense and actual mood. An event that is ongoing at the speech moment has not been completed. Hence there is a correlation between present tense and incompletive (imperfective or progressive) aspect and, by implication, between past tense and completive (perfective or non-progressive) aspect. A consequence of these correlations is that temporal distinctions may be expressed by morphosyntactic categories that have wider modal or aspectual functions.

As an example of the correlation between future tense and non-actual mood, consider Lakhota, which at first glance appears to be another language with a future vs. non-future system. According to Boas and Deloria, the particle *kta* (~ *kte*) is used to express events in the future; no particle expresses present or past. 'In simple declarative sentences present and past are not distinguished. If it is required to indicate time more accurately adverbs ... must be added' (1941:156). Examples of this distinction, from Rood and Taylor (1972), are:

(6)  a. Ma-khúžį
        1SG-sick
        'I was sick/am sick'

  b. Ma-khúžį kte
        1SG-sick   FUT
        'I will be sick'

But the particle *kta* has a range of usage that goes beyond pure future to unrealized but potential events. It can mark deontic mood (obligation) as well as future, as in (7a), and can be used with the subordinate clause of governing verbs like 'want', as in (7b).

(7)  a. Yį́-kta iyéčheča
        go-FUT perhaps
        'It is likely that he will go/He ought to go'

  b. He   itháčhą-kta čhį́
        that chief-FUT    want
        'That one wants to be chief'

In Lakhota, then, future tense is expressed by a morpheme with additional modal functions.

Chamorro illustrates the correlation of tense with both mood and aspect.[3] There are two moods in Chamorro, realis and irrealis; morphologically these moods are distinguished primarily by their subject agreement patterns (the irrealis may additionally be marked by the preverbal particle *pära*). The irrealis is used for clauses subordinate to certain modal verbs and for the consequent of counterfactual conditionals, as in:

(8)    a. Debi di u-guäha       guafi
          ought   3SG(IRR)-exist fire
          'There ought to be a fire'

       b. Kumu hu-tungu'        mohon esti, bai
          if      1SG(REALIS)-know as if   this FUT
          u-fañúñuli'          atchu'
          1SG(IRR)-carry(PROG) stone
          'If I had known this, I would have been carrying a stone'

Consistent with the correlation above, it is also used for future events:

(9)    Pära u-guäha      guput lämu'na
       FUT 3SG(IRR)-exist party tonight
       'There is going to be a party tonight'

Chamorro also has an aspectual opposition of neutral vs. progressive. The progressive aspect (marked morphologically by reduplication of the stressed CV) designates events in progress and iterative events, while the neutral aspect (with no overt morphological marking) designates other types of events. Because of the correlation between tense and aspect above, events that overlap the speech moment are typically expressed by the progressive, events anterior to the speech moment by the neutral aspect (NL):

(10)    a. Mämaigu'  si   Dolores
          sleep(PROG) ART Dolores
          'Dolores is sleeping'

       b. Maigu'  si   Dolores
          sleep(NL) ART Dolores
          'Dolores slept'

However, the temporal value of the aspectual distinction is by no means obligatory, as will be discussed below under aspect.

### 1.4 *Metrical tense*
In a few languages, tense distinctions not only characterize the relationship between the event frame and the, tense locus, but are also

weakly metrical, in the sense that they provide an approximate and subjective measure of the interval between the frame and the tense locus.

A particularly well-developed set of metrical past tenses is found in the Wishram–Wasco dialect of Chinook, which distinguishes four: remote *ga(l)*-, far *ni(g)*-, recent *na(l)*-, and immediate *i(g)*- (Silverstein 1974):

(11)    a. *ga*-č-i-u-x̣
           'he did it some time ago'

        b. *ni*-č-i-u-x̣
           'he did it long ago'

        c. *na*-č-i-u-x̣
           'he did it recently'

        d. *i*-č-u-x̣
           'he just did it'

Although no precise time measures can be given, the recent past is likely to be used for an interval of a week or so, the far past for an interval of months; the remote past is used for more distant events, including mythical events in the past.

The Bantu language ChiBemba has a system of four metrical tenses that are nearly symmetrical in past and future (Givón 1972). Some examples, with appropriate characterizations of the time intervals, are:

(12)    a. remote past
           ba-*àlí*-bomb-*ele*
           'they worked (before yesterday)'

        b. removed past
           ba-*àlíí*-bomba
           'they worked (yesterday)'

        c. near past
           ba-*àcí*-bomba
           'they worked (today)'

        d. immediate past
           ba-*á*-bomba
           'they worked (within the last three hours)'

(13)    a. immediate future
           ba-*áláá*-bomba
           'they'll work (soon, within three hours)'

   b. near future
      ba-*léé*-bomba
      'they'll work (later today)'

   c. removed future
      ba-*kà*-bomba
      'they'll work (tomorrow)'

   d. remote future
      ba-*ká*-bomba
      'they'll work (after tomorrow)'

These metrical tense distinctions can in principle be further cross-classified by aspectual distinctions such as perfect vs. perfective vs. imperfective, although not all distinctions are possible in all metrical tenses (the examples above are perfective). There is also an asymmetry between past and future in the distribution of aspectual distinctions; past tenses allow more aspectual distinctions than the future.

### 1.5 *Event as tense locus*
The discussion above concerned events whose temporal reference is determined with respect to the speech moment. Tense is more complicated in complex syntactic structures describing two events, where (the description of) one event is syntactically subordinate to the other. In such cases the subordinate (or secondary) event can be characterized temporally both with respect to the matrix (or primary) event and with respect to the speech moment. This raises two issues.

   First, the temporal freedom of the secondary event. In certain constructions a language may restrict the temporal range of the secondary event with respect to the primary event or with respect to the speech moment. A trivial example of such a restriction is that imposed by particular lexical subordinating conjunctions with temporal value, such as English *after* (implying that the secondary event must be anterior to the primary event), *while* (the secondary and primary events overlap), and *before* (the secondary event must be posterior), or their equivalents in other languages.

   A more sophisticated example of a restriction on temporal range is provided by Hua, which has a technique of combining clauses known as clause-chaining (Haiman 1980). There are two basic varieties of clause-chaining. One allows variable temporal reference; the other requires the temporal reference of the secondary event to be the same as that of the primary event with respect to the speech moment as tense locus. For this variety of clause-chaining, the temporal reference of the secondary event (= non-final predicate in linear order) must be past when the primary event (= final predicate in linear order) is past, present if present, and future if future. The clause expressing the secondary event is not morphologically marked for tense.

The second issue concerns the selection of tense morphology for the secondary event. In principle there are three possibilities: (i) The secondary event may be characterized directly with reference to the speech moment, a strategy termed absolute tense; (ii) The secondary event may be characterized with reference to the primary event (relative tense); (iii) The secondary event may select morphology that reflects both its temporal relation to the primary event *and* (indirectly) the temporal relation of the primary event to the speech moment (sequence of tenses). Particular languages select different strategies, but it is worth pointing out that they may select different strategies for different types of secondary events, and that strategies may compete in some constructions.

A classic example of relative tense is provided by Southern Paiute (Sapir 1930); in this language the temporal reference of secondary events expressed by adverbial clauses is determined relative to the primary event. The morphological expression of relative tense is combined with the expression of switch reference (that is, whether the subject of the adverbial clause is coreferential or not with the subject of the matrix clause). This yields four possibilities: -ci- 'same subject, anterior', -kai- 'same subject, simultaneous', -kka- 'different subject, anterior', and -ku- 'different subject, simultaneous':

(14)    a. Mai-*ci*-ʔŋʷ(a) immi-ŋʷaʔai-ʔŋʷa payï-kki-va·
find-TNS-3    2-with-3            return-here-FUT
'Having found him with you, he will come home'

   b. Yaγa-*kai*-ca-aŋ(a) ivi-ŋu
cry-TNS-PAST-3       drink-MOMENTANEOUS
'While he cried, he drank'

   c. Su·va-aŋa tɔnna-*kka*-nni tɔyɔkki-va·
if-3           hit-TNS-1        run-FUT
'If I hit him, he will run'

   d. Yaʔai-*ku*-ca-aŋa-nni kïmma-ŋʷittuγʷa-ŋu
die-TNS-PAST-3-1       other-toward-MOMENTANEOUS
'While he was dying, I went away'

In (14b) and (14d), -ca- is a sentence enclitic that specifies the tense of the primary event.

The use of the relative tense strategy is not necessarily dependent on special morphology. Russian uses ordinary tense morphology for secondary events expressed by finite subordinate clauses (for the imperfective aspect, the tenses are past, present, and future). Depending on clause type and other factors, tense morphology for the secondary event may be selected via the absolute (direct reference to the speech moment) or relative (reference to the primary event) strategy. Finite adverbial clauses and relative clauses necessarily use absolute tense; for a relative clause, see (15), in which the past tense is used for a secondary event that is simultaneous with the primary event when both are anterior to the speech moment:

(15)     Molodoj kloun, u  kotorogo trjaslis'/     *trjasutsja
        young    clown by whom   tremble(PAST)/ *tremble(PRES)
        ruki, ušel
        hands left
        'The young clown, whose hands were trembling, left'

Subject and object complement clauses, however, typically use relative tense, although there is considerable variation. Some factors governing the variation are described below. (In the examples below the secondary event is simultaneous with the primary event, and both are past with respect to the speech moment. Use of past morphology for the secondary event indicates absolute tense, while use of present morphology indicates relative tense.)

   (i) Construction type. Reported speech and indirect questions require relative tense (present morphology, under the conditions specified above); other constructions at least marginally allow absolute tense (past morphology):

(16)   a. Ja sprosil, počemu u  nego trjasutsja/     *trjaslis'
         I  asked  why    by him tremble(PRES) *tremble(PAST)
         ruki
         hands
         'I asked why his hands were trembling'

    b. Ja zametil, čto  u  nego trjasutsja/    ?trjaslis'
         I  observed that by him  tremble(PRES)/?tremble(PAST)
         ruki
         hands
         'I observed that his hands were trembling'

   (ii) Syntactic position. Postposed subordinate clauses (as above) prefer relative tense; preposed clauses, which are syntactically more autonomous, allow absolute tense more freely.

(17)    Čto u  nego trjasutsja/       trjaslis'        ruki,
        that by him   tremble(PRES)/ tremble(PAST) hands
        ja srazu       zametil
        I  right away observed
        'That his hands were trembling I noticed immediately'

(iii) Subordinating conjunction. The conjunction *čto* 'that' reports the
secondary event as a static fact and prefers relative tense; the conjunction *kak* 'how' reports the event as a dynamic process and is neutral
between relative and absolute tense. Compare (16b) above with (18).

(18)    Ja zametil, kak u  nego trjasutsja/        trjaslis'       ruki
        I  observed how by him   tremble(PRES)/ tremble(PAST) hands
        'I observed how his hands were trembling'

Other factors besides these influence the choice between relative and
absolute tense strategies for complement clauses in Russian. The
generalization behind most of these factors is that relative tense is
favored if the secondary event is syntactically and semantically subordinate (and expresses the point of view of the matrix subject); absolute
tense is favored if the secondary event is syntactically and semantically
autonomous. Finally, the choice between relative and absolute tense is
one place where it becomes relevant to make further discriminations in
the type of overlap between two basically simultaneous events, mentioned above in section 1.1. The secondary event may start before, but
end in the middle of, the primary event; it may encompass it completely;
and so on. These distinctions exert a subtle influence on the choice of
tense strategy.
    Another strategy for selecting tense of a secondary event is the one
termed sequence of tenses, found in English. In sequence of tenses the
secondary event carries some indication of its temporal relation to the
primary event (anterior, simultaneous, posterior) and – at least when
the primary event is anterior to the speech moment – a mark of the tense
of the primary event as well. Thus, the past, present perfect, present,
and future tenses of the simple sentences in (19) become past perfect,
past perfect, past, and future-in-the-past in (20), where they are
subordinated to a verb of reported speech.

(19)    a. I was at work

        b. I have been at work

        c. I am at work

        d. I will be at work

(20)     a. John said he had been at work

        b. John said he had been at work

        c. John said he was at work

        d. John said he would be at work

The use of the sequencing strategy is to some extent variable; in informal English it competes with relative tense. The choice between the two depends on many of the same factors that govern the choice of relative vs. absolute tense in Russian.

The discussion above concerned tense specification in secondary events; in these contexts the tense locus is not necessarily taken to be the speech moment. Another tense strategy in which the tense locus is not identical to the speech moment – this time involving primary events – is the narrative mode termed the historical present, the use of the present tense to narrate events anterior to the speech moment. This device, which is so widespread and familiar that it needs no exemplification, has the function of making the narration more vivid and immediate.

The historical present is commonly explained in terms of markedness (as the unmarked tense, the present can supposedly substitute for other, more marked tenses), but this interpretation does not account for the specialized narrative value of the historical present. It is more reasonable to view it as specialized strategy for selecting the tense locus. On this view, the historical present might be characterized as reflexive tense, in that the tense locus for each event is the frame of the event, and the locus moves forward with each new frame that is selected in the narration.

In closing the discussion of tense, we should point out that we have given a relatively restrictive definition of tense – the relationship between the event frame and a reference locus in time. Other semantic operations that are sometimes termed tense (specifically, the perfect and the progressive) will be considered below, as instances of aspect.

## 2 Aspect

### 2.1 *Framework for aspect*
Aspect characterizes the relationship of a predicate to the time interval over which it occurs.[4] This definition is intended to include two distinct types of relationship. First, change. Predicates describe states, situations, properties, and so on, that can either remain constant or else change over time. The notion of change is central to aspect.

Second, as defined earlier, an event is composed of a predicate and some time interval selected by the speaker, which we termed the event frame. In order to qualify as an event, the predicate must minimally occur over the event frame, but there is more than one way to satisfy this requirement. Notably, the predicate can occur wholly within the event frame, or it can occur over a larger interval of time that includes the frame. In addition, it appears that frames can be nested, in that individual subframes can be added together to form larger, inclusive macroframes. Aspect characterizes the different relationships of a predicate to the event frame.

One of the interesting properties of aspect is that the same concepts are relevant at different levels of semantic structure. Although the boundaries between different levels are not always clear, here we distinguish four nested levels: (a) the verb and its inherent aspectual properties; (b) the predicate, defined here in the narrow sense of a verb plus its major syntactic arguments (subject and objects); (c) the proposition, the predicate in relation to the event frame; and (d) the narrative/textual, the proposition in the context of a connected set of propositions. An example of these nested levels is:

(21)    verb:            angry
        predicate:       John got angry at a stranger
        proposition:     John got angry at a stranger on the bus today
        narrative:       John got angry at a stranger on the bus today,
                             and then apologized

The semantic parameters discussed in this section are intended to have variable scope, so that in principle they can characterize any of the different levels mentioned above. In practice, the most important distinction is that between the proposition level and the verb and predicate levels; the latter two may be referred to together as the lexical level. As the discussion of event frames above is intended to suggest, it is the proposition level that is particularly relevant to aspect that is encoded by bound morphology on the verb form.

### 2.1.1 Dynamicity

In a very general sense, any predicate can be understood as describing a situation or state of affairs at a given moment of time. The state of affairs can either remain constant over successive moments of time, or else it can change. An event exhibiting little or no change over time can be termed a state, while one that does change can be termed a dynamic event or a process (other terms are also used).

Particular verbs typically describe basic states or processes, although it is usually possible to modify the value of dynamicity for a given predicate. Examples of stative verbs include those describing properties ('tall', 'happy', 'rich') and cognition/perception ('know', 'see', 'understand'). Examples of processes include verbs such as 'read', 'bake', 'beat', 'run', 'burn', and so on.

A commonly invoked criterion for distinguishing processes from states involves agency: if an event has an agent (a conscious, willful, responsible instigator), then it is a process rather than a state. By this criterion 'smell', for example, would be stative in 'the food smells good to me' but processual in 'I smelled (= sniffed) the food'. A number of operational tests for stativity are based on agency: states do not occur in the imperative (*'know the answer!') or subordinated to certain governing verbs (*'Sue persuaded/forced/allowed/required John to know the answer'), because both of these modal contexts require an agent who is responsible for the event; states do not co-occur with manner adverbs describing agency, such as 'assiduously', 'deliberately', 'intentionally', 'laboriously'. The criterion of agency is useful, but provides only a one-way implication: an event with an agent is dynamic, but there are events without agents that are not stative, to judge from the fact that they occur in the progressive ('the knot is slipping', 'crime is increasing').

In some languages states have special morphosyntactic properties; for example, intransitive verbs have different agreement patterns in Chamorro depending on whether they describe states or processes. More importantly, the opposition between states and processes can play a role in the selection of aspectual morphology, specifically the progressive. The progressive asserts that an event is dynamic over the event frame. By definition, then, processes but not states can appear in the progressive.

By varying the dynamicity of a given predicate, it is possible to alter its ability to appear in the progressive.

The basic mechanism for converting a process verb to a state is to remove the sense of change over time, and present the verb as a property of its arguments. For example, 'open' is a process in 'John is opening the window' or 'the valve is now opening', but it can also be presented as a static property, as in 'the key opens the door' or 'the window opens onto the garden'. A verb can be presented as a property by modalizing it (that is, viewing it over possible occasions), as in 'the oven bakes too hot' or 'he runs a six-minute mile' (= 'on any occasion he is able to run a six-minute mile'). Related to this, iterating a process over a number of actual occasions creates a macroevent that can be interpreted as a property – that is, as a state. Thus, in 'he occasionally worked/?was working overtime' the macroevent is a static property of

John, even though the verb 'work' describes a process on any particular occasion.

Conversely, a stative verb can be converted to a process by adding a sense of actual or possible change. Three particular mechanisms for accomplishing this can be distinguished. First, if the proposition presents the state as having different degrees of manifestation that change over time, the state can be interpreted as a process, and thus can select progressive morphology. Compare stative 'I understand/?am understanding this problem' vs. 'I am understanding my problems more clearly every day'.

Second, as suggested by the discussion of agency above, interpreting the subject as an agent turns a state into a process ('you are being obnoxious').

Third, a stative verb can be turned into a process if the concept of change is modalized; that is, if there is a possibility of change in the state in some potential future world. For instance, 'live' can be interpreted either as a state (in which case it appears in the non-progressive) or as a process (in which case it appears in the progressive). But the process sense is more natural if there is an indication that the situation is temporary, as in 'John is living/*lives with his parents until he finds a place of his own'. Similarly, verbs of position are more likely to be interpreted as stative (and use non-progressive morphology) if the state is assumed to be permanent, but as dynamic (and use progressive morphology) if the state is accidental, temporary, or subject to change: 'New Orleans lies/*is lying on the Mississippi River' vs. 'The book is lying/?lies on the table'.

Dynamicity is a fundamental aspect parameter that shows up at various levels of semantic structure, not only at the lexical and proposition levels. At the narrative level, events may be presented as static facts or dynamic processes relative to other events. For example, in object complement clauses subordinate to verbs of perception in Russian, there is a choice between two complementizers, čto 'that' vs. kak 'how', illustrated above in the discussion of relative tense; in both of these examples the verb is an inherent process. The complementizer čto presents the process as a static fact with respect to the event of perception (roughly, 'I observed (the fact) that his hands were shaking'), while kak presents it as a dynamic process (roughly, 'I observed how his hands were shaking' or 'I observed his hands shaking').

### 2.1.2 Closure
A basic concept in aspect can be described in terms such as boundedness, limitation, holicity, completion, and the like. While all of these

terms have some currency, they are sometimes taken to have slightly different meanings, so we will use the neutral and deliberately abstract term 'closure'.

On the proposition level, as we discuss below, closure means simply that an event comes to an end before some temporal point ('John painted until the sun went down') or within the confines of some temporal interval ('John painted from morning until night', 'John painted seventeen houses within three days'). Thus, closure at the proposition level means that an event is limited, bounded, or wholly contained within the event frame.

At the predicate level, the meaning of closure differs for processes and for states.

A process may either have the potential of continuing indefinitely, or it may have associated with it a natural boundary or limit on the degree of change, such that when the limit is reached, the event cannot continue. Traditionally a process without an inherent limit is called atelic, one with a limit is called telic (from Greek *telos* 'limit, end, goal'). Using the terminology proposed here, a process without limit is open at the predicate level; one with a limit is closed.

The notion of inherent limit depends both on the semantic content of a verb and on the content of its arguments at the predicate level. Verbs of motion, such as 'walk' or 'roll', are telic when spatial limits are specified but atelic otherwise; compare atelic 'John walked in the city', 'Sue rolled the hoop along the sidewalk' vs. telic 'John walked from Madison Avenue to 91st Street', 'Sue rolled the hoop off the sidewalk onto the street'. Some verbs describe atelic processes when intransitive, but when transitive characterize a complete change of state in the direct object; compare atelic 'John painted', 'Sue wrote' vs. telic 'John painted the house', 'Sue wrote a letter'. And in general, verbs that describe an effect on an argument (direct object or intransitive subject) can be made telic by specifying that the argument is affected completely; compare atelic 'The fire burned', 'The fire burned the log' vs. telic 'The fire burned out', 'The fire burned the log up'. As the last set of examples suggests, languages commonly have a morphological means of deriving telic verbs using affixes or particles with spatial meaning.

Applied to states, closure implies a complete change of state, specifically inception rather than cessation. Thus, languages that have a morphological category (traditionally called perfective) to specify closure for processes often use the same category to signal inception of a state. The perfective form of stative verbs like 'see', 'be pregnant', 'remain', 'be dead' will mean 'catch sight of', 'become pregnant', 'begin to remain', 'die'.

Table 4.1. *A classification of predicates*

| Open | Closed |
|------|--------|
| *state* | *inception of state* |
| pregnant | become pregnant |
| see | catch sight of |
| remain | begin to remain |
| dead | die |
| *atelic process* | *telic process* |
| travel | travel from $x$ to $y$ |
| burn | burn up/out/through |
| read | read the book |
| look for | find |

Combining closure with dynamicity, we get the classification of predicates shown in Table 4.1.

### 2.1.3 *Aspect at the proposition level*

The discussion of aspect parameters above concentrated on aspect at the lexical (both verb and predicate) level of semantic structure. In some languages verbal morphology is in fact used to directly encode aspectual values at this level. For example, in Chamorro the difference between states and processes at the verb level is marked by a difference in agreement morphology, as discussed below. In many languages prefixes or verbal particles (typically with spatial meaning) are used to mark closed processes at the predicate level. More generally, however, languages that encode aspect by obligatory choices of verbal morphology make reference to aspect parameters at the level of the proposition.

At the proposition level, events are evaluated with respect to some temporal point or interval that serves as the basis for narration. This point or interval, which we have called the event frame, can be named explicitly by an adverbial phrase ('yesterday', 'tomorrow', 'now', 'at two o'clock', 'on Sunday', 'last year', 'when', 'while', and so on), or left unspecified and implicit in the narration. The frame can be identical to the speech moment (in which case the event will necessarily include the frame), but this is not required. An event can be evaluated over its frame for either of the non-quantitative aspect parameters, dynamicity and closure, and languages differ as to which evaluation they make.

On the one hand, a language may choose to evaluate whether an event is dynamic over the event frame. This in effect means two things. First, the frame is internal to the event or, equivalently, the event goes on before, during, and after the frame. Second, the event must be dynamic; that is, it must be a process rather than a state. A language-particular morphological category that signals that an event is dynamic over the event frame is traditionally termed progressive, as opposed to non-progressive, or neutral.

To illustrate, a verb like '(be) sad' is a state, so it will not exhibit progressive morphology regardless of whether the event frame is internal ('She was sad when he came home') or external ('She was sad until he came home'). A verb like 'paint' is a process, so it can exhibit progressive morphology if the frame is internal ('He was painting at two o'clock/when I came home'), but non-progressive morphology if the frame is not internal, for example if it serves as a temporal limit for the event ('He painted and then went home').

On the other hand, a language may choose to evaluate whether an event is closed over the frame. This in effect means two things. First, the frame is not internal to the event, which is to say that the frame is an upper temporal limit for the event (if the frame is a point) or it contains the whole event (if the frame is an interval). Second, the predicate has an inherent limit that is reached by the event of the event frame; that is, the predicate must be telic rather than an atelic process or state. A language-particular morphological category that signals closure in this sense (inherent limit actually reached within the event frame) is traditionally termed perfective, and a category that signals absence of closure is termed imperfective.

To illustrate, a verb like 'draw' without a direct object is an atelic predicate, so it could not exhibit perfective morphology regardless of whether the frame is internal or external. In combination with a specific direct object, as in 'draw a circle', it is a telic predicate. If the event frame is internal, the verb cannot exhibit perfective morphology, so the translation of 'He was drawing a circle when I came home' will be imperfective. If the frame is external, the verb may or may not be perfective, depending on whether the inherent limit is reached within the frame. If both conditions are met, then perfective morphology will be used; for example, in the translation of 'At two o'clock he drew the circle and then left'.

To sum up, in order to be encoded as progressive (in a language that has a progressive category), an event must be dynamic, and must include the frame. In order to be encoded as perfective (in a language that has a perfective category), an event must be telic, and must be included in the frame.

There is a third language-particular morphological category that refers crucially to the event frame, a category traditionally termed the perfect. Although this category clearly involves a frame, the rest of its characteristics remain elusive. Described informally, a perfect describes an event that occurs before the event frame and leaves a result that continues to hold up to the frame. If this informal description is taken as definitional, it suggests that the perfect characterizes a complex event, which consists of an event located prior to the event frame, the frame itself, and perhaps a stative interval connecting the event to the frame. However, a simpler interpretation is also conceivable, according to which the perfect simply describes an event whose predicate occurs over some interval disjoint from and anterior to the event frame.

Note that the terms perfective and perfect refer to different views of the event, which in some cases may overlap. Thus, 'He drew the circle' would be perfective but not perfect (since no continuing result is mentioned); 'He has been drawing circles' would be perfect but not perfective (since the series of iterated subevents is open); and 'He has drawn the circle' is both perfective and perfect.

There is considerable variation across languages in the range of events encoded by morphological categories that are termed perfect. Tentatively adopting the complex interpretation given above, it is possible to state, and to some extent motivate, some cross-linguistic generalizations regarding the use of the perfect.

In terms of the predicate, the perfect is formed more readily for telic than for atelic processes (and more readily for processes than for states), presumably because telic processes are more likely to result in a stative interval (e.g. one can say 'He has drawn a picture' (telic) but not ?'He has drawn' (atelic)). In terms of the stative interval, there is a metrical consideration dictating that short intervals are encoded as perfect in preference to long ones (for example, the perfect in Old French is said to have been restricted to intervals of approximately one day). In terms of the event frame, languages that exhibit distinct tenses for the perfect typically use them to characterize the temporal relation of the frame rather than the predicate *per se*; thus, a present perfect ('He has now arrived') describes a past event whose stative result continues to a frame in the present (= the speech moment); a past perfect (pluperfect) describes an event in the distant past whose result continues up to some frame in the past ('He had already drawn the circle when I came home'). Perhaps as a consequence of this, the perfect in many languages cannot be used in combination with an adverb explicitly specifying the time of the occurrence of the predicate *per se*.

## 2.1.4 *Iterativity*

The discussion above dealt with events for which the event frame was a homogeneous interval of time. In contrast to these, events are sometimes composed of a multiple number of essentially equivalent sub-events that are iterated over time (or in some cases, over possible occasions in possible worlds). Such events have a complex structure, in which individual events (each with its own event frame) collectively form a larger, inclusive macroevent.

On the predicate level a verb like 'bake' in combination with a singular direct object is understood as characterizing a unique event: 'He baked a cake'. A proposition involving the same verb can be iterative, for example if it includes a quantifying adverbial and an indefinite plural direct object: 'He often baked cakes'. A verb such as 'blink' is often understood to designate an inherently iterative event. For this reason some languages have special derivational morphology for turning an inherently iterative verb into a semelfactive (= unique occurrence), on the order of 'blink once'.

The repetition of subevents is usually understood to be distributed over time, but if the subevents are indefinite both in number and in their position along the temporal dimension, repetition can also be viewed as extending over possible worlds. Consequently, iterativity may interact with non-actual mood. In English, for example, iteration in the past can be realized either by an independent verb (*used to*) or by irrealis mood (*He would bake cakes (on occasion)*).

There are several parameters along which iteration can vary. Most obviously, iteration can be quantitatively large ('numerous times') or small ('a couple of times'). Iteration may be definite ('four/seven times') or indefinite ('several times'). An event can be iterated more or less regularly ('occasionally', 'now and then' vs. 'usually', 'always'), and the iterated subevents may be understood as distinct and individuated ('on many (different) occasions') or collectivized ('many times together'). In particular languages these variations on the parameter of iterativity play a role in the selection of aspectual morphology.

Iterative events can be expressed by distinct morphology (for example, in Lithuanian) or by the same morphology used for non-iterative events. In the latter case, given that iterative events have a complex structure, aspect can be evaluated in terms of either the macroevent or the individual subevents, or both together. At the level of the macro-event, an iterative is usually stative (implying non-progressive) and open (implying imperfective). Individual subevents can be evaluated for dynamicity or closure over their frames. In English, for example, aspect seems to involve both levels. Generally the non-progressive is used for iteratives over discrete temporal occasions, both because the macro-event is stative and because the individual subevents are closed over their frames (*On Saturdays I often work/?am working in the garden. The* *mail usually arrives/*is arriving late*). But the progressive is possible either if the subevents are in progress over their frames (*On Saturdays I am often working in the garden when she returns*) or if the macroevent is viewed as a process that changes over time (*These days the mail is arriving later and later*).

### 2.1.5 *Durativity*

Iterativity quantifies the event. A second type of aspectual quantification is durativity, the explicit measurement of the duration of the event frame. To judge from English and other languages, it is possible to measure the duration of both open (imperfective) and closed (perfective) events, as in *John read the book for an hour* (open) vs. *John read the book in an hour* (closed). The morphological expression of duration, however, varies from language to language. English expresses the difference between open and closed events primarily in the duration phrase; Mokilese uses the same measure phrase, but different verbal aspects, for the two types of events; and Russian employs different verbal aspects as well as different measure phrases. Given that all three languages can measure duration whether the event is open or closed, aspect is apparently determined independently of duration. This observation runs contrary to the assumption that there is a direct correlation between aspect and durativity, in particular that perfective events are inherently punctual or non-durative.

We turn now to consider some language-particular aspect systems, with the intent of showing that they can be described in a reasonably efficient and coherent fashion in terms of the general framework outlined above. Four languages are discussed: Russian, ChiBemba, Chamorro, and Mokilese.

### 2.2 *Russian*

Russian has two aspect categories, traditionally termed the perfective and the imperfective.[5] These categories are morphologically encoded via several patterns of prefixation and/or suffixation. Most commonly, simplex (i.e. unaffixed) verbs are imperfective, since they typically refer to atelic processes; an example is *motat'* 'wind, shake, tire (fig.)'. Although most such verbs do not have unique perfective counterparts, they can accept a variety of spatial prefixes to form derived perfective verbs with specialized meaning. Thus, corresponding to *motat'* are the derived perfectives *v-motat'* 'wind in(to)', *vy-motat'* 'exhaust', *za-motat'* 'wind around; tire out', *iz-motat'* 'exhaust', *na-motat'* 'wind a quantity', *ot-motat'* 'reel off', *pere-motat'* 'rewind', *raz-motat'* 'unravel', *s-motat'* 'wind up, together'.

Typically, each derived perfective verb can itself be suffixed to form a corresponding derived imperfective; thus, *v-matyvat'* 'wind in(to) (imperfective)', *ot-matyvat'*, *pere-matyvat'*, etc. (Imperfectives derived from this verb are additionally marked by ablaut of the root vowel.) Observe that each derived imperfective verb has a unique perfective counterpart, whereas most simplex imperfectives do not. Consistent with this, simplex imperfectives have an aspectual character somewhat different from that of derived imperfectives.

A significant feature of Russian aspect is that the imperfective has a considerably wider range of usage than the perfective.

Lexical states are expressed by the imperfective, as in (22):

(22)   a. Veterennikov molčal
          Veterennikov silent(IMPERF)
          'Veterennikov was silent'

       b. Srednjaja škola No. 13 otkryvalas'     na ulice Lenina
          middle    school       open(IMPERF) on street Lenin
          'Middle school No. 13 faced (lit. opened on) Lenin Street'

Atelic processes are expressed by (simplex) imperfectives, even when the event is included in the frame (it is *not* in progress over the frame):

(23)   a. Žgučaja ironija klokotala      v ego grudi
          burning irony  rumble(IMPERF) in his  breast
          'A burning irony rumbled in his breast'

       b. V prošlom godu na odnom iz zasedanij Politbjuro
          in last     year at one    of meetings Politburo

          mučitel'no iskali        otvety na èti    voprosy
          painfully  seek(IMPERF) answer to these questions
          'Last year at one of the meetings of the Politburo they sought answers to these questions'

For telic processes, the choice of aspect depends on whether the event is closed with respect to its frame. If the frame is internal to the event, the event is necessarily open with respect to it and the imperfective must be used. In (24), the frame is established by the 'when' clause:

(24)   Kogda tanki dostigli      kanala, fašisty kak raz
       when  tanks reach(PERF) canal    fascists just then
       vzryvali           most
       blow up(IMPERF) bridge
       'When the tanks reached the canal, the fascists just then were blowing up the bridge'

As a consequence, only the imperfective can be used to indicate an actual event that is ongoing at the speech moment; that is, the perfective cannot refer to an actual event in the present tense. If the frame includes the event, the event may nevertheless be open if it was attempted but not carried through to its limit. This conative sense of the imperfective is illustrated in (25a) with a simplex verb, and in (25b) with a derived verb:

(25)   a. Kalif   bagdadskij rubil        emu golovu, a    on vse-taki
          caliph Baghdad     cut(IMPERF) him head     but he still

          živ
          alive
          'The Caliph of Baghdad cut off (= tried to cut off) his head,
          but he is still alive'

       b. Fašisty vzryvali            most, no im    ne udalos' èto
          fascists blow up(IMPERF) bridge but them not succeed that
          'The fascists blew up (= tried to blow up) the bridge, but
          they did not succeed

If, finally, a telic event is closed with respect to the frame (in that the frame includes the event and the event reaches its inherent limit), then the perfective is used. In (26a–b) the frame is established by a 'when' clause; in (26a) the 'when' clause gives the upper limit for the primary event (expressed by the matrix clause), while in (26b) the 'when' clause gives the initial limit for the primary event.

(26)   a. Kogda otgremeli       poslednie vystrely, my (uže)
          when   resound(PERF) last        shots      we already

          pokinuli         rajon
          abandon(PERF) region
          'When the last shots died down, we already abandoned
          (= had already abandoned) the region'

       b. Kogda tanki dostigli      kanala, fašisty vzorvali
          when   tanks reach(PERF) canal    fascists blow up(PERF)

          most
          bridge
          'When the tanks reached the canal, the fascists blew up the
          bridge'

In (27) below, a past event frame has been established in the narration, and the two events that are mentioned occurred at some time earlier than that frame. Because both events are closed, they are expressed by the perfective. Note that in English a retrospective aspectual form (here, a pluperfect) would have to be used; as this example suggests, Russian does not distinguish a retrospective category in its aspectual morphology.

(27)   Rovno god  do    ètogo francuzskoe pravitel'stvo podlomilo
       exactly year before that   French       government  bend(PERF)

       koleni i    podpisalo akt o     peremirii
       knees and sign(PERF) act about truce
       'Exactly a year before that, the French government threw
       (= had thrown) itself on its knees and signed (= had signed) a
       truce'

We turn now to the quantitative parameters. When the duration of an event is specified by means of an adverbial, prepositionless accusative, the imperfective must be used. Note that the event in the example below is sequentialized between two closed events, a fact that might otherwise be expected to lead to the use of the perfective:

(28)   Rogov vzjal     šariki i   dolgo razgljadyval,   daže
       Rogov take(PERF) balls and long  examine(IMPERF) even
       ponjuxal
       sniff(PERF)
       'Rogov took the balls and examined(IMPERF) them for a long
       time, and he even sniffed them'

Although the motivation for this constraint is usually taken to be self-evident, the issue is complicated by the fact that the perfective can be used with an adverbial phrase that measures duration (preposition *za* 'within' plus the accusative):

(29)   Za    (èti) dve minuty on razgljadel     vse dokumenty
       within those two minutes he examine(PERF) all  documents
       'Within (those) two minutes he examined all the documents'

This suggests that the measurement of duration is independent of aspect.

To describe iterative events, it is necessary to consider the aspectual character of the macroevent, the aspectual character of its individual subevents, and the quantificational relationship between the two.

If the individual subevents are not closed telic events (for example, if they are attempted but not completed), the imperfective must be used:

(30)   Oni triždy proryvalis'/    *prorvalis'  iz    okruženija,
       they thrice escape(IMPERF)/ *escape(PERF) from surround

no im    èto ne udalos'
but them this not succeed
'Three times they escaped (= tried to escape) being surrounded, but they did not succeed'

If the individual subevents are closed, the choice of aspect depends on
several properties of the quantification. If the number of subevents is
large and/or indefinite, the imperfective is required:

(31)    Oni často proryvalis'/    *prorvalis'    iz    okruženija
        they often escape(IMPERF)/ *escape(PERF) from surround
        'Often they escaped being surrounded'

Even if the number of subevents is few, the imperfective is still favored
if the subevents are loosely related and distributed over a large temporal
interval:

(32)    Oni triždy proryvalis'/    ?prorvalis'    iz    okruženija
        they thrice escape(IMPERF)/ ?escape(PERF) from surround

        letom    sorok  pervogo goda
        summer forty   one       year
        'Three times they escaped being surrounded in the summer of
        '41'

The perfective, however, is fully possible if the subevents are interpreted as collective, an interpretation that is favored by a closed
measure phrase ((33a)) or by a retrospective point of view ((33b)):

(33)    a. Oni triždy proryvalis'/    prorvalis'    iz    okruženija
           they thrice escape(IMPÉRF)/ escape(PERF) from surround

           za      odin mesjac
           within one  month
           'They escaped being surrounded three times within one
           month'

        b. K ètomu vremeni oni  uže      triždy proryvalis'/
           by that  time    they already thrice escape(IMPERF)/

           prorvalis'  iz    okruženija
           escape(PERF) from surround
           'By that time they had already escaped being surrounded
           three times'

To summarize aspect usage in Russian, then, an event is expressed by
the perfective only if it meets a set of conjunctive conditions: it must be

a unique telic process that is actually closed on its frame. If the event fails to meet any one of these conditions, the imperfective will be used.

### 2.3 *ChiBemba*

The tense–aspect system of ChiBemba is superficially extremely complex, in that it distinguishes twenty-four morphological tense–aspect forms (Givón 1972). On closer inspection, however, the system reduces to a relatively small number of tense–aspect categories.

Some of the twenty-four morphological forms involve a category that is not strictly tense–aspect, but rather information or focus. This category distinguishes propositions that focus on some circumstance of the event (for example, a manner adverb) from those that do not; it is not included in the discussion below.

The distribution of the aspect categories is sensitive to tense. As mentioned in 1.4, ChiBemba has present, past, and future tenses; the past and future tenses include metrical distinctions of the sort 'within three hours of the speech moment', 'on the same day', 'on the adjacent day', and 'not within the same or adjacent day'. There are minor differences in aspect among the different metrical tenses. More importantly, however, there are significant differences among the three basic tenses of past, present, and future.

In some (although not all) past tenses there is a three-way distinction of perfective, perfect, and imperfective aspects. The perfective is used for events that are completed. The perfect is used for events that have enduring results, although apparently the events do not have to be completed. The imperfective is used primarily for events in progress over some frame in the past (as specified by the particular metrical tense), but it appears from the somewhat scanty description in Givón that it can also express iterative events; hence the term imperfective rather than the more restricted term progressive. The examples in (34) are from the remote past tense which is the most richly developed metrical past tense. (NB In the examples, PERF = perfective aspect; PERFECT is printed in full.)

(34)   a. ba-*àlí*-bomb-*ele*
          'they worked(PERF) (before yesterday)'

       b. ba-*àlí*-bomba
          'they had worked(PERFECT) (before yesterday)'

       c. b-*àléé*-bomba
          'they were working/kept on working/worked repeatedly (IMPERF) (before yesterday)'

It is noteworthy that the tense of a perfect event in ChiBemba is determined by the time at which the event actually occurs rather than the frame from which it is retrospectively viewed. This is a typologically unusual property for the perfect, but it is perhaps not so surprising given that the tense system of ChiBemba in general is metrical.

Events in the future can be expressed in the perfective or (if progressive or iterative) in the imperfective, but not in the perfect. Examples from the remote future:

(35)   a. ba-*ká*-bomba
          'they will work(PERF) (after tomorrow)'
       b. ba-*káláá*-bomba
          'they will be working/keep on working/work repeatedly (IMPERF) (after tomorrow)'

In the present, there is no possibility of a perfective or perfect, so events are necessarily treated as imperfective. The morphological form that corresponds to the imperfective in past and future tenses is restricted, however, to events in progress; iterative events are expressed by a distinct habitual category:

(36)   a. ba-*léé*-bomba
          'they are working(PROG IMPERF)'
       b. ba-*là*-bomba
          'they repeatedly work(ITERATIVE IMPERF)'

In short, the superficially rich aspect system of ChiBemba reduces to familiar distinctions: perfect vs. non-perfect (past only) and perfective vs. imperfective (past, future). Both progressive and iterative senses are expressed by imperfective morphology in the past and future, but are morphologically distinguished from each other in the present.


### 2.4 *Chamorro*

In Chamorro, a Western Austronesian language, there are two morphological aspect categories: a neutral category, which consists simply of the basic verb form, and a distinct category marked by reduplication of the stressed cv of the verb. The latter, reduplicated form can tentatively be called progressive, although one of the main interests of Chamorro aspect is the extent to which this category can be used for situations not ordinarily construed as events in progress. A second noteworthy feature of Chamorro aspect is the contrast in the aspectual properties of states and processes. Our discussion begins with processes and turns to states later.

As noted in 1.3, Chamorro does not have a morphological category of tense, in that present and past events are not morphologically distinguished from each other, and future events are expressed by a more general irrealis mood. The examples here are limited to realis mood. The distinction between atelic and telic processes is unimportant in Chamorro compared with the distinction between processes and states. Consequently, the neutral aspect is used not only for telic events but also for atelic events that do not include the frame (the event is not in progress over the frame):

(37)    a.  Malagu yu' nigap
           run(NL) I    yesterday
           'I ran yesterday'

       b.  Lao ti  ha-dúlalak    yu' i   ga'lagu
           but not 3SG-chase(NL) me the dog
           'But the dog did not chase me'

The choice of aspect for processes depends primarily on the relation of the predicate to the event frame. The usage can be illustrated with complex sentences involving adverbial conjunctions meaning 'when' or 'while', in which each event defines the frame for the other.

If the two events are sequential, they appear in the neutral aspect:

(38)    Änai in-na'chotchu un biahi i   masoksuk na ga'lagu,
        when 1PL-feed(NL)  one time the skinny        dog

        ha-tutuhun    mattu gi  gima'-mami käda birada
        3SG-begin(NL) come LOC house-our   each round trip
        'After we fed the skinny dog once, he began to come to our house every time'

If an event is simultaneous with another event, it appears in the progressive. In (39a) the secondary event (expressed by the subordinate clause) includes the entirety of the primary event (expressed by the matrix clause). The secondary event is progressive, while the primary event is in the neutral aspect. In (39b) the primary event is progressive because it includes the secondary event, which is expressed by the neutral aspect:

(39)    a.  Änai mamómokkat yu', maloffan un amigu-hu
           when walk(PROG)    I    pass(NL) a  friend-my
           'While I was walking, one of my friends passed by'

       b.  Änai h-um-anao yu' guätu, istaba    si  Sandy na
           when SG-go-NL   I    there IMPERFECT ART Sandy COMP

manayúyuda
help(PROG)
'When I went over there, Sandy was helping'

If the two events mutually overlap, both appear in the progressive:

(40)    a. Mientras manayúyuda gui', manlitráratu    yu'
           while    help(PROG)    she photograph(PROG) I
           'While she helped, I took pictures'

        b. Mientras um-atgumémentu häm, man-ma-pópo'lu
           while    SG-argue(PROG)    we   PL-PASS-put(PROG)
           i    néngkanu' gi lamäsa
           the food    LOC table
           'While we were arguing, the food was being put on the table

We turn now to the quantitative parameters. When duration is explicitly specified, the neutral aspect must be used:

(41)    a. Tudu dia man-mama'tinas/*man-mama'títinas pära i
           all    day PL-cook(NL)/    *PL-cook(PROG)    for the
           giput
           party
           'All day they cooked for the party'

        b. Pues um-atgumentu-nñaihun/*um-atgumentu-nñäñaihun
           so    SG-argue-awhile(NL)/    *SG-argue-awhile(PROG)
           häm
           we
           'So we argued for a while'

Iterative events show some variation. In principle, such events can be expressed by either the neutral or the progressive aspect. In (42a), from a narrative text, there is virtually free alternation in aspect; in (42b), speakers freely allow either form. Possible further conditions on the choice of aspect here are not clear.

(42)    a. ma-na'kabalis    i    kareta, ma-na'kabábalis    i
           PASS-COMPLETE(NL) the car    PASS-COMPLETE(PROG) the
           kareta man-ma-na'yi todu, est    todu man-ma-pienta,
           car    PL-PASS-add(NL) all    already all    PL-PASS-paint(NL)
           tódudu esti guini ni    ma-na'fankabábalis i    kareta yan
           all    this here COMP PASS-complete(PROG) the car    and

lokkui' man-ma-tétes
also     PL-PASS-test(PROG)
'(a factory where) the car is assembled, the car is assembled (and) everything added, everything is painted, all this is where the cars are assembled and also tested'

b. ... i    pigua'    pupulu, yan afuk ni    ma-na'fandänña'/
   the betelnut, leaf    and lime COMP PASS-combine(NL)/

ma-na'fandädanña' pues ma-ngangas/  ma-ngángangas
PASS-combine(PROG)then PASS-chew(NL)/ PASS-chew(PROG)
'... the betelnut, leaf, and lime which are combined and then chewed'

The use of what is otherwise a progressive category for iteratives is surprising, given that iteratives in other languages are usually considered stative, and prefer the non-progressive aspect (note, for example, that a progressive would be inappropriate in the English glosses to (42a–b)). One possible interpretation is that an iterative event is intermediate between a state and a process: it is stative in that the macroevent is relatively uniform over its frame, but dynamic in that there is change in individual subevents. An iterative event that holds on some frame can therefore be construed either as stative (hence the neutral aspect) or as dynamic (hence the progressive).

A curious property of iteratives emerges when the iteration is explicitly indicated by adverbs of the type *sessu* (*di*) 'often', *käda birada* 'all the time, every time'. With such adverbs, the progressive is only marginally acceptable, although without an adverb either aspect would be acceptable:

(43)   a. Yänggin malangu gui', guahu sessu fuma'tinas/
          when    sick    she  I    often cook(NL)/
          ?fuma'títinas i    sena
          ?cook(PROG) the dinner
          'When she is sick, I often cook dinner'

       b. Sessu di    ha-tagu'/    ?ha-tátagu'    yu' pära i
          often COMP 3SG-send(NL)/?3SG-send(PROG) me to    the
          tenda
          store
          'Often he would send me to the store'

(44)   a. Yänggin malangu gui', guahu fuma'tinas/ fuma'títinas
          when   sick   she  I    cook(NL)/  cook(PROG)
          i    sena
          the dinner
          'When she is sick, I cook dinner'

       b. Ha-tagu'/     ha-tátagu       yu' pära i   tenda
          3SG-send(NL)/3SG-send(PROG) me to   the store
          'He would send me to the store'

Evidently, a principle of dissimilation governs the use of the progressive, at least for iteratives, which are not in progress in the strict sense: if the iteration is specified independently of aspect, then the neutral form rather than the progressive is used. This dissimilative principle is supported by the continuative verb *sigi di* 'keep on', which does not allow a progressive verb as its complement:

(45)   a. Sigi yu' di     um-éssalao/  *um-é'essalao   ya
          keep I   COMP SG-shout(NL)/*SG-shout(PROG) and
          hu-agang/     *hu-á'agang    si   tata-hu
          1SG-call(NL)/*1SG-call(PROG) ART father-my
          'I kept on shouting and calling for my father'

       b. Um-é'essalao yu' ya  hu-á'agang   si   tata-hu
          SG-shout(PROG) I    and  1SG-call(PROG) ART father-my
          'I was shouting and calling for my father'

Iterative conditionals are consistent with the above description, but they also show the importance of considering the aspect of the subevents in the condition ('if') clause and the consequent ('then') clause. If, for example, the subevents overlap, the progressive is required:

(46)   Guäha na biahi na    yänggin machócho'chu'/*macho'chu'
       exist       time COMP when   work(PROG)/    *work(NL)
       yu', ha-kuentútusi/  *ha-kuentusi   yu'
       I    3SG-talk to(PROG)/*3SG-talk to(NL) me
       'Sometimes when I am working, she talks to me'

If, however, neither subevent is in progress with respect to the other, there is a difference in aspect for the condition and the consequent clauses. The consequent clause allows either aspect (consistent with the use of either aspect for independent iterative macroevents), but the condition clause strongly prefers neutral aspect (given that the subevent in the condition is not in progress with respect to the subevent in the consequent):

(47)   Pues ha-tattiyi/    ha-tattítiyi    häm guätu gi  gima'
       so   3SG-follow(NL)/ 3SG-follow(PROG) us   there LOC house

       yänggin mattu/    ?máfattu    häm tatti
       when   come(NL)/?come(PROG) we   back
       'So he follows us to the house when we come back'

We turn now to states. States in Chamorro have morphosyntactic properties distinct from processes, and independent of morphological aspect. Some but not all states have a fossilized prefix *ma-* (*mapotgi* 'pregnant', *masoksuk* 'skinny', *maolik* 'good, well' but *ñalang* 'hungry', *díkiki'* 'small', *bulachu* 'drunk'). More importantly, states are distinguished from processes by the number agreement that they exhibit with singular subjects in the realis mood: processes are marked with the infix *-um-* (prefix *mu-* before sonorants), while states lack this infix. Compare the following:

(48)   a. H-um-aohao/h-um-anao/s-um-aga   i ga'lagu
          SG-bark(NL)/ SG-go(NL)/ SG-stay(NL) the dog
          'The dog barked/went/stayed'

       b. Masoksuk/ mapotgi/    ñalang/    bulachu   i
          skinny(NL)/pregnant(NL)/hungry(NL) drunk(NL) the

          ga'lagu
          dog
          'The dog is skinny/pregnant/hungry/drunk'

There are also a few exceptional verbs that are semantically processes (and behave as processes with respect to aspect), but contain the fossilized prefix *ma-*, on account of which they do not select the number agreement *-um-* (e.g. *malagu* 'run', *mata'chung* 'sit'). Except for these, states are distinguished from processes by the non-plural number agreement marker *-um-*.

As the examples in (49) suggest, states do not ordinarily occur in the progressive, even when the event includes the frame:

(49)   a. Malangu yu' änai g-um-uäha  guput
          sick(NL) I    when SG-exist(NL) party
          'I was sick when the party occurred'

       b. Bulachu  giu' änai mattu    si  Rosa
          drunk(NL) he   when come(NL) ART Rosa
          'He was drunk when Rosa came back'

There are, however, some semantic conditions under which verbs describing states allow the progressive: (i) if the state is conceptualized as having an agentive subject:

(50)    Lokkui' hunggan, hu-kumprendi        ha'   na   siempri
        also    yes        1SG-understand(NL) EMPH COMP indeed
        bíbisi      hao gi che'cho'-mu
        busy(PROG) you LOC work-your
        'And yes, I do understand that you are really keeping busy at
        your job'

or (ii) if the state increases in intensity:

(51)    a. Ya esta      mämaipi
           and already hot(PROG)
           'And it was getting hotter'

        b. Bulálachu    yu' änai h-um-alum   gui'
           drunk(PROG) I    when sG-enter(NL) he
           'I was getting drunker when he came in'

In these two cases the state described by the verb is at least weakly
conceptualized as a process.
    The progressive can also give the specific sense of 'still in α state,
despite expectations' or 'no longer in α state, despite expectations':

(52)    a. Ya esta pa'gu mapópotgi      ha'
           and until now   pregnant(PROG) EMPH
           'And even now (the dog) is still pregnant'

        b. Esta pa'gu ti    ñáñalang
           until now   not hungry(PROG)
           'He still was not hungry'

This usage of the progressive suggests a modalized interpretation. In the
speaker's view, the history of a stative event belongs to a set of possible
worlds in which the event could be expected to change. Although there
is no change in the actual history of the event, there is change across
possible histories of the event. Evidently, this modalized type of change
is sufficient to permit the use of the progressive for states.
    Finally, states can be semantically converted to inceptive processes
(marked morphologically by -um- with singular subjects). The neutral
aspect is used for these derivatives when the inception is closed:

(53)    Gi  mä'pus na simana mu-malangu yu'
        LOC past       week  sG-sick(NL)   I
        'Last week I got sick'

The progressive is used when the inception is in progress or, somewhat
exceptionally, when it is iterated:

(54)   a. I   díkiki' na ga'lagu esta    y-um-óyommuk
          the small    dog     already sɢ-fat(ᴘʀᴏɢ)
          'The little dog is getting fat'

       b. Ya esta      mu-mämaipi
          and already sɢ-hot(ᴘʀᴏɢ)
          'And it was getting hot'

       c. Ti mu-malálangu yu' yänggin malangu gui'
          not sɢ-sick(ᴘʀᴏɢ)  I   when   sick(ɴʟ) she
          'I used not to get sick when she was sick'

In summary, the aspect system of Chamorro basically consists of an opposition of progressive vs. neutral. The progressive is restricted to processes that include the event frame; it is not used with lexical states except when they are construed as processes or involve a modalized sense of change across possible histories. One surprising feature is the regular (although not obligatory) use of the progressive for iterative events, a fact that can perhaps be explained by the complex structure of iteratives: an iterative macroevent is basically stative, but its subevents may be dynamic. Finally, with respect to iteratives Chamorro shows a dissimilative principle of aspect encoding, which favors the neutral aspect if iteration is independently specified.

### 2.5 Mokilese

A somewhat different realization of the same aspect parameters is found in Mokilese (Oceanic, Micronesian). Mokilese formally distinguishes three aspect categories, which may be called imperfective, progressive, and perfective (Harrison 1976). Formally the imperfective is simply the stem form of the verb. The progressive is specified by cvc reduplication. The perfective is expressed by a postverbal directional particle, typically -*da* 'up', -*di* 'down', or -*la* 'away, off'.

The usage of these categories is as follows: the progressive is used to assert specifically that the event is in progress with respect to the frame. The frame can be the speech moment (the neutral interpretation of (55a)), some point in the past ((55b)), or some point in the future ((55c)). The frame can also be specified by another event ((55d)).

(55)   a. Ngoah raprapahki ih   me
          I        look(ᴘʀᴏɢ) him here
          'I am in the process of looking for him here'

       b. Ngoah raprapahki ih    aio
          I        look(ᴘʀᴏɢ) him yesterday
          'I was in the process of looking for him yesterday'

    c. Ngoah nen raprapahki ih   lakapw
       I      FUT look(PROG) him tomorrow
       'I will be in the process of looking for him tomorrow'
    d. Ngoah raprapahki ih   anjoauo ih japahldo
       I      look(PROG) him time   he come back
       'I was looking for him when he came back'

The imperfective seems to have a wide range of usage, as indicated by the glosses in (56):

(56)    a. Ngoah rapahki    ih   me
       I      look(IMPERF) him here
       'I am looking for him here'
    b. Ngoah rapahki    ih   aio
       I      look(IMPERF) him yesterday
       'I looked/was looking/tried to look for him yesterday'

The English gloss that is most regularly given for the Mokilese imperfective is the progressive. This suggests that the imperfective as well as the progressive can be used for dynamic events in progress over a frame. Evidently, the progressive emphatically asserts that an event is in progress over the frame, while the imperfective allows but does not require the event to be in progress.

The imperfective is regularly used for events that are attempted but not completed. Note the conative sense in (56b) above, or in (57) below:

(57)    Ngoah poahj      noai pehnno
       I      reach(IMPERF) my  pen
       'I am reaching for (= trying to reach) my pen'

In some cases the English gloss for a Mokilese imperfective suggests that the event may be interpreted as closed and completed, although the imperfective does not insist on this interpretation:

(58)    Ngoah kang     raisso
       I      eat(IMPERF) rice
       'I ate the rice'

In contrast to the imperfective, the perfective specifies that the event is telic and closed with respect to a frame. Compare the imperfective in (56b) above with the perfective in (59a), or the imperfective in (57) with the perfective in (59b):

(59)    a. Ngoah rapahkih-da ih   aio
       I      look-PERF  him yesterday
       'I looked for (and found) him yesterday'

b. Ngoah poahj-da   noai pehnno
  I       reach-PERF my  pen
  'I reached/got hold of my pen'

c. Arai pirin kang-la  raisso
  they FUT  eat-PERF rice
  'They will eat up the rice'

One presumes that a perfective verb cannot be interpreted as ongoing at the speech moment; nor does it seem to be possible to form a progressive of a perfective.

A single verb stem can potentially occur with more than one suffix, so there is not necessarily a unique form of the perfective for a given verb; some contrasts with the basic three suffixes are:

(60)    a. Ngoah dolih-da  epwi rohssok
       I       pick-PERF some flowers
       'I gathered up some flowers'

    b. Ngoah dolih-di   rohsso
       I       pick-PERF flower
       'I plucked the flower'

    c. Ngoah dolih-la   rohssok
       I       pick-PERF flowers
       'I picked (all) the flowers'

Here it may be instructive to point out the contrast with Russian. In both languages affixes with spatial meaning can be added to verbs, creating perfective verbs with different senses for each affix. In Russian these prefixed perfective verbs can usually generate corresponding imperfectives with the same sense, but in Mokilese no further imperfectives can be formed.

Both imperfective and perfective can be combined with durative measure phrases (specified by the suffix *-ki* on the verb plus a separate time expression), but with different senses. With an imperfective the time expression measures the duration of an open event, while with a perfective it specifies the duration of a closed event:

(61)    a. Ngoah kauj-ki        ih  awahioaw
       I       chase(IMPERF)-DUR him hour
       'I chased him for an hour'

    b. Ngoah kauj-kih-di     ih  awahioaw
       I       chase-DUR-PERF him hour
       'I chased him down in an hour'

Here again, one can note the similarity and contrast with Russian. In both languages the imperfective combines with an open interval of duration, and the perfective with a closed interval that contains the closed event. In Mokilese this difference is expressed only by verbal aspect; in Russian it is expressed both by aspect and by different time expressions.

It is not clear how iterative events are evaluated aspectually in Mokilese, but it appears that a perfective can occur in an iterative context; if so, the perfective characterizes the closure of the individual subevent:

(62)    Rehn phroj ngoah kin    pwohr-da kiloak wonow
        day   each   I    HABIT  rise-PERF clock  six
        'Every day I get up at six o'clock'

Lexical states in Mokilese (as in Chamorro) have distinct aspectual properties. States normally occur in the neutral (imperfective) form, even when they include the event frame (as in (63a)). The progressive is used for states that are intensive and dynamic (as in (63b)) or for states that continue despite expectations (as in (63c), in which the lexical item requires double reduplication). The perfective indicates inception of a state (as in (63d)):

(63)    a. Oai ohlahu moadoak
           my  wound  hurt(IMPERF)
           'My wound hurts'

        b. Oai ohlahu moadmoadoak
           my  wound  hurt(PROG)
           'My wound is hurting (= is acting up)'

        c. Pahrangkije pe    pwespwespwes
           iron            still warm(PROG)
           'This piece of iron is still warm'

        d. Ih lioas-ka
           he angry-PERF
           'He got angry'

In summary, the Mokilese aspect system makes three divisions in the evaluation of dynamic events with respect to the frame. At one extreme, the progressive explicitly asserts that an event is in progress over the frame; at the other extreme, the perfective explicitly characterizes an event as closed on the frame. The imperfective is used for the intermediate cases, when neither the dynamic character of an event nor its closure with respect to the frame is emphasized. States have distinct aspectual properties. Iterative events appear not to be treated in any special way, and there is no evidence for a retrospective (perfect) aspect.

## 2.6 *Typology*

At this point one can ask whether there are any cross-linguistic generalizations governing the structuring of aspect systems. On the basis of the examples presented above (and others), there appear to be relatively few facile generalizations. Overall, it appears that the aspect parameters can be treated more or less independently in their expression as morphological aspect categories. Still, the following interpretation is suggested by the languages discussed above (as well as English).

The basic issue in an aspect system is the relationship between the predicate and the frame in an event. As suggested above, there are two possibilities: either the frame is internal to the event (the predicate goes on before, during, and after the frame), or the frame includes the event (the predicate occurs only within the frame). A given language will choose to define one of these two possibilities in relatively narrow terms, in the sense that it will impose additional semantic restrictions; the opposite possibility will be defined in broad terms, and will be expressed with the same morphology used for other aspectual values. The four aspect systems illustrated above, along with English, can be typologized according to this principle.

Russian can be considered an example of one type. In Russian the perfective is the narrowly defined category. Its usage is subject to two conditions: the frame must limit, or contain, the event – that is, the event must be closed at the proposition level; and, additionally, the predicate must be telic – that is, it must also be closed at the predicate level. Conversely, the broadly defined category, the imperfective, expresses a variety of events: those that are not closed at the proposition level (progressives) or at the predicate level (atelic processes); states; and iteratives. Given that the aspect system of Russian is organized around closure, it can be termed a closure language.

ChiBemba likewise takes closure as its narrow category, in the sense that the expression of open (progressive) events is combined with the expression of iterativity, at least in the past and future. In this way ChiBemba can also be viewed as a closure language.

In contrast to closure languages, a language may choose to take as narrowly defined the situation in which the event includes its frame. Although not discussed here, English treats its progressive as the narrowly defined category. Two conditions must be met to use the progressive: the event must include the frame (it must be in progress);

and the event must be a process. The alternative category, the neutral form, is used for both telic and atelic processes that are not in progress over the frame, and also for states and (usually) for iteratives. In view of this, English can be characterized as a dynamicity language.

The categorization of Chamorro and Mokilese in this typology is slightly problematic. In Mokilese it is clear that dynamicity is taken as a narrow category, inasmuch as the morphological progressive (reduplicated form) is only optionally used for events that include the frame, and is not used for states. On the other hand, it also appears that closed events are treated narrowly, inasmuch as there are distinct perfective forms. The morphologically basic form, for which the neutral term imperfective is appropriate, seems to cover the range of both dynamic and closed events (at least to some extent) as well as statives and duratives. Mokilese, then, appears to satisfy both parts of the typology.

In Chamorro it appears that dynamicity, expressed by the reduplicated form, is the narrow category, although this form is also used optionally for iteratives. Chamorro can then be tentatively identified as a dynamicity language, although it is clear that its progressive is used for a wider range of events than the progressive of English or Mokilese.

States are often treated as a distinct category (Chamorro), but to the extent that they are incorporated into the aspect system used for processes, their treatment follows from the choice of dynamicity or closure as the narrow category. In closure languages, states are imperfective (Russian). In dynamicity languages, states are non-progressive (English, Mokilese, Chamorro).

The treatment of a retrospective relation between event and frame (the perfect) appears to be independent of dynamicity and closure. A morphologically distinct perfect category may or may not be present in either a dynamicity linguage (present in English, absent in Mokilese) or a closure language (present in ChiBemba, absent in Russian).

Of the two quantitative parameters, durativity appears to be unimportant. It may be that any discussion of durativity should be subordinated to closure, since languages commonly distinguish durativity for open vs. closed events, and impose corresponding restrictions on aspect (Russian and Mokilese).

Iterativity is relatively more important. In some languages iterativity is given a distinct morphological expression (Lithuanian). And in those languages where its morphological expression is combined with the expression of closure or dynamicity, iteratives can be evaluated either at the level of the individual subevents (Mokilese) or at the level of the macroevent (Russian), or at both levels simultaneously (English, Chamorro).

## 3 Mood

### 3.1 *Framework for mood*

Of the three categories discussed here, mood has the greatest internal complexity.[6] As the concept of event was defined earlier, a predicate is associated with an event world (or set of worlds) in which the predicate occurs. Mood characterizes the actuality of an event by comparing the event world(s) to a reference world, termed the actual world. An event can simply be actual (more precisely, the event world is identical to the actual world); an event can be hypothetically possible (the event world is not identical to the actual world); the event may be imposed by the speaker on the addressee; and so on. Whereas there is basically one way for an event to be actual, there are numerous ways that an event can be less than completely actual. For this reason our discussion of mood is concerned principally with different types of non-actuality. As before, we direct our attention primarily to categories that are overtly signaled by bound morphology on the verb.

If we focus on verbal morphology, we find that languages commonly distinguish between actual and non-actual events, or – to use morphological terms – between realis and irrealis mood. (Realis is basically equivalent to indicative, and irrealis is equivalent to subjunctive, conditional, hypothetical, and the like.) Languages also tend to distinguish a morphological imperative. Although a few languages make further modal distinctions (such as indicative vs. subjunctive vs. optative in Attic Greek), these seem to consist of imposing a finer division on the basic notions just mentioned. In this respect the typology of mood is relatively straightforward.

It is also clear, however, that languages differ significantly as to which events are evaluated as actual (and expressed morphologically by the realis mood) vs. non-actual (and expressed by the irrealis mood). To describe this variation, we define below two basic parameters of non-actuality, or modes, in terms of which the actuality of an event can be characterized. The modes apply to primary events (in the sense of events expressed syntactically by matrix clauses) as well as to secondary events (expressed syntactically by subordinate clauses). Each mode may incorporate one or both of the following:

(i) Source. A mode may include a source from whose point of view the event is characterized as actual or non-actual. For primary events the source is typically the speaker; it is the speaker who identifies the event as actual, or imposes it on the addressee, or denies responsibility for its truth, and so on. For secondary events the source is typically the subject of the matrix clause. For example, with governing verbs of intention ('want', 'try') or obligation ('order', 'forbid'), the subject of that verb provides the source of modality for the subordinate clause.

(ii) Target. A mode may include a participant target who is responsible for the actuality of the event. For primary events the target is typically the subject. In imperatives, for example, the target is the addressee, who also happens to be the subject of the clause (we include in the category of 'subject' subjects with no overt morphosyntactic realization). For secondary events the participant target is usually both an argument of the matrix clause and the subject of the subordinate clause. With governing verbs of intention, for instance, the target is the matrix subject and the subject of the subordinate clause; with verbs of transferred modality ('ask', 'order', 'deny'), the target is the matrix direct or indirect object and the subject of the subordinate clause.

### 3.2 *Epistemic mode*

The epistemic mode characterizes the actuality of an event in terms of alternative possible situations, or worlds. At any point in time, there is an actual world, and there are also a number of alternative worlds that could exist at that time. (In one sense there is always an infinite number of such worlds. To describe the epistemic mode in language, it is appropriate to restrict the notion of alternative worlds to those that the speaker considers to be in some sense reasonably close to the actual world.) The epistemic mode characterizes the event with respect to the actual world and its possible alternatives. If the event belongs to the actual world, it is actual; if it belongs to some possible alternative world (although not necessarily to the actual world), it is possible; and so on.

Two subtypes of epistemic mode are often distinguished: necessity (the event belongs to all alternative worlds) and possibility (the event belongs to at least one alternative world). These subtypes are illustrated by one sense of the English modal auxiliaries; consider *John must be in Phoenix by now* (= in all alternative worlds that one could imagine at this time, John is in Phoenix) and *John can/may be in Phoenix now* (= there is at least one world one could imagine in which John is in Phoenix).

Because necessity and possibility are concepts familiar from logic, it is tempting to view the epistemic mode as one area of language in which logical concerns are reflected fairly directly. There are, however, several respects in which language-particular realizations of the epistemic mode may differ from a strictly logical treatment.

First, if we exclude modal auxiliaries, particular languages tend to be less concerned with distinguishing necessity from possibility than with distinguishing different types of possibility. Here mood interacts with tense. Situations in the past or present are relatively certain, so that possible events in the past or present are either actual (they have occurred or are occurring) or definitely non-actual (they have not occurred or are not occurring, though it is conceivable that they could). For the past and present tenses, then, there is a relatively clear bifurcation between actuality and counterfactuality. For the possible but counterfactual event, we use the term hypothetical.

Situations in the future are inherently uncertain as to actuality. Any future event is potential rather than actual, and there are more degrees of possibility, depending to some extent on the speaker's (or source's) convictions: a future event may be evaluated as relatively certain, merely possible, conceivable but unlikely, and so on. For this variety of possible event, we use the term potential.

The future is thus a semantic category where tense and mood merge. In practice many languages do not distinguish morphologically between future tense and potential (irrealis) mood. Where a difference is made, the future tense is used for events that are presumed to be certain to occur, and the irrealis mood for events that are potentially possible but not presumed to be certain.

Particular languages may of course structure these types of epistemic non-actuality in various ways. In particular, there is no guarantee that the difference between hypothetical and potential will be encoded morphologically. The difference does, however, appear to be expressed directly in Lakhota, where *tkhá* is used for counterfactual but hypothetically possible (HYP) events, and *kta* (~*kte*) for potential events (Boas and Deloria 1941):

(64)   a. Leháyela ma-tʔá tkhá
          now       1SG-die HYP
          'I could have/almost died'

       b. Tʔí-kte-šni
          die-FUT-not
          'He will not die'

The potential *kta* is also used to express obligation, so that *kta* in its obligational sense can be combined with the counterfactual/hypothetical *tkhá*:

(65)   Wa-kʔú-kta tkhá
       I-give-FUT   HYP
       'I should have given her (but I didn't)'

Second, particular languages tend to place less emphasis on the possibility/necessity of an event in absolute terms than on its possibility/necessity under certain conditions. The most familiar realization of this relation is the ordinary conditional sentence of the type 'if α, then β', although the condition may also be reduced to a deictic ('otherwise, ...', 'if so, ...'). Conditional sentences are discussed further in section 3.5 below.

### 3.3 *Epistemological mode*

Given that the epistemic mode characterizes the actuality of an event *per se*, it does not include a participant target or, strictly speaking, a source. In practice, however, it is hard to be sure that the speaker (as source) is totally absent when an event is characterized as possible. For example, some of the various sentential adverbs with epistemic function are relatively independent of the speaker ('possibly', 'necessarily'), but others are not ('conceivably').

The epistemic mode can be contrasted with a related mode, the epistemological mode, which differs only in that it more clearly involves a source.

The epistemological mode evaluates the actuality of an event with respect to a source. The event may be asserted to be actual, or else its actuality may be dependent on the source in one of several ways. Some of the relevant submodes here include: (i) experiential, in which the event is characterized as experienced by the source; (ii) inferential or evidential, in which the event is characterized as inferred from evidence; (iii) quotative, in which the event is reported from another source; and (iv) the submode in which the event is a construct (thought, belief, fantasy) of the source.

Languages often have verbal morphology that encodes the epistemological status of an event. In Takelma, for example, the inferential mood is used 'to imply that it is not definitely known from unmistakable evidence that the event really took place, or that it is inferred from certain facts (such as the finding of the man's corpse or the presence of a bear's footprints in the neighborhood of the house), or that the statement is not made on [the speaker's] own authority' (Sapir 1912:158). Compare the realis mood in (66a), with a distinct realis stem, with the inferential in (66b), with a different stem used for all non-actual moods and a special inferential suffix -k'-:

(66)    a. Menà yap'a t'omō-k'wa
           bear   man   kill(REALIS)-3HUMAN OBJ
           'The bear killed the man'

b. Menà yap'a dõm-k'wa-k'
bear man kill(IRR)-3HUMAN OBJ-INFERENTIAL
'It seems that the bear killed the man/The bear must have, evidently has, killed the man'

Particular languages occasionally use the same morphology to encode the epistemic and epistemological modes, suggesting that these modes are concerned with similar types of non-actuality. On the one hand, a language may express certain epistemically non-actual events with morphology used basically for epistemological uncertainty. In Takelma, for example, the future differs from other moods in that it cannot be negated simply by adding a negative adverb. Instead, negated future events are expressed by the inferential mood plus the negative adverb (both future and inferential use the irrealis stem):

(67)  a. Yaná-ʔt'
        go(IRR)-3SG(FUT)
        'He will go'

      b. Wede yanà-k'
        not  go(IRR)-INFERENTIAL
        'He will not go/Evidently he didn't go'

On the other hand, a language may express epistemologically uncertain events with morphology used basically for epistemic non-actuality. This type of encoding is common when the uncertain event is syntactically subordinate to a verb of belief or reported speech. Choice of morphological mood in these cases often reveals the speaker's attitude toward the event's actuality: realis mood is neutral, whereas irrealis expresses a lack of conviction about the event (ranging from doubt to knowledge to the contrary). In German, for example, the irrealis mood is used in the past tense to express counterfactual conditionals, among other things. In the present tense the irrealis can be used in clauses subordinate to world-creating, quotative, inferential, and experiential matrix verbs; in contrast to the realis, the irrealis expresses the speaker's doubt or uncertainty about the truth of the event:

(68)  a. Er glaubt/ behauptet/ vermutet/ fühlt, dass er krank
        he believe/ maintain/ suspect/ feel  that he sick

        ist
        be(REALIS)
        'He believes/maintains/suspects/feels that he is sick (and perhaps he is)'

b. Er glaubt/ behauptet/ vermutet/ fühlt, dass er krank
he believe/ maintain/ suspect/ feel   that he sick

sei

be(IRR)

'He believes/maintains/suspects/feels that he might be sick
(but that's only his belief/opinion/suspicion/feeling)'

### 3.4 *Deontic mode*

#### 3.4.1 *Deontic vs. epistemic*

The deontic mode characterizes an event as non-actual by virtue of the
fact that it is imposed on a given situation. Given the actual world at any
point in time, there are a number of worlds that could conceivably
develop out of that world. The deontic mode restricts these subsequent
worlds with respect to an event, such that the event has to belong to
some or all of the subsequent worlds.

As in the epistemic mode, two subtypes of deontic mode are often
distinguished: obligation (the event must hold in all subsequent worlds)
and permission (the event may hold in some subsequent world). These
subtypes are illustrated by the non-epistemic sense of the English modal
auxiliaries, as in *John must go to Phoenix* (= in all worlds developing out
of the given world, John goes to Phoenix) and *John may go to Phoenix*
(= there is some world subsequent to the given world in which John
goes to Phoenix).

There is considerable parallelism between the epistemic and deontic
modes. Both can be described in terms of alternative worlds, and both
have parallel subtypes produced by quantifying over these worlds. Thus,
epistemic necessity is parallel to deontic obligation, and epistemic
possibility is parallel to deontic permission. As a morphosyntactic
realization of this parallelism, modal auxiliaries in many languages,
notably English, often have both epistemic and deontic senses, and they
can usually be ranked in a single hierarchy from necessity/obligation to
possibility/permission, along the lines of 'must' ⩾ 'will' ⩾ 'can' ⩾ 'may'.
Given the parallelism, it is appropriate to comment on the similarity and
difference between the two modes.

The epistemic mode deals with alternative worlds with respect to a
given world at a given time point; the alternative worlds are those that
could exist instead of the given world. The deontic mode also deals with
a given world and with alternative worlds, but the alternative worlds are
those that could develop out of the given world. For either mode, the
given world and time point can be located anywhere on the temporal
dimension. As a result, both the epistemic and the deontic modes can be

applied to events in any tense; notably, there are future epistemic propositions ('John will be in Phoenix tomorrow' = at a given time tomorrow, in all alternative worlds John is in Phoenix) and future deontic propositions ('tomorrow John will have to go to Phoenix' = at a given time tomorrow, in all worlds subsequent to that, John goes to Phoenix). The crucial difference between the two, then, is that the epistemic mode deals with a set of alternative worlds at a given time, while the deontic mode deals with a set of alternative worlds that develop out of a given world and time.

In addition, there are two further properties that typically, but not necessarily, distinguish between the epistemic and deontic modes.

First, the deontic mode often includes a source of obligation/permission (for example, the speaker). But an event can also be imposed without any explicitly named or understood source; consider 'John must finish his dissertation' (= it is necessary for John to finish his dissertation). Conversely, as noted above, the epistemic mode sometimes includes a source from whose point of view the event is evaluated as possible.

Second, the deontic mode typically includes a participant target who can be held responsible for the event (for example, the subject and/or semantic agent). But an event can also be imposed without being imposed on any particular target, as in 'let there be light' or 'there must be no smoking'.

### 3.4.2 *Primary events in the deontic mode*
When the deontic mode is applied to primary events – that is, events expressed by syntactically independent clauses – a number of distinct senses can be distinguished, depending on the variables discussed earlier (source, target, and strength of modality). Some of these senses are: (i) imperative (the speaker commands the addressee to realize the event); (ii) exhortative (the speaker exhorts the addressee to participate in realizing the event along with the speaker); (iii) voluntative or desiderative (the speaker expresses intention or deliberation to realize the event); (iv) optative (the speaker desires an event of some participant); (v) jussive (the speaker allows an event); (vi) obligative or debitive (the event is required of some participant); (vii) permissive (the event is allowed of some participant); and (viii) abilitative (the event is within the ability of some participant). These different senses of the deontic mode may be expressed by distinct morphological moods (or by other morphosyntactic means, such as auxiliaries), although a given morphological mood will usually express some combination of the deontic senses listed above.

The imperative mood encodes what is perhaps the quintessential form of the deontic mode: the speaker is the source that imposes an event on the addressee. In many languages the imperative has morphological properties radically distinct from other verbal forms. In Biloxi, for example, the imperative differs from other verb forms in encoding information about the age and sex of speaker and addressee: there are distinct forms for commands to a child; commands from male adult to male adult; from male to female; from female to male; and from female to female (Dorsey and Swanton 1912).

Although the imperative usually obligates the addressee to perform the event, imperative forms can also be used to permit the addressee to perform the event. In Lakhota, for example, the imperative forms used by female speakers explicitly distinguish between obligation and permission (Boas and Deloria 1941).

Particular languages need not exhibit a one-to-one map between a morphological imperative and events imposed by the speaker on the addressee. The imperative can be used for other modal functions, as in Russian, where it can be used for counterfactual conditions:

(69)   Pribud'      ja na vokzal, menja by  posadili v  tjur'mu
       arrive(IMP) I  at station  me    IRR put      in prison
       'I arrive at the station (= if I arrived at the station), they would
       have thrown me in jail'

Conversely, other morphological moods can be used to encode events imposed by the speaker. In Attic Greek, for example, both the imperative and the optative are used to express commands, with different degrees of strength of imposition (Goodwin 1965 [1875]):

(70)   a. Ekselthōn tis        idetō
          going out  someone see(IMP)
          'Let someone go out and see'

       b. Ekselthōn tis        idoi
          going out  someone see (OPTATIVE)
          'May someone go out and see'

In the limiting case a language may not have a distinct morphological imperative. Palauan uses its single irrealis mood in the non-past tense for commands, as well as for exhortative and desiderative senses (Josephs 1975):

(71)   a. Mo-lim          a   kerum!
          2SG(IRR)-drink ART your medicine
          'Drink your medicine!'

b. Do-mẹngur ẹr  tiang
   1PL(IRR)-eat LOC here
   'Let's eat here'

c. Ku-rael          ẹl    mo ẹr  a    blik
   1SG(IRR)-travel COMP go  LOC ART my house
   'Perhaps I should go home'

### 3.4.3 *Secondary events in the deontic mode*

When the deontic mode is applied to secondary events – that is, events expressed by syntactically subordinate clauses – the source is the subject or agent of the matrix verb. The target is the subject or agent of the subordinate clause, but it may have either of two relations to the matrix clause. With matrix verbs of the type 'make', 'force', 'ask', 'prohibit', 'prevent', 'order', 'allow', 'let', and so on, the target is the direct or indirect object of the matrix clause as well as the subject of the subordinate clause. With matrix verbs of the type 'try', 'attempt', 'intend', 'promise', 'want', 'decide', 'refuse', 'agree', and the like, the target is identical to the source; that is, it is the subject/agent of both clauses. Thus, there is an analogy between the deontic mode applied to secondary events and the deontic mode applied to primary events: the case with 'order' or 'allow' is analogous to the imperative and the jussive, while the case with 'try' or 'intend' is analogous to the voluntative/desiderative.

Secondary events in the deontic mode are often expressed by an irrealis mood. In Lithuanian and many other Indo-European languages, for example, events imposed by the subject of the matrix clause on the object of the matrix clause can be expressed by an infinitive or by the irrealis:

(72)  a. Aš prašau jo  eiti     namo/kad eitụ    namo
         I  ask      him go(INF) home/that go(IRR) home
         'I asked him to go home'

      b. Aš įsakiau jam eiti     namo/kad eitụ
         I  order   him go(INF) home/that go(IRR) home
         'I ordered him to go home'

Curiously enough, Palauan does *not* use its irrealis mood for secondary events in the deontic mode, even though these are the subordinate-clause counterparts of the commands illustrated above in (71a):

(73)   a. A   sensei   a   dilu ęr   ngak mę ak mo         ęr   a
          ART teacher ART told LOC me   and I   go(REALIS) LOC ART

          Guam
          Guam
          'The teacher told me to go to Guam'

       b. A   sensei   a   kilęngę mę a   ngalęk a   mo
          ART teacher ART permit and ART child   ART go(REALIS)

          ęr   a   Hawaii
          LOC ART Hawaii
          'The teacher gave permission for the child to go to Hawaii'

In summary, we have identified two basic parameters of non-actuality, the epistemic mode and the deontic mode. The epistemic mode evaluates the actuality of an event, while the deontic mode expresses the imposition of actuality. Other modes – notably, the epistemological – can be derived from these by varying the source and/or target of modality.

We now turn to a more detailed consideration of mood in one classic type of syntactically complex construction – the conditional sentence.

## 3.5 *Conditional sentences*

### 3.5.1 *Introduction*

The typical conditional sentence consists of a condition (the event described by the 'if' clause) and a consequent (the event described by the 'then' clause). Both condition and consequent can in principle be evaluated for their degree of (epistemic) actuality.[7]

The actuality of the consequent is, of course, related to the actuality of the condition. The relationship involved is usually taken to be necessity; so 'if $\alpha$, then $\beta$' means that $\beta$ necessarily occurs when $\alpha$ occurs. In practice, though, the relationship can be weakened, so that a conditional sentence can mean 'if $\alpha$, then certainly/probably/perhaps $\beta$'.

The condition itself must in some way be less than fully actual – as Goodwin states, 'the Greek has no form implying that a condition *is* or *was* fulfilled, and it is hardly conceivable that any language should find such a form necessary or useful' (1965 [1875]:140). This requirement produces an asymmetry with respect to tense.

Because events in the past or present are relatively certain, 'the question of fulfilment has already been decided' for past or present conditions, as Goodwin notes (1965 [1875]:139). One way to introduce the necessary non-actuality in the condition is to iterate over a number of occasions, as discussed above under aspect. Aside from iteration, a conditional relationship can be established in the past or present only if the condition is contrary to actuality but hypothetically possible ('if α – as is not the case, but might have been, – then β'). With iterated conditionals excluded, past and present conditionals in effect reduce to the counterfactual hypothetical case.

Because events in the future are inherently uncertain, 'the question as to the fulfilment of a future condition is still undecided', as Goodwin says (1965 [1875]:140). Consequently, conditional statements about the future can vary considerably in their actuality, perhaps depending on the speaker's convictions: 'if α – as is certain/probable/possible/highly unlikely, – then β'.

In short, the requirement that a condition be less than fully actual has two practical consequences. Past and present conditions reduce essentially to counterfactual conditions; future conditions are neither actual nor counterfactual, but rather potential.

Particular languages vary considerably in their morphosyntactic realization of mood in conditional sentences, as is shown below.

### 3.5.2 *Russian*
Russian has two morphological moods besides the imperative: a realis mood (with tense distinctions) and an irrealis (marked by *by* plus the morphological past tense of the verb). In counterfactual conditionals both the condition and the consequent are expressed in the irrealis:

(74)   Esli by ja pribyl        na vokzal, menja by posadili v tjur'mu
       if      I  arrive(IRR) at station   me         put(IRR) in prison

       'If I had shown up at the station, they would have thrown me in prison'

In potential conditionals both the condition and the consequent are expressed in the realis (for example, perfective non-past):

(75)   Esli ja pribudu        na vokzal, menja posadjat    v tjur'mu
       if    I  arrive(REALIS) at station   me      put(REALIS) in prison

       'If I arrive at the station, they will throw me in prison'

### 3.5.3 *Chamorro*
Chamorro has two morphological moods, realis and irrealis, which are distinguished primarily by different forms of subject agreement. (In the examples below, which contain intransitive verbs describing processes, realis is marked by postverbal subject pronouns and the non-plural infix *-um-*, whereas irrealis is marked by preverbal subject agreement and

absence of *-um-*.) The irrealis mood is used for future events and certain other non-actual events; the realis is used otherwise.

Counterfactual and potential conditionals are treated identically with respect to mood. The condition of both types is expressed in the realis, although counterfactual conditions are marked additionally by the particle *mohon* 'as if, supposedly'. The consequent of both types appears in the irrealis:

(76)   a. Kumu b-um-aila       hao mohon, bai u-kanta
          if      SG-dance(REALIS) you as if      FUT ISG(IRR)-sing
          'If you had danced, I would have sung'

       b. Kumu b-um-aila       hao, bai u-kanta
          if      SG-dance(REALIS) you FUT ISG(IRR)-sing
          'If you dance, I will sing'

### 3.5.4 *Takelma*

The morphological moods of Takelma include a realis mood (termed aorist by Sapir 1912) and a number of non-actual moods: future, imperative, inferential, conditional, and hypothetical. The moods are distinguished by differences in person and differences in the morphophonemic shape of the verb stem; one stem is used for the realis, another stem (glossed IRR below) is used for all other moods.

All conditions, whether counterfactual or potential, appear uniformly in the conditional mood. (Takelma in general differentiates consistently between syntactically subordinate clauses and matrix clauses, and there is morphological evidence that the conditional mood is in fact an irrealis form for subordinate clauses.) Consequents distinguish counterfactual from potential: the hypothetical mood is used for counterfactual consequents, the future for potential consequents.

(77)   a. Gī ge     yú-kʻiʔ        eītʻeʔ bōu yaná-ʔ
          I  there be(IRR)-COND ISG    then go(IRR)-3SG(HYP)
          hagà
          in that event
          'If I had been there, then in that event he would have gone'

       b. Ākʻ yaná-kʻiʔ        gī honoʔ yaná-tʻē
          he  go(IRR)-COND I too      go(IRR)-ISG(FUT)
          'If he goes, I too will go'

### 3.5.5 *Palauan*

Palauan distinguishes between two moods which we call realis and irrealis (Josephs (1975) uses the equivalent term hypothetical for the latter). Morphologically the realis mood is characterized by a verb marker with varying shape; the irrealis mood is characterized by subject agreement. Both moods distinguish past vs. non-past tense as well as perfective vs. imperfective aspect. In conditional sentences, the condition is expressed in the irrealis, while the consequent is expressed in the realis. In both the condition and the consequent, past tense is used for counterfactuals, non-past tense for potential conditionals:

(78)  a. A lę-bilskak            a   udoud a   dęmak   e
         if 3SG(IRR)-give me(PAST) ART money ART my father then

         ak mlo            ęr  a   Guam
         I   go(REALIS PAST) LOC ART Guam
         'If my father had given me the money, I would have gone to Guam'

      b. A lę-bęskak            a   udoud a   dęmak,   e
         if 3SG(IRR)-give me(NONPAST) ART money ART my father then

         ak mo            ęr  a   Guam
         I   go(REALIS NONPAST) LOC ART Guam
         'If my father would give me the money, I would go to Guam'

Curiously, the irrealis mood appears in the condition only if the conjunction is *a* 'if'. It is not used with other conjunctions, such as *a lsękum* 'if perhaps' and *a kmu* 'if as seems unlikely', both of which have presuppositions of less actuality than plain *a* 'if'. Compare:

(79)  a. A lę-me            a   Droteo, e   ng me kie ęr  a
         if 3SG(IRR)-come ART Droteo  then he FUT stay LOC ART

         blik
         my house
         'If Droteo comes (as is probable), he'll stay at my house'

      b. A lsękum a   Droteo a   me,            e   ng me kie
         if          ART Droteo ART come(REALIS) then he FUT stay

         ęr  a   blik
         LOC ART my house
         'If Droteo should come (as is possible), he'll stay at my house'

      c. A kmu a   Droteo a   me,            e   ng me kie ęr
         if       ART Droteo ART come(REALIS) then he FUT stay at

         a   blik
         ART my house
         'If Droteo were to come (as is unlikely), he'll stay at my house'

By the same token, the irrealis mood is required in strictly temporal subordinate clauses when the morpheme *a* is the final morpheme of a complex adverbial conjunction, such as *er se ẹr a* 'when', *ẹr a uche ẹr a* 'in front of (the time when), before', *ẹr a uriul ẹr a* 'in back of (the time when), after'; the subordinate clause appears in the non-past tense:

(80)  a. Ak milsuub          er se ẹr a lẹ-mad
         I   study(REALIS PAST) when     3SG(IRR)-die(NONPAST)

         a    dengki
         ART electricity
         'I was studying when the electricity went out'

      b. A  sẹchẹlik   a    mirrael          ẹr a uche ẹr a
         ART my friend ART leave(REALIS PAST) before

         ku-mẹngur
         1SG(IRR)-eat(NONPAST)
         'My friend left before I ate'

      c. Ak mlo            mẹchiuaiu ẹr a uriul ẹr a
         I   go(REALIS PAST) sleep         after

         lo-rael                    a    Toki
         3SG(IRR)-leave(NONPAST) ART Toki
         'I went to sleep after Toki left'

The use of the irrealis for potential and counterfactual conditions may thus be somewhat deceptive. It remains true, however, that in counterfactual conditionals there is no distinct specification of counterfactuality in the *mood* of either the condition or the consequent.

### 3.5.6 *Attic Greek*

In Attic Greek, both the condition and the consequent of counterfactual conditionals have a realis past tense form (aorist for past events, imperfect for present events). The consequent is additionally marked with the particle *an*:

(81)  Ei touto eprakse,          kalōs an eskhen
      if this  do(REALIS AORIST) good     hold(REALIS AORIST)
      'If he had done this, it would have been good'

In potential, reasonably certain conditionals, the condition appears in an irrealis mood (subjunctive) and the consequent in realis future:

(82)  Ean prassēi    touto, kalōs heksei
      if  do(SJNCT) this    good hold(REALIS FUT)
      'If he does this, it will be good'

In both types of conditionals, then, the consequent appears in a realis mood. Potential conditions appear in an irrealis mood, while counterfactual conditions appear in a realis mood – a reversal of what one might expect. One possible way of rationalizing this distribution is to suggest that the irrealis moods in Greek (subjunctive and optative) are used for events with uncertain modality; since counterfactual events are definitely not actual (but only hypothetically possible), they are definite in their modality, and – in Greek – expressed in the realis.

### 3.5.7 *Summary*
Looking back over this survey, we can observe considerable diversity in the language-particular treatment of mood in conditional sentences. This diversity can be typologized according to the treatment of mood in the condition and the consequent. Either the condition and the consequent can be treated identically (by a kind of mood harmony), or they can be differentiated in mood. Russian and Greek belong to the first type, in that counterfactual conditionals exhibit one mood in both condition and consequent, whereas potential conditionals exhibit a different mood. (The actual moods involved appear to be reversed in the two languages.) Takelma belongs to the second type, in that conditions in this language appear in a special irrealis mood for subordinate clauses; consequents appear in either the hypothetical or future moods. Chamorro also appears to belong to the second type, in the sense that it has realis in the condition, but irrealis in the consequent; counterfactuality is not specified by morphological mood at all, but only by an adverb in the condition.

The classification of Palauan in terms of this typology is problematic. In terms of morphological mood, it belongs to the second type, since it uses irrealis in the condition and realis in the consequent; this, however, is a relatively superficial result of the particular subordinating conjunction that is chosen. Palauan specifies the difference between counterfactual and potential conditionals through tense, and there is tense harmony between the condition and the consequent; in this sense, Palauan belongs to the first type.

## 4 Conclusion

By way of concluding our discussion of tense, aspect, and mood, we would like to mention two general issues that deserve further investigation: the relationship of tense, aspect, and mood to one another; and the relationship between event (verbal) categories and participant (nominal) categories.

Perhaps the most striking property of tense, aspect, and mood is that all make reference to a point on the temporal dimension. Tense characterizes the location of an event with respect to a point in time (called the tense locus here). Aspect characterizes the dynamicity or closure of an event with respect to a point or interval in time (the event frame). The tense locus is usually fixed at the speech moment, while the event frame is obviously variable. This suggests that tense and aspect could be subsumed under a single category of tense–aspect which characterizes the relationship between an event and salient points on the temporal dimension.

Mood characterizes the relationship between an event and alternative worlds that might exist at a point in time. The actual world that is opposed to alternative worlds is analogous to the temporal reference point that serves as tense locus or event frame, in the sense that it provides a standard from whose point of view the event can be evaluated. This suggests that mood is a semantic operation analogous to tense–aspect, although it differs in that it deals with events and worlds rather than with events and time.

Perhaps as a consequence of the similarity between tense–aspect and mood, these categories interact morphosyntactically in some concrete ways. Perhaps the most obvious restrictions have to do with the morphosyntactic elaboration of categories: for example, realis mood makes more tense distinctions than irrealis; imperfective aspect makes more tense distinctions than perfective, and neutral aspect makes more tense distinctions than perfect or progressive; past tense makes more aspectual distinctions than present or future.

Among the more interesting of these interactions are two that we mention here. First, non-actual modality, and the deontic mode in particular, appears to induce perfective aspect more than does actual modality. For example, Tagalog distinguishes perfective vs. imperfective aspect and realis vs. irrealis mood (Schachter and Otanes 1972). The irrealis imperfective is used for ordinary future events ((83)), while the irrealis perfective is used for imperatives – that is, for deontic modality ((84)):

(83)    Wawalis-an        mo ang sahig
        sweep(IRR IMPERF)-LOC you SUBJ floor
        'You will sweep the floor'

(84)    Walis-an        mo ang sahig!
        sweep(IRR PERF)-LOC you SUBJ floor
        'Sweep the floor!'

Second, the use of adverbial conjunctions suggests that tense and mood relate pairs of events in analogous ways. Many languages have certain conjunctions that can be used for both temporal sequentiality and conditional modality (e.g. 'when', 'whenever'); both uses tend to induce perfective aspect in the clause expressing the secondary event. Conversely, other conjunctions are used for both temporal simultaneity and concessive modality (e.g. 'while'); both uses tend to induce imperfective aspect in the clause expressing the secondary event.

There are also parallelisms in the semantic categories used to describe events and those used to characterize participants. Evidently, iteration of events corresponds to number in participants; closure of events corresponds to the holistic interpretation of a set of participants; and an analogy can be drawn between the actuality of events and the definiteness/referentiality of participants.

The morphosyntactic interaction between event categories and participant categories – notably aspect and case – is well-known. It is often the case that ergative case marking (or agreement) occurs in the perfective or perfect aspect, while nominative case marking occurs in the imperfective or non-perfect aspect. A different type of interaction between aspect and case marking occurs in Finnish. In Finnish the partitive case is used instead of the accusative for two types of direct objects: the partitive object of a closed event, and any object of an open event, particularly an event in progress (Eliot 1890). (This distinction in aspect is not otherwise expressed by verbal morphology.) This is an illustration of the parallelism between closure of events and holisticity of participants suggested above.

These interactions could conceivably be accounted for in a more unified and better elaborated theory of tense, aspect, and mood.

NOTES

* We are especially indebted to Edith Moravcsik, Dwight Bolinger, and Peter Merrill for their comments on earlier versions of this chapter. We would also like to thank the following people, who served as our linguistic consultants for this project: Priscilla Anderson-Cruz, Manuel F. Borja, John Guerrero, Anicia Q. Tomokane, and Frank Tomokane (Chamorro); Nelja Dubrovič, Sergej Zamaščikov, and Vladimir Skomarovskij (Russian); Mykolas Drunga and Livija Lipaitė (Lithuanian); and Vera Wheeler (German). Examples from these languages are taken from our fieldnotes.

1 For general discussions of tense, see Bull (1960) and Jespersen (1965 [1924], chapters 19 and 20).

2 The morpheme-by-morpheme glosses given for examples in this chapter ignore material not relevant to the discussion at hand.

3 The Chamorro examples are taken from our fieldnotes. For other discussions of tense, aspect, and mood in Chamorro, see Costenoble (1940) and Topping (1973).

4 For general discussions of aspect, see Bull (1960), Comrie (1976a), and Dowty (1979, chapters 2 and 3). Additional recent studies can be found in Hopper (1982) and Tedeschi and Zaenen (1981).

5 Our discussion of Russian aspect is based on our fieldnotes as well as on the studies of Bondarko (1971), Forsyth (1970), Isačenko (1968), and Rassudova (1968).

6 For general discussions of mood, see Jespersen (1965 [1924], chapter 23) and Lyons (1977, chapters 16 and 17).

7 For general discussions of conditionals, see Dowty (1979, chapter 2) and McCawley (1981, chapters 10 and 11).

# 5 Deixis

## STEPHEN R. ANDERSON and EDWARD L. KEENAN

## 0 Introduction

Following standard usage, we consider as *deictic expressions* (or *deictics* for short) those linguistic elements whose interpretation in simple sentences makes essential reference to properties of the extralinguistic context of the utterance in which they occur. Given the sentence *John loves me*, for example, we cannot tell who is being loved unless we know who is uttering the sentence. *Me* is thus a deictic – its referent is understood of necessity to be the person who utters or asserts the sentence in which it appears.

The principal kinds of information which are expressed by deictics in language are: (i) Person, (ii) Spatial location, and (iii) Time reference. (Grammatical) person deictics are expressions which make essential reference to the speaker (*Sp*) or the addressee (*Adr*) of the utterance; spatial deictics are items which specify the spatial location of an object relative to the location of the *Sp* or the *Adr*; and temporal deictics are expressions which identify the time of an event or state relative to the time at which the utterance occurs. Thus, in the utterance *Did you write this yesterday?* the pronoun *you* is a person deictic, since it refers to the *Adr*; the demonstrative *this* is a spatial deictic, since it refers to something whose location is described by reference to the spatial location of the *Sp*; and the adverb *yesterday* is a temporal deictic, since it refers to a time one day prior to the day on which the sentence is uttered. The past tense form *did* is also a temporal deictic, since it specifies the time of writing as prior to that at which the utterance occurs.

In this chapter, we are primarily concerned with specifying in more detail the variety of linguistic forms which deictic expressions may take, and the variety of kinds of person, spatial, and temporal information which may be systematically structured by such forms. Our interest is less in the formal mechanisms by which deictic elements are expressed than in the types of system which are found in natural languages. For some discussion of the former issue, see chapters III:3 and I:1.

We also limit our attention primarily to items which are deictic when used in (what we naively determine to be) simple sentences. We can note, however, that many items which are deictic in simple sentences cease to be interpreted deictically when they appear in various types of complex structure. For example, the past tense in *He was sick* is deictic, since it refers to an event or state which obtained prior to time of the utterance. When the same tense marking occurs in *John will say that he was sick* (said for example as an attempt to anticipate John's excuse for not having attended some meeting in the future), however, we interpret the state as past merely with regard to the time of John's speaking, not with regard to that of the utterance. We refer to this phenomenon as *relative* (or *relativized*) deixis, and will return to it in the final section of this chapter.

### 1.0  Person deixis

The basic person deictics are expressions which necessarily refer to the speaker(s) or addressee(s) of the utterance in which they occur. Person deictics may encode information of several different sorts concerning the identification of *Sp* and *Adr*, including: the sex of the referent; the number of individuals represented by the referent; the social status of the referent; the social and personal relations obtaining between the referents (specifically, between the *Sp* and the *Adr* – less commonly, between the *Sp* and third parties referred to by the *Sp*).

Among linguistic items which express this information, we would of course wish to include first and second person pronouns. This is true regardless of their grammatical function (subject, direct object, etc.), including possessive and vocative forms. The deictic function of first and second person elements is also independent of whether the 'pronominal' form is an independent word, a clitic, or simply an inflectional affix: thus, there is no reason not to treat inflectional marking on verbs or on nouns marked for their possessors (in languages like Finnish) as deictic.

While the deictic function of first and second person forms is self-evident, it is worth noting that in many languages these also acquire a non-deictic role. In a sentence such as *When you're hot, you're hot* the second person pronouns are impersonal: non-deictic in that their interpretation does not depend directly on any feature of the non-linguistic context of the utterance. They are thus analogous in function to elements such as French *on* or German *man*. In other languages, this impersonal function (while kept distinct) is also clearly integrated into the pronoun system. In Breton, for example, impersonal forms are given a distinct verbal inflection (IMPRS):

(1)      Ne c'heller    ket beva gant dour sklear hag ear    an
         NEG can(IMPRS) NEG live  by   water clear  and air [of] the

amzer
weather
'You can't live on the plain water and the free air'

There is no pronominal form corresponding to this impersonal in Breton, but as a verbal inflection it is entirely parallel to (while distinct from) the three 'standard' persons and two numbers. Such a special category for impersonal forms is unusual; this function is generally filled either by a special form which is grammatically third person singular (like French *on*), or by a second person form. In a language like English, however, second person sentences with this non-deictic function do not generally differ formally from those in which the same forms refer essentially to the *Adr*.

Not only first and second person pronouns may be deictic, but also other terms of address. These are titles which may be understood as specifying information concerning the social status of the addressee relative to the speaker, or other mutual social relationships. In fact, the choice of language register is usually deictic in our sense. It may depend on the topic being discussed, but it also depends on social relations obtaining between *Sp* and *Adr*. This is a global property, not usually localizable in some particular, discrete part of speech and will have consequences at all levels of structure, including syntax, phonology, and vocabulary.

We have confined our attention thus far to first and second person deictic elements, but traditional grammatical descriptions generally do not distinguish between these and 'third person' forms. From the point of view adopted here, however, the existence of third person deictics is conceptually more complicated. On the one hand, demonstrative pronouns (such as English *this*, *that*, *these*, and *those*) as well as full NPS which are specified by demonstrative adjectives (with or without additional locative deictic specification, as for example *this card*, or *those men over there*) are clearly enough deictics, and will be treated below under the category of spatial deixis. The personal third person pronouns (e.g. English *he*, *she*, *it*, *they* and their related forms), however, as well as full NPS specified by the definite article *the* may also be used deictically, as when we say (pointing to a linguist slumped over his typewriter) *He's exhausted* or *The poor guy's exhausted*.

*He* or the definite article, however, are often anaphoric rather than deictic, with the referent of *he* or the definite NP established earlier in the discourse. For that reason, we will characterize third person personal pronouns and NPs involving definite articles as 'weak' deictics. In several languages (e.g. Japanese, Hindi, Malagasy) the third person pronouns are closely related in form to the more clearly demonstrative pronouns, especially when they have inanimate referents.

As noted above in chapter III:3, some languages have one more than the traditional three categories of 'person'.. Occasionally, such grammatical 'fourth person' categories have little to do with deictic systems: in Eskimo, for example, this inflectional category is used in subordinate structures to indicate a third person participant coreferential with the subject of a matrix clause. Although this category is otherwise integrated into the system that can be used for deictic expression of person in the language, it has no independent deictic force. Elsewhere, however, 'fourth person' forms may represent a distinct deictic category. In the Algonquian languages, for example (cf. Hockett 1966 for a clear description of the person/number marking system of Algonquian), non-first-or-second person participants within a local section of a discourse must belong to distinct deictic categories (unless they are conjoined). Thus, in 'I went for a walk and saw a bear chasing an elk', *bear* and *elk* cannot both be third person. In order to satisfy this condition, the language distinguishes 'obviative' or fourth person forms from 'proximate' or third person ones. In some instances, indeed (e.g. Potawatomi), the language recognizes yet another, 'further-obviative' or 'fifth person' form. The differences among these depend on the *Sp*'s and *Adr*'s attitudes, which then shape the discourse: whatever referent is most central to the focus of interest at a given point will generally be treated in third person, with others relegated to fourth person (or 'obviated'). As the focus of a story changes, the grammatical form by which a given referent is designated may change as well.

Designation of a referent as 'further from the focus of interest' clearly depends on factors of the extralinguistic context of utterance. Under some specified circumstances, the choice of obviative or proximate form is grammatically fixed, however. In a noun phrase containing a possessive construction, for example, the possessor is treated as proximate and the possessed as obviative (regardless of discourse factors which might operate in the opposite direction). The contrast between *John's father*, where obviation is grammatically determined, and *John saw Bill*, where it is free subject to attitudes shaping the discourse, demonstrates the difference between deictic and non-deictic uses of the same grammatical category.

Another language in which such a grammatical 'fourth person' is to be found is Navajo (as well as other Athabaskan languages; for a discussion of Navajo, cf. Akmajian and Anderson 1970). This language uses the fourth person forms (which must always, unlike third person forms, refer to human participants) for a variety of purposes: sometimes as impersonals, sometimes to refer to entities not identified internal to the sentence in which they appear, and sometimes for disambiguation (since third and fourth person participants must be distinct in reference). Again, there are some complex conditions under which the grammar determines the choice of fourth versus third person, but under many other circumstances extralinguistic factors determine this choice as they do the obviation category described above for Algonquian.

We turn now to some representative examples of the expression of gender, person and number, social status, and social and personal relations in person-deixis systems.

## 1.1 *Person and number*

Apparently, all languages make a morphemic distinction between a first person singular pronoun ('I') and at least one first person plural form ('we'). The greatest range of number distinctions we know of in the lexicon of a language is four, illustrated from Fijian in Table 5.1.

Table 5.1 *Fijian subject pronouns:*

| | Person | | |
| --- | --- | --- | --- |
| Number | First | Second | Third |
| Singular | au | iko | koya |
| Dual (inclusive) (exclusive) | kedaru keiru | kemudrau | rau |
| Trial (inclusive) (exclusive) | kedatou keitou | kemudou | iratou (eratou) |
| Plural (inclusive) (exclusive) | keda keimami | kemuni | ira (era) |

Alternate forms (most of which have not been noted here) exist in several cases. The dual and trial endings seem clearly related to the words *rua* 'two' and *tolu* 'three'. We note that Pawley and Sayaba (1971) reconstruct the same range of person and number distinctions for both Proto-Eastern and Proto-Western Polynesian, except that no distinct second person trial form is reconstructed.

A specifically trial or paucal form distinct from both duals and other plurals is also attested in New Guinea (in e.g. Gadsup; cf. Frantz 1973) and Australia (in e.g. the languages of the Djeragan family; cf. Wurm 1972). As noted by Greenberg (1966), the existence of a trial form implies the existence of duals, though of course the converse is not true:

many languages, such as Classical Arabic and Proto-Indo-European, attest duals and plurals but not trials.

It is possibly somewhat more common for a language to fail to distinguish number in second person pronouns than in first. Thus in the most basic pronominal form in the standard dialect, English does not distinguish between singular and plural forms for *you*, though in some forms with less wide distribution it does: compare, for example, *yourself* and *yourselves*. We can note that in other forms traditionally called pronominal (e.g. relative, reflexive, and interrogative pronouns), person distinctions that are made in the basic forms (those used for independent subject forms) may be neutralized. In fact, it is apparently universally true that no language marks person in interrogative pronouns. If it did, indeed, a question such as *Who* [first person] *left early?* would be self-answering. For other forms, the point is somewhat more interesting. In the case of reflexives, for example, languages may mark person in the reflexive pronouns as well as the basic forms (e.g. English, Russian, Hebrew); but it may also be the case that a single, constant, reflexive form serves for all persons (e.g. in Hindi, Kannada, Malagasy).

Note further that person inflection on verbs ('agreement') may carry deictic information which is not independently present in the sentence. Thus, in (2) from Spanish, the apparent subject is third plural, whereas the person marking on the verb is first plural:

(2)    Las mujeres protesta*mos*    pero los hombres ...
       the women  complain(1PL) but   the men ...
       'We women complain, but the men ...'

And from Warlpiri (Australia), we have:

(3)    Ngarrka  ka-rna    purla-mi
       man(ABS) PRES-1SG shout-NONPAST
       'I (a man) am shouting'

In first person plural forms, it is not uncommon to find morphemic distinctions that depend on whether or not the referent of *we* includes or explicitly excludes the *Adr*. Such *inclusive/exclusive* distinctions commonly extend also to clitics, personal affixes, and possessive forms as well. Note the translation differences in the Malagasy examples below, where EXCL = exclusive, INCL = inclusive:

(4)    a. (i) H-andeha izahay        (ii) ny  trano-nay
              FUT-go    we (EXCL)          the house-ours (EXCL)
              'We (but not you)            'our house (but not yours)'
              will go'

b. (i) H-andeha isika          (ii) ny tranon-tsika
     FUT-go     we (INCL)       the house-ours (INCL)
     'We (including you)      'our house (including yours)'
     will go'

Combinations of pronominal forms, especially first and second person ones, are not uncommonly subject to rather unpredictable, idiosyncratic constraints of a language-particular nature. For example, in French both direct and indirect object pronouns are usually presented in the form of clitic pronouns in preverbal position:

(5)    a. Il nous a  vus
        he us    has seen
        'He has seen us'

    b. Il vous a    parlé
       he you has spoken
       'He has spoken to you'

    c. Il les    a    mangés
       he them has eaten
       'He has eaten them'

However, two or more such clitics are acceptable only if, at most, one of them is first or second person:

(6)    a. *Il nous vous presentera
       he us    you    introduce(FUT)
       'He'll introduce us to you'

    b. Il vous les    presentera
       he you   them introduce(FUT)
       'He'll introduce them to you'

The difference between (6a) and (6b) is usually described by saying that in the structure of the French verb, there is only one positional 'slot' for the object clitics *me*, *te*, *se*, *nous*, and *vous*. Once this is filled by, for example, *nous*, there is no longer any position in which *vous* can appear. In (6b), on the other hand, *vous* and *les* occupy different positions, and thus can co-occur.

We should distinguish this language-particular morphological restriction from what appears to be a universal constraint against using ordinary pronouns and noun phrases for referring to the same individual twice within a single clause. Thus, in a sentence such as *John saw him*, the referent of *him* cannot be John, though it is otherwise free. By the same principle, *I saw me* is impossible, as is *I saw us*. Similarly, while English *we* can be either exclusive or inclusive under ordinary conditions, in *We saw you*, *we* can only be interpreted exclusively (i.e. as excluding the *Adr* from the class of those who did the seeing). Thus, even intersecting reference, as well as absolute identity, is precluded between two ordinary referring expressions in the same clause.

Of course, when both reference and person/number are identical, languages generally provide a special set of reflexive (and possibly also reciprocal) forms which are restricted to this situation. In English, *I saw myself* thus fills the gap created by the impossibility of *\*I saw me*. Since the reference is only overlapping, and not identical, however, *\*I saw ourselves* is just as bad as *\*I saw us*: there is really no simple way to express this meaning in English. In many languages, only some of the reflexive forms are distinct from ordinary anaphoric pronouns; thus, while French has reflexive *se* (as in *Il s'est vu* 'He saw himself') as opposed to non-reflexive *le/la/les* (as in *Il l'a vu* 'He saw him'), the first and second person forms are not distinct. The form *me* can thus be either reflexive (as in *Je me suis vu* 'I saw myself') or non-reflexive (as in *Il m'a vu* 'He saw me'). A sentence such as *Nous nous avons vus* is thus not an exception to the constraint mentioned above (in connection with the sentences in (6)), since the first *nous* is a subject form, and only the second, reflexive *nous* is assigned to the object clitic position.

Occasionally at least, sequences of pronouns referring to different persons and numbers may 'collapse' into a single *portmanteau* form. For instance, in Kapampangan (Philippines; cf. Mirikitani 1972) three persons and two numbers (singular and plural) are distinguished, with inclusive and exclusive first plural forms. We might expect, therefore, that subject and object would be represented separately in sentences with transitive verbs, like those in (7) below:

(7)     a. Binasa mya    namam?
           read    you+it too
           'Did you read it too?'

        b. Saupan da kang maglinis bale
           help    I  you  clean    house
           'I'll help you clean the house'

        c. O  sige, bayaran ku ne
           all right pay      I   already+it (= na 'already'+ya 'it')
           'All right, I'll pay it already'

In (7a) the two distinct pronouns 'you+it' are represented by a single form. Not all combinations of pronouns in Kapampangan are represented by portmanteau forms, however, as shown by (7b). In this case, there is good reason to believe that the portmanteau forms result from straightforward (if fossilized) phonological coalescence: (7c) shows that a pronominal element may also coalesce with another sentence element in some cases. Such portmanteau forms are much commoner in the domain of bound verbal morphology. A great many languages in which verbs agree with their objects as well as their subjects display such a pattern, as illustrated in the following (partial) paradigm from Mohawk (cf. Bonvillain 1973):

(8)  a. wa?-*ko*-hlo:li?     '*I* told (it to) *you*'
     b. wa-*hi*-hlo:li?      'I told him'
     c. wa-*hsek*-hlo:li?    'You told me'
     d. wa-*hts*-hlo:li?     'You told him'
     e. wa-*hak*-hlo:li?     'He told me'
     f. wa-*hya*-hlo:li?     'He told you'

Conjunctions of pronouns may also be subject to unexpected constraints (sometimes of a prescriptive or normative, as opposed to strictly grammatical, sort). Thus, *John and I* sounds better to our ears than *I and John* (perhaps at least partly due to the efforts of our former English teachers). More interestingly (though still a relatively minor phenomenon), what is semantically a first singular conjunct may in some languages be treated formally as a first plural one. In Malagasy, for instance, where we would expect (9a) we may hear, at least in some dialects, (9b) instead:

(9)  a. Rakoto sy  aho . . .
        Rakoto and I
        'Rakoto and I . . .'

     b. Rakoto sy  ahay
        Rakoto and we (exclusive)
        'Rakoto and I . . .'

The expression of person may not be independent of the expression of tense. In terms of bound morphology, this is a familiar enough situation: in French, for example, the first person singular ending on first conjugation verbs in the present tense (indicative mood) is *-e*; in the future it is *-(er)ai*; in the incomplete past ('imparfait') it is *-ais*; in the 'passé simple' it is *-a*; etc. (endings are given here in their orthographic forms in order to avoid controversy concerning their phonological characterization; it is their distinctness, rather than their identity, which interests us here). Somewhat more surprisingly, perhaps, what holds for bound morphology in such cases may hold for apparently independent pronominal forms elsewhere. Thus, in Iai (Melanesian; cf. Tryon 1968) we have:

(10)    a.  Ogeme mokut
           I(PRES) sleep
           'I am sleeping'

        b.  Ogema mokut
           I(FUT)  sleep
           'I will sleep'

        c.  Oge    mokut
           I(PAST) sleep
           'I slept'

Superficially at least, it appears that pronouns in this language carry tense marking.

Like other elements of language, of course, the form used to convey a particular person/number category in a given case may not be specifically limited to this use, but may cover a range of persons and numbers which are (elsewhere) distinguished in the language. A simple but familiar case is that of German [zi:], which may be (a) a second person polite form (written *Sie*); (b) a third person plural; or (c) a third person singular feminine form (both of the latter written *sie*). In this case, it is probably appropriate to think of uses (b) and (c) as merely accidentally homophonous, while (a) and (b) perhaps represent a genuine syncretism. More extensive and complex cases are not hard to find, however. In Vietnamese (cf. Cooke 1968), *mình* may be a first person form (used chiefly by females to intimates of either sex); a second person term (used chiefly with spouse or intimates of the opposite sex); an impersonal term (as in questions like *What (is one) to do?*); and finally as an inclusive first plural form (used when speaking to equals or slightly inferior intimates). Cooke (1968) also cites several 'pronominal' forms in Thai which may be used for either second or third person (usually with differences in meaning or conditions of use).

As a rather different sort of example we cite also the so-called '*poly-focal*' forms in New Guinea languages. The basic pronominal series may distinguish three persons and three numbers (singular, dual and plural). Various agreement markers, however, divide the person/number space differently. For example, in Bena-Bena (cf. Young 1971) verbs in subordinate clauses (called 'medial verbs' in the literature on New Guinea languages) take a tense suffix and a final suffix indicating whether the subject of that verb is the same as the subject of the verb in the next clause, or whether it is different. We note that the basic pronominal system of Bena-Bena distinguishes three persons and three numbers (singular, dual and plural). On the other hand, simple past tense medial verbs whose subjects are the same as that of the next

Table 5.2 *Past medial verb forms: Bena-Bena 'pierce'*

| Person | Number | | |
|--------|--------|------|--------|
|        | Singular | Dual | Plural |
| First  | fi-'ohu-to | fi-'ohu-to | fi-'ohu-to |
| Second | fi-'ohu-to | fi-'ehi-te | fi-'ehi-te |
| Third  | fi-'ohu-to | fi-'ehi-te | fi-'ehi-te |

clause have one of only two forms. One of these forms is used if the subject of the medial verb is either second or third person, dual or plural. The other is used if the subject of the medial verb is either first person (any number) or singular (any person). This is illustrated in Table 5.2. Note that both the past tense suffix and the same-subject suffix exhibit this two-way distinction. The two forms (*fi-'ohu-to* and *fi-'ehi-te*) may both be glossed as 'pierce-past-same subject'.

### 1.2 *Gender*
Person deictics may code information concerning the sex (semantic gender) or arbitrary class (grammatical gender) of their referents. While this is most common for third person terms, where commonly two or three (masculine, feminine, neuter) genders may be distinguished, it is also reasonably well attested for first and second person forms. The second person subject pronouns of Modern Hebrew exemplify this situation:

(11)             *Singular Plural*
        *Masculine* atah      atem
        *Feminine*  at        aten

Gender distinctions are probably less common in first person pronouns than in the second person. It seems to be true that gender marking in first person is only possible if gender is also marked in second person; and that second person forms only distinguish gender if third person forms do as well. Even where the pronoun forms do not distinguish gender themselves, however, such distinctions are clearly attested in inflectional person marking. Thus, while both Hebrew and French have only one first person singular pronoun, gender 'agreement' in the predicate may force a masculine or feminine reading, as in the examples from Hebrew in (12):

(12)    a. Ani medaber
             I    speak(MASC SG)
             'I (male) speak'

        b. Ani medaberet
             I    speak(FEM SG)
             'I (female) speak'

or from French in (13):

(13)    a. Je suis vieux
             I    am  old(MASC SG)
             'I (male) am old'

        b. Je suis vieille
             I    am  old(FEM SG)
             'I (female) am old'

Further examples can be found among the mind-boggling proliferation of first person pronouns cited by Cooke (1968) for Thai, which includes several that discriminate male from female first person. To take but one example, *kramɔm'* (lit. 'crown of the head') is used by males addressing lesser royalty, while *kramɔm' chàn'* or *mɔm' chán'* is used by women in the same circumstances. A final observation on number is due to Greenberg (1966), who noted that languages commonly make fewer distinctions in the plural numbers than in the singular. English *he/she/it* vs. *they* is representative here – this is an instance of the general principle (enunciated in a number of places by Roman Jakobson) that more marked categories tend to be less differentiated internally than less marked ones.

### 1.3 *Social rank and relationship of participants*
Person deictics commonly code information concerning the social status of the speaker, the addressee, or a third party referred to, as well as the social or personal relationship between them. More specifically, person deictics may reflect whether *Sp* and *Adr*, *Sp* and third party, or *Adr* and third party are of the same or different social rank, sex, or age group; kin related in designated ways; personally intimate, etc. Such information may be reflected in the choice of first, second or third person deictics; it may be reflected in the title of address or in the use (or non-use) of particles or affixes indicating respect or deference (*honorifics*); it may even be reflected in the choice of vocabulary used.

A systematic account of the kinds of social information coded deictically and the possible forms of encoding would border on a study of universal anthropology or sociology and go well beyond what could be presented here (even if we had the knowledge to provide such an account). We therefore content ourselves with a few examples from the more prominent systems known to us.

Perhaps the classic cases of deictic systems which encode social and related distinctions are those of East Asian languages. Extremely rich systems are indicated by Cooke (1968) for Thai, Burmese and Vietnamese, three languages related areally but not genetically. For Thai alone, Cooke lists 25 first person forms. A few of these are dialectal variants, some are borrowings (a remarkable fact in itself, since deictics are a part of the vocabulary of a language which is not generally thought to be subject to much influence of this sort), some are plural, but still most of those listed could be used, depending on context, as translations of the English first person singular pronoun. Without attempting to exhaust Cooke's (1968) list, we give a few of the translations provided for the correct use of the various first person singular forms: 'adult or adolescent male speaking to inferior or female intimate'; 'non-intimate deferential terms used by adult females speaking to superiors'; 'male commoner addressing royalty of any but the highest ranks'; 'highly deferential, male addressing high-ranking non-royalty'; 'child or young woman speaking to intimate'; 'polite term used by males speaking to equals or superiors'; 'Buddhist priest speaking to non-intimate layman or lower-ranking priest'; 'a strong non-restraint term, especially male speaking to intimate male' (where non-restraint indicates a term whose usage implies freedom from the restraints of more proper usage), etc.

Many of the 'pronominal' forms for all persons in these languages are either internally complex or else independently exist as kin terms (father, grandfather, respected uncle, etc.) or as simple common nouns (master, slave, body, self, etc.). Nonetheless, all items listed by Cooke (1968) would translate 'ordinary' pronominal usage in English. Some of the internally complex terms evidently render literally the concept of deference expressed by the term. For example, the higher ranking of the interlocutors seems to be represented as resting his foot on the head of the inferior. Adopting the other's point of view, the inferior might refer to himself when speaking to royalty then as 'crown of my head', and one of the terms used for addressing royalty translates literally as 'dust underneath sole of royal foot'.

On the other hand, a complex class or rank system is not necessary for the use of address and reference forms which codify relations of sex, familiarity and the like. In a Malagasy peasant village, where we find little social differentiation, there are still (in addition to neutral terms of address such as *ianao* 'you (sg.)' and *ianareo* 'you (pl.)') forms such as *ialahy* 'you (sg.)' which can only be used to address males, and *indriaku* 'you' which is only used to address females. Both are more familiar than the neutral terms. Yet another common term is *ise* 'you' which indicates 'quite intimate' relationship. This is most commonly used when speaking to a member of the opposite sex, but in fact it may occasionally be used between members of the same sex.

Malagasy also appears to make at least limited use of prefixes which might be translated as 'same sex as' and 'different sex from'. Thus the two ways to translate 'my brother' in (14) below vary with the sex of the referent of *my*: in (14a) the speaker is male, while in (14b) the speaker is female:

(14)    a. ny  raha+lahi-ko
           the same sex+male-my
           'my brother'

        b. ny  ana+dahi -ko
           the different sex+male-my
           'my brother'

Analogous forms exist for 'sister'.

Indicators of respect and deference are not limited in their occurrence to independent pronominal forms, but may occur as well as part of the bound morphology of a language. A rather limited case is illustrated by the verbal forms of a number of European languages, especially their imperatives. Many of these languages make a pronominal distinction between familiar and polite forms (e.g. French *tu* vs. *vous*, German *du* vs. *Sie*, Danish *du* 'you (sg.), familiar' vs. *I* 'you (pl.), familiar' vs. *De* 'you, polite'. This same distinction may be reflected in their verbal forms, as in the imperative: cf., for example, French *parle* (familiar) vs. *parlez* (polite).

A more complex system is that evidenced by modern Nahuatl (for details of which we refer the reader to Hill and Hill 1978). We indicate here some of the types of social relations between participants in a discourse which may be coded in the grammar and morphology of the language, and some of the means by which these relations are coded.

There are four different sorts of social relations between *Sp* and *Adr* that may be signaled (in a variety of ways) by the forms used by the *Sp*. These are: (1) intimacy; (2) neutral or somewhat formal relations; (3) honor (shown by *Sp* to *Adr*); and (4) 'compadrazgo' (obtaining between persons standing in a ritual relation of kinship by virtue of being parent/godparent or godparent/godparent of the same child). We will refer to these as level 1, level 2, etc.

These respect levels are marked in various ways, in (a) forms of direct address, such as second person pronouns and titles of address; (b) as affixes on verbs, in which case the respect level may pertain either to the subject or to the object of the verb; (c) as affixes on imperative forms of the verb; (d) affixally in possessive constructions, in which case the degree of respect shown usually pertains to the possessor, but sometimes to the possessed; and (e) on inflected postpositions. We illustrate briefly the first case:

(15)            'you (SG)'
        level 1: teh(huatl)
        level 2: tehhuatzīn
        level 3: māhuizotzin
        level 4: īmāhuizotzin

We may note that third person pronouns distinguish the first three respect levels as well. As an example of the marking of respect levels on verbs, we can consider the various forms that can be taken by a sentence such as *You have it*, where the subject is the addressee:

(16)            'You(SG) have it'
        level 1: ticpīa
        level 2: ticompīa
        level 3: ticonmopīalīa
        level 4: quimopīalīa

The level 2 affix -*om*-/-*on*- may in other contexts indicate motion away from *Sp*. Level 3 appears to be formed from level 2 by the addition of the infix -*mo*-, which apparently has elsewhere a reflexive meaning, plus a non-final 'transitivizing' suffix. Level 4 is formally in the third person, rather than the second, and it is the use of such third person forms in direct discourse which signals this respect level.

In systems such as that from Nahuatl just discussed, the indicators of social relationship are primarily associated with terms referring in some way or another to the *Sp* or *Adr*, such as pronouns, or verbal affixes referring to first or second person participants. An unusual variation on this is the system of verbal affixes marking the so-called 'familiar voice' forms of verbs in Basque (cf. Lafitte 1962). These affixes mark the degree of respect shown by *Sp* to *Adr*: an unusual feature of the system is that they do *fail* to appear exactly when the subject of the verb is second person (i.e. exactly when *Adr* is already coded by a subject-marking affix on the verb). There are thus five different forms of a (non-second-person) verb in Basque: one representing respect (corresponding to French *vous*); a neutral form; two representing a substantial degree of familiarity (one for addressing males and one for females); and one representing an even greater degree of intimacy. These affixes are not used to the same extent in all dialects of the language, and conditions for their use vary somewhat (as is quite typical with elements of this sort dependent on social structure). An example of the forms involved is given in (17).

(17)    'Familiar voice' forms of Basque *nago* 'I remain':
    a. nagozu   (polite)
    b. nagok    (familiar, used with male *Adr*)
    c. nagon    (familiar, used with female *Adr*)
    d. nagochu  (intimate)
    e. nago     (neutral form)

Similar forms exist for the other tense/aspect categories of the Basque verb.

The final type of 'social deictic' category we consider here is the character of systems based on a choice of vocabulary and syntactic constructions. In a number of languages, a division between two (or more) registers of speech has extensive consequences for the vocabulary employed on a given occasion, with the choice dependent on extra-linguistic factors of the situation. In Samoan, for example, there is a special oratorical style characterized not only by a considerable special vocabulary but also by a range of construction types somewhat different from normal conversational style. This phenomenon is probably charac-teristic of all languages, to some extent – wherever 'formal' situations arise, they tend to demand special locutionary effects. In situations such as that in Samoan, however, the distinction seems to be somewhat categorical (rather than a continuous gradation between more and less formal styles).

Another example of a difference between 'high' and 'low' linguistic style that seems to be categorical is furnished by Javanese (cf. Horne 1961). In this language, there are two clearly distinguished social levels: *Krama* (or *Keromo*), the 'formal' style; and *Ngoko*, the 'informal' or 'plain' style. *Krama* is used when speaking with someone higher in social or official status, including older members of one's own family, or to strangers or those not well-known to the *Sp*; *Ngoko* is used only in speaking with someone clearly lower in status than the *Sp*, including younger members of the *Sp*'s own family. The difference between the two styles is quite extensive (though not total; there are a large number of shared lexical items, and most of the syntax is the same for both styles), affecting a substantial part of the lexicon and some of the bound morphology as well. Sentences (18a,b) below illustrate the sorts of differences in question; they correspond completely, except for the difference in language-level.

(18)  a. *Krama*: Kulo saweg    maos buku Djawi
             I    be(PROG) read  book Javanese
             'I'm reading a Javanese book'

     b. *Ngoko*: Aku lagi     motjo buku Djowo
             I    be(PROG) read   book Javanese
             'I'm reading a Javanese book'

Undoubtedly the best-known system of linguistic elements deictically marking social relationship is found in Japanese, where the relevant distinctions pervade the grammar. We do not attempt to describe this here, since the distinctions made and the sorts of formal realization they receive primarily involve types instantiated by the languages discussed above and below. There are also elaborate possibilities, however, for showing respect to people spoken about, and for indicating respect levels *between* people spoken about. There are also affixes that can appear on various parts of speech in polite conversation: thus, *cha* 'tea', but *o-cha* with a use that is parodied by English gloss 'honourable tea' which might be put into the mouth of a stereotyped Japanese character in a film. For thorough discussion of respect level marking in Japanese, and the contextual determinants of its use, we refer the reader to Harada (1976) and Inoue (1979).

A particularly dramatic sort of categorical style distinction reflected in the vocabulary is characteristic of a number of languages of Australia, and has been discussed in the literature under the name of 'mother-in-law' languages. We cite here briefly the situation that obtains in the language Guugu Yimidhirr.

In this language there are large-scale differences in the linguistic forms that are used for communication when *Sp* and *Adr* stand in certain kin relations. If *Adr* is a family relation of a male *Sp*'s wife, such as a father-in-law or brother-in-law, then many of the ordinary forms of speech are replaced by others, whose use with that meaning is specific to communication between in-laws. Everyday language and joking style is appropriate not only with a male *Sp*'s wife, but with any *potential* wife as well, such as the wife's younger sisters or other women of the appropriate kin relation. By contrast, *Sp* could use the special language as a sign of respect with a potential brother-in-law or father-in-law. Women are less constrained to use the special language with their in-laws, possibly because they become members of their husband's moiety after marriage. As Haviland points out, traditionally one was not supposed to speak to one's mother-in-law at all, so for Guugu Yimidhirr, 'brother-in-law' language would actually be a more appropriate designation than 'mother-in-law' language. The reader is referred to Haviland (1979) for a much more thorough description of the language and of the exact nature of the kin relationships involved.

In narrow linguistic terms the brother-in-law language differs from the ordinary language in the following ways: first, while some forms such as *badhurr* '(type of) fruit' are used in both ordinary and brother-in-law language without difference in meaning, there are many nouns and verbs which are specific to the brother-in-law language. Thus, *balin-ga* 'echidna (a porcupine-like animal)' in the brother-in-law language becomes *nhalngarr*. On the other hand, some words in the ordinary language, especially those in the semantic domain of sexual activity such as *gulun* 'penis' have no equivalent at all in the brother-in-law language. In general, the brother-in-law language has a basic vocabulary which is much reduced compared with that of the ordinary language. Thus, the brother-in-law language may have a special word which 'translates' several words from the ordinary language. For example, the ordinary language names about ten different kinds of kangaroo, but has no generic term covering all sorts of kangaroo. The brother-in-law language has such a generic term, and uses it for any of the ten different types distinguished in the ordinary language. Similarly the brother-in-law language has a generic word for the verb 'go' and uses it in various combinations with other words to translate the specific items of the ordinary language meaning 'go', 'float, sail', 'limp', 'paddle', 'wade', etc. A case of more specific interest to the study of deictics is the brother-in-law term of direct address. The ordinary language distinguishes second person singular, dual and plural forms; in the brother-in-law language the second person plural form is used in all cases, reminiscent of the use of the plural forms in European languages in polite or formal discourse to address a single individual.

In addition to these linguistic differences in a narrow sense, speech between brothers-in-law is also associated with a variety of extralinguistic factors: for example, they may speak to each other through third parties; when speaking to one another they do not face each other directly, but rather sit crosswise; or they may speak in subdued tones. We again refer the reader to Haviland's (1979) work for more extensive and detailed discussion of these points; treatment of similar systems in other Australian languages will be found in Dixon (1972) and (for an 'initiation language') Hale (1971).

As a final note, since this is a chapter on deixis, we cannot resist pointing out the meaning of the language name Guugu Yimidhirr itself. First, *-dhirr* is a kind of comitative suffix (meaning 'with, having') which transforms nominal elements into more adjectival ones. *Yimi* itself is a demonstrative form, 'this', so Yimidhirr means roughly '*yimi*-having'.

*Guugu*, in turn, means 'word, language'. We might thus translate Guugu Yimidhirr as 'language with *yimi* for *this*'. It is thus one of the few languages in the world which is actually named after a deictic element.

## 2.0  Spatial deixis

The elements most commonly cited as 'deictics' are those designating spatial location relative to that of the speech event. All languages identify locations by reference to that of the *Sp*. It is also possible to determine locations by reference to that of the *Adr*, and many (but not all) languages utilize this possibility as well.

As a particularly clear instance of the anchoring of deictic notions by reference to the speaker, we may consider the system of verbal deictic prefixes of Abaza (cf. Allen 1956:164ff, on which the discussion below is based; for comparative notes dealing with the other languages of the Northwest Caucasian family, cf. Dumézil 1975). Verbs in this language can take one of two prefixes (placed immediately after the verb-initial pronoun position marking agreement with the absolutive noun phrase of the clause, and before the other preverbal prefixes): either ʕa or na. The former of these can be glossed roughly 'hither', and the latter 'thither'. They appear in contrasts such as those in (19):

(19)    a.    (i)   ʕágra          'to bring'
              (ii)  nágra          'to take'
              (iii) gará           'to carry'
        b.    (i)   ʕáyra          'to come here'
              (ii)  náyra          'to come there'

These two prefixes are clearly inflectional in character: they can be added to essentially any verb with which their meaning is appropriate without any change in meaning to the verb stem.

In general, ʕa indicates that the motion described by the verb proceeds toward the speaker (and the somewhat less common na that it proceeds away from the speaker). It appears that just in situations where the *Sp* is not involved, the reference point can be the *Adr* instead. This means that ʕa is used commonly when the subject of the sentence is second or third person, and the object is first person; or when the subject is third person and the action is directed toward the second person. Sentences (20a,b,c) illustrate this.

(20)    a.  yʕasɔ́ytd          'He gave it to me'
        b.  yʕasɔ́t            'Give it to me!'
        c.  yʕawɔ́ltb          'She will give it to you'

The interesting bit of complexity (from an English-centered point of view) in this system comes when we consider examples such as those in (21):

(21)   a. yʕawzə́sʕʷd          'I wrote to you'
       b. yʕawə́stxb           'I will give it back to you'
       c. yʕawáshʷd           'I told it to you'

All of these examples have a first person subject, but a second person object; how is it then possible that the prefix ʕa is appropriate in these cases? Allen (1956) shows, however, that these examples can in fact be understood in the same terms as earlier ones, once we recognize that they are only appropriate when describing situations in which, *at the time of the action*, the *Sp* was not located where he is at the time of speaking, but rather elsewhere, and the *Adr* (again, at the time of the action) was located at (or nearer to) the present location of *Sp* and *Adr*. Thus, (21a) is appropriate when describing the fact that, for example, *Sp* sent a letter home (where he is now) when he was away on a trip; (23b) could be used to promise that *when you come here* I will give it back to you; and (23c) to describe a situation in which I, who was then elsewhere, told something to you, who were then here. Thus, the reference of the notion of 'hither' remains firmly anchored by the *present* location of the *Sp*, regardless of whether he occupies the same location at the time of the action related. The failure of this element to undergo relativization of deixis (cf. section 4 below) is rather striking, and makes the 'speaker orientation' of the notion involved particularly sharp.

It is important to note that spatial references serve as the basis, in most languages, for a variety of metaphorical extensions into other domains. For example, if the meaning of English *this* is taken to be primarily 'near to the speaker', expressions such as *at this time*, *in this way*, etc. capitalize on extensions of 'nearness' to domains other than literal spatial location. Furthermore, notions such as 'near to the speaker' may be interpreted not only in the literal, physical sense, but also by extension to 'psychological proximity', i.e., vividness to the mind of the speaker, and often to 'temporally close', i.e., in the immediate past or future of the speaker.

Yet another complication in this domain is the fact that in some languages, some deictic terms are anchored by reference to the (presumed) location of the subject or actor, rather than of the *Sp*. This extension falls midway between the central basis of deictic notions and the special problem of 'relativized deixis' described below in section 4. Craig (1979) shows how the same deictic elements make reference to the

*Sp* in intransitive verbs of motion such as 'climb here', 'climb there', 'come up', 'go up', etc.; and make reference to the actor/subject in transitive verbs of motion such as 'push', 'pull', 'put in', 'take out', etc.

Spatial deictic notions are expressed in a variety of parts of speech. Perhaps most central (and probably universal) are locative adverbs (e.g. *here, there*). From these, we may consider it a short step to demonstrative adjectives (e.g. '*this* pencil') and demonstrative pronouns (e.g. 'I don't like *that*'). Less commonly, a number of languages exhibit elements we can call *presentatives*, which are used to indicate an item's location or to signal its appearance in (or relative to) the observational field of the *Sp*. Examples of such items are French *voici/voilà* 'here is ...'/'there are ...', Latin *ecce* 'behold ...', etc. In addition, a language may have bound verbal morphology indicating whether the action described in a sentence proceeds into or away from the 'space' of the *Sp/Adr* (as in the case of the Abaza prefixes considered above). Verbal roots themselves can also have deictic meaning, as in English *come, go, bring, take*, etc.

A variety of interesting problems arise in describing spatial reference implicit in particular lexical items in individual languages. Consider, for example, the verbs *come* and *go* in English. The most basic sense of *come* is apparently 'motion toward the *Sp*', and of *go*, 'motion away from the *Sp*' (though the range of usage of these items, especially in embedded contexts where the notion of 'relativized deixis' comes into play, is exceedingly difficult to describe: cf. Fillmore 1966 for discussion). They thus correspond roughly to the two basic demonstrative categories of the language, 'here' vs. 'there', 'this' vs. 'that'. One might expect that in languages with more complex deictic systems for the expression of spatial reference, additional categories of these systems might be reflected in the lexicon. This is in fact the case in some instances. Palauan (cf. Josephs 1975), for example, has three basic verbs of motion: *me* 'come', *eko* 'go', and *mo* 'go'. The difference between these latter two is that *eko* indicates motion toward the *Adr*, while *mo* is used to describe motion away from both *Sp* and *Adr*. These three lexical items thus form a system parallel to that of the Palauan demonstrative adjectives, which has *tia* 'this (near *Sp*)' vs. *tilęcha* 'that (near *Adr*)' vs. *se* 'that (far from *Sp* and *Adr*)' for singular non-animates, with other forms for plurals and animates. The corresponding place adverbs are *ęr tia* 'here (near *Sp*)', *ęr tilęcha* 'there (near *Adr*)', and *ęr se* 'there (distant)'.

The variety of forms with such spatial deictic references is quite considerable. As far as we can determine, however, the deictic notions involved are not different in *type* from those that can be studied in the limited, relatively closed systems of demonstrative elements: a grammatical class which is generally distinguishable from the rest of the lexicon of a language. We therefore confine ourselves here to such systems. The examples below are organized by reference to the principal dimension of location relative to $Sp$: first in terms of the number (and character) of distinctions recognized along a primary dimension of distance from $Sp$, and then in terms of additional, cross-classifying dimensions which can be added to this basic one.

### 2.1 *Minimal systems of spatial deictics*
### 2.1.1 *One-term systems*

In principle, a language might have only a single item which could function as a demonstrative pronoun or adjective and which would simply indicate something like 'present to $Sp$' or 'present in the extralinguistic context of the utterance', without commitment to its distance from the speaker, visibility to the speaker, etc. While we know of no unequivocal one-term demonstrative systems in this sense, Czech seems to come quite close. The commonly used *ten* may function either as a demonstrative adjective or as a demonstrative pronoun, and may be used for items which are either close to or far from the speaker. It is thus non-committal as to relative distance from the speaker, and a candidate for the status of a 'one-term' deictic system. In more formal discourse, however, it appears that there is a near/far distinction between *tento* and *onen*, although a statistical study conducted by Meyerstein (1972), to which we owe our discussion of this system, showed that *onen* is rather infrequently used. Similarly, in quite colloquial speech Meyerstein lists four near forms and two far forms, but again the only one commonly attested in her corpora is *tenhle* 'near'.

Another possible example of a 'one-term' deictic system is French *ce* (/*cette*/*cet*), which does not encode any sort of distance distinction. However, the use of *ce* is commonly supplemented by suffixal *-ci* 'here' and *-là* 'there'. Thus, while *cette maison* 'DEM house' is neutral with respect to distance from the speaker, *cette maison-ci* indicates one reasonably close to the speaker, while *cette maison-là* indicates one rather farther away or less immediately identifiable to the speaker.

Actually, a 'one-term' deictic system would be little different from a definite article. In fact, we find the definite article used in some circumstances in English with vaguely deictic force: we may say, for example, looking at a car accident, *The Ford didn't stop at the light.* Here the Ford in question is understood to be present to the speaker and the addressee, but no commitment is made concerning how far it may be from either.

Table 5.3 *Modern Hebrew near-to-speaker forms*

|  | Singular | Plural |
|---|---|---|
| Masculine | ha-yeled ha-zeh<br>the-child the-this | ha-yeladim  ha-ele<br>the-children the-these |
| Feminine | ha-yalda ha-zot<br>the-child the-this | ha-yeladot  ha-ele<br>the-children the-these |

### 2.1.2 *Two-term systems*

All languages known to us exemplify at least two distinct categories along the basic spatial deictic dimension. Standard English *this* vs. *that* (and the corresponding plural forms), *here* vs. *there* thus constitute a minimal (but not at all unusual) system. Another example, displaying a bit more internal structure, is furnished by Modern Hebrew.

As expected, the fundamental distinction made in the Hebrew deictic system is between forms indicating 'near to speaker' and those indicating 'far from speaker'. The two sets are not morphologically related, and the far-from-speaker forms seem to be used much less frequently. We give the near-to-speaker forms in Table 5.3.

Note that the gender distinction present in the singular forms of the demonstrative adjective/pronoun is neutralized in the plural. This is another instance of the principle referred to at the end of section 1.2. Note also that the definite article *ha-* is clearly distinct from the demonstrative adjectives. The demonstrative adjectives, like other adjectives in Hebrew, agree in definiteness with the head of the phrase in which they appear, in the sense that both the head and the adjective carry separate markers of definiteness (cf. *ha-yeled ha-gdol* 'the big boy, lit. the-boy the-big').

The far-from-speaker forms are constructed from the independent personal pronouns and the definite article as given in Table 5.4.

Table 5.4 *Modern Hebrew far-from-speaker forms*

|  | Singular | Plural |
|---|---|---|
| Masculine | ha-yeled ha-hu<br>the-child the-he | ha-yeladim  ha-hem<br>the-children the-them(MASC) |
| Feminine | ha-yalda ha-hi<br>the-child the-she | ha-yeladot  ha-hen<br>the-children the-them(FEM) |

As mentioned, these distal forms are much less commonly used than, for example, the corresponding distal demonstrative *that/those* in

English; moreover, the feminine plural forms in particular seem quite unusual.

### 2.1.3 *Three-term systems*

Many languages (e.g. Latin, Japanese, Southern Sotho, Turkish, and Spanish) present three basic demonstrative adjectives/pronouns. In these systems the first term represents something which is close to the *Sp* (as noted above, either in literal, spatial terms, or temporally, or perhaps mentally: vivid to his mind). The third term represents something which is remote relative to the space occupied by *Sp* and *Adr*. The systems differ in the interpretation given to their middle terms, often in ways which are not clearly described in the literature. Excluding cases where the middle term's interpretation cannot be determined from existing descriptions, we may distinguish two major types of system: (a) those in which the middle term marks objects as being in some sense close to or identifiable by the *Adr*; and (b) those in which the middle term indicates an object which is simply farther from the *Sp* than would be indicated by the first term of the system, but closer than would be indicated by the third. We refer to these two types as *person oriented* and *distance oriented* systems, respectively.

In the examples which follow we may classify Spanish and Southern Sotho as distance oriented systems; Japanese and Palauan, on the other hand, display person oriented systems. Both Latin and Turkish have also been classed (cf. Lyons 1977) as person oriented systems, though Frei (1944) disputes this for Latin, and Bastuji (1976) disputes this for Turkish. Frei also cites Old Church Slavonic *sy*, *ty*, and *ony* as a person oriented deictic system.

### 2.1.3.1 *Distance oriented three-term systems.* 

Spanish distinguishes three demonstrative adjectives/pronouns as follows (masculine singular forms): *este*, *ese*, *aquel*. The basic semantic distinctions among them seem basically to be ones of relative distance from the *Sp*, with *este* referring to items which are close, *ese* to items farther away, and *aquel* to items which are rather remote, clearly less present to *Sp* and *Adr* than items marked with *ese*.

Southern Sotho (cf. Doke and Mofokeng 1967) exhibits a more elaborate system, but one which employs the same basic three-way contrast as Spanish. Again, there are three basic demonstrative categories in any given circumstance. The first indicates something close to the speaker, the second something rather farther away (but not noted by the authors as specifically close to *Adr*), and the third something quite far from both, but generally still visible nonetheless. It is perhaps notable

that the second form is also used to refer to things previously mentioned, and also as the anaphoric element in relative clauses (e.g. *motho
eo ke-mo-tsebang* 'The person I know, lit. person that I-him-know').

Southern Sotho nouns come in 13 classes distinguished by the form of
a noun class prefix. The first 12 classes can be arranged into six
singular/plural pairs; the thirteenth class is that of abstract nouns, with
no corresponding plural class. For each prefix there is a demonstrative
base or root: three different demonstrative adjectives or pronouns in
each case are formed by adding a suffix to the appropriate root. There
are thus actually $3 \times 13 = 39$ actual demonstrative forms. In fact, each
demonstrative also has a regularly constructed emphatic form, yielding
a total of 78 different demonstrative adjectives/pronouns. Without
indicating the morphological segmentation, we give the forms for classes
7 and 8 (where 8 is the plural class corresponding to 7) in Table 5.5.

Table 5.5 *Southern Sotho demonstrative adjectives/pronouns classes 7
and 8*

|  | Class 7 (singular) | Class 8 (plural) |
|---|---|---|
| *near speaker* | | |
| unemphatic | seē | tseē |
| emphatic | sena | tsena |
| *farther* | | |
| unemphatic | seō | tseō |
| emphatic | seno | tseno |
| *quite far* | | |
| unemphatic | sanē | tsanē |
| emphatic | sela | tsela |

We note that the demonstrative bases (e.g. *se-* and *tse-* above) are
identical to the relativization concord element on verbs (i.e. to the
'relative pronoun').

That it is not proximity to the addressee which is relevant in
contrasting the second and third terms of this system is suggested by the
fact that when contrasting two objects, any series may be contrasted
with any other in terms of their *relative* distance from the *Sp*, without
necessary consistency in the real-world locations of the objects involved.
Also, as noted above, the unemphatic second-series forms are commonly used as previous reference markers, again without dependence on
real-world location.

The three-way distinction in the demonstrative adjectives/pronouns
is paralleled by a three-way distinction in locative particles/adverbs:

(22)        near speaker
*unemphatic emphatic*
moō       mona

farther
*unemphatic emphatic*
moō       monō

quite far
*unemphatic emphatic*
manē      mola

Finally, we may note that Southern Sotho also admits of a two-way distinction in manner adverbs: *jŏana* 'thus, in this manner' vs. *jŏalo* 'thus, in that manner'.

In fact, it is not necessary to go beyond English to attest a three-term distance oriented system. In Scottish dialects, as in earlier stages of the standard language, the form *yon* and its derivatives are distinguished from *this* and *that* in what seems to be a straightforward distance oriented system. The demonstrative differences are of course paralleled by similar ones in the locative adverbs: *yonder* vs. *here* and *there*.

2.1.3.2 *Person oriented three-term systems.* In clear contrast to the distance orientation of the systems we have just considered, we can recall the Palauan demonstrative system cited above, whose 'middle term' refers explicitly to proximity to the *Adr*. The deictic demonstratives of Japanese also show an orientation to the category of person. The three demonstrative adjectives of Japanese are (a) *kono*, which indicates 'near *Sp*'; (b) *ano*, which indicates 'far from both *Sp* and *Adr*'; and (c) *sono*, used for objects near to the *Adr* (or at least easily identifiable by the *Adr*). We note that – as adjectives – these demonstratives are unlike other adjectives in Japanese in that they do not distinguish past and non-past tenses.

Corresponding to the three-way distinction in the demonstrative adjectives (or specifiers) we find a morphologically related series of three demonstrative pronouns: (a) *kore* 'this (near *Sp*)'; (b) *are* 'that (distant from both *Sp* and *Adr*)'; and (c) *sore* 'that (near to *Adr*)'. The locative adverb series also shows the same three-way distinction, although the morphological pattern is not quite so neat: (a) *koko* 'here (near *Sp*)'; (b) *asoko* 'there (distant)'; and (c) *soko* 'there (near *Adr*)'. Consistently then, the 'middle-distance' or *so-* forms indicate a location near to the *Adr*, rather than simply an intermediate distance between the *ko-* and the *a(so)-* forms. The only exception to this general principle is that in discourse, when referring to previously mentioned things anaphorically, the *sono* series is used.

2.1.3.3 *Other three-term systems.* Virtually all of the demonstrative systems known to us that employ three terms disperse them along a single dimension in the ways just illustrated. In some cases, it is difficult to assign a particular system to one or the other of 'person oriented' and 'distance oriented' systems, however. Turkish, for instance, makes a three-way distinction among *bu*, *şu*, and *o*. These may function as demonstrative pronouns or adjectives, with *o* serving in addition as the ordinary third person pronoun. Each may be suffixed by *-ra* to yield one of the corresponding demonstrative adverbs: *bura*, *şura*, and *ora*. Of these three, *bu* (and its derivatives) clearly pertains to the (physical or mental) space of the *Sp*. *O* equally clearly refers to things which are remote from both *Sp* and *Adr*, and is the form used for marking something which has been previously mentioned in the discourse.

The use of *şu* and its derivatives, however, is somewhat more problematic. Lyons (1977) identifies this with 'close to *Adr*'. It appears that historically Turkish had a basic two-term system (*bu* and *ol*), each member of which had a more emphatic form built with a prefix *ş* (i.e., *şu* and *şol*). The form *şol* has since died out.

Bastuji (1976) argues that currently the form *şu* is still in fact an expressive variant of *bu*, but that it does express some addressee-orientation in direct address such as imperatives:

(23)    Bakın şu    avuç-lar-ıma!
        look at these hand-PL-my
        'Look at my hands!'

Arguably the speaker's hands are closer to the *Sp* than to the *Adr*, and the effect of *şu* here would be in some way to reinforce the attention drawn to the *Adr*. It appears, then, that *şu* is not purely and simply a demonstrative meaning 'near *Adr*' (as opposed to 'near *Sp*'): in certain contexts it does pertain to things in the (physical or psychological) space of both *Adr* and *Sp*, and there serves in some way to emphasize reference to the *Adr*.

In at least one case, a system employing three terms does so as a variant of a basically two-term system. In Nama Hottentot the demonstrative system basically opposes *nee* 'this' and *//nāá* 'that', with the former used for persons or things actually near the *Sp*, and the latter for items that are not. The term *//nāá*, however, can only be used in relatively neutral deictic settings, and in particular, it cannot be used to make an overt contrast with *nee*. When it is desired to say, for example, this one *and that one*, the distal demonstrative used is the form *náú*. This latter form is only used for contrastive purposes, and in fact can be used to contrast *either* with *nee* or with //*nãã*:

(24)    a.  nee kxòep tsíí náú kxòep
            this man   and that man
            'this man and that one'

        b.  //nãá kxòep tsíí náú        kxòep
            that   man   and that (other) man
            'that man and that other one'

This use of a specifically contrastive category in the Nama Hottentot deictic system is reminiscent of the proximate/obviative or 'fourth person' systems of Algonquian and Navajo cited above in section 1.0.

### 2.1.4 *Systems with more than three terms*

Under the category of person above (section 1.0) we have already discussed one system with more than three terms, the Algonquian obviation system. It is not clear, however, that this is a genuine instance in which the basic dimension of spatial deixis (proximity to $Sp$) is extended to a fourth value parallel to the first three. It has sometimes been noted, however, that there are languages that utilize more than three points along this dimension. Frei (1944) cites Tlingit, Welsh, and Breton as examples of systems with four terms.

In the case of Tlingit, Story and Naish (1973) make it clear that the system of demonstrative adjectives/pronouns makes a four-way distinction of the type we have characterized as distance oriented above. Thus, *yáa* 'this (one) right here' is clearly 'close to $Sp$'; *héi* 'this (one) nearby' is characterized by moderate distance from $Sp$ without reference to the *Adr*; *wée* 'that (one) over there' is again not identified by the location of the *Adr*; and *yóo* 'that (one) far off (in space or time)', the fourth term, is simply remote from the speech situation. Tlingit also displays a fourth person inflectional form in its verbal system, but this seems primarily to be used impersonally (similar, as one might expect, to one important use of fourth person forms in the Athabaskan languages), and has no apparent connection with the four terms of the deictic system.

Contrary to what is suggested by Frei (1944), we can find no significant evidence for a four-term deictic system in Welsh or Breton. Breton, for example, distinguishes three degrees of proximity in a distance oriented system by demonstrative suffixes:

(25)  a.  e-r    plas-mañ
          in-ART place-this
          'in this place'

      b.  e-n    dez-se
          on-ART day-that
          'on that day'

      c.  e-r    coat-hont
          in-ART woods-yon
          'in yonder wood'

It is interesting to note, from a formal perspective, that these demonstrative elements are final in their noun phrase, while the articles appear in noun-phrase initial position; this situation is quite uncommon, since articles and demonstratives generally have a great deal in common formally. In any event, each of the three demonstrative categories has a corresponding pronoun (*hemañ*, *hennezh*, and *henhont*, for the masculine singular forms) and a locative adverb. The fourth term given for this system by Frei, *eno*, does not appear to exist in any of the modern dialects as a distinct deictic category. In Welsh as well, the supposed fourth term of the system seems to be represented simply by a variant form with deictic properties similar to one of the others; Welsh (and Breton) can be said to have inherited a complex set of deictic elements based on multiple roots with various etymologies, but apparently the wealth of available forms have not been synthesized into a single system with more than three members along the same dimension.

A language that does exemplify a four-term system, however, is Sre (a Montagnard language spoken in Vietnam; cf. Manley (1972) for a description). This system appears to contrast with the Tlingit one in that it is person, rather than distance oriented. The four demonstrative pronouns are: (a) *dɔ* 'near *Sp*'; (b) *dɛn/gɛn* 'near hearer'; (c) *nɛ* '*Sp* and *Adr* are together; object is not close to them'; and (d) *həʔ* 'remote, out of sight (either spatially or temporally)'. In addition to these terms, there is another element *daʔ*, used solely as the second (farther) element of a contrast. When contrasted with *daʔ*, *dɔ* simply designates the relatively closer of the objects contrasted, without commitment as to spatial location relative to the participants in the speech situation. This element *daʔ*, used only for contrast, is thus similar to the 'third term' of the Nama Hottentot system discussed above.

We can also note that, unlike the case in most systems, where the intermediate term of the deictic series is often a general anaphoric element, in Sre it is the most distant demonstrative, *həʔ*, which often functions as a definite article (or rather, as a previous reference marker: 'the one we have been talking about').

Both Tlingit and Sre augment the basic three-term system by a fourth term indicating increased remoteness from the speech situation. This case is actually quite similar to that of languages which simply recognize an additional dimension, that of visibility: such languages will be discussed below, and Tlingit and Sre could perhaps be regarded as cases in which this additional dimension is limited in relevance to a single term. Other four-term systems, however, do not seem to be similarly reducible. In Quileute (cf. Andrade 1933), for example, the set of demonstratives referring to visible locations is as follows:

(26)    a. x̣o´ʔo 'near speaker'
        b. so´ʔo 'near addressee'
        c. sa´ʔa 'at a comparatively short distance from both'
        d. á:čaʔa 'at a long distance'

Apparently these four terms make use of the dimension of distance from $Sp$ and $Adr$ in a somewhat different way from the Tlingit and Sre systems, since the 'extra' term of the set denotes something which is (roughly) equidistant from both, rather than something remote or invisible from the speech situation.

For completeness' sake, we note that in addition to these elements, Quileute also has a set of three demonstratives used for invisible objects – one for an object nearby and indefinite in extension; one for objects whose location is known; and one for objects whose location is unknown. This set of elements is apparently quite orthogonal to those the language deploys along the basic deictic dimension of distance from $Sp$ and $Adr$, and falls properly among the systems considered below in section 2.2.

Another language which has been said to have a four-way contrast of the sort illustrated by Quileute is CiBemba. Actually, however, Welmers (1973:286f) observes that this language has a *five*-way contrast along the basic deictic dimension:

(27)    a. ú-nó 'this (immediately adjacent to or on the $Sp$)'
        b. ù-yú 'this (nearer the $Sp$ than the $Adr$)'
        c. ù-yóò 'this (equally near or relevant to both)'
        d. ù-yó 'that (immediately adjacent to or on the $Adr$)'
        e. ù-lyà 'that (away from both)'

Systems with more than five terms along the basic deictic dimension are exceedingly rare. We will note one such system below, that of Malagasy, the only one with which we are familiar.

## 2.2 *Systems with more than one dimension of contrast*

The systems we have considered up to this point have all made deictic contrasts along a single dimension, that of distance from *Sp*. This is of course both the most familiar and the most common state of affairs in deictic systems, but in some parts of the world additional dimensions of contrast are integrated into the same system, leading to substantially richer inventories of categories.

One additional dimension, employed by a few languages, is that of new information vs. previously mentioned items. Hausa, for example (cf. Welmers 1973:287) distinguishes only two degrees of distance along the primary dimension of distance from *Sp*, similar to Modern English. Within each of these categories, however (in addition to a possible gender contrast), the item referred to is marked for whether or not it has been previously mentioned:

(28)  a. wánnàn 'this (new)'

  b. wáncàn 'that (new)'

  c. wànnán 'the one previously mentioned'

  d. wàncán 'that other (mentioned) one'

The forms given here are masculine ones; as noted, parallel ones exist for referring to feminine nouns.

We have seen above, in connection with systems such as that of Nama Hottentot, that it is possible to introduce additional terms into a deictic system which are distinctively used for contrastive purposes. In Woleaian (cf. Sohn 1975), this parameter is apparently used as an additional dimension superimposed on the basic spatial one. In this language, the basic terms of the demonstrative system are (a) *ye* 'this (near *Sp*)', (b) *mwu* 'that (near *Adr*)', (c) *la* 'that (nearer *Adr* or away from both)', and (d) *we* 'that (unseen but in minds of *Sp* and *Adr*)'. An additional suffix, *-iy*, marks items which the *Sp* is inside of at the time of the utterance. Both *mwu* and *la* in this system have the meaning of 'near *Adr*'. However, each of these demonstratives can be suffixed with *-l*, in which case they are taken as specifying contrastive location (in comparison to some other possible referent, as when pointing out one member of a group). In the set of these contrastive demonstratives, *mwuul* has only the sense of 'near *Adr*', while *laal* has only the sense of 'away from both *Sp* and *Adr*'.

The added dimensions we have just considered have not been directly related to physical location or position relative to the speech situation, but rather to other discourse factors (previous mention and contrast). Another additional dimension, common in a number of languages in diverse parts of the world, is a contrast in terms of whether or not the object in question is visible to the *Sp*. A language in which this contrast plays a significant role is Kwakwa'la (cf. Boas 1947). In this language every noun phrase is overtly marked for its deictic status in a rather complex way: the marking appears both in the form of a preceding determiner element (generally postclitic on whatever comes before in the sentence) and in the form of a following suffix (postclitic on the first full word of the noun phrase). Not all categories of the system have distinct prenominal determiners in all environments, nor do they all have distinct postnominal suffixes in all cases, but the combination of prefix and suffix gives a unique interpretation to the deictic status of virtually all noun phrases in the language.

Since our interest here is with the set of categories the language recognizes, rather than with the formal mechanics by which these categories are marked, we will not illustrate the marking of full noun phrases in Kwakwa'la. The same categories are also reflected in the set of demonstrative pronouns used as anaphoric substitutes for full noun phrases, which appear as clitics on the preceding sentence element. These pronouns encode not only deictic status (obligatorily; there is no neutral third person form unmarked for deixis) but also grammatical category in a system distinguishing subject forms from 'object' and 'instrumental' forms.

The basis of the system is a three-term contrast along the primary dimension of distance from *Sp*, of the type we have called 'person oriented'. Superimposed on this distinction is the additional one of visibility to the *Sp*, resulting in a set of six terms. We give these pronominal demonstratives below (in a transcription slightly different from Boas'):

(29)  

| Demonstrative of | Subject | Object | Instrumental |
|---|---|---|---|
| 1st person, visible | -k | -qək- | -sək |
| 1st person, invisible | -ga? | -x̣ga? | -sga? |
| 2nd person, visible | -ux̣w | -qw | -sux̣w |
| 2nd person, invisible | -u? | -qu? | -su? |
| 3rd person, visible | -iq | -q | -s |
| 3rd person, invisible | -i? | -qi(?) | -si(?) |

As will be evident from this chart, the category of invisibility is generally marked by a suffixed [?], confirming its status as a dimension orthogonal to the primary one of distance from *Sp*. In addition to these six categories, Boas (1947) reports that the Bella Bella (or Heiltsukw) dialect adds a seventh: that of 'something that was in view but is no longer in view'.

The category of visibility is not by any means the only additional physical dimension that can be superimposed on a deictic system, however. A number of languages of New Guinea, as well as some in Australia, make use of a dimension of height relative to the *Sp*. In Daga (cf. Murane 1974), for example, there is a series of fourteen basic demonstrative elements:

(30)
| | | | | | |
|---|---|---|---|---|---|
| oea | 'overhead' | ea | 'underneath' | ata | 'same level' |
| ao | 'up, high' | ae | 'down, low' | ase | 'same level, far' |
| uta | 'higher (near)' | ita | 'lower (near)' | ma | 'near *Sp*, this' |
| utu | 'higher (far)' | isi | 'lower (far)' | ame | 'near *Adr*, that' |
| use | 'higher (remote)' | ise | 'lower (remote)' | | |

There are a number of ways we might organize this system in terms of deictic dimensions, but clearly the first two columns of (30), together with the first two elements in the third column, contrast on a dimension 'above *Sp*' vs. 'below *Sp*' vs. 'same level as *Sp*'. The elements *uta/utu/use* and *ita/ita/isi/ise* contrast on a distance oriented three-term basic dimension, while *ma* vs. *ame* appears to represent a person oriented contrast in terms unmarked for relative height.

In addition to the basic contrasts represented in (30), Daga also indicates several other deictic dimensions: (a) the suffix *-p(a)/-pe* can be added to any of the terms in (30) to mark non-visibility; (b) the suffix *-t/-m* can be added to any term except *ame* to mark visibility explicitly; (c) the suffix *-na* can be added to any term in (30) to mark vague or approximate location; (d) the suffix *-i(si)ra* can be added to some of these terms to indicate direction toward; and (e) the suffix *-me(pe)* can be added to one of the terms in (30) to mark previous mention of an object, creating a deictically specified anaphoric demonstrative pronoun.

Orientation by height with respect to the *Sp* is attested in several languages, not all of them in New Guinea. Abkhaz, for example (cf. Dumézil 1975), is a language close related to Abaza. One difference between them, however, is that Abkhaz supplements the Abaza verbal particles for 'hither' vs. 'thither' (considered above in section 2) with two others for 'upward' vs. 'downward'. Height is not the only possible dimension of this sort, however. Some languages also instantiate a deictic contrast based on geographical or environmental features. In Dyirbal (cf. Dixon 1972), we find a complex system of deictic markers which appear suffixed to noun markers (or determiners). One set of these marks a contrast of height relative to the speaker (as in Daga):

(31)   gali 'down (vertically)'
       gala 'up (vertically)'
       galu 'straight in front (with reference to the way *Sp* faces)'

Another set of markers, however, indicates a rather different sort of contrast:

(32)  baydi   'short distance downhill'        dayi   'short distance uphill'
      bayda   'medium distance downhill'      daya   'medium distance uphill'
      baydu   'long distance downhill'        dayu   'long distance uphill'

      balbala 'medium distance downriver'     dawala 'medium distance upriver'
      balbulu 'long distance downriver'       dawulu 'long distance upriver'

              guya    'across the river'
              bawal   'long way (in any direction)'

In this system there is a contrast of 'river' vs. 'hill'. According to Dixon, the former refers to water-features in general, and the latter to 'cliff', 'tree', etc. Within each series (in both (31) and (32)) we can distinguish three formal categories, marked by *-i/-a/-u*. It appears that the function of this distinction in (31) is rather different from its function in (32). We can regard this contrast as, in general, 'short distance' vs. 'middle distance' vs. 'long distance' (with expression for 'down' corresponding to 'short distance', 'up' to 'middle distance', and 'straight ahead' to 'long distance'). As Dixon (1972:263) points out, 'we can only see a short distance down (to the ground); a fair distance up; and a longer distance straight ahead'. He supports this suggestion with forms in a related language, possibly cognate with those in (31) but signaling simply a 'here'/'there'/'yonder' contrast.

We now provide a summary of the deictic system of Malagasy, which is a particularly rich one. We consider first the system of locative adverbs, as they display the greatest amount of structure among the language's spatial deictics. There is a series of seven deictics distinguished along the primary spatial dimension of distance from the *Sp*:

(33)    Close to speaker          Increasingly far from speaker
        ←————————————————————————————————————→
        ety     eto     (eo)     etsy     eny     eroa     ery

The element *eo* is included in parentheses since it has taken on a specialized meaning of 'inside of'.

These deictics not only function as locative adverbs, as in (34a), but also obligatorily accompany full noun phrases used to specify a location, as in (34b). They may also be used as predicates, as in (34c):

(34)    a. Mipetraka eto   Rakoto
           sit (=live) here Rakoto
           'Rakoto lives here (or is sitting here)'

b. Mipetraka eto   Antsirabe Rakoto
   live      here Antsirabe Rakoto
   'Rakoto lives (here) in Antsirabe'

c. Mbola tsy eto   Rakoto
   still   not here Rakoto
   'Rakoto is still not here'

In addition to marking seven degrees of relative distance from the *Sp*, the Malagasy locatives may also be inflected for 'non-visible' and for tense. To form the non-visible series, the initial *e-* in the series above is replaced by *a-*. Thus, note the difference in meaning between (35a) and (35b):

(35)  a. Mipetraka eny   Antsirabe Rakoto
       live      there Antsirabe Rakoto
       'Rakoto lives (there) in Antsirabe'
       (*Sp* can see Antsirabe, which is not far away)

    b. Mipetraka any   Antsirabe Rakoto
       live      there Antsirabe Rakoto
       'Rakoto lives (there) in Antsirabe'
       (*Sp* does not see Antsirabe; it is not too far away)

Each of the visible or invisible deictics above may also take an initial *t-* indicating that the object referred to was at the distance indicated in the past; the forms we have given thus far have been present tense forms. Future tense is formed by the use of a prefix *ho-*. Consider the following contrasts:

(36)  a. N-andeha t-any       Antsirabe Rakoto
       PAST-go   PAST-there Antsirabe Rakoto
       'Rakoto went to Antsirabe'

    b. M-andeha any   Antsirabe Rakoto
       PRES-go   there Antsirabe Rakoto
       'Rakoto is going to Antsirabe'

(37)  a. N-ipetraka t-any       Antsirabe Rakoto
       PAST-live   PAST-there Antsirabe Rakoto
       'Rakoto lived in Antsirabe'

    b. M-ipetraka any   Antsirabe Rakoto
       PRES-live   there Antsirabe Rakoto
       'Rakoto lives in Antsirabe'

    c. H-ipetraka ho-any   Antsirabe Rakoto
       FUT-live   FUT-there Antsirabe Rakoto
       'Rakoto will live in Antsirabe'

The demonstrative adjective/pronoun system also marks six (but not seven) degrees of distance from the *Sp*, as follows:

(38)    Near *Sp*          Increasingly far from *Sp*

←――――――――――――――――――――――→

ity    io    itsy    iny    iroa    iry

These forms do not, however, inflect for the distinction between visible and invisible, or for tense. They do, however, incorporate a number distinction. Thus, to form the plural correspondents of (38), the infix *-re-* is inserted after the initial *i-* of the demonstrative. Interestingly, this plural marker is the same one that distinguishes singular *ianao* 'you' from plural *ianareo* 'you'; and other than the number difference in the first person pronoun *izahay* 'we (exclusive)' and *itsika* 'we (inclusive)', number is not marked morphologically anywhere else in the language.

Formally, it is worth noting that the demonstrative adjectives are normally constructed so as to frame the nouns they modify:

(39)    a. ity   trano fotsy ity
           this house white this
           'this white house'

        b. iny   tranon-dRakoto   iny
           that house-(of)Rakoto that
           'that house of Rakoto's'

While the demonstrative adjectives do not productively inflect for the distinction between visible and non-visible shown in the locative adverbs, many of the forms do take a *-za-* infix in the same position as the plural *-re-* infix. This yields forms like *izao, izany*, etc., which are most naturally used for objects which are not in fact visible at the moment of speaking. They are also commonly used as pronominal forms referring to events or states, as the demonstrative pronoun *that* in *Mary's sick – That's too bad*.

Finally, we may note that despite the extensive system of spatial deictics, Malagasy possesses a definite article *ny*. This element is comparable in function to English *the*, though it is also used actively to form nominalizations of verb phrases, adjective phrases, and even adverbs such as the locative ones. Thus, *ny mbola tsy tonga* 'the still not come' would be used naturally to mean 'the one(s) who had not yet arrived', and *ny eto* 'the here' would be used to mean 'the one(s) who is/are here'. Moreover, in addition to the definite article *ny*, Malagasy also possesses a previous reference marker *ilay*, whose initial *i-* suggests some relation with the demonstratives, but which is in fact normally used to refer to some object whose existence has been previously established in the discourse or to an object previously acknowledged by the *Sp* or *Adr* in the extralinguistic context of the discourse. If this element is construed as a demonstrative, then, it is neutral with respect to most of the dimensions of the Malagasy deictic system.

We close this section with a brief sketch of the spatial demonstrative system of Eskimo, reputedly the world's most exuberant development of this aspect of linguistic structure. An initial dimension organizing this system is described in various references as 'extended' (indicating either large expanses of land or water, or objects that are lengthy or moving), vs. 'restricted' (indicating objects that are stationary, or moving within a confined area, and fairly small in extent, relatively near, and visible), vs. 'obscured' (indicating objects that are farther away and not clearly in sight). Based on this primary opposition, we give in Table 5.6 the set of demonstratives described by Reed *et al.* (1977), for the Alaskan Yup'ik dialect.

Table 5.6 *Alaskan Yup'ik Eskimo demonstrative pronouns*

| Extended | Restricted | Obscured | |
|---|---|---|---|
| man'a | una | | 'this (near speaker)' |
| tamana | tauna | | 'that (near listener)' |
| | | imna | 'the aforementioned one' |
| ukna | | | 'the one approaching speaker' |
| aûgna | ingna | amna | 'the one going away from speaker' |
| agna | ikna | akemna | 'the one across there' |
| qaûgna | kiûgna | qamna | 'the one inland, inside, upriver' |
| qagna | keggna | qakemna | 'the one outside' |
| un'a | kan'a | camna | 'the one below, toward river' |
| unegna | ugna | cakemna | 'the one downriver, by the exit' |
| paûgna | pingna | pamna | 'the one up there, away from river' |
| pagna | pikna | pakemna | 'the one up above' |

Some of these elements have other specialized meanings; some other specialized meanings that have been reported for other dialects (e.g. 'the one to the right (or left) of *Sp*', 'the one to the north (south, east, west) of *Sp*') are not cited for Alaskan Yup'ik, but are apparently quite consistent with a system of this sort. There are, in addition, a number of suffixes which can be added to the deictic elements in Table 5.6, yielding even more specific and precise locational information.

### 3.0 Temporal deixis

While the representation of spatially deictic notions in language often forms a highly structured, complex system at the heart of the grammar, deictic notions of time do not generally have the same degree of centrality. We therefore provide only a very brief sketch below of some of the ways in which temporal reference is structured. We begin by noting the nature of the linguistic representation of temporal concepts, and proceed to mention the areas of grammar in which they are realized.

### 3.1 *The character of temporal units and relations*

The following discussion is based rather directly on Fillmore (1975), to which we refer the interested reader for much more detailed treatment of the relevant notions.

Time is generally thought of as a unidirectional stream, such that any two events can be uniquely and necessarily related by their ordering along a single dimension. One event is either *earlier*, *simultaneous with*, or *later* than another, and of course many references to temporal relations are explicitly in these terms. In other instances, however, the dimension of time is conceptualized as analogous to a spatial one, and we may say that an event is *ahead of* or *behind* another in time.

Basically, there are two distinct ways of representing the passage of time (and therewith the relations between events differing in time): one may either think of 'the world' as constant, and of time as flowing past it from the future into the past; or one may think of time itself as constant, and of 'the world' as passing through it from the past into the future. In the terms of the first metaphor, we may speak of 'the coming' week, as opposed to the weeks 'gone by'; in the terms of the 'moving world' metaphor, on the other hand, we may speak of 'the week ahead'. In obvious ways, we may speak of one time as 'near' to another, or of events as 'far apart' in time as well as in space. These spatial metaphors are quite frequently the basis, in rather direct ways, of temporal references in natural languages.

Among expressions referring to temporal elements, we can distinguish between those that concern time points (like 'twelve o'clock') and time periods (like 'this afternoon'). The latter, of course, can be uniquely specified in terms of their beginning and ending points. Furthermore, time periods can be divided into those that designate simply a fixed length of time, and those that are fixed by reference to some recurring cycle of fixed points. 'December', for example, is such a calendric unit, while 'a fortnight' seems to have only a non-calendric use.

Of course, in addition to reference to points or intervals of time, seen from 'outside' the temporal dimension itself, we also must recognize what is perhaps the most important and pervasive distinction in temporal reference: that separating the present, the past, and the future. It is this distinction that is essentially deictic, and the deictic character of other temporal terms derives from their reference to it.

## 3.2 *The formal representation of temporal deixis*

Temporal reference appears in grammar in three distinct ways, though only two of these are generally developed. The first, and least common realization of time distinctions, is in terms of a demonstrative system similar to that found in most languages for spatial deixis. Secondly, languages generally make deictic time distinctions in the verbal category of tense; and thirdly, of course, all languages have (varying numbers of) lexical items that are to some extent deictic in their temporal character.

### 3.2.1 *Temporal demonstratives*

Similar to such locational adverbs as 'here' and 'there', languages quite generally have such temporal adverbs as 'now' and 'then': the former referring to 'proximal' time, and the latter to 'distal' time. In English, this can be either in the past or in the future: the question of whether there are languages with a three-term system of temporal adverbs, distinguishing 'now' from 'then-past' and 'then-future' is difficult to resolve without a clearer conception of the difference between purely lexical distinctions (in which these contrasts are of course quite common) and grammaticized ones.

Most languages, however, do not have a system of temporal demonstrative adjectives parallel to (but distinct from) the spatial demonstratives ('this', 'that', etc.). Quite typically, the spatial expressions are imported directly into the temporal domain by means of the metaphorical representation of time as a spatial dimension referred to above: this is the case when we say 'This week, I'm not working' or 'I didn't go home that evening'. Sometimes, the reference involved can be clearly understood by means either of the 'moving time' or the 'moving world' metaphors. For instance, in Woleaian (cf. Sohn 1975), the demonstratives *tog* 'hither, to the *Sp*' and *lag* 'thither, away from the *Sp*' are employed in temporal expressions. A form such as *rag ye tog* 'next year' is thus literally 'the year (coming) hence', and *rag ye lag* 'last year' is literally 'the year (going) away': a clear use of the 'moving time' metaphor.

In the great majority of cases, the system of spatial demonstratives is imported into the temporal domain without any particular modification. An especially direct example is furnished by the deictic demonstratives of Wik-Munkan (cf. Sayers and Kerr 1964). Here, a set of elements is constructed along three orthogonal dimensions. The first of these is a basic three-term, distance oriented system of the sort we have seen in a number of cases above. Superimposed on this is a further dimension, distinguishing points from intervals at each of the three degrees of distance from *Sp*. Finally, to a base composed of elements marking each of the first two dimensions, one adds a suffix indicating either (a) direction (*-pal*); (b) location in a time-dependent fashion: that is, location at some fixed point in time (*-ngul*); or (c) time-independent location (*-man*). The distinction between these two latter categories is not entirely clear from the available description, but is not central to our point here.

The important feature of this system is that it is applicable equally to point/interval locations in space and in time, relative to the location of the *Sp*. Compare the examples in Table 5.7.

Table 5.7 *Wik-Munkan demonstratives*

| Form | Spatial sense | Temporal sense |
|---|---|---|
| inman | right here | right now, today |
| inpal | from here | from now |
| anpal | from there (distant) | from then (on) |
| anman | around there | around now |
| nanpal | from there (near) | from then (recent) |
| nanman | there (close), that place | now (general), any near time |

Some of these terms have apparently acquired special meanings so that the spatial and temporal senses are not always mutually predictable, but by and large the isomorphism between deictic notions in the two domains is maintained.

In these (and indeed in most) systems, the spatial basis of the temporal deictic forms is quite apparent. It is much less common for a language to employ demonstratives with specialized temporal senses that are not (in any obvious way) based on the metaphor of time as space. The only systems we are aware of with specialized temporal demonstratives are found in languages of the Micronesian family, and even here it is usually a set of spatial demonstratives which are employed. In Mokilese (cf. Harrison 1976) for example, we find a three-term, person oriented system of spatial demonstratives (with some additional dimensions, which need not concern us here). From this system, the basic element *-e* 'this; near *Sp*' is employed with time words exclusively to mark future time (e.g. *wihkke lakapw* 'next week (lit. week-future tomorrow)'); the element *-oawe* 'that; near *Adr*' exclusively to mark the present (e.g. *wihkkoawe* 'this week'); and the element *-o* 'that; distant' to mark the past (e.g. *wihkko aio* 'last week (lit. week-past yesterday)').

There is no particularly direct basis for the notion that the future is near to the *Sp*, the present near to the *Adr*, and the past near to neither (at least as far as the standard spatial metaphor for time is concerned), and it appears that these elements (a relatively small subset of the entire demonstrative system; the others have no temporal uses) have become specialized as a set of time deictics. It is also important to distinguish this state of affairs from that seen above in section 2.2 for Malagasy. In that language, spatial deictics agree with the time of the action, and thus include a temporal parameter; but this usage is primarily a matter of an *agreement* category (in the sense of chapter III:3) marked on a basically spatial element, rather than an *inherent* category of temporal deixis. Mokilese, by contrast, marks time as the primary content of a (sub)set of its demonstratives, rather than by agreement with the tense of the main verb or the like.

Other Micronesian languages have slightly different systems of the same basic sort. In Kusaiean (cf. Lee 1975), there is a basic system of four demonstratives: *uh* 'this (near *Sp*)'; *an* 'that (near *Adr*)'; *oh* 'that (distant)'; and *ah* 'that (previously mentioned, regardless of location)'. Of these, it is *ah* ('previously mentioned') that is specialized with time words to indicate the past; *an* ('near *Adr*') that indicates the future; and *uh* ('near *Sp*') either the present or the future (i.e., non-past). The element *oh* ('distant') has no temporal use. If this system is based on a spatial metaphor, it is clearly a different one from that functioning in Mokilese.

Finally, in Trukese (representing yet another distinct subgroup from Mokilese and Kusaiean within the Micronesian family) we find yet another system, involving some elements which are apparently used only with temporal sense. According to the description given by Dyen (1965), Trukese has a basic four-term spatial demonstrative system: *jeej* 'this (near *Sp*)'; *na* 'that (near *Adr* or previously mentioned)'; *naan* 'that (distant)'; and *joob* 'that (out of sight, but known to exist)'. In addition to these, however, there are two further elements: *jewe* 'that (past)', and *jeen* 'that (future; something which is to be seen, taken, etc.)'. These latter elements are not limited in their use to time words proper, but rather indicate that the referent of their associated noun phrase (whatever it is) has its existence (or at least its discourse-interest) primarily in the past or the future, rather than in the immediate present context of the speech event.

These are the only instances of which we are aware in which deictic elements indicate inherent categories of temporal reference, other than by the extension of a transparently spatial metaphor. We pass on now to areas of the grammar in which temporal reference is rather more common.

### 3.2.2 *The category of tense*

Of course, most languages represent an inherent category of temporal reference whose interpretation is necessarily deictic, in the notion of tense. The most basic indication of this sort is by reference to the time of the speech event: the distinction of present, past, and future (or some combination of these categories, as in languages with a 'non-past' tense, like Japanese, or a 'non-future', like Lardil and a number of other Australian languages). Within this categorization, languages may make a number of further distinctions between relatively proximate and relatively distant times. It is rather less common to find inflectional categories referring to particular (rather than relative) times, but it is not unknown: the Australian language Tiwi (cf. Osborne 1974), for example, inflects verbs for whether the action referred to took (or will take, or is taking) place in the morning or in the evening. For more extended remarks on the category of tense, however, cf. chapter III:4 immediately preceding.

### 3.2.3 *Temporal deixis in the lexicon*

Most languages have at least a few words, such as English *home*, *come* and *go*, *foreign*, *local*, *indigenous*, etc., that incorporate spatial references that can only be interpreted (in general) by reference to extra-linguistic features of the situation of an utterance. Less 'lexicalized' (and thus more 'grammaticized') elements such as *this* and *that*, *here* and *there*, however, probably carry the bulk of the burden of indicating deictic location. By contrast, as we have seen, most languages have little or no specialized grammatical apparatus (beyond a limited number of tense distinctions) for indicating deictic time, and thus the bulk of such reference is due to the properties of particular lexical items. Besides *now* and *then*, we have *today*, *yesterday*, and *tomorrow*; days of the week (as in *I'm going there Tuesday*) and other names for calendric units, and a host of others. Many languages display systems with richer sets of deictically anchored day names; Hausa, for instance, has distinct lexical items for naming not only one day in either direction from the present, but three in either direction; Chinantec is said (Fillmore 1975) to go four days in each direction. Some languages, on the other hand, make fewer (or different) distinctions than English: according to Welmers (1973) the major dialects of Igbo use a single form (*écí*) to indicate either 'tomorrow' or 'yesterday' (i.e. a time one day from the present in either direction). A full study of such possibilities for temporal deictic reference in lexical items, like the corresponding study for spatial deixis, would go well beyond the scope of this chapter. The basis for such a study (some of which is outlined by Fillmore 1975) is the classification of time references suggested above in section 3.0: we do not pursue it further here.

## 4.0 Relativized deixis

The essential characteristic of deictic expressions is that their semantic values depend on the real-world context in which they are uttered. But this may not be so when the sentence in which the deictic appears is itself embedded in more complex utterances. Recall our earlier example, repeated in (40):

(40)  a.  He was sick
      b.  Dan will say he was sick

The past tense in (40a) is (absolutely) deictic, in that it specifies a period of time prior to the time of the utterance. In (40b), however, this same sentence does not specify a time prior to the utterance, but rather one prior to the event 'Dan will say'. Since that event is itself future relative to the time of uttering (40b), the past tense element in the embedded clause may or may not be referring to a time prior to the utterance of the entire sentence. The time of 'He was sick' has been *relativized* to that of 'Dan will say'.

For a spatial example, consider (41) below:

(41)  a.  Dan is coming to the office now
      b.  Dan says he will come to the office tomorrow

In (41a), the usual interpretation of the verb *come* requires that Dan be on his way to the office, and that the *Sp* be there at the time of utterance. In (41b), however, while it is still required that Dan proceed to the office, the *Sp* need not be there himself when (41b) is uttered: rather, the most natural interpretation is that he *will* be there tomorrow when Dan arrives. As Fillmore (1966, 1975) has shown, the interpretation of *come* and *go* in English is actually extremely complicated, but one aspect of this complexity is the fact that the deictic locations implicit in these lexical items may be interpreted relative to the location of the *Sp* and *Adr* under some circumstances other than those of the utterance of the sentence itself.

The nature of this process of relativization, and the syntactic and discourse contexts which condition it, are highly complex and poorly understood even for a language as well studied as English: the literature in this area is generally a part of philosophy rather than of linguistics. *A fortiori*, we are not able to characterize the full range of possibilities which may occur across languages here, and will have to content ourselves with merely illustrating a few of the types of relativized interpretation which languages exhibit and with respect to which languages may vary.

### 4.1 *Relativization of deixis in indirect discourse*

One of the most likely contexts across languages in which the interpretation of deictics may be relativized to that of other sentence elements is that of reported speech (and, by extension, in utterances reporting thoughts, beliefs, etc.). Compare, for example, the direct quote in (42a) with its report in (42b):

(42)     a. 'I will go' Dan said

        b. Dan said that he would go

The embedded sentence in (42b), (*that*) *he would go*, expresses the content of Dan's speech: that is, it expresses the information contained (explicitly) in the direct quote in (42a). To describe certain differences among languages in the interpretation of relativized deictics, it will be convenient to describe (in the terms of Jakobson 1957) the 'shift' from the use of the deictic elements in (42a) in comparison with their reported speech counterparts in the embedded sentence in (42b). For instance, in reported speech (in English), the first person singular pronoun shifts to a third person singular pronoun; and the future tense form *will* shifts to *would*. Note that, while *would* has many uses in English, one of the principal ones is to serve as a future relative to a past. In isolation, in fact, *He would go* is not a grammatical sentence. English thus has certain 'tense' forms which are distinctive to such relativized uses. The shifted form of *I* in (42b), namely *he*, is by contrast not a distinctively relativized form of the first person singular pronoun, since *he* occurs independently in simple sentences with a third person singular meaning (just the meaning it has in (42b) as well). Other languages, however, may differ from English in both of these respects.

In a number of West African languages, for example (e.g. Yoruba, a Kwa language; Kera, a Chadic language; and Aghem, a Grassfields Bantu language), the first person singular pronouns may shift to distinctive relativized forms, referred to in the literature as *logophoric* pronouns. Consider the following examples from Aghem (taken from Hyman 1979):

(43)     a. Wìzɨ́n  mɔ̀  dzὲ  ñi'á ò  mɔ̀  bvὺ nò
        woman PAST say  that 3SG PAST fall
        'The woman said that he/she(≠ the woman) fell'

b. Wìzín  mɔ̀ dzè n̄ɨ á é   mɔ̂ bvʉ̀ nò
woman PAST say that she PAST fall
'The woman said that she(= the woman) fell'

The pronoun *é* in (43b) does not exist as a single main clause pronoun in the language synchronically (though historically it represents a third person singular object pronoun which was later displaced by the demonstrative pronoun *wín*). Its function in embedded clauses is to indicate essential coreference with a noun phrase in a higher clause. In distinction to English, then, the shifted form of first person singular pronouns in Aghem is a distinctively relativized form.

On the other hand, again in contrast with English, languages may *not* have distinctive shifted tense forms. Thus, compare (42) above with their translations into modern Hebrew:

(44)   a. 'Ani elex'    Dan amar
         I     go(FUT) Dan said
         ' "I will go" Dan said'

       b. Dan amar she-hu  yelex
          Dan said  that-he go(FUT)
          'Dan said that he would go'

Clearly, the first person singular pronoun *ani* has shifted to a third person singular form *hu*, as in English, but otherwise the same future tense found in the direct quote is also used (subject to phonologically conditioned variation) in the reported speech of (44b). There is thus no distinctive form for the future relative to the past in Hebrew. Hebrew has only three tenses (present, past, and future), and in general we observe much less tense shifting than in English. For example, in simple 'if–then' sentences in English (and French, among others), if the 'then' clause is future, the 'if' clause is neutralized to present: cf. *if he comes I'll leave*. In Hebrew, by contrast, such sentences translate literally as 'if he will come I will leave'.

Our impression is that English shifts a great deal with regard to person and time deixis, whereas not uncommonly in other languages we find that the form of deictics used in direct quotes is carried over into reported speech (as was the case with future tense in the Hebrew example just considered). This is the case, for example, in Aghem (cf. Hyman 1979):

(45)   Wìzín  'vú ndzè à wín n̄i'á é   ŋgé  'lɨghá wò
       woman that say to him that she much like  you
       'The woman said to him that she liked him a lot'

Note that the use of the logophoric pronoun *é* would seem to force an indirect discourse interpretation; nonetheless the direct quote deictic form *wò* 'you' is used with intended coreference to *wín* 'him' in the main clause.

Similar facts can be attested from a number of unrelated languages, including Persian (cf. Rastorgueva 1964): ·

(46)    Be šoma xäbär dad-ø    ke  be koja   xab-äm räft
        to  you  know gave-3SG that to where will-1SG go
        'He informed you where he would go'

Kannada (cf. Bhat 1978):

(47)    Nanage bahuma:na bandideyendu ra:ju tilisidda:ne
        me to   prize          come has thus Raju informed has
        'Raju has informed (me) that I have won a prize'
    *or* 'Raju has informed (me) that he (= Raju) has won a prize'

and Navajo (cf. Akmajian and Anderson 1970):

(48)    a. Jáan beʔesdzą́ą́ ʔáyóí-yóʔní ńtéé? Bill hatsiʔ
           John wife(3SG) 3SG-loves  but  Bill daughter(4SG)
           ʔayóí-ʔájóʔní haɫní
           4SG-loves     said
           'John loves his wife, but Bill told (someone else) that he (John) loves his (John's) daughter'
        b. Jáan beʔesdzą́ą́ ʔáyói-yóʔní ńtéé? Bill ʔéi nitsiʔ
           John wife(3SG) 3SG-loves  but  Bill 4SG daughter(2SG)
           ʔayóí-ʔííníʔ haɫní
           2SG-love     said
           'John loves his wife, but Bill told him (John) that he (John) loves his (John's) daughter'

In sentence (48a) above, the first clause is in the third person, but the coreferential deictics in the second clause are in the 'fourth' person by virtue of the Navajo obviation system (noted above in section 1.0), to keep them distinct from the third person forms referring to the main subject (Bill). Obviation thus serves as a systematic person shift, yielding unique forms similar in function to the Aghem logophoric pronouns (although this is not their only use, as we have already noted). In (48b), on the other hand, since the subject of the embedded clause in the second conjunct (as well as the coreferential possessive marker) is the same as the indirect object of the verb of saying, these forms are shifted into second person forms, rather than fourth (obviative). This takes place despite the fact that the indirect object pronoun itself (*ʔéi*), with which they are coreferential, is a fourth person form.

These remarks have primarily been concerned with the systematic shifts in person marking elements that occur in embedded (particularly indirect discourse) contexts. We have also pointed to the fact that languages often have systematic principles shifting tense as well, however. Indeed, traditional grammars quite generally give rules for (at least some such) shifts of tense, under the heading of 'sequence of tense' rules. It is beyond the scope of the present chapter to survey such phenomena; for some further remarks on this topic see chapter III:4.

In general, then, it appears that person and time deictics in indirect discourse contexts may either shift or not, depending on the language, and if they do shift it may be either to independently existing forms of the same category or to special forms employed by the language particularly for relativized deixis. It must, of course, be emphasized that a serious and systematic survey of the range of possible deictic shifts and the contexts that govern them remains to be done.

### 4.2 *Relativization of spatial and time deictics*
Spatial deictics seem to behave rather differently from the person deictic elements considered in the previous section. In extended discourse (but not specifically in reported speech), the distal (= not close to *Sp*) spatial deictics may function to corefer with something already mentioned in the discourse, as in the following English examples:

(49)    a.      John just went to Chicago

        b.  (i) What's he going to do there (*here)?
           (ii) That (*this) is an awfully windy city

Note that, as a response to (49a), the forms in (49b) with proximal demonstratives are only possible if the speaker is in fact presently in Chicago, so that the deictic can be interpreted absolutely. Only the distal demonstrative is possible if the interpretation is to be derived from the discourse, despite the discourse 'proximity' of the mention of 'Chicago'.

It is quite general that distal spatial deictics can be used in this anaphoric fashion, taking their reference relative to something specified in the discourse rather than absolutely from the circumstances of the speech act. Languages with more than one distal form may differ, however, in which is used most typically in this role. Some languages, furthermore, have distinct forms for such discourse-anaphoric deictics. An example is Woleaian (cf. Sohn 1975): in this language, in addition to the basic three-term deictic system (with additional dimensions as well: cf. section 2.2 above), there are two additional elements *we* (singular) and *kawe* (plural) used for referring to previously mentioned elements or old information, without regard to actual location.

In contrast with person and temporal deictics, the relativization of spatial deictics is not general in English in reported speech.

(50)    *Some student said that nobody liked that student

(50) cannot be interpreted with both instances of *student* referring to the same person, since it is not possible to use *that* in such a relativized deictic way. We can also recall the system of deictic verbal prefixes in Abaza cited above in section 2.0, where the impossibility of interpreting the 'hither' prefix with respect to the location of the action, as opposed to the present, absolute location of the *Sp*, was quite clear.

English spatial deictics, in fact, despite certain appearances to the contrary, do not appear to have shifted forms of any sort in reported speech. For example, (51b) cannot be used to report (51a):

(51)    a. 'I'll put the book here/in this drawer', John said

          b. John said that he would put the book there/in that drawer

In (51b), the reference of *there* or *in that drawer* must be understood either in terms of a location or a drawer present in the speech context of (51b) (that is, as absolutely deictic, similar to the only possible interpretation of (49b) with proximal demonstratives above). Otherwise, the reference of those terms is understood as anaphoric to some location or drawer presented in the previous discourse. If it were possible for *there* to serve as a shifted form of *here*, then (51b) would also have the meaning of 'John said he would put the book in the place he was indicating when he said "I'll put the book here"' – a meaning the sentence does not in fact have.

The possibility of shifting or relativizing the reference of temporal deictic lexical elements is quite complex, and little studied. For some speakers, a sentence like (52b) cannot be used to report (52a):

(52)    a. 'I'll do it tomorrow', John said

          b. John said that he would do it the day after

For such speakers, it is not possible to interpret *the day after* (or *the next day*) in (52b) as meaning the day after John made the quoted utterance in (52a). Other speakers, however, allow such relativization of temporal expressions. Some lexical items, such as French *le lendemain*, uniquely specify such a relative interpretation. Further, temporal expressions involving reference to positional terms generally allow or even require relative interpretation:

(53)    a. 'I'm going to finish this paper on Friday', John said

      b. John said that he would finish the paper on Friday

      c. 'I'm going to finish the paper this Friday', John said

      d. John said he would finish the paper this Friday

      e. John said he would finish the paper that Friday

Sentence (53b) may be taken as a report of (53a), referring to a Friday determined by reference to the time of John's utterance (typically, the immediately following one). For some speakers, however, (53b) can also be used to report John's intention to finish the paper by a Friday determined with reference to the time of the speech act: quite possibly, a very different Friday. (53d), in contrast, has only this absolute interpretation, as we would expect since it contains a proximal demonstrative. It thus cannot be used to report (53c) unless the two speech acts occur within the same week. In (53e), finally, it is only the relativized interpretation that is available.

Clearly, the approach to these problems even in well-studied languages like English has only begun, and attempts to formulate valid cross-linguistic descriptions would be quite premature. If field workers are aware of the general distinction between absolute and relative interpretation of deictic elements, however, considerably more information may become available on this topic in the future.


## 5 Conclusion

We have surveyed above the principal systematic areas of grammar in which the extralinguistic context of the utterance determines the interpretation of linguistic elements: the categories of person, social relations, spatial demonstratives, and temporal reference. We have seen that a relatively small inventory of possible contrasts (though a larger one than is obvious from the study of English and other European languages alone) is exploited across languages. In some cases, such grammaticized deictic systems are quite central to the nature of the language: the system of spatial demonstrativeness in Kwakw'ala, for example, was taken by Boas to be a pervasive feature of utterances in this language of major typological significance. Other languages employ the same notions to a considerably smaller extent (except in their lexicons), although a minimal person/number system and at least a two-term spatial demonstrative system seem to be universal.

# 6 Causative verb formation and other verb-deriving morphology*

BERNARD COMRIE

## 0 Introduction

In this chapter, we are concerned with that part of derivational morphology dealing with the formation of new verbs, whether from existing verbs (sections 1–3) or from other parts of speech (section 4). Special attention has been given to causative verbs (section 2); causatives are a source of great interest at present, not only because of the important role they play in the derivational morphology of many languages, but also because of the way their analysis requires a complex approach combining syntax, semantics, and morphology. Many of the general problems in dealing with derivational morphology can be illustrated in a particularly clear way with examples of causatives, and this we have tried to do in section 2. Section 4 (verbs derived from other parts of speech) and, to a lesser extent, section 3 (verbs derived from verbs without valency change), are intended primarily to illustrate some of the kinds of semantic relations that hold between derived verbs and the forms they are derived from, rather than to provide a complete and systematic classification of such relations: such an account seems impossible, at least for the present.

General problems that will occur throughout this chapter, as indeed throughout this volume, include the dividing-line between derivational morphology and syntax and inflectional morphology on the one hand, between derivational morphology and the lexicon as a structured list on the other. A second set of problems is concerned with the direction of derivation. In many instances, the direction of derivation is clear from the forms: one form has an affix that is lacking in the other, from which it can be considered to be derived. Often, however, one finds that each form has a different affix, or that there is no segmentable morpheme difference (the difference being shown, for instance, by vowel alternation); in such cases it is often difficult to decide whether one form should be derived from the other, or whether a reciprocal derivation should be established, or whether perhaps both forms should be derived

Table 6.1. *Derivational relationships among some Russian verbs*

| I | | II | III |
|---|---|---|---|
| 'sit' | sidet' (sidi-) | i. $\begin{cases} \text{sadit' (sadi-)} \\ \text{sažat' (sažaj-)} \end{cases}$ | sadit'-sja (sadi- ... -sja) |
| | | p. po-sadit' (po-sadi-) | sest' (sjad-) |
| 'lie' | ležat' (leži-) | i. klast' (klad-) | ložit'-sja (loži- ... -sja) |
| | | p. po-ložit' (po-loži-) | leč' (ljag-) |
| 'stand' | stojat' (stoi-) | i. stavit' (stavi-) | stanovit'-sja (stanovi ... -sja) |
| | | p. po-stavit' (po-stavi-) | stat' (stan-) |

from some third form that does not exist as a separate word in the language. For the sake of convenience, we have used direction of derivation as one of our criteria in classifying verbal derivation below (e.g. transitives from intransitives, intransitives from transitives), but the problems inherent in generalizing this criterion should not be lost sight of.

To illustrate the range of problems that can occur, Table 6.1 shows three series of derivationally related Russian verbs. The first set is concerned with sitting position, the second with lying position, the third with standing position. Each series is divided into three, as indicated by the roman numerals: I indicates a state (e.g. 'to be in a sitting position'), III entry into a state (e.g. 'to assume a sitting position'), and II the causative equivalent of III (e.g. 'to put someone/something into a sitting position'). Within II and III, forms for both imperfective (i.) and perfective (p.) aspect are given. In each instance, both the infinitive and the non-past stem are given. The semantic relations are perfectly regular; the formal relations are irregular to an extent that involves most of the problems discussed above. Although aspect is usually considered an inflectional category in Russian, the prefixes and suffixes used to mark aspectual distinctions (such as perfective *po-*) function otherwise as derivational affixes, and such aspectual pairs as *sadit'-sja/sest'*, *ložit'-sja/leč'*, *stanovit'-sja/stat'* have formal relations well outside the usual gamut of Russian inflectional morphology. In column II, one finds a regular formal and semantic relation between *sadit'* and *po-sadit'*, between *stavit'* and *po-stavit'*, but no formal relation between *klast'* and *po-ložit'*. From a formal viewpoint, *klast'* is a distinct lexical item, although its semantic function strongly calls for integration into the overall system shown in Table 6.1. Russian, incidentally, has no simple verb *\*ložit'*; the tendency for *sadit'* to be replaced by *sažat'* may soon mean that the simple verb *sadit'* will also be non-existent. Statement of the direction of derivation is complicated by vowel alternations (e.g. *lež-*, *lož-*, 'lie') and alternation of theme suffixes (e.g. *-e-* and *-i-* in *sid-e-t'*, *sad-i-t'*), which means that different forms often contain exactly the same number of morphemes. In some instances, direction of derivation seems to be readily dictated by morphological complexity, for example *po-sadit'* is derived from *sadit'* by prefixing *po-*, and *sadit'-sja* from *sadit'* by suffixing *-sja*. But generalization of these derivational processes would suggest that the perfective in column III should be *\*po-sadit'-sja*, a form which, like *\*po-ložit'-sja* and *\*po-sta(no)vit'-sja*, does not exist; the actual form is *sest'*. Indeed, apart from the anomalous *klast'*, the forms *sest'*, *leč'*, *stat'* contain fewer morphemes than any of the other forms, having no theme suffix between the stem and the infinitive ending *-t'*. Overall, then, it is not possible to say without reservation that the column III forms are derived from the corresponding column II forms.

The Russian examples in Table 6.1 illustrate the kind of lack of formal systematicity that one is particularly likely to find with such common words of the basic vocabulary. Although much of derivational morphology is far more regular than this – and we have concentrated on such examples below – field-workers investigating derivational morphology in detail should not be surprised if they encounter subparts of the derivational morphology of comparable idiosyncrasy.

In discussing Table 6.1, we did not present English glosses for all of the Russian forms. In fact, while Russian has a distinction in form for each of columns I, II, and III, the corresponding English forms often cover two or three of these columns. Thus *to stand* is the same for I, II, and III. Although *to seat* exists as a separate form for column II, *to sit* can be used in this sense, as well as for columns I and III. Only with *to lie* (I and III) versus *to lay* (II) does English (at least, Standard English) have an absolute distinction. This is a situation which will recur frequently in the discussion below: where many other languages utilize derivational processes, English often has no formal distinction at all (e.g. *to stand*), or uses completely non-productive and idiosyncratic formal relationships (e.g. *sit/seat*, *lie/lay*), or simply has different lexical items (e.g. *kill* as causative of *die*). For this reason, English examples figure little in the discussion below.

The Russian examples of Table 6.1 illustrate the situation where one has semantic regularity with morphological irregularity. Sometimes, one finds the inverse of this. For instance, Classical Arabic has a number of verbal derivatives (traditionally, fifteen, including the basic form or first derivative), all using the same root (usually consisting of three consonants, symbolized here $c_1c_2c_3$). Each derivative has the same morphological pattern for all verbs, but some patterns carry a number of possible meanings, and a particular derivative of a particular verb may well have an idiosyncratic meaning. Thus the third derivative has the form $c_1\bar{a}c_2ac_3a$, for example *kātaba* 'correspond with' (taking as direct object the person corresponded with; cf. basic *kataba* 'write'), *xādaʕa* 'try to deceive' (cf. *xadaʕa* 'deceive'), *fāxara* 'compete with someone for praise' (cf. *faxara* 'praise'), *xāšana* 'treat harshly' (cf. *xašuna* 'be harsh'). Although such semantic features as 'conative' ('to try to V') and 'reciprocal' can be factored out of a number of third derivatives, the combinations are by no means predictable, and where there is no corresponding first derivative (basic verbal form), the relation to the root noun is often very idiosyncratic: *sāfara* 'to travel' (cf. *safar* 'journey'), *sāḥala* 'make for the coast' (cf. *sāḥil* 'coast'), *ʕāyana* 'see with one's eyes' (cf. *ʕayn* 'eye').

## 1.0 Verbs formed from verbs with valency change

One often finds that a given verb can occur with a different number or arrangement of its noun phrase arguments in semantically well-formed sentences, as in the following English examples:

(1)    John is boiling the water

(2)    The water is boiling

(3)    Mary is reading the book

(4)    Mary is reading

(5)    Mary is reading the book to John

In these examples, the form of the English verbs *boil* and *read* does not change to show the different actual valencies of the verbs in the different sentences. Many languages, however, have derivational processes of varying degrees of systematicity to indicate such changes of valency. Occasionally, even English has such derivationally related verbs:

(6)    Trees fall

(7)    Lumberjacks fell trees

Below, we examine such derivational relations in more detail. For convenience of exposition, we treat separately valency changes where the subject is not involved in the change (section 1.1) and valency changes where the subject is involved (section 1.2).

### 1.1 *Valency change: objects only*

With many verbs, semantically well-formed sentences can be constructed where the number and type of object noun phrases varies, without any change in the subject of the sentence. For instance, the verb *read* can appear with only a direct object (*Mother is reading a book*), with no object at all (*Mother is reading*), or with an indirect object, usually in addition to the direct object (*Mother is reading a book to John*). In English, as so often, these differences in valency are not marked by any change in the forms of the verb; in many languages, verbs are marked for such changes in valency, either in all instances or, in some languages, only for certain lexical verbs. Such formal coding of differences in valency can indicate either (a) a decrease in the number of objects, or (b) an increase in the number of objects, or (c) a rearrangement of the objects, relative to the valency of the basic non-derived verb. Types (a) and (b) (increase and rearrangement of valency) often utilize the same formal mechanism, and in some instances it is difficult to separate them, as will be seen in some of the examples below; in particular, where rearrangement involves transforming some peripheral argument of the verb (e.g. an instrument phrase) into an argument more closely bound to the verb (a direct object), the effects of valency-increase and valency-rearrangement are often indistinguishable. Similarly, some instances of valency-rearrangement are similar to valency-decrease.

### 1.1.1 *Valency-increase and valency-rearrangement*

In German, a number of verbs in their basic form take an oblique (prepositional) object, but in addition there are derivationally related (prefixed) verbs, with essentially the same lexical meaning, taking a direct object; the number of objects is in either case one, but differences in verbal derivational morphology permit different coding of this object, for example:

(8)     Hans bittet um Hilfe
(9)     Hans er-bittet Hilfe

        'Hans asks for help'

In other instances, the basic verb can take two objects, one direct and the other oblique; the oblique object is usually omissible. The derived verb also takes two objects, but the other way round: the noun phrase that is direct object of the basic verb becomes oblique object of the derived verb (and is usually omissible), while the noun phrase that is oblique object of the basic verb becomes direct object of the derived verb, and is not omissible, for example:

(10)    Hans pflanzt Bäume (im Garten)
        'Hans plants trees (in the garden)'

(11)   Hans be-pflanzt den Garten (mit Bäumen)
       'Hans plants the garden (with trees)'

As can be seen from the glosses to these examples, English too has the possibility of rearranging the objects of many verbs (*to plant X in Y, to plant Y with X*), but typically without any change in the verb. Russian behaves here like German, for example:

(12)   Ivan sejet/posejal pšenicu (v pole)
       'Ivan sows/sowed wheat (in the field)'

(13)   Ivan zaseivajet/zasejal pole (pšenicej)
       'Ivan sows/sowed the field (with wheat)'

The verb in (12) is *sejat'* (imperfective)/*po-sejat'* (perfective), that in (13) is the derivationally related verb *zaseivat'* (imperfective)/*za-sejat'* (perfective). The change in arguments between (12) and (13) is much as in the English glosses: *pšenicu* 'wheat' is accusative (direct object) in (12) and *v pole* 'in [the] field' is a prepositional phrase; in (13), *pole* is accusative (direct object), while *pšenicej* 'with wheat' is instrumental, which in Russian does not require a preposition.

Although the range of semantic arguments permitted by such basic verbs as German *pflanzen* or Russian *sejat'* is the same as the range of semantic arguments permitted by the derived verbs *bepflanzen* and *zaseivat'*, this does not necessarily mean that sentences containing, for instance, *sejat'* and *zaseivat'* have exactly the same meaning, only that the semantic roles expressed by the noun phrases are the same. In (13) with *zaseivat'*, for instance, just as in its English gloss, there is the implication that the whole of the field was sown with wheat; whereas in (12) with *sejat'*, as in its English gloss, there is no such implication, and it is quite possible that only a small amount of wheat was sown in a small part of the field. Derivationally related verbs with different arrangements of objects may therefore give rise to sentences with differing meaning, although the semantic roles are the same with both basic and derived verb.

The examples just discussed from German and Russian are primarily of valency-rearrangement, although the rearrangement of the arguments does entail differences in which arguments can optionally be omitted. We shall now turn to some clear examples of valency-increase. In Chukchee, a number of verbs require no change in derivational morphology when they are used with or without a direct object, as in the following examples:

(14)   ənpənačg-a   rʔeyip-ərkən-in pagtəlgən
       old man-ERG drill-PRES-he/it sledge runner
       'The old man is drilling the sledge-runner'

(15)   ənpənačg-ən rˀeyip-ərkən
       old man-ABS drill-PRES
       'The old man is drilling'

(Chukchee has ergative case marking of noun phrases, so the case marking of the subject is different in the two sentences. Verbs agree with subject and direct object, so the inflections on the verb are also different.) Many verbs, however, do require coding of valency changes. Increased valency can be marked, for instance, by the prefix *r(ə)-*, often accompanied by a suffix, such as *-v*, *-et/-at*, or *-ŋet/-ŋat*; the choice of suffix is lexically determined. Thus *vaŋe-k* 'to sew' (*-(ə)k* is the infinitive ending) is basically intransitive; if a direct object is to be added, the derivationally related verb *rə-vaŋe-v-ək* is used. Similarly, *viliv-ək* 'to sell, trade' is basically intransitive, the derivationally related transitive verb is *rə-viliv-et-ək*:

(16)   ətləg-ən   viliv-ərkən ŋoten-velətkora-k
       father-ABS sell-PRES   this-shop-in
       'Father trades in this shop'

(17)   ətləg-e   rə-viliv-et-ərkəni-net    ənn-ət
       father-ERG  -sell  -PRES-he/them fish-ABS PL
       'Father sells fish'

   A very systematic means of coding valency-increase is found in Wolof. A given verb has a certain basic valency (no object, e.g. *dem* 'go'; one object, e.g. *dyàng* 'read'; or two objects, e.g. *dyaay* 'sell'). Decrease in valency relative to this basic valency is not marked:

(18)   Mungi    dyàng tééré bi
       PRES(3SG) read   book the
       'He is reading the book'

(19)   Mungi dyàng
       'He is reading'

(20)   Di na  nyu la  dyaay suma xar
       FUT AUX 3PL you sell   my    sheep
       'They will sell my sheep to you'

(21)   Di na nyu dyaay suma xar
       'They will sell my sheep'

(22)   Di na nyu la dyaay
       'They will sell to you'

(23)    Nyungi    dyaay
        PRES(3PL) sell
        'They are selling'

Where, however, a verb has more objects than is permitted by its basic valency, this must be coded by adding the suffix -al for each additional object. The precise semantic role of the additional objects can vary, determined in part by lexical specification, but common semantic roles are accompaniment, recipient, benefactive:

(24)    Nga       dem
        AUX(2SG) go
        'You went'

(25)    Kan nga dem-al?
        'Who did you go with?'

(26)    Mungi dyàng tééré bi                                    (= (18))
        'He is reading the book'

(27)    Mungi     dyàng-al eleew yi      tééré-ém
        PRES(3SG) read-      pupil the(PL) book-his
        'He is reading his book to the pupils'

(28)    Di naa        toogal nenne bi
        FUT AUX(1SG) seat    child   the
        'I will seat the child

(29)    Di naa la toogal-al nenne bi
        'I will seat the child for you'

One of the best-known derivational processes leading to increase or rearrangement of objects is the prepositional (applicative) verb form in Bantu languages, although parallel formations also exist in many other languages. In Swahili, for instance, the addition of the applicative suffix (APPL) increases the verb's valency by one. The commonest semantic roles of the additional noun-phrase argument are benefactive (or, with semantically appropriate verbs, the opposite of this, i.e. 'to someone's detriment'), recipient, motion towards. The additional argument functions as (closest) direct object to the applicative verb, while a direct object of the basic verb loses many of its direct object properties, including the possibility of being encoded as an object prefix before the verb stem. Examples are:

(30)    Mtoto a-li-kimbia
        child   he-PAST-run away
        'The child ran away'

(31)     Mtoto a-li-m-kimbi-lia                    mama   wake
         child   he-PAST-her-run away-APPL mother his
         'The child ran away to his mother'

(32)     Musa a-li-andika              barua
         Musa he-PAST-send-APPL letter
         'Musa sent a letter'

(33)     Musa a-li-ni-andik-ia              barua
         Musa he-PAST-me-send-APPL letter
         'Musa sent me a letter'

(34)     Ni-me-lima          shamba
         I-PERF-cultivate plantation
         'I have cultivated the plantation'

(35)     Ni-me-m-lim-ia              Musa shamba
         I-PERF-him-cultivate-APPL Musa plantation
         'I have cultivated the plantation for Musa'

In some instances, there are synonymous or nearly synonymous equivalents to the applicative construction using the basic form of the verb and
an oblique object (with a preposition, often complex, e.g. *kwa ajili ya*
'for (the sake of)'), for example:

(36)     Nimelima shamba kwa ajili ya Musa
         'I have cultivated the plantation for (the sake of) Musa'

In such instances, one can speak of rearrangements of objects, rather
than of increase in valency. However, such paraphrases are not always
available, so that there are instances of clear increase in valency. This is
one place where the distinction between valency-increase and valency-
rearrangement is difficult to maintain absolutely.

    Another language which has applicative verb forms increasing the
valency is Classical Nahuatl:

(37)     Ni-tlaōco-ya
         I-be sad-
         'I am sad'

(38)     Ni-mitz-tlaōco-lia
         I-you-be sad-APPL
         'I am sad for you, sorry for you'

(39)     Ni-c-pāca
         I-it-wash
         'I wash it'

(40)    Ni-c-no-pāqui-lia
        I-it-myself-wash-APPL
        'I wash it for myself'

(41)    Ni-mitz-tla-pāca-ltia
        I-you-something-wash-CAUSE
        'I make you wash something'

(42)    Ni-mitz-no-tla-paca-lti-lia
        I-you-myself-something-wash-CAUSE-APPL
        'I make you wash something for me'

In the examples given so far of increase of valency, the semantic correlate of the additional argument has been fairly nebulous: although there is a tendency for it to be interpreted as a benefactive or a recipient, other interpretations may be forced by the context (e.g. 'to the detriment of') or by language-specific rules (e.g. motion towards with intransitive verbs of motion in Swahili; accompaniment with many intransitive verbs in Wolof). Sometimes, however, processes for increasing verbal valency are more specific in their semantic function. In Wolof, for instance, the verbal suffix -e enables an instrumental noun phrase (otherwise constructed with the preposition ag) to appear as a direct object:

(43)    Mungi    lekk ag   kuddu
        PRES(3SG) eat   with spoon
(44)    Mungi lekk-e kuddu

        'He is eating with a spoon'

In Luganda, the suffix -is is used in this way, as an alternative to the preposition na (n' before a vowel):

(45)    John yatta enkoko n'   ekiso
        John killed chicken with knife
(46)    John yatt-isa ekiso enkoko

        'John killed the chicken with a knife'

Luganda also has an applicative suffix corresponding to that illustrated above for Swahili, with primarily benefactive meaning:

(47)    John yatt-ira mukazi enkoko
        'John killed the chicken for the woman'

(It is not, incidentally, possible in Luganda to have both instrumental and benefactive suffixes simultaneously on a single verb.) The instrumental verbal suffix in Wolof and Luganda is so regular in its use that it more properly belongs to syntax, rather than to derivational morphology.

### 1.1.2 *Valency-decrease and valency-rearrangement*

In many languages, a derivational marker must be used when some argument of a verb is omitted, either in all instances, or for specific lexical items, or according to other criteria. In Russian, for instance, many verbs that normally take a direct object can also be used without a direct object, for example *čitat'* 'to read', *nesti* 'to lay (eggs)', *kusat'* 'to bite'. Where there is no direct object, *čitat'* requires no change in derivational morphology, whereas *nesti* and *kusat'* require the so-called reflexive suffix *-sja* (after vowels *-s'*):

(48)   Boris čitajet knigi
       'Boris reads books'

(49)   Boris čitajet
       'Boris reads'

(50)   Kury nesut jajca
       'Hens lay eggs'

(51)   Kury nesut-sja
       'Hens lay'

(52)   Sobaka kusajet počtal'ona
       'The dog bites the postman'

(53)   Sobaka kusajet-sja
       'The dog bites'

For some verbs that take *-sja* to show valency-reduction (omission of the direct object), the suffix *-sja* is used only where the situation referred to is a habitual situation, but not, for instance, where a specific instance is referred to. One such verb in Russian is *kusat'* (perfective *ukusit'*) 'to bite', in contrast to *nesti* (perfect *snesti*) 'to lay (eggs)':

(54)   Kurica snesla jajco
       'The hen has laid an egg'

(55)   Kurica snesla-s'
       'The hen has laid'

(56)   Sobaka ukusila počtal'ona
       'The dog has bitten the postman'

(57)   Sobaka ukusila/*ukusila-s'
       'The dog has bitten'

Examples similar to those from Russian can be given for Swedish (with the so-called passive suffix -s, etymologically a reflexive pronoun, like Russian -sja) and Hungarian (detransitivizing suffix -kod(ik)/-köd(ik)):

(58)    Hund-en  biter mig
        dog    the bites me
        'The dog bites me'

(59)    Hunden bit-s
        'The dog bites'

(Note that the present tense ending -(e)r is lost before -s.)

(60)    Knuffa mig inte!
        'Don't push me!'

(61)    Knuffa-s inte!
        'Don't push!'

(62)    A csősz gyaláz egy gyereket
        'The parkkeeper curses a child'

(63)    A csősz gyaláz-kodik
        'The parkkeeper uses abusive language'

This formal relationship between transitivity and aspect is even clearer in Yidiɲ (Dixon 1977:273–93), where the same suffix -:d$^y$i- is used both to indicate derived intransitivity and to indicate a continuous situation:

(64)    Yin$^y$d$^y$u:ŋ bun$^y$a:ŋ    mayi         buga-ŋ
        this(ERG)   woman(ERG) vegetables(ABS) eat-PRES
        'This woman is eating vegetables'

(65)    Yiŋu     bun$^y$a       buga-:d$^y$i-ŋ
        this(ABS) woman(ABS)  eat-:d$^y$i-PRES
        'This woman is eating'

(66)    ŋan$^y$an$^y$ bama:l    bun$^y$d$^y$a-:d$^y$i-n$^y$u
        I(ACC)   people(ERG) hit-:d$^y$i-PAST
        'People kept on hitting me'

(Yidiɲ has ergative case marking for non-pronouns, so that bun$^y$a:ŋ is ergative in (64) as subject of a transitive verb, bun$^y$a is absolutive in (65) as subject of an intransitive verb, while bama:l is again ergative as subject of a transitive verb.)

In Dyirbal, overt marking of lexically transitive verbs that have no direct object is obligatory in all instances:

(67)     Balam wud$^y$u baŋgul yaṛa-ŋgu d$^y$aŋga-n$^y$u
        CL     fruit  CL       man-ERG eat-TNS
        'The man eats the fruit'

(68)     Bayi yaṛa d$^y$aŋgay-mari-n$^y$u
        CL   man eat-         -TNS
        'The man eats'

(Dyirbal also has ergative case marking of non-pronouns, so that (68) has the absolutive case *yaṛa* where (67) has ergative *yaṛa-ŋgu*.) In Dyirbal, this process is so regular, systematic, and productive, that it belongs in the domain of syntax rather than of derivational morphology. The derived intransitive is often referred to as the 'antipassive' voice.

As a final example of a language marking derived intransitivity, we may cite Nivkh, where the morpheme that codes derived intransitivity is the prefix *p$^h$-*, also used as a reflexive prefix:

(69)     Ńi larq ot-t′
        I   shirt sew
        'I am sewing the shirt'

(70)     Ńi p$^h$-ot-t′
        'I am sewing'

Although most examples relevant to this section concern basic verbs that take a direct object, omitted with the derived form, it is possible for a language to use derivational morphology to indicate the absence of some other object. In Georgian, for instance, the combination of prefix *i-* and suffix *-eb* can be used both to show the omission of a direct object (e.g. of *xed(av)* 'see') and of an indirect object (e.g. of *h-ķben* 'bite', which in Georgian takes an indirect object):

(71)     Uķan i-xed-eb-i
        behind -see- -2SG
        'You look behind'

(72)     ʒaɣli i-ķbin-eb-a
        dog   -bite- -3SG
        'The dog bites'

Similar to omission of the direct object is the situation where the direct object of the basic verb appears as an oblique object of a derived verb, i.e. valency-rearrangement rather than valency-decrease. An example from Russian, again with the suffix *-sja/-s'* on the verb, would be:

(73)    Boris vstretil Ninu
        'Boris met Nina'

(74)    Boris vstretil-sja s Ninoj
        'Boris met up with Nina'

The simple verb *vstretit'* 'to meet' takes a direct object, whence in (73) the accusative *Ninu*. The derived verb *vstretit'-sja* takes the preposition *s* 'with' (which governs the instrumental case in Russian, whence *Ninoj*).

In some instances where one has derivationally related verbs, the one having one more argument than the other, the direction of derivation is unclear – conceivably, there is no direction of derivation. In the following examples from Nenets, the transitive and intransitive from *pad-* 'write' simply have different suffixes, there is no formal reason for deriving the one from the other (Tereščenko 1973:192):

(75)    Ńe ŋaćeki jun? padar-m? pad-bi
        girl        letter-ACC        write-
        'The girl writes a letter'

(76)    Ńe ŋaćeki pad-na
        'The girl is writing'

### 1.2 *Valency change including subjects*

Having examined valency changes among object noun phrases, we may now turn to examples where subjects are also included in the change. The commonest type here is the derivational relationship between an intransitive verb and a transitive verb where the subject of the intransitive verb is the same as the direct object of the transitive verb, i.e. $s_i v^{intr}$ and $s_j v^{tr} DO_i$, for example *The water boils* and *John boils the water*. (English, as often, has no overt difference between transitive and intransitive verb.) The direction of derivation, where clear from the presence of further affixes on the derived form, can be either (a) from intransitive to transitive; (b) from transitive to intransitive; (c) non-directional, in that either (i) each member has a different affix, or (ii) the difference is expressed by internal change rather than by affixation. A given language may combine several of these: thus Swahili has (a) (e.g. *hama*, transitive *ham-isha* 'move'), (b) (e.g. *vunja*, intransitive *vunj-ika* 'break'), and (c.i) (e.g. intransitive *chem-ka*, transitive *chem-sha* 'boil'). An example of (c.ii) would be Lithuanian intransitive *lūž-ti*, transitive *lauž-ti* 'to break'. Where the direction of derivation in such cases is from intransitive to transitive, the derived transitive is often referred to as 'causative' (e.g. Swahili *hamisha*). Where the direction is from transitive to intransitive, the derived intransitive may be referred to as 'anticausative' (e.g. *vunj-ika*). Although the derivational relationship between transitive and intransitive, with interchange of transitive object and intransitive subject, is the most widespread one involving subjects, there are other possible relationships, as illustrated in the following sections.

### 1.2.1 *Valency-increase (causative)*

Here, the basic verb forms a sentence that describes some situation; the derived verb has a different subject, and the sentence with the derived verb indicates that the referent of this new subject brings about (or, more weakly, fails to prevent) the situation described by the sentence containing the basic verb. This derived construction is referred to as 'causative', and various facets of this construction are discussed in section 2; here, we simply give some illustrative examples. The causative verb may be a transitive verb formed from an intransitive; but it may also, in many languages, be formed from a basic verb already of higher valency, in which case the derived causative always has (at least potentially) one more noun phrase argument than the basic verb. The following examples are from Turkish (causative suffix *-t* or *-dir/-tir*, the latter with vowel harmony variants):

(77)    Hasan öl-dü
        Hasan die-PAST
        'Hasan died'

(78)    Ali Hasan-i    öl-dür-dü
        Ali Hasan-DO die-CAUSE-PAST
        'Ali caused Hasan to die/killed Hasan'

(79)    Müdür  mektub-u imzala-di
        director letter-DO  sign-PAST
        'The director signed the letter'

(80)    Dişçi  mektub-u müdür-e    imzala-t-ti
        dentist letter-DO  director-IO sign-CAUSE-PAST
        'The dentist made the director sign the letter'

(81)    Müdür  Hasan-a mektub-u göster-di
        director Hasan-IO letter-DO show-PAST
        'The director showed the letter to Hasan'

(82)    Dişçi   Hasan-a  mektub-u  müdür   tarafından
        dentist Hasan-IO letter-DO   director by
        göster-t-ti
        show-CAUSE-PAST
        'The dentist got the director to show the letter to Hasan'

The basic verbs are the one-place predicate *öl* 'die', two-place *imzala* 'sign', and three-place *göster* 'show'. The causative sentence in each instance has one more argument. In (82), *tarafından* is a postposition, belonging with *müdür*. The syntax of the noun phrase arguments of the causative verb is discussed in section 2.3.

In Turkish, unlike many languages that have derived causatives, the derivational process is iterative, i.e. one can form causatives of causatives:

(83)    Mehmet Hasan-ı   Ali-ye öl-dür-t-tü
        Mehmet Hasan-DO Ali-IO die-CAUSE-CAUSE-PAST
        'Mehmet made Ali kill Hasan'

The next set of examples is from Chukchee, where the causative has the prefix $r(ə)$-, often also a suffix (apparently lexically determined):

(84)    Qaa-t              melev-g?et (phonetically: melekv?et)
        reindeer-ABS PL heal-3PL
        'The reindeer got better'

(85)    ətləg-e     qaa-t              rə-melev-ninet
        father-ERG reindeer-ABS PL   -heal-he/them
        'Father cured the reindeer'

(86)    Ekke-te čə?-miməl pəl-nin
        son-ERG cold-water drink-he/it
        'The son drank cold water'

(87)    ətləg-e     akka-gtə rə-lpə-ŋen-nin  čə?-miməl
        father-ERG son-IO       -drink-  -he/it cold-water
        'The father gave his son cold water to drink'

(The alternation *ekke-/akka-* 'son' is conditioned by vowel harmony. The verb *pəl-ək* 'to drink' has an irregular medial alternant *-lp-.*) Some Chukchee verbs, for example *məle-k* 'break in two', use exactly the same form for both causative and non-causative, like English *boil, break.*

Finally, here are some examples from Wolof (causative suffix *-al*):

(88)   Nenne bi di na          toog
       child  the FUT AUX(3SG) sit
       'The child will sit down'

(89)   Di naa          toog-al   nenne bi                (= (28))
       FUT AUX(1SG) sit-CAUSE child   the
       'I will make the child sit down'

### 1.2.2 *Valency-decrease (anticausative, reciprocal, reflexive)*

The commonest type here is the anticausative, i.e. derivation of an intransitive verb ($s_iv^{intr}$) from a transitive verb ($s_jv^{tr}DO_i$), as with Swahili *vunj-ika* 'break (intransitive)' from *vunja* 'break (transitive)'. (We are not aware of any language that has a corresponding systematic derivational procedure for reducing the valency of verbs with more than two arguments.) Some further examples are given below:

Russian (anticausative suffix *-sja/-s'*):

(90)   Anton otkryl dver'
       'Anton opened the door'

(91)   Dver' otkryla-s'
       'The door opened'

Hungarian (various anticausative suffixes, including *-ód(ik)/-őd(ik)*:

(92)   Zoltán cukrot old a vízben
       'Zoltan dissolves sugar in the water'

(93)   A cukor a vízben old-ódik
       'The sugar dissolves in water'

Nivkh (anticausative prefix $p^h$-):

(94)   Jeskinivx magazin arkt-t'
       salesman shop        close
       'The salesman closed the shop'

(95)   Magazin $p^h$-arkt-t'
       'The shop closed'

The anticausative is similar in many ways to the passive: in both constructions, typically the direct object of the basic verb appears as subject of the anticausative or passive, for example *Anton opened the door*, anticausative *The door opened*, passive *The door was opened*, cf. Russian *Anton otkryl dver'*, *Dver' otkryla-s'*, *Dver' byla otkryta*. In some (though by no means all) languages, the subject of the basic verb can appear as an agentive phrase in the passive, i.e. there is valency-rearrangement, rather than valency-decrease: thus English *The door was opened by Anton*, Russian *Dver' byla otkryta Antonom*. Passive and anticausative differ in that, even where the former has no agentive phrase, the existence of some person or thing bringing about the situation is implied, whereas the anticausative is consistent with the situation coming about spontaneously. Since the passive falls within the domain of syntax rather than of derivational morphology, we shall not discuss it further here, but simply refer the reader to chapters 1.5 and 1.6.

Reciprocal verbs, as in English *John and Mary met* as opposed to *John met Mary*, introduce a more complex valency change involving subjects. With the reciprocal verb, subject and direct object of the basic verb are combined into a single compound subject: formulaically, basic $S_i V^{tr} DO_j$, reciprocal $S_{i\text{-and-}j} V^{intr}$. The valency of the verb is, of course, reduced, from transitive to intransitive:

Russian (reciprocal suffix -*sja*/-*s'*):

(96)    Anton vstretil Ninu
        'Anton met Nina'

(97)    Anton i Nina vstretili-*s'*
        'Anton and Nina met'

Swedish (reciprocal suffix -*s*):

(98)    Ingrid mötte Ingmar på bron
        'Ingrid met Ingmar on the bridge'

(99)    Ingrid och Ingmar mötte-s på bron
        'Ingrid and Ingmar met on the bridge'

Turkish (reciprocal suffix -(*i*)ş, with vowel harmony variants):

(100)   Sultan Şehrazad-i        sev-er
        sultan Scheherazade-DO love-PRES
        'The sultan loves Scheherazade'

(101)   Sultan ve  Şehrazad       sev-iş-ir-ler
        sultan and Scheherazade love-RECIP-PRES-3PL
        'The sultan and Scheherazade love one another'

Finally, within this subsection, we may consider reflexive verbs that are formed by derivational processes from non-reflexive verbs. In the non-reflexive verb, subject and direct object are distinct (non-coreferential). In the reflexive equivalent, only the subject is expressed overtly, but the reflexive affix (or other derivational marker) indicates that the subject noun phrase functions equally as direct object.

Russian (reflexive suffix *-sja/-s'*):

(102)     Mat' pomyla rebenka
        'The mother washed the child'

(103)     Rebenok pomyl-sja
        'The child washed (himself)'

Hungarian (several reflexive suffixes, including *-kod(ik)/-köd(ik)*):

(104)     A nő       fésül        egy gyerek-et
        the woman combs hair of a    child-DO
        'The woman combs a child's hair'

(105)     A gyerek fésül-ködik
        'The child combs his (own) hair'

Nivkh (reflexive prefix $p^h$-):

(106)     Ńi $p^h$-ōla    d'u-d'
        I-REFL-child wash
        'I wash my (own) child'

(107)     Ńi $p^h$-sud'
        I    REFL-wash
        'I wash (myself)'

(In Nivkh, the initial consonant of verbs is subject to regular changes when a prefix is added, whence the alternation *d'u-/su-* 'wash'. Note that $p^h$- also functions as a possessive reflexive prefix, as in $p^h$-*ōla* 'one's own child'.)

Dyirbal (reflexive suffix *-yiri*):

(108)     Bala yugu baŋgul yaṛa-ŋgu buyba-n
        CL    stick CL      man-ERG hide-TNS
        'The man hides the stick'

(109)     Bayi yaṛa buyba-yiri-nʸu
        CL    man hide-REFL-TNS
        'The man hides (himself)'

English typically has either no overt marker of reflexivity (*The mother washes the child*, *The child washes*), or uses a reflexive pronoun, *myself*, *yourself*, etc., i.e. a direct object noun phrase rather than verbal derivational morphology (e.g. *The child washes himself*, *The child dries himself*).

### 1.3 *Parallels in marking valency change*

The reader will probably have noted that in the exposition in section 1, which is arranged by semantic and syntactic criteria rather than formal criteria, some affixes in certain languages recur in several individual sections, for example Russian *-sja/-s'*, Swedish *-s*, Nivkh *pʰ*-, Chukchee *r(ə)-* (with or without a suffix), Wolof *-al*. On the other hand, some of the affixes treated are more specific in their function, such as the Swahili causative, the Swahili applicative, the Turkish reciprocal, i.e. some languages do make formal distinctions corresponding to distinct entries in our taxonomy. But when we look at suffixes that have, from the viewpoint of our classification, several disparate functions, then it is often possible to give a more general characterization of the range of these functions. For instance, all the uses of Russian *-sja/-s'* discussed above (reduction or rearrangement of valency by removing the direct object, anticausative, reciprocal, reflexive) can be grouped together under the general characterization: *-sja/-s'* indicates that the direct object of the basic verb to which it is attached is absent (Babby 1975). For convenience, the examples illustrating the various functions are grouped together here:

(110)   Sobaka kusajet-sja                    $(= (53))$
        'The dog bites'                       (deletion of DO)

(111)   Boris vstretil-sja s Ninoj           $(= (74))$
        'Boris met up with Nina'             (DO appears as oblique object)

(112)   Dver' otkryla-s'                      $(= (91))$
        'The door opened'                     (anticausative)

(113)   Anton i Nina vstretili-s'            $(= (97))$
        'Anton and Nina met'                  (reciprocal)

(114)   Rebenok pomyl-sja                     $(= (103))$
        'The child washed himself'            (reflexive)

(115)   Dver' otkryvajet-sja švejcarom
        'The door is opened by the doorman'   (passive)

The systematicity of this derivational process does, however, vary somewhat in Russian from one set of examples to another, being very systematic with the passive, somewhat less so for the anticausative – a few verbs, like *povoračivat'* (perfective *povernut'*) 'to turn', in the sense of 'to change the direction of trajectory', can be used transitively and intransitively (anticausative) without *-sja/-s'* – and idiosyncratic where only direct object deletion is involved, since most verbs, like *čitat'* 'to read', *jest'* 'to eat', can occur without a direct object without requiring (or, indeed, allowing) *-sja/-s'*.

The Swedish suffix *-s* and the Nivkh prefix *p$^h$-* can be given similar general characterizations in terms of absence of the direct object:

Swedish:

| | | |
|---|---|---|
| (116) | Hunden bit-s | (= (59)) |
| | 'The dog bites' | (deletion of DO) |
| (117) | Ingrid och Ingmar möttes på bron | (= (99)) |
| | 'Ingrid and Ingmar met on the bridge' | (reciprocal) |
| (118) | Jag kalla-s Ingmar | |
| | 'I am called Ingmar' | (passive) |

Nivkh:

| | | |
|---|---|---|
| (119) | Ńi p$^h$-ott' | (= (70)) |
| | 'I am sewing' | (deletion of DO) |
| (120) | Magazin p$^h$-arktt' | (= (95)) |
| | 'The shop closed' | (anticausative) |
| (121) | Ńi p$^h$-sud' | (= (107)) |
| | 'I wash (myself)' | (reflexive) |

One finds similar examples with valency-increase. Some affixes, etc., have very specific functions, like Turkish *-dir/-t* (causative), Luganda *-is* (instrumental object). Others have a wider range of functions, like the applicative suffix in Bantu languages and Classical Nahuatl (addition of an extra object, often but by no means always benefactive). Sometimes the affix has an even wider range of functions: thus Chukchee *r(ə)-* (with or without suffix) and Wolof *-al* simply indicate an increase by one of the valency of the verb, which may mean simply addition of another object, but may also mean a rearrangement of arguments involving the subject. The relevant examples are collected together for convenience:

Chukchee:

| | | |
|---|---|---|
| (122) | ətləge rə-viliv-et-ərkəninet ənnət | (= (17)) |
| | 'Father sells fish' | (addition of DO) |
| (123) | ətləge qaat rə-melevninet | (= (85)) |
| | 'Father cured the reindeer' | (causative) |

Wolof:

| | | |
|---|---|---|
| (124) | Kan nga dem-al? | (= (25)) |
| | 'Who did you go with?' | (comitative) |

(125)    Di naa toog-al nenne bi                                          (= (89))
        'I will make the child sit down'                          (causative)

One specially interesting feature of Wolof is that it is possible to increase the valency of a basic verb by two, using the suffix -al twice, so that one can combine, for instance, causative and benefactive:

(126)    Di naa la toog-al-al nenne bi                                    (= (29))
        'I will make the child sit down for you'

In addition to formal relations among different valency-changing functions, one also finds formal relations between valency-changing and other derivational processes, some of which recur in quite unrelated languages. Above (see examples (53) and (66)), we noted a relationship between reduced valency and continuous or habitual aspect, as in Yidiɲ and Russian. Another recurrent relationship is between causative and intensive: thus the causative of Swahili *chanja* 'chop', namely *chanj-isha*, can mean either 'cause (someone) to chop' or 'chop energetically'; possibly this is related to the intensity (force) that is often implied in forcing someone to do something. Sometimes, however, other meanings of usually valency-changing affixes seem quite idiosyncratic, as when adding the reciprocal suffix *-iş* to Turkish *gel* 'come' produces *gel-iş* 'develop (intransitive)'.

## 2.0 Causative verbs

In this section, we shall look in greater detail at the derivation of causative verbs, a topic already mentioned briefly in section 1.2.1. Causative constructions involve a range of problems, many of which fall, strictly speaking, outside the brief of this particular chapter (derivational morphology of verbs). Nonetheless, an adequate presentation even of the derivational morphology of causatives requires constant reference to other parameters of causative constructions, so that in sections 2.1 and 2.2 we discuss these various parameters, to return in greater detail in section 2.3 to the valency changes associated with causatives.

If we take a sentence containing a non-causative verb (or other predicate) to be describing a certain situation $s$, then a sentence containing the corresponding causative verb will describe a situation $s^{caus}$ where some entity (person, thing, abstract force) either brings about situation $s$ or, at the very least, fails to prevent $s$. Syntactically, one of the main differences between non-causative and causative constructions will be the increased valency (or potential valency) of the latter, since in addition to the participants in $\phi$ there will also be the actant that brings about $\phi$.

### 2.1 *Analytic, morphological, and lexical causatives*

There are three basic ways in which such a causative situation may be expressed, relative to the non-causative situation, namely analytic (or syntactic), morphological (or synthetic), and lexical. By an analytic causative construction, we mean one that uses regular syntactic devices of the language for forming complex sentences out of simplex sentences without fusing together the predicates of those simplex sentences; in the case of causative constructions, this means that the predicate expressing the idea of causation will be separate from the predicate of $\phi$. If we take $\phi$ to be *Sam slid off the roof*, then corresponding analytic causatives in English would be *Mary brought it about that Sam slid off the roof*, *Mary caused Sam to slide off the roof*, *Mary made Sam slide off the roof*, where the idea of causation is expressed by the verbs *bring about, cause,* or *make.* A morphological causative means that the predicate of $\phi$ undergoes some derivational process in order to express causativity, there being no separately expressed predicate of causation, as in (128) below from Turkish, where (127) represents $\phi$; the derivational process is the addition of the suffix *-dür*:

(127)   Hasan öl-dü                                                    (= (77))
        'Hasan died'

(128)   Ali Hasan-i öl-dür-dü                                          (= (78))
        'Ali brought it about that Hasan died, killed Hasan'

The alternative English gloss to this last sentence exemplifies lexical causatives. The verb used in describing $\phi$ in English is here *die*, but to indicate that Ali brings about $\phi$ we may use a completely different lexical item, namely *kill*, which has no morphological resemblance to *die*; *kill* is thus the lexical causative of *die*.

Although we have here given clear examples of the distinction between synthetic, morphological, and lexical causatives, one should not be surprised to find borderline cases between synthetic and morphological or morphological and lexical. In French, for instance, one causative construction uses the predicate *faire* 'to make' plus the infinitive of the basic verb, for example *faire courir* 'to make run', *faire manger* 'to make eat'. This appears to be an analytic construction, as with English *cause* or *make*, but for many purposes *faire* plus infinitive behaves like a single predicate, i.e. like a morphological causative. For instance, a single French predicate may not take two subjects or two direct objects, and this restriction applies equally to the *faire* construction:

(129)    Paul fit manager les pommes à/par Pierre
         Paul made to-eat the apples to/by Pierre

(130)    *Paul fit Pierre manger les pommes

         'Paul made Pierre eat the apples'

(131)    Paul lui    /?*le  fit    manger les  pommes
         Paul to him/  him made to eat   the apples
         'Paul made him eat the apples'

The distinction between morphological and lexical causatives can be even more difficult to draw, since in principle one could treat lexical causatives as morphological causatives involving suppletion, i.e. *kill* would be causative of *die* just as *went* is past tense of *go*. This analysis can probably be justified where one has just a few suppletive pairs alongside a range of clearly morphological causatives (cf. the position of Russian *klast'* 'to lay' in Table 6.1 at the beginning of this chapter); elsewhere, it probably tells more about the linguist who advocates it than about the language he is describing. Conversely, where one has only a few pairs whose members are clearly similar to each other, though not related by regular processes, such as English *lie/lay, fall/fell*, there may be little to gain by treating them as part of a limited derivational process rather than as distinct lexical items, especially where members of the pair also diverge semantically: thus *fell* in English, in literal use, normally only refers to causing trees to fall by cutting them down, and does not have the general meaning 'cause to fall'.

At this point we may also mention the question of productivity – does the formation of causatives extend right across the lexicon, and is it applicable to newly introduced verbs? In general, formation of analytic causatives is completely productive. Formation of lexical causatives is by definition non-productive, since there is no regular pattern to be extended to new items. The degree of productivity of morphological causatives varies immensely from language to language, from languages like English with only a few fossilized pairs (*lie/lay, sit/seat*) to languages like Turkish where virtually any verb (including a causative verb) can form a causative.

## 2.2 Semantics of causation

Where one has a causative situation, involving a causer (person, thing, force) and a situation brought about, then one relevant semantic parameter is the degree of closeness between the cause (i.e. the causer's action) and the effect (resultant situation). For instance, in English both *John broke the stick* and *John caused the stick to break* imply that the stick broke, but there is a potential semantic difference between them. *John broke the stick* implies an immediate connection between John's action and the breaking of the stick, for example he broke it by standing on it, or by snapping it with his fingers, whereas *John caused the stick to break* suggests rather a mediated chain of events, for example, John pushed against the lever that released the weight that fell on the stick . . . There is a similar distinction between *kill* and *cause to die*. Although an absolute distinction between mediated and immediate causation is difficult to draw, one often finds that, where a language has both analytic and morphological or lexical constructions, the former implies less direct causation than the latter, as in the Russian sentences paralleling those just given for English:

(132)   Anton slomal paločku
        'Anton broke the stick'

(133)   Anton sdelal tak, čtoby paločka slomala-s'
        'Anton brought it about that the stick broke'

A similar distinction is sometimes found between non-productive (lexicalized or virtually lexicalized) and productive morphological causatives, the former implying greater closeness between cause and effect, for example in Nivkh (productive morphological causative in *-gu*):

(134)   Lep   če-d'
        bread dry(INTRANS)-
        'The bread dried'

(135)   If  lep    seu-d'
        he  bread  dry(TRANS)-
        'He dried the bread'

(136)   If  lep    če-gu-d'
        he  bread  dry(INTRANS)-CAUSE-
        'He caused the bread to get dry (e.g. by forgetting to cover it)'

Thus the scale analytic – morphological – lexical causative correlates with the scale mediated – direct causation.

Another aspect of the relation between causer and effect is the difference between causative proper and permissive meaning. With the causative proper, the causer brings about a resultant situation which might well not have come about without him, for example *I made John climb the tree*. With the permissive, the causer has, or at least can be supposed to have, the power to prevent a situation from coming about, but in fact he does not prevent it, for example *I let John climb the tree*. What is common to both types is the control imputed to the causer over whether the situation comes about or not. Analytic causative constructions generally have distinct predicates for causation proper and permission, for example English *cause*, *make* versus *allow*, *let*; though there are exceptions, for example German *lassen*. Lexical causatives typically express causation proper, but morphological causatives often cover the range of both causation proper and permission, as in the following Nivkh example:

(137)   Ńi atik-ax              pʰ-əmək    vi-gu-d'
        I  younger brother-CAUSEE own-mother go-CAUSE-
        'I made/let my younger brother follow my mother'

Semantic features of causation proper and of permission are combined in the assistive, as in English *I helped John to climb the tree*, i.e. the situation of John's climbing the tree may or may not have come about without me, but I helped bring it about. A causative ranging across all three meanings is illustrated in this Georgian example, where the causative is expressed by prefix *a-* and suffixes *-in-eb*:

(138)   Mama švil-s   çeril-s    a-çer-in-eb-s
        father son-IO letter-DO  -write- - -3SG
        'The father makes/helps/lets his son write the letter'

In some languages, although the causative verb can cover a wide range of degrees of coercion in this way, differences in degree of coercion can be expressed by differences in the rest of the construction, as in the following Japanese examples (causative suffix *-(s)ase*):

(139)   Taroo ga   Ziroo o  ik-ase-ta
        Taroo SUBJ Ziroo DO go-CAUSE-PAST
(140)   Taroo ga Ziroo ni(IO) ik-ase-ta

        'Taroo made Ziroo go'

Sentence (139), with the direct object postposition *o*, implies greater coercion (e.g. Taroo forced Ziroo to go); (140), with the indirect object postposition *ni*, implies less coercion (e.g. Taroo persuaded Ziroo to go, got Ziroo to go by asking him nicely). See further sections 2.3.1–2.

## 2.3 *Causative verbs and valency change*

Since the causative situation always implies one more actant than the non-causative equivalent, namely the causer, the potential valency of a causative verb is one greater than that of its non-causative equivalent. The causer, apparently universally, appears as subject of the causative verb. Since few languages tolerate predicates with more than one subject noun phrase, this means that the subject of the non-causative verb (the cause) cannot appear as a subject of the causative verb: if it appears at all, it must appear as some other syntactic argument of the causative construction. The other possibility is for the cause to be omitted, where it is indefinite or recoverable from context, especially where we have the causative of a transitive or ditransitive verb, as in the following examples from Songhai (Sonrai) (causative suffix -*ndi*):

(141)   X nga tasu di
        X eat rice the
        'X ate the rice'

(142)   Ali nga-ndi    tasu di
        Ali eat-CAUSE rice the
        'Ali got someone to eat the rice'

(143)   X neere bari  di  Musa se
        X sell    horse the Musa IO
        'X sold the horse to Musa'

(144)   Ali neere-ndi bari di Musa se
        'Ali got someone to sell the horse to Musa'

(This sentence could also mean 'Ali got Musa to sell the horse', as causative of *Musa neere bari di* 'Musa sold the horse', with recipient unspecified, since in Songhai the overt causee appears as indirect object of the causative of a transitive verb; see (178) below.)

In discussing valency changes brought about by causativization, it is useful to work with a three-way valency distinction among the basic non-causative verbs: intransitive (no direct object), monotransitive (direct object, but no indirect object), and ditransitive (direct object and indirect object); other kinds of object (oblique objects) are rarely relevant. In some languages, one finds that, of these three classes, morphological causatives can be formed only from verbs with lower valency. For instance, Latin has intransitive–monotransitive pairs of the type *fugere* 'to flee' – *fugāre* 'to put to flight', *līquere* 'to melt (intransitive)' – *liquēre* 'to melt (transitive)', but no such pairs with a basic (mono- or di-) transitive and its causative. Chukchee forms causatives from intransitives (e.g. *melev-ǝk* 'to get better', *rǝ-melev-ǝk* 'to cure') and from a few monotransitives (e.g. *lʔu-k* 'to see', *rǝ-lʔu-ŋet-ǝk* 'to show') but not from ditransitives. Turkish allows causatives of all three types (e.g. *öl* 'die', *öl-dür* 'kill'; *imzala* 'sign', *imzala-t* 'cause to sign'; *göster* 'show', *göster-t* 'cause to show'). The inverse hierarchy, i.e. a language allowing only causatives of transitives, or only causatives of ditransitives, seems not to occur.

We may now look more systematically at what valency changes occur when causatives are formed from, respectively, intransitive, monotransitive, and ditransitive verbs. Given that these are the basic types of verbs with one, two, and three arguments respectively, one might expect that the extra argument introduced by causativity would lead to intransitives becoming monotransitives, and monotransitives becoming ditransitives. This does indeed happen in many, though not all, languages. One feature that does seem to be common to languages with morphological causatives is that it is always the causee that has to change its syntactic relation in order to fit in with the increased valency of the causative verb: the causee is subject of the basic verb, but cannot remain as subject of the causative verb, this position being usurped by the causer. However, some syntactic subject properties may still be retained, in individual languages, by the causee. In Japanese, for instance, the reflexive pronoun *zibun* refers to the subject. With a non-derived verb, the reference of *zibun* is clear. In the following examples, note that Taroo is male, Hanako female:

(145)   Taroo ga   Hanako ni zibun no  hon  o   watasi-ta
        Taroo SUBJ Hanako IO self   GEN book DO hand-PAST
        'Taroo handed Hanako his/*her book'

In (145), *zibun* can only refer to the subject *Taroo*. With the morphological causative, however, *zibun* can refer to either the causee (as subject of the basic verb) or the causer (as subject of the causative verb):

(146)   Taroo ga   Hanako ni zibun no  huku  o   ki-sase-ta
        Taroo SUBJ Hanako IO self   GEN clothes DO wear-CAUSE-PAST
        'Taroo made Hanako put on his/her clothes'

In (146), *zibun* can refer to either Taroo or Hanako. Thus a construction with the causative of a verb with valency *n*, even when the morphology of its arguments is identical to that of a simple verb with valency *n* + 1, may still differ syntactically from a non-causative construction of valency *n* + 1.

## 2.3.1 *Causatives of intransitive verbs*

In the causative of an intransitive verb, the causer appears as subject, and the causee usually as direct object, as in this Turkish example:

(147)   Hasan öl-dü                                                    (= (77))
        'Hasan died'

(148)   Ali Hasan-ɨ öl-dür-dü                                          (= (78))
        'Ali caused Hasan to die, killed Hasan'

This applies also to verbs which take one or more objects none of which is a direct object, such as the Turkish verb *başla* 'start', which requires an indirect object only:

(149)   Çocuk okul-a     başla-dɨ
        child   school-IO start-PAST
        'The child started [attending] school'

(150)   Öğretmen çocuğ-u okul-a     başla-t-tɨ
        teacher   child-DO school-IO start-CAUSE-PAST
        'The teacher made the child start school'

In some languages, usually alongside constructions where the causee appears as a direct object, one also finds constructions where the causee appears as a non-direct object, either as an indirect object or as an oblique object, as in Hungarian:

(151)   Én köhög-tet-te-m         a  gyerek-et
        I  cough-CAUSE-PAST-1SG the child-DO

(152)   Én köhög-tet-te-m a gyerek-kel(INSTR)
        'I made the child cough'

Sentence (151) has a direct object causee, sentence (152) an oblique (instrumental) object causee. The sentences are not absolutely synonymous: (151) implies direct coercion, with the boy having little or no choice in the matter; (152) implies rather that I got the boy to cough by asking him to do so, i.e. he still retained control over whether or not he coughed. With the non-direct object, then, the causee retains at least partial agentivity. Compare the Japanese examples (139–40) above, repeated here:

(153)   Taroo ga Ziroo o ik-ase-ta                                     (= (139))
        'Taroo made Ziroo go'

(154)   Taroo ga Ziroo ni ik-ase-ta                                    (= (140))
        'Taroo got Ziroo to go'

Sentence (153), with the direct postposition *o*, implies greater coercion than does (154), with the indirect object postposition *ni*.

## 2.3.2 *Causatives of monotransitive verbs*

Causatives of monotransitive verbs usually have the same valency as a basic ditransitive verb: the causer appears as subject of the causative verb, the causee as its indirect object, while the direct object of the basic verb remains as direct object of the causative, as in the following examples from Turkish and Chukchee, respectively:

(155)    Müdür mektub-u imzala-dɨ                    (= (79))
         'The director signed the letter'

(156)    Dişçi mektub-u müdür-e imzala-t-tɨ           (= (80))
         'The dentist made the director sign the letter'

(157)    Ekke-te čəʔ-miməl pəl-nin                    (= (86))
         'The son drank cold water'

(158)    ətləg-e akka-gtə rə-lpə-ŋen-nin čəʔ-miməl    (= (87))
         'The father made the son drink cold water'

Some languages, however, either allow or require causatives of monotransitives to have both the causee and the direct object of the basic verb appear in the form of direct objects, as in examples (159–60) from Sanskrit (direct object in the accusative) and examples (161–2) from Swahili (direct object after the verb without any preposition or postposition):

(159)    Bhṛtyaḥ       kaṭaṁ       karoti
         servant(NOM) mat(ACC) prepares
         'The servant prepares the mat'

(160)    Rāmaḥ         bhṛtyaṁ  . kaṭaṁ       kārayati
         Rama(NOM) servant(ACC) mat(ACC) prepare(CAUSE)
         'Rama makes the servant prepare the mat'

(161)    Msichana a-li-u-funga        mlango
         girl        she-PAST-it-open door
         'The girl opened the door'

(162)    Mwalimu a-li-m-fungu-zisha      msichana mlango
         teacher he-PAST-her-open-CAUSE girl        door
         'The teacher made the girl open the door'

In such double direct object constructions, not all direct object properties need adhere to both direct objects. In Swahili, for instance, a verb has only one position for a direct object prefix, and in the causative of a transitive verb this position is occupied by a prefix referring to the causee, not to the direct object of the basic verb. In (161), the object prefix *u-* relates to *mlango* 'door', the only direct object; in (162), the object prefix *m-* relates to *msichana* 'girl', the causee, and there is no possibility of having *u-* in addition to or instead of *m-*.

Another deviation from the most straightforward type (causee as indirect object) is where the causee appears as some oblique object, often, though not always, the same as is used to express the agent in a passive construction. This construction is sometimes found alongside the indirect object causee, as in French:

(163)  Pierre mangea les pommes
       'Pierre ate the apples'

(164)  Paul fit manger les pommes à/par Pierre                    (= (129))
       'Paul made Pierre eat the apples'

Sometimes it occurs alongside the double direct object construction, as in an alternative to Sanskrit (160):

(165)  Rāmaḥ      bhṛtyena      kaṭaṁ      kārayati
       Rama(NOM) servant(INSTR) mat(ACC)  prepare(CAUSE)
       'Rama made the servant prepare the mat'

Sometimes, it is the only possibility for the causative of a transitive verb, as in Finnish:

(166)  Muurari-t      rakens-i-vat      talo-n
       bricklayer-PL build-PAST-3PL house-DO
       'The bricklayers built the house'

(167)  Minä rakennut-i-n              talo-n      muurare-i-lla
       I    build(CAUSE)-PAST-1SG house-DO bricklayer-PL-on
       'I had the bricklayers build the house'

In some languages, it may be possible to argue that such constructions should be analyzed as causatives of passives (i.e. 'Paul caused the apples to be eaten by Pierre'), even though there is no overt passive morphology, especially if restrictions on the use of this construction parallel restrictions on the passive, and if the causee appears in the same form as the passive agent (e.g. with *par* in French, the instrumental in Sanskrit). Elsewhere, however, this analysis has no real motivation; in Finnish, for instance, apart from causative constructions, the adessive case (in *-lla/-llä*, basic meaning 'on') is never used to mark a passive agent.

Where the oblique object causee alternates with a direct object or indirect object causee, there are often semantic differences between the alternants, the oblique object being more agentive than the direct or indirect object, as in Kannada (Peter Cole, personal communication):

(168)    Nānu    bisketannu tinde
         I(SUBJ) biscuit(DO) ate
         'I ate a biscuit'

(169)    Avanu    nanage bisketannu tinnisidanu
         he(SUBJ) me(IO) biscuit(DO) ate(CAUSE)
         'He made me eat a biscuit, fed me a biscuit'

(170)    Avanu nanninda(INSTR) bisketannu tinnisidanu
         'He got me to eat a biscuit'


### 2.3.3 Causatives of ditransitive verbs

Probably no language has a class of 'typical' four-place predicates, so there is no natural valency-type for the causative of a ditransitive verb, in the sense that the ditransitive type is a natural valency-type for the causative of a monotransitive verb. Many languages express the causee, with the causative of a ditransitive, as some oblique object, often the same as a passive agent, for example Turkish:

(171)    Müdür Hasan-a mektub-u göster-di                    (= (81))
         'The director showed the letter to Hasan'

(172)    Dişçi Hasan-a mektub-u müdür tarafından göster-t-ti   (= (82))
         'The dentist made the director show the letter to Hasan'

The postposition tarafından also marks passive agents:

(173)    Adam kadın    tarafından döv-ül-dü
         man   woman   by            hit-PASS-PAST
         'The man was hit by the woman'

In languages that allow such oblique objects as causees even with the causative of a monotransitive verb, such as French, this introduces no new data-type. Turkish is interesting here, however, in that most speakers of Turkish do not allow tarafından with the causative of a monotransitive, i.e. alongside (156) one cannot say:

(174)    *Dişçi mektub-u müdür  tarafından imzala-t-tı
          dentist letter-DO director by      sign-CAUSE-PAST
         'The dentist made the director sign the letter'

Since monotransitive verbs are no less passivizable in Turkish than are ditransitives, both having passive agents with tarafından, this suggests that Turkish causative constructions with tarafından should not be analyzed as causatives of passives, otherwise the ungrammaticality of (174) is unexplained.

Languages that permit double direct objects with causatives of monotransitives equally permit them, as might be expected, with causatives of ditransitives, as in Swahili:

(175)   Maria a-li-m-lip-isha                Johni pesa    kwa watoto
        Maria she-PAST-him-pay-CAUSE John money to    children
        'Mary made John pay the money to the children'

Where a language expresses the causee of a monotransitive as an indirect object, it often allows double indirect objects in the causative of a ditransitive – this seems to be much more frequent, relative to the number of languages allowing indirect object causees at all, than doubling of direct objects. Many speakers of Turkish allow this construction (cf. (172)):

(176)   Dişçi   müdür-e    mektub-u Hasan-a  göster-t-ti
        dentist director-IO letter-DO  Hasan-IO show-CAUSE-PAST
        'The dentist made the director show the letter to Hasan'

Native speakers often vary as to whether such double indirect object constructions are permissible, though this hesitation often seems due more to euphonic or other stylistic considerations. No speaker of Turkish would hesitate over rejecting a causative construction with two direct objects.

A final possibility, attested in Songhai, is for there to be no way of including both the causee and the indirect object of the basic verb, i.e. Songhai has no causative formed from sentence (177).

(177)   Ali neere bari   di  Musa se
        Ali sell   horse the Musa IO
        'Ali sold the horse to Musa'

Causatives of ditransitive verbs are possible, for example *neere-ndi* 'cause to sell', but in the resultant sentence one must omit either the causee or the indirect object of the basic verb (or, of course, both), so that the causative sentence has at most one indirect object; only the context will tell whether this is the causee or the indirect object of the basic verb:

(178)   Garba neere-ndi bari   di  Musa se              (cf. (144))
        Garba sell-CAUSE horse the Musa IO
        (i) 'Garba made [someone] sell the horse to Musa'
        (ii) 'Garba made Musa sell the horse'

Table 6.2. *Typical valency relations between basic and causative verbs*

|  | Basic | Causative |
|---|---|---|
| Intransitive | SUBJ | SUBJ<br>DO |
| Monotransitive | SUBJ<br>DO | SUBJ<br>DO<br>IO |
| Ditransitive | SUBJ<br>DO<br>IO | SUBJ<br>DO<br>IO<br>OBL |

### 2.3.4 *Causatives and valency: conclusions*

Although we have seen much variation across languages in the valency of causative verbs relative to non-causative verbs, yet still there is a certain general tendency that emerges – a pattern from which languages tend to deviate surprisingly little, and in very restricted ways. If we set up a hierarchy Subject – Direct object – Indirect object – Oblique object (OBL), then we can state this general tendency as follows: the causee occupies the leftmost (topmost) position of the hierarchy that is not already filled by some argument of the causative verb. This is illustrated for intransitive, monotransitive, and ditransitive verbs in Table 6.2.

## 3 Verbs formed from verbs without change of valency

### 3.1 *State and change of state*

Many languages have a derivational relationship between verbs denoting being in a certain state ('stative') and verbs denoting entry into that state ('ingressive'), for example Russian *sid-e-t'* 'to be in a sitting position', *ses-t'* (present stem *sjad-*) 'to adopt a sitting position'. English often uses the same verb in both senses, for example *sit*, or else has morphophonemically unrelated verbs, for example stative *wear* (clothes), ingressive *put on* (clothes). Some languages go even further than English in this respect, for example Classical Arabic, which has just the one verb *labisa* for both 'wear' and 'put on'.

In some languages the direction of derivation is from ingressive to stative, as in Chukchee, with a stative suffix -(ə)*tva*, for example *vakʔo-k* 'adopt a sitting position', *vakʔo-tva-k* 'be in a sitting position', *tenmav-ək* 'get oneself ready', *tenmav-ətva-k* 'be ready'. Other languages have typically the inverse derivation. Thus Russian forms many ingressives with the prefix *za-*, for example *spat'* 'to sleep', *za-sypat'* 'to fall asleep'. The simple verb does not have to be stative, but can also be a verb describing a dynamic process, in which case *za-* indicates the start of this process, for example *pet'* 'to sing', *za-pet'* 'to start singing, burst into song'.

Specific derivational processes indicating exit from a state (or process) are also found, formed either from the stative or the ingressive verb. In Swahili such derived verbs are called 'conversives', for example *v-u-a* 'take off (clothes)' from *va-a* 'put on (clothes)', *lev-uk-a* 'become sober' from *lew-a* 'be drunk'.

Here we may also mention the derivational process found in some languages to indicate that some situation in itself indefinitely protractable is in fact working towards some definite end-point; the derived form may be called 'telic'. Thus the German simple verb *kämpfen* 'to fight', as in *Die Partisanen kämpften für ihre Freiheit* 'The partisans fought for their freedom', gives no indication of the outcome of the struggle, whereas the telic derivative *er-kämpfen* incorporates the successful outcome of the struggle, as in *Die Partisanen erkämpften ihre Freiheit* 'The partisans fought for [and won] their freedom'. In this example, there is also a slight change of valency: *kämpfen* takes an oblique object (introduced by the preposition *für* 'for'), whereas *erkämpfen* takes a direct object.

### 3.2 *Aspectuals*

Derivationally related verbs often express differences in the internal temporal structure of the situation described, for example whether it lasted a long time or a short time, whether it was repeated at intervals, etc. Such semantic correlates of verbal derivation may be referred to as 'aspectuals' or 'Aktionsarten'. In Russian, for instance, prefixes can often indicate the (subjective) length of time for which a situation persists, for example *stojat'* 'to stand' (neutral), *po-stojat'* 'to stand' (for a short time), *pro-stojat'* 'to stand' (for a long time). Gombe Fulani has a suffix -(*i*)*law* indicating that an action happens quickly, for example *ʔo-maḅḅilawii-nde* 'He shut it quickly'. Another related possibility is a means of indicating a momentary event, i.e. one that takes place so quickly that it cannot be decomposed temporally. Russian has many such verbs in -(*a*)*nu-*, for example *kašlj-anu-t'* 'to give a cough' (cf. *kašlj-a-t'* 'to cough'), and Hungarian in -(*a*)*n*/-(*e*)*n*, for example *zörren* 'give a knock' (cf. *zörög* 'knock'). Hungarian also has some verbs with the inverse of this, indicating a state, process, or series of events that goes on for a long time, for example *áll-dogál* 'stand about, loiter' (cf. *áll* 'stand').

Some languages have special iterative derivatives, indicating that an event is repeated several times, for example Hungarian *nevet-gél* 'give a series of laughs' (cf. *nevet* 'laugh'). In Gombe Fulani, iterativity is expressed by means of reduplication, for example *ʔo-ḍaani-ḍaaninto* 'He keeps on falling asleep'. A more specific iterative derivative refers to a single repetition of an event, as with English *re-write* (cf. *write*, i.e. 'write again'), Gombe Fulani *winnd-it-o* 'write again, rewrite' (cf. *winnda* 'write'), *mak-it-o* 'rebuild' (cf. *maka* 'build').

Semantically related to the iterative is the distributive, whereby a given type of event is repeated, but applied to a different entity each time. Thus Russian has verbs like *po-vskakat'* 'to jump up one at a time', for example *Učeniki povskakali* 'The pupils jumped up one at a time', versus *Učeniki vskočili* 'The pupils jumped up' (possibly all at once). With distributives, one typically finds that the distributiveness applies to the subjects of intransitive verbs, but to the direct objects of transitive verbs, as in Russian *On po-zapiral dveri* 'He locked the doors one at a time', versus *On zaper dveri* 'He locked the doors' (possibly all at once).

### 3.3 *Manner*

Derivative verbs exist in many languages to indicate the manner in which an event occurs. Some such examples have already been met in section 3.2, as aspectuals, for example the Gombe Fulani *-(i)law* meaning 'quickly'. A frequent type of manner derivative is the intensive, indicating that an action is carried out with force, with greater than expected intensity. Thus from Zulu *buza* 'ask' we can form *buz-isisa* 'ask insistently', from *thanda* 'love' *thand-isisa* 'love exceedingly'; Arabic *kasara* 'break' gives (by doubling the second consonant) *kassara* 'smash to pieces'. Sometimes the meaning relates rather to the quantity of actants affected by the situation, as with the Gombe Fulani suffix *-(i/u)d*, indicating that all the subjects of an intransitive verb, or all the objects of a transitive verb, are affected, for example *Ɓe-nastidii fuu* 'They all came in', *Gujjo nastidii shuuḍi ʔamin fuu* 'The thief entered all our huts'.

The opposite meaning, i.e. attenuative, is also found. In Zulu, this is formed by reduplication, for example *ndiza* 'fly', *ndizandiza* 'fly a little'. In Russian, the prefix *pri-* often adds attenuative meaning, for example *nažat'* 'to press', *pri-nažat'* 'to press lightly'.

Finally, many languages have a system of derivational morphology for indicating the direction in which an action takes place, either in absolute terms (e.g. 'up', 'down', 'away'), or in relative (deictic) terms (e.g. 'towards the speaker', 'away from the speaker'). One such system is found in Georgian, where relative (deictic) direction is indicated by *mo-* (towards speaker or hearer) and *mi-* (Ø- after another directional) (away from speaker or hearer, or not involving speaker or hearer), absolute direction by a variety of prefixes, as in the following derivatives of *-dis* 'He goes/comes/travels':

| | | | |
|---|---|---|---|
| *mi-dis* | 'he goes' | *mo-dis* | 'he comes' |
| *a-dis* | 'he goes up' | *a-mo-dis* | 'he comes up' |
| *ča-dis* | 'he goes down' | *ča-mo-dis* | 'he comes down' |
| *še-dis* | 'he goes in' | *še-mo-dis* | 'he comes in' |
| *ga-dis* | 'he goes out' | *ga-mo-dis* | 'he comes out' |
| *gada-dis* | 'he goes across' | *gad-mo-dis* | 'he comes across' |
| *ça-dis* | 'he goes away' | *ça-mo-dis* | 'he comes away' |

Further examples are Russian *s"-jexat'-sja* 'to come together', *raz"-jexat'-sja* 'to separate, travel apart', from *jexat'* 'to go, come, travel'.

## 4 Verbs formed from other parts of speech

### 4.1 *Verbs formed from adjectives*

Adjectives are, from a semantic viewpoint, very similar to verbs, especially stative verbs, and in many languages even a formal distinction is hard to draw. Thus, the kinds of relations found in deriving verbs from adjectives are often very similar to those found in deriving verbs from (especially stative) verbs.

In some languages which do have a verb/adjective distinction, it is sometimes possible to derive a verb from an adjective where the verb simply has the meaning 'to be Adjective', for example Russian *bel-e-t'* 'to be white' from *bel-* 'white'. (The usual citation form of Russian adjectives is the masculine singular nominative attributive form, with the ending *-yj/-ij/-oj*, i.e., here, *bel-yj*.) In the imperfective aspect, *bel-e-t'* can also be ingressive, expressing entry into a state, i.e. 'to become white'; in the perfective aspect, 'to become white' is the only meaning of *po-bel-e-t'*. Some other de-adjectival verbs in *-e-t'* and other suffixes (e.g. *-nu-t'*) have only the ingressive meaning, for example *molod-e-t'* 'to become young', cf. *molodoj* 'young', *mjak-nu-t'* 'to become soft(er)', cf. *mjag-k-ij* 'soft'. Often, the sense is not so much 'to become Adjective' as 'to become more Adjective', or at least both meanings are possible. Thus *mjaknut'* can mean either 'to become soft' (something was hard but is now soft) or 'to become softer' (something was hard, but is now less so, or was already fairly soft, but is now more so). This is equally true of its English de-adjectival gloss *soften* (intransitive).

Transitive (causative) equivalents to such ingressives often exist, with the meaning 'to make (more) Adjective', for example *bel-i-t'* 'to make white, bleach', *s-mjag-č-at'* 'to make soft(er), soften (transitive)'.

In Russian, which has no regular and productive pattern for forming causative verbs, although the intransitive and transitive de-adjectivals both have the same root (allowing for morphophonemic alternations), the selection of affixes for the de-adjectivals is lexically determined. In languages that have a regular and productive causative suffix, this suffix can be used, as with Classical Nahuatl -lia, for example cual-ti 'become good' (where -ti is a verbalizing suffix), (tē-)cual-ti-lia 'make (someone) good'.

## 4.2  Verbs formed from nouns
The range of verbs that can be formed from nouns is immense, and here we must content ourselves with a structured set of illustrative examples.

### 4.2.1  Predicate nouns
Verbs formed from predicate nouns are similar to those formed from adjectives. Thus one can form verbs meaning 'to be Noun', like Ancient Greek basileúein 'to be a king, reign', from basileús 'king', or Russian carstvovat' 'to reign', from car' 'tsar, emperor'. Sometimes, the meaning is not so much literally 'to be Noun', but rather 'to be like Noun', 'to behave like Noun'. Thus carstvovat' can be applied not only to tsars, but also (without any sense of metaphorical extension) to the rule of any other kind of monarch or regime. Russian xozjajničat', from xozjain 'master', has usually the meaning 'to lord it over', i.e. 'to behave like a master'.

Ingressive denominal verbs are also found, as in Classical Nahuatl tēmachtih-cā-ti 'become a teacher' from tēmachtih-qui 'teacher', tlahuēli-lō-cā-ti 'become a rogue' from tlahuēlilō-c 'rogue'. (Here and below, the final morphemes of Classical Nahuatl nouns are absolutive suffixes.) Sometimes, the meaning is 'to become like Noun' rather than 'to become Noun', for example Classical Nahuatl tlīl-ihui 'become black' from tlīl-li 'ink', i.e. 'become like ink'.

Transitive derivatives may also exist, with causative meaning, as with Classical Nahuatl (tē)tlahuēlilō-cā-ti-lia 'cause (someone) to become a rogue, corrupt (someone)'. Sometimes such transitive denominals mean 'to treat someone as Noun', as in Classical Nahuatl (tē-)mahuiz-tla, from mahuiz-tli 'person worthy of awe', meaning 'to honor (someone)', i.e. 'to treat (someone) as a person worthy of awe'.

### 4.2.2  Arguments of predicates and adverbials
Many languages can form verbs from nouns with the meaning 'to have Noun'. Thus Classical Nahuatl, from the noun xio-tl 'skin sore', can form the verb xio-ti 'to have skin sores'. In Chukchee, this is a

completely productive process, using the prefix *ge-*/*ga-*, though if one were to draw a dividing-line between verb and adjective in Chukchee, these formations would probably be adjectives rather than verbs. Thus from the noun *qora-ŋə* (stem *qora-*, *qaa-*) 'reindeer' one can form *ga-qora-* 'have a reindeer', for example *ga-qora-ygəm* 'I have a reindeer', *ga-qora-len* 'he has a reindeer'. Malay has similar derivatives, for example *bĕr-bini* 'have a wife' from *bini* 'wife'. The causative equivalent to this pattern would be verbs meaning 'cause to have Noun', 'to provide with Noun', such as German *be-waffn-en* 'to arm' from *Waffen* 'weapon'; the conversive also exists, *ent-waffn-en* 'to disarm', i.e. 'to cause not to have Noun'.

A further type has the meaning 'to produce/manufacture Noun'. In Chukchee this is fully productive, with the prefix *t(e/a)-* and suffix *-ŋ*, for example *te-kupre-ŋ-ək* 'to make nets' from *kupre-n* (stem *kupre-*) 'net'. Classical Nahuatl also has such formations, for example *tamal-oa* 'make tamales' from *tamal-li* 'tamale'.

A number of related denominal formations can be grouped under the general heading of 'instruments', i.e. 'to use Noun to do something (to someone or something)', 'to do something (to someone) as a result of Noun'. Examples from German include *ver-gift-en* 'to poison', i.e. 'to kill with poison (*Gift*)', *ver-hunger-n* 'to starve', i.e. 'to die because of hunger (*Hunger*)', *er-heirat-en* 'to obtain something via marriage (*Heirat*)'. Classical Nahuatl examples are *āyacach-oa* 'play a gourd-rattle' from *āyacach-tli* 'gourd-rattle', *(tla-)izta-huia* 'salt (something)' from *izta-tl* 'salt', i.e. 'flavor something with salt'. Compare also Malay *bĕ-layar* 'to sail', i.e. 'travel with the help of a sail', from *layar* 'sail'. The precise relationship between the noun stem and the action described can be quite varied, as illustrated by these examples, and also for instance English *en-case* 'put in a case', where the noun indicates a receptacle.

We may also mention here verbs derived from adverbials that are not nominal, for example Classical Nahuatl *(tla-)īlihuiz-huia* 'do (something) inconsiderately', from *īlihuiz* 'inconsiderately'.

The noun can also indicate the destination, as in Russian *pri-zeml-i-t'-sja* 'to land' (e.g. of airplane), cf. *zemlja* 'land', French *a-lun-ir* 'to land on the moon', cf. *lune* 'moon', Malay *mĕn-darat* 'to land', cf. *darat* 'land'.

Verbs can also be formed from time-expressions, for example Russian *zim-ova-t'* 'to spend the winter (somewhere)' from *zima* 'winter', Classical Nahuatl *cem-ilhui-tia* 'to spend one day (somewhere)' from *cem-ilhui-tl* 'one day', Malay *bĕr-malam* 'spend the night' from *malam* 'night'.

Finally, verbs can be formed from nouns expressing some emotion, and mean 'to feel such-and-such an emotion (towards someone)', for example Swahili *hurum-ia* 'to pity' from *huruma* 'pity', German *ver-abscheu-en* 'to abhor' from *Abscheu* 'disgust'. Although morphologically the direction of derivation is from noun to verb, the semantic relation is rather that between a verb and its derived action nominal, a topic that is discussed fully in the next chapter.

Combinations of derivational processes are often possible, though there are many language-specific restrictions (apart from restrictions arising from semantic incompatibility). For instance, Turkish forms causatives of causatives, for example *öl-dür-t* 'cause to cause to die, cause to kill', whereas Nivkh does not, despite the transparently agglutinative and regular nature of its causative formation (suffix *-gu*). Some examples of complex formations in Turkish are: *ak* 'white', *ağ-ar* 'become white', *ağ-ar-t* 'make white' (causative of ingressive of adjective); *tanɨ* 'know', *tanɨ-ş* 'know one another', *tanɨ-ş-tɨr* 'cause to know one another, introduce socially' (causative of reciprocal of verb); and *daya* 'prop up', *daya-n* 'prop oneself up', *daya-n-ɨş* 'engage with others in propping oneself up, practise mutual aid', *daya-n-ɨş-tɨr* 'cause to practise mutual aid' (causative of reciprocal of reflexive of verb).

NOTE

* This work was supported by the Center for Applied Linguistics and, in part, by a Social Science Research Council (London) grant for the investigation of the linguistic typology of the non-Slavic languages of the Soviet Union.

# 7 Lexical nominalization*

BERNARD COMRIE and SANDRA A. THOMPSON

## o Introduction

The term 'nominalization' means in essence 'turning something into a noun' (see chapter 1:1 for the internal and contextual characterization of 'noun'). In this chapter we will be concerned both with what forms can turn into nouns and with what kinds of nouns result from these operations.

The organization of this chapter, then, will be as follows: section 1 will be a discussion of derivational devices which create nouns from lexical verbs and adjectives. The resulting nouns may be the name of the activity or state designated by the verb or adjective, or may represent one of their arguments. Thus, we may categorize them as follows:

- A. Name of activity or state
  - 1. action/state nouns
- B. Name of an argument
  - 2. agentive nouns
  - 3. instrumental nouns
  - 4. manner nouns
  - 5. locative nouns
  - 6. objective nouns
  - 7. reason nouns

As we shall see, the difference between the forms in Class A and those in Class B is that the A forms retain certain properties of the verbs or adjectives they are related to, while those in B typically behave syntactically like other nouns in the language, bearing only morphological and (often unpredictable and idiosyncratic) semantic relations to the associated verb or adjective. Section 2 will be a somewhat more lengthy treatment of devices by which entire predicates and propositions can be turned into noun phrases; included there will be a discussion of the types of devices found, the verbal and nominal categories represented in the nominalization, the syntactic collocations of action nominals, and the functions of such nominalizations. Section 3 will briefly take up nouns derived from nouns, and Section 4 summarizes the discussion.

## 1 Processes for forming nouns from lexical verbs and adjectives

### 1.1 *Action/state nominalization*

Most languages in the world make use of one or more devices for creating action nouns from action verbs and state nouns from stative verbs or adjectives, meaning the fact, the act, the quality, or occurrence of that verb or adjective. English has a rich array of suffixes for this purpose, a few of which are illustrated below:

(1)    create → creation
       arrive → arrival
       stupid → stupidity
       quiet → quietness

In Lakhota, a Sioux language of South Dakota (Buechel 1939: 176), there is a prefix *wó* (where the stem-final *ã* of the verb may change to *-e* by a general rule):

(2)    gnayã́      → wógnaye
       to deceive    deception
       wiyuškĩ    → wówiyuškĩ
       to rejoice    rejoicing

In Semitic languages, derivation from one lexical class to another takes the form of various modifications of a three-consonant (= triliteral) root. Thus, in Hebrew, for example, the root *y-š-v* means 'to sit', *yašav* is 'sat', while *yešiva* means '(state of) sitting'. Similarly, *x-l-t* is 'to decide', *hexlit* is 'decided', and *haxlata* is 'decision'.

In some vo languages, an action/state noun can be formed from a verb phrase consisting of a transitive verb and its object by reversing the order of the verb and the object. In English this strategy is very productive with *-ing*:

(3)    drive a truck    → truck-driving
       trim a tree      → tree-trimming
       hunt for a house → house-hunting

A very similar process can be observed in Gwari, a Kwa language of Nigeria (see Hyman and Magaji 1970), as well as in many other Kwa languages:

(4)    sī shnamá     → shnamásī
       buy yams        yam-buying
       zhnī tnútnû   → tnutnúzhni
       do work         work-doing

It has been suggested (Givón 1971) that the order Object–Verb in such nominalizations in English and Gwari can be explained by appealing to earlier stages of Germanic and Kwa. which can be shown independently to have had the order Object–Verb in simple sentences.

Some languages have different derivational processes for different semantic types of action/state nouns. A distinction which many languages make is that between a nominalization designating a process and one designating a non-process. Thai is such a language: the nominalizers *kaan* and *khwam* differ in that the former derives process nouns while the latter derives non-process nouns.

(5)     chyâ    → *kaan* chyâ
        believe    believing (process)
              → *khwam* chyâ
                belief (non-process)

In fact, *kaan* cannot occur with stative attributive verbs (there is no separate category of adjective in Thai):

(6)     dii     → *khwam* dii
        good       goodness
              → *\*kaan* dii
        suǎj    → *khwam* suǎj
        beautiful  beauty
              → *\*kaan* suǎj

These action/state nouns, then, are those which name the activity or state designated by the verb or adjective, those which we labeled as Class A above. In the following sections we will discuss the types in Class B, those which create the name of one of the arguments of the verb or adjective. The first type we shall consider is the agentive noun.

### 1.2 *Agentive nominalization*
A number of languages have a productive process whereby action verbs can be made into nouns meaning 'one which "verbs"'. We will refer to this process by the traditional label 'agentive nominalization' even though, strictly speaking, the noun need not be in an 'agent' relationship with the verb from which it is derived. In English, for example, the suffix *-er* derives nouns meaning 'one which "verbs"' from both agentive and non-agentive verbs:

(7)     a. sing → singer
        b. hear → hearer

In English, however, this process is constrained in certain ways: for example, *-er* may not be added to adjectives, and there are many stative verbs with which it cannot occur:

(8)      tall→ *taller
                tall *one*
         fall→ *faller
                *one* that $\begin{cases}\text{falls}\\\text{fell}\end{cases}$

But in Tagalog, the process is unconstrained: any verb or adjective may become a noun meaning 'one which "verbs"', simply by being used in a nominal slot in the sentence without any modification in its form (Schachter and Otanes 1972:150ff):

(9)
         Iyon ang $\begin{cases}bago\\\text{new}\\bumagsak\\\text{fell}\end{cases}$
         that TOP

         That's the $\begin{cases}\text{new one}\\\text{one that fell}\end{cases}$

Here are some further examples, where even the aspectual distinctions of the verb are maintained:

(10)   a. Magsasalita
             speak(CONTEMPLATED)
       b. Nagsasalita              si    Rosa
             speak(IMPERF)         ART Rosa
       c. Nagsalita
             speak(PERF)

             Rosa $\begin{cases}\text{will speak}\\\text{is speaking}\\\text{spoke}\end{cases}$

(11)
                                a. magsasalita
                                     speak(CONTEMPLATED)
       Nakita ko ang            b. nagsasalita
       saw    I   TOP                speak(IMPERF)
                                c. nagsalita
                                     speak(PERF)

       I saw the one who $\begin{cases}\text{will speak}\\\text{is speaking}\\\text{spoke}\end{cases}$

The situation in Modern Hebrew is slightly different: there the agentive nominalization is morphologically indistinct from a verbal form, but it is specifically the participial form of the verb that serves this function:

(12)     šamar          → šomer
         (he) guarded    he guards/is guarding/a guard

In Zulu (Kunene 1974), an agentive noun can be formed by prefixing to a verb root the prefix which occurs on all nouns in the human class, *um(u)*, and replacing the verbal suffix *-a* by an *-i*:

(13)     -cula → *um*-cul-*i*
         sing    singer

In some languages, agentive nominalization can also be used to modify another noun. Mandarin Chinese is such a language; compare the expression translated by a relative clause in (b) with the agentive nominalization in (c):

(14)     a. *Full sentence*
            Tā chǎo - fàn
            he cook - rice
            'He cooks'
         b. *Relative clause*
            chǎo - fàn de   rén
            cook - rice NOM person
            'a/the person who cooks'
         c. *Agentive nominalization*
            chǎo - fàn - de
            cook - rice - NOM
            '(a) cook'

## 1.3 *Instrumental nominalization*

In some languages there is a (typically morphological) process for forming from an action verb a noun meaning 'an instrument for "verbing"'. In Wappo, a California Indian language (as well as in a number of other American Indian languages), this process is very productive. A suffix *-(e)ma* 'for the purpose of' is added to the verb root:

(15)     yoʔ-      → yokema
         sit          for the purpose of sitting = chair
         kač-      → kačema
         plow (v)    for the purpose of plowing = plow (N)
         lat-      → latema
         whip (v)    for the purpose of whipping = whip (N)

Lakhota (Buechel 1939: 176) has a similar process: an -*i* is prefixed to a transitive verb root to form instrumental nouns:

(16)    kahinta  → icahinte
        to sweep   broom
        kasleca  → icaslece
        to split    wedge

In some languages, the form which yields instrumental nouns is indistinguishable from that which forms agentive nouns. Thus, in Diola, a Western Atlantic language of the Niger-Congo family (J. D. Sapir 1965), we find the suffix -*a* used both for instruments, as in (a), and for agents, as in (b):

(17)    a. -lib        → ɛlib-a
           make slices    knife
        b. -tɛp        → atɛb-a
           build          builder

English, of course is similar: -*er* is used for both functions:

(18)    *Agentive*:
        sing → singer

(19)    *Instrumental*:
        slice → slicer
        mow → mower

### 1.4 *Manner nominalization*

Some languages have a special derivation pattern for forming nouns which mean 'way of "verbing"' from verbs. In Turkish, the suffix -(*y*)*iš* performs this function (where the form of the vowel may change according to regular rules of vowel harmony; Lewis 1967: 172–3):

(20)    a. yürü-       → yürüyüš
           to walk        way of walking
        b. ye-         → yeyiš
           to eat         way of eating
        c. yap-ıl-     → yapılıš
           to make(PASS)  way of being made

In some languages, the action noun is indeterminate between a fact/occurrence interpretation and a manner interpretation. English gerunds are like this: *his walking* can refer either to the fact or occurrence of his walking or to the way he walks. The action nouns in

Hebrew are similar. Similarly in Zulu, the verbal noun with an infinitival prefix can have both of these interpretations (Kunene 1974). Thus:

(21)     -hamba → uku-hamba
        walk     INF-walk =  i. the fact of walking
                                  ii. the way of walking

## 1.5 *Locative nominalization*

Some languages have devices for creating from a verb a noun which means 'a place where "verb" happens'. Many Bantu languages have such a device; here are examples from Si-Luyana (Givón 1970):

(22)     a. lóta   → li     - lot   - elo
           dream   CL 5/6 - dream - OBL = place of dreaming

        b. móna  → li     - mon  - eno
           see    CL 5/6 - see   - OBL = place of seeing

Sundanese, an Austronesian language of West Java, uses a discontinuous morpheme *paŋ . . . an* for this function (Robins 1959:358):

(23)     a. diuk   → *paŋdiukan*
          to sit    place of sitting = seat

        b. sare  → *paŋsarean*
          to sleep  place of sleeping = bed

In Hungarian (Edith Moravcsik, p.c.), the same suffix used for agentive and instrumental nominalization can form place nouns (-*ó* or -*ő* depending on vowel harmony):

(24)     a. ír      → író    (agentive)
          to write   writer

        b. hegyez   → hegyező (instrumental)
          to sharpen    sharpener (for pencils)

        c. társalog → társalgő (locative)
          to converse place of conversing = parlor

        d. mulat    → mulató (locative)
          to have fun   place for having fun = bar

## 1.6 *Objective nominalization*

Some languages have an affix which forms nouns designating the result, or the typical or 'cognate', object of an action, such as -*um* in Diola (J. D. Sapir 1965):

(25)     -lib      → lib*um*
        make slices   cuts, slices

Many Bantu languages have a similar device for creating a noun from a verb, where that noun means the object that results from an action. In Zulu, and in Si-Luyana, for example, a prefix for nouns in one of the non-human noun classes and the suffix -o will turn a verb into such a noun (Kunene 1974 and Givón 1970):

(26)    *Zulu*:

    a. -cabanga → um        - cabang - o
        think        CL PREFIX - think    - NZR = thought

    b. -cula → i            - cul  - o
        sing        CL PREFIX - sing - NZR = congregation/hymn

(27)    *Si-Luyana*:

    a. -lóta   → lu-lot-o
        dream    a dream

    b. -ìmba → lw-imb-o
        sing      a song

In Sundanese, the suffix -*an* is one affix that performs this function (Robins 1959:347):

(28)    a. inum    → inuman
            to drink    drink/alcohol

    b. omoŋ    → omoŋan
        to say        word/saying

    c. iŋət    → iŋətan
        to think    thought

In some languages, there is a process for taking a verb and forming a noun from it which names not the typical object nor the result of the activity denoted by the verb, but a noun with the passive meaning, that is, 'thing/person that is "verbed"'. In Si-Luyana, for example, either a human or a non-human noun-class prefix may be added to a passive verb to form an objective noun (Givón 1970:74–5):

(29)    -móna → mu    - mon - wa
        see       CL 1/2 - see  - PASS  = one who is seen

        → si       - mon - wa
        CL 7/8 - see   - PASS  = thing which is seen

### 1.7  *Reason nominalization*

Sundanese is an example of a language in which a noun meaning 'the reason for "verbing"' can be created from a verb (Robins 1959:351):

(30)  a. dataŋ         → paŋdataŋ
         to arrive          reason for arrival

      b. daek          → paŋdaek
         to be willing     reason for being willing

      c. indit         → paŋindit
         to leave           reason for leaving

## 1.8 *Predictability and productivity*

Languages typically show rather low predictability with respect to their noun formation processes. In some, such as Hebrew, for example, there is no general way to predict the form of the action nominal from the form of the triliteral root. In English, there is slightly more predictability. For example, almost any polysyllabic verb ending in *-ate* will form its action noun by adding *-tion*, as in *create/creation*. Similarly, most adjectives ending in *-able* or *-ible* form nouns in *-ity*: *respectable/respectability*. But there is no way to predict, for example, that *refuse* will take *-al* while *accuse* will take *-ation* or that *true* will add *th*.

Similarly, in Zulu, while many verbs freely form agentive nouns, as in (13), there is no apparent way to predict that certain other verbs cannot form such agentive nouns, as shown in (32) (Kunene 1974:120–1):

(31)    -lima       → um-lim-i
        cultivate   cultivator
        -diala      → um-dial-i
        play        player
        -cula       → um-cul-i
        sing        singer

(32)    -fulela     → *um-fulel-i
        thatch          thatcher
        -bhaceka → *um-bhacek-i
        plaster         plasterer

Semantically, it is very common to find a deverbal noun taking on special and unpredictable meanings precisely because it is a noun and as susceptible to idiosyncratic semantic change as any other lexical item. One very typical type of semantic specialization is the concretization of action nouns. Thus, in English, *proposal* may refer either to the fact or activity of proposing or to an actual statement or piece of writing in which an act of proposing is conveyed. However, *refusal* is much less amenable to a concrete interpretation:

(33)    His proposal }
        ?His refusal  } was fourteen pages long

An example of this type of semantic unpredictability in Hebrew involves the verbs *avad* and *pa'al* both meaning roughly 'work' and their agent noun counterparts *oved* and *po'el*. While the *avad* verb generally takes an animate subject and includes physical labor as well as mental effort, the agent noun *oved* is used for white-collar workers; the verb *pa'al* is used of mechanisms or systems (a watch, a new method) in the sense of work as 'function, operate', but its morphologically related agent noun *po'el* refers to a blue-collar or manual laborer.

Finally, we note one further type of unpredictability: a derivational process is often blocked just in case the language happens to have a lexical item already filling the 'slot' which the derived form would occupy. It is for this reason, for example, that the English agentive *-er* nominalization process does not apply to verbs such as *study*: the English lexicon already contains *student*. (For some discussion of the question of productivity in derivational morphology, see Thompson 1974.)

## 2 Processes for forming noun phrases from predicates and propositions

### 2.1 *The 'action nominal'*
In this section we will discuss various phenomena associated with the so-called 'action nominal', that is, a noun phrase which contains, in addition to a noun derived from a verb, one or more reflexes of a proposition or a predicate. For example, in English, the term 'action nominal' could refer to a noun phrase such as

(34)    the enemy's destruction of the city

in which *the enemy's* is a reflex of the subject and *of the city* is related to the object of the proposition:

(35)    The enemy destroyed the city

The term could also be used to refer to a noun phrase such as

(36)    the loud chanting in the quad

in which *loud* relates to the adverb *loudly* and the prepositional phrase to its counterpart in the predicate:

(37)    chanting loudly in the quad

The derived noun itself in the action nominal is formed by the process which creates action/state nouns from action or stative verbs, described just above in 1.1. It is a 'non-finite' verb form in the sense that it does not manifest any of the tense and/or agreement morphology found with verbs functioning as predicates in ordinary simple sentences. We shall examine the syntactic properties of action nominals in languages of various types, comparing the action nominal on the one hand with sentences expressing approximately the same information content and on the other hand with non-derived noun phrases, i.e. comparing action nominal syntax with sentential (verbal) syntax and with nominal syntax. Perhaps the main result of this investigation, providing also a framework within which to structure the discussion, is that action nominals typically have some of the syntactic characteristics of both sentences and non-derived noun phrases, i.e. they occupy an intermediate position between these two categories; the extent to which action nominals are verbal or nominal varies considerably from language to language, as will be seen below. The intermediate status of action nominals between verbs and nouns can probably be used as one of the defining criteria of an action nominal. (For further illustration of the approach to the syntax of action nominals presented here, see Comrie (1976b).) We may illustrate this briefly with an example from English. If we compare the noun phrases in (38), sentence (39), and the action nominal construction in (40) below

(38)     the enemy's weapons/the weapons of the enemy

(39)     The enemy destroyed the city

(40)     the enemy's destruction of the city

then we observe that despite the close parallelism among the three types of constructions, the action nominal, like an ordinary noun, is modified by an adjective, as in (42), although the corresponding verb would have a manner adverb, as in (41); further, its internal structure parallels that of an ordinary noun phrase in that it takes genitive attributes, while in a sentence, subject and direct object are not marked by any preposition or ending:

(41)     The enemy destroyed the city rapidly

(42)     the enemy's rapid destruction of the city

Some speakers of English, it is true, can also keep a bit of verbal syntax by using a manner adverbial with the action nominal:

(43)     ?the enemy's destruction of the city rapidly

With the so-called gerundive nominal in English, the internal structure is almost completely verbal (prepositionless direct object, manner adverbial):

(44)     The enemy('s) destroying the city rapidly surprised everyone

Even here, however, there is one (optional) feature of noun phrase syntax, in the possibility of having the subject in the genitive, i.e. as if it is an attribute to a noun rather than a verbal form. Thus the English derived nominal has very few verbal characteristics, the gerund very few nominal characteristics.

The discussion of this section is divided into two parts. In the first, we examine whether and how verb-internal categories (e.g. tense, aspect, voice) are retained in action nominals, in relative isolation from other constituents of the action nominal noun phrase; we are not, of course, here interested primarily in the phonetic shape of morphological categories, but rather in whether or not those categories can be expressed as categories in the action nominal. Once we determine that a given category is expressed in the action nominal, we may then ask whether it is expressed in the same way as it would be in the corresponding verb or noun. In the second part, we discuss the possibilities for combining verbs/nouns/action nominals with other constituents of the sentence/noun phrase, in particular: the valency of verbs/nouns/action nominals (the number and type of subjects, direct objects, other objects, genitival attributes, etc., that a verb/ noun/action nominal may take), and also some wider collocational possibilities, for instance of verbs with manner adverbials and nouns with adjectives. Finally, we note briefly some data that seem to fall somewhat outside the present framework, namely properties of action nominals that seem to distinguish them from both verbs and non-derived noun phrases.

### 2.1.1 Verbal and nominal categories

2.1.1.1 *Verbal categories.* In this section, we shall examine the extent to which such typically verbal categories as tense, aspect, voice, transitivity, and negation are retained in action nominals; since these categories are not typical of noun phrases in general, retention of such categories in action nominals is evidence of the (partial) verbal nature of such action nominals. We might expect the verbal category of mood to appear in action nominals as well, but in fact, as we are not aware of languages where mood is retained in action nominals (indeed, mood in any non-finite verbal form seems relatively rare), we are led to assume that as far as mood is concerned action nominals simply do not retain this verbal category. When we speak of a verbal category being retained in an action nominal, we mean of course its retention *as a morphological category* (that is, actually expressed by a bound morpheme) in the action nominal. It is no doubt often possible to give a close paraphrase by lexical means of verbal categories in action nominals – for example *your current failure to pay your bills* (compare present tense) – but such lexical paraphrases do not constitute morphological categories. As a final introductory point, it should be noted that total loss of or partial neutralization of some or all of the verbal categories of tense, aspect, mood, and voice is also characteristic of non-finite verbal forms that are usually still considered part of the verbal paradigm (e.g. participles, gerundives). Thus we seem here to be dealing with a cline of expressibility of verbal categories: finite verbs can express the most such categories, non-finite verbs fewer, action nominals still fewer, and other noun phrases fewest of all.

2.1.1.1.1 *Tense.* The English action nominal provides a good example of the loss of tense *vis-à-vis* verbal forms. Corresponding to the basic past/non-past distinction, for example *the enemy destroyed the city* versus *the enemy is destroying the city*, we have only the one action nominal, *the enemy's destruction of the city*. In appropriate contexts, present or past time reference may be forced or preferred, but there is no overt category of tense. (For instance, (45) below would probably be assigned present time reference, and (46) past time reference):

(45)    The enemy's destruction of the city is causing consternation

(46)    The enemy's destruction of the city caused consternation

In English, non-finite verbal forms also show some neutralization of tense opposition; actually the past/non-past distinction is combined with the perfect/non-perfect aspectual distinction to give a single opposition, past-or-perfect versus non-past, for example:

(47)    Having heard so many lies from you before, no-one is prepared to believe what you're saying now

The paraphrase with a finite verb would be: *Since they have heard so many lies* ... (perfect).

(48)    Having heard so many lies from you at the previous meeting, no-one is prepared to believe what you're saying now

The paraphrase with a finite verb would be: *Since they heard so many lies* ... (past).

(49)    Walking down the street, I usually meet many other students from the institute

The paraphrase with a finite verb would be: *When I walk/am walking down the street* ... (present – more strictly, relative present, see below).

With the action nominal, not even this much of a tense distinction may be made.

In some languages, however, tense distinctions can (or even must) be made, at least with some action nominals. In Turkish, for instance, the action nominal in -dik is non-future, whereas that in -ecek is future, for example (Lewis 1967:254):

(50)    Çocuk-lar-a asağiya    inip                    kendisi-ni sokak-ta
        child-PL-to  downwards having descended her-DO      street-in

        bekle-*dik*-leri-ni   söyle-di
        await-VN-their-DO  say-3SG PAST

        'She told the children that they went (had gone) down and waited for her in the street'

(51)    Çocuk-lar-a asağiya inip    kendisi-ni sokak-ta
        bekli-*yecek*-leri-ni    söyle-di
        'She told the children that they would go down and wait for her in the street'

Although the range of tense distinctions here is not identical to that found with finite verbs (for instance, in that there is no past/non-past distinction), still the future/non-future distinction is possible, indeed required. Actually, the distinction here is primarily one of relative tense: the -ecek verbal noun refers to a situation subsequent in time to that of the verb on which it is dependent, and the -dik verbal noun to a situation prior to or simultaneous with that of the verb on which it is dependent. The interpretation of the tense category as relative rather than absolute tense is very common generally with non-finite verbal forms: thus if in examples (47–9) above one were to replace the main verbs *is* (*prepared*) and *meet* by their past tense equivalents *was* (*prepared*) and *met*, then the participial forms would be, respectively, perfect, past, and present relative to the past time reference of the main verb, i.e. paraphrasable as, respectively, *since they had heard . . ., since they had heard . . .* (English does not distinguish overtly between perfect-in-the-past and past-in-the-past), *when I walked/was walking*.

2.1.1.1.2 *Aspect.* In some languages which have an aspectual distinction (e.g. perfective versus imperfective), the categorial distinction is usually lost with verbal nouns, as in Russian, where, for example, corresponding to the imperfective *pisat'* and perfective *napisat'* 'to write' there is only the one action nominal *pisanie*:

(52)    *Pisanie* takix statej daet mnogo radosti
        'The writing of such articles gives much pleasure'

In this sentence, the sense may be either that pleasure is given by the fact of involvement in the act of writing (imperfective), or that pleasure is given by the fact that one has completed the act of writing (perfective). In a few instances, Russian does seem to have a morphological distinction in action nominals corresponding to that found in verbs: for example corresponding to the verbal pair *rassmatrivat'* (imperfective)/ *rassmotret'* (perfective) 'to examine' we have action nominals *rassmatrivanie* and *rassmotrenie*. However, the difference between such action nominals is lexical rather than aspectual: *rassmotrenie* refers primarily to examination or scrutiny as a legal term, whereas *rassmatrivanie* is the semantically neutral action nominal of the pair. In Polish, on the other hand, we find that the aspectual distinction imperfective/perfective is quite widespread with action nominals, so that corresponding to the verbal pair *czytać* (imperfective)/*przeczytać* (perfective) 'to read' we have the action nominals *czytanie/przeczytanie*:

(53)     *Czytanie* tej książki dało dużo radości
         'The reading of this book gave much pleasure'

*Czytanie* here refers to the process of reading which gave pleasure.

(54)     *Przeczytanie* tej książki dało dużo radości

With *przeczytanie*, reference is to the totality of the act of reading which resulted in giving pleasure. In both Polish and Russian, non-finite verbal forms (infinitives, participles, and verbal adverbs) do show aspect, so that failure to show aspect in the action nominal is a clear loss of a verbal category; in Russian, this loss is much more widespread than in Polish.

2.1.1.1.3 *Voice*. In many languages, there is no overt morphological distinction corresponding to that between active and passive verbal forms, as can be seen from the English ((55–8)), Russian ((59–62)), and Maori ((63–6)) examples below:

(55)     The enemy destroyed the city

(56)     the enemy's *destruction* of the city

(57)     The city was destroyed by the enemy

(58)     the city's *destruction* by the enemy

(59)     Vrag razrušil gorod
         'The enemy destroyed the city'

(60)     *razrušenie* goroda
         'the *destruction* of the city'

(61)    Gorod byl razrušen vragom
    'The city was destroyed by the enemy'

(62)    *razrušenie* goroda vragom
    'the destruction of the city by the enemy'

(63)    Ka patu te tangata i   te   whekė
    PCL kill  the man    DO the octopus
    'The man killed the octopus'

(64)    te *patunga*  a te   tangata i   te   wheke
    the killing    of the man     DO the octopus
    'the man's killing of the octopus'

(65)    Ka patua    te  wheke e  te  tangata
    PCL kill(PASS) the octopus by the man
    'The octopus was killed by the man'

(66)    te *patunga* o te  wheke e  te  tangata
    the killing   of the octopus by the man
    'the killing of the octopus by the man'

The forms *destruction, razrušenie,* and *patunga* ('killing') occur both where one would have active verbs and where one would have passive verbs. However, if we look not simply at the morphology, but also at the syntax of such constructions, in particular at the valency (number and kind of noun phrase arguments) of the action nominal relative to the valency of active and passive verbs – note in particular the expression of the passive agent – then we see that there is motivation for saying that in these languages the syntactic active/passive distinction is maintained, although it is not maintained morphologically. We shall return to this phenomenon below.

In other languages, however, the active/passive distinction with the action nominal is made both syntactically and morphologically: in Turkish, the passive suffix is *-il*, and the introduction of the agent, though somewhat unnatural with the Turkish passive, is possible:

(67)    Hasan mektub - u  yaz  - dɨ
    Hasan letter   - DO write - 3SG PAST
    'Hasan wrote the letter'

(68)    Hasan - ɨn  mektub - u  yaz  - ma - sɨ
    Hasan - GEN letter   - DO write - VN - his
    'Hasan's writing of the letter'

(69)   Mektub (Hasan tarafından) yaz  - ıl    - dı
       letter    Hasan by         write - PASS - 3SG PAST
       'The letter was written by Hasan'

(70)   mektub - un  (Hasan tarafından) *yaz  - ıl   -ma - sı*
       letter   - GEN Hasan by          write - PASS - VN - his
       'the letter's writing (being written, the writing of the letter) by
       Hasan'

In claiming that traces of voice in action nominal constructions are
instances of verbal non-nominal syntax in the action nominal, we are of
course assuming that non-derived noun phrases do not and cannot
exhibit the same phenomena. This might seem to be called into question
by data from English, where even with non-derived nouns like *book* we
have a range of possibilities similar to that of a derived noun like *refusal*:

(71)   Shakespeare's latest book

(72)   the latest book by Shakespeare

(73)   John's refusal (to approve the plan)

(74)   the refusal by John (to approve the plan)

In particular, the *by*-phrase in (72) would seem to indicate that even
non-derived noun phrases allow a passive agent (cf. Chomsky 1970: 206–
7). However, whatever analysis is given to noun phrases like (72) in
English, the 'passive of a non-derived noun phrase' analysis is not
generalizable to (all) other languages, since there are many languages
where non-derived nouns like *book* do not allow a passive agent
although action nominals do. Thus in Russian we have:

(75)   kniga Tolstogo
       'Tolstoy's book'

(76)   *kniga Tolstym
       'the book by Tolstoy'

(77)   čtenie Ivana
       'Ivan's reading'

(78)   čtenie knigi Ivanom
       'the reading of the book by Ivan/Ivan's reading of the book'

In such languages, passive-like features of action nominals are more
clearly instances of verbal, not nominal, syntax.

2.1.1.1.4 *Transitivity.* A somewhat similar distinction which, in some languages, is made with verbs but not action nominals is that between transitive and intransitive members of a verbal pair. In English there is typically no distinction even with the verb – for example *open* (transitive) versus *open* (intransitive), so that there is no *loss* of distinction in the action of the nominal:

(79)    the opening of the door (cf.: someone opened the door)

(80)    the opening of the door (cf.: the door opened)

In Russian, this distinction must be made with the verb, and cannot be made with the action nominal:

(81)    Kto-to    otkryl   dver'
        'Someone opened the door'

(82)    Dver' otkryla-s'
        'The door opened'

The intransitive verb has the 'reflexive' suffix -*s'*/-*sja*, which never occurs with action nominals:

(83)    otkrytie dveri                              (cf. both (81) and (82))
        'the opening of the door'

(84)    *otkrytie-s'/*otkrytie-sja dveri
        'the opening (by itself) of the door'

In Polish, on the other hand, the distinction is made with both verbs and the action nominal (the *się* here is the reflexive morpheme, corresponding to the Russian *sja* above):

(85)    Ktoś otworzył drzwi
        'Someone opened the door'

(86)    Drzwi otworzyły sie
        'The door opened'

(87)    otwieranie drzwi
        '(someone's) opening of the door'

(88)    otwieranie się drzwi
        'the (possibly spontaneous) opening of the door'

2.1.1.1.5 *Negation.* As a final verbal category in terms of which to view action nominals, let us consider negation.

Logically, there are three ways in which an action nominal could be negated: (i) in the same way as sentences, (ii) in the same way as nouns, (iii) in a way different from that found with either nouns or verbs. Thai shows case (i), English exemplifies both case (i) and case (ii), while Modern Hebrew presents us with case (iii).

Action nominals in Thai are negated in exactly the same way as are sentences, with the preverbal *may*:

(89)    a. John *may* ʔaan - naŋsɨɨ
         John NEG read - book
         'John doesn't study'

      b. Kaan *may* ʔaan - naŋsɨɨ khɔɔŋ John
         NZR  NEG read  book  of     John
         'John's not studying'

In English, sentences are negated with *not*, while nouns are negated with *non-*:[1]

(90)    a. Harry is *not* my brother

      b. This is a *non*-party

In action nominals, the sentential negator *not* is rigidly excluded and only the nominal negator *non-* can be used, suggesting again that the English action nominal is rather close to the noun end of the nominal–verbal scale:

(91)    Gloria's $\left\{ \begin{array}{c} \text{*not} \\ \text{non-} \end{array} \right\}$ participation in the meeting surprised me

The more verbal gerund may occur with either, though *not* is preferred if adjuncts are present:

(92)    *Gloria's *not* participation

(93)    a. Gloria's *not* running
      b. Gloria's *non*-running
      c. ?Gloria's *non*-running in the marathon

In written Modern Hebrew, a negative prefix *iy-*, which is used neither for negating sentences nor nouns, is found in action nominals:

(94)    a. Hem *lo*  amdu   al zxut-am
         they NEG insisted on right-their
         'They didn't insist on their right'

      b. *iy* - amidat  - am  al zxut - am
         non - insistence - their on right - their
         'their non-insistence on their right'

2.1.1.1.6 *Summary*. Thus of the typically verbal categories of mood, tense, aspect, voice, transitivity, and negation, we see that mood is (?nearly) always absent from the action nominal; tense usually so (though some languages have some tense differentiation here); and aspect rather less usually so. Voice as a morphological category tends (but only tends) to be absent, although there are often grounds for retaining it as a syntactic category with action nominals, and transitivity tends not to be expressed. Negation can typically be expressed, but the negative marker itself may be a verbal negative morpheme, a nominal negative morpheme, or a special form found only in nominalizations.

2.1.1.2 *Nominal categories*. The main categories that we shall look at in connection with the action nominal are case, number, and definiteness. If other noun phrases of a language show these categories, then so, in general, do action nominals; indeed, with respect to case and definiteness in particular, this is almost a defining characteristic of action nominals. Thus the use of the definite article with action nominals in English and Classical Arabic parallels its use with other noun phrases:

(95)     the bread

(96)     the arrival

(97)     John's bread

(98)     John's arrival

(99)     al-xubzu
         'the bread'

(100)    al-qatlu
         'the killing'

(101)    xubzu zaydin
         'Zaid's bread'

(102)    qatlu zaydin
         'Zaid's killing'

Note that in both English and Arabic the possessor (*John*/*Zaid*) can be understood as either the agent or the patient of the proposition expressed by the action nominal.

Number is more difficult to signal in action nominals, since certain non-derived noun phrases, in particular abstract noun phrases (e.g. *the weather*) do not show number, and since action nominals fall into this class, they would be expected not to show number for this reason, quite irrespective of their characterization in terms of nominal and verbal categories. Number is normally shown only when it can be understood as signaling 'occurrences', or 'cases' of 'verb-ing', as with English *murders* for individual acts of murder, or *protestations* for individual occurrences of protesting.[2]

The case category might seem relatively trivial, but in fact some languages demonstrate the *partially* nominal character of certain action nominals by allowing them to stand in only a restricted number of cases, rather than the full gamut of cases allowed to other noun phrases. In this respect, the Turkish verbal noun in *-mek* is very much a noun, but not completely so: it may stand in any case except the genitive (Lewis 1967:167–9). Finnish has a number of forms (traditionally called 'infinitives') which are nouns derived from verbs, although only a limited number of cases of these nominalizations are used, often with specialized meanings. For instance, the so-called second infinitive occurs only in the inessive and instructive cases. The basic meaning of the inessive is to indicate 'place in which', for example *talo* 'house', *talo-ssa* 'in (the) house'. The inessive of the second infinitive indicates an action simultaneous with that of the main verb:

(103)    Meidän kirjoittae-ssa-mme    hän luki  kirjaa
         our     writing-INESSIVE-our  he   read book
         'While we were writing (during our writing) he was reading a book'

(The suffix *-mme* in this example is a first person plural possessive ending, correlating with the (omissible) genitive pronoun *meidän*.) The basic meaning of the instructive is to express adverbials of manner or means (e.g. *omin avuin* 'by one's own abilities'), and the instructive of the second infinitive also indicates the manner in which the action of the main verb is carried out:

(104)    Pullo lensi suhiste-n          halki    ilman
         bottle flew whistling-INSTRUCTIVE through air
         'The bottle flew whistling through the air'

With the category of case, then, we find further evidence that there are forms intermediate between noun and verb (or, more generally, non-noun). There is also a diachronic aspect to such intermediate forms, in that there are many instances where they represent an intermediate historical stage in the verbalization of nominal forms. For instance, the infinitive in *-ti* (or *-t'*) in most Slavic languages derives historically from the locative case of a verbal noun; in Old Church Slavonic, and still to a limited extent in Slovenian, this contrasts with the old accusative of this verbal noun in *-t"b* (or *-t*), but in the modern Slavic languages the infinitive has been completely integrated into the verbal paradigm and has virtually all of the typically verbal categories (apart from person and number, like most non-finite forms), and none of the typically nominal categories.

### 2.1.2 *Syntactic collocation*

2.1.2.1 *Valency.* Perhaps the most interesting evidence for the hybrid verbal–nominal nature of the action nominal comes from the expression of subject and direct object with the action nominal; other kinds of objects (marked objects) provide, in general, less interesting material, since they usually occur in the same form with both verb and action nominal, as in the following English and German examples:

(105)   Harry objected *to Bill's solution*

(106)   Harry's objection *to Bill's solution*

(107)   Willi spottet *über den Armen*
        'Willi makes fun of (lit. over, about) the poor chap'

(108)   Willis Spott *über den Armen*
        'Willi's mockery of the poor chap'

With subject and direct object (unmarked adjuncts), however, there is a greater extent to which the action nominal, despite its clear semantic relation to a sentence, accommodates itself to noun phrase syntax.

2.1.2.1.1 *Subjects and objects assimilate to* NP *syntax: English.* The relevant aspects of sentence syntax in this section are simply that a sentence contains a verb preceded by a subject (with no overt case marker, apart from such pronouns as *I/me* with a nominative/ accusative distinction), and possibly (depending primarily on which lexical verb is under discussion) followed by a direct object (again with no overt case marker, apart from the above-mentioned pronouns):

(109)   John arrived

(110)   The enemy destroyed the city

As far as noun phrase syntax is concerned, and we are here dealing firstly with non-derived nouns, instead of adjuncts lacking any overt marker we find instead the possibility of a preposed noun phrase with the ending *'s* (Saxon genitive) and of a postposed adjunct with the preposition *of* (Norman genitive):

(111)    John's car

(112)    the roof of the house

The Saxon genitive is, essentially, in complementary distribution with the definite article, i.e., were it not for the *John's* of *John's car* we should have *the car*.

Turning now to action nominals, and using as examples those corresponding to (109–10) above, we see that the internal structure is much more similar to that of a noun phrase:

(113)    John's arrival

(114)    the enemy's destruction of the city

Moreover, if the Saxon genitive is absent, the definite article appears:

(115)    the arrival

(116)    the destruction of the city (by the enemy)

Although the internal structure is more similar to that of a noun phrase, with Saxon and Norman genitive rather than 'nominative' and 'accusative', yet still there is a close correlation between the two kinds of genitive in these action nominals and the subject/direct object distinction with sentences: Saxon (prenominal) genitive corresponds to subject (preverbal), while Norman (postnominal) genitive corresponds to direct object (postverbal):

(117)    the enemy – destroyed – the city
         the enemy's – destruction – of the city

This is an absolute correspondence where both genitives are present, i.e. *the enemy's destruction of the city* cannot be the derived nominal of *the city destroyed the enemy*.

In action nominal constructions with only one genitive, the interpretation of that genitive as corresponding to subject or direct object of the verb is more complex, except, of course, with action nominals of intransitive verbs, where the genitive cannot correspond to a (non-existent) direct object. Taking the Saxon genitive first, we find that in general where the action nominal corresponds to a verb that *requires* a direct object, then in the absence of a Norman genitive the Saxon genitive must be interpreted as corresponding to a direct object:

(118)    Bill's execution

(cf. (*someone*) *executed Bill*, not *Bill executed someone*, as there is no *\*Bill executed*). Where, however, the action nominal corresponds to a verb that does not require, but only allows, a direct object, then there is a tendency for only that interpretation to be possible where the Saxon genitive corresponds to the subject of the verb, often in defiance of real-world probability:

(119)    John's reading

(cf. *John reads*);

(120)    Shakespeare's reading

(cf. *Shakespeare reads*, not (*someone*) *reads Shakespeare*, despite the greater likelihood of a discourse being about someone's reading of Shakespeare);

(121)    ?the book's reading

(grammatical, though nonsensical in any literal interpretation, if it corresponds to *the book reads*; ungrammatical if it corresponds to (*someone*) *reads the book*). There are still some unaccounted-for examples left over – for example both *John's performance* (cf. *John performed*) and *the play's performance* (cf. (*someone*) *performed the play*) are possible – but the general tendency described remains. With the Norman genitive, there seems to be at best a tendency for this posthead genitive to be interpreted as object of the action nominal, although the subject interpretation is rarely completely excluded, as in *the shooting of the hunters*. We shall see below that some other languages have a tendency to discriminate between genitives interpreted as subject and those interpreted as direct object of an action nominal in ways similar to that discussed here for English.

### 2.1.2.1.2 *Subjects and objects retain sentence syntax*

a. *Tamil* and *Avar*. At the opposite extreme from English (where subjects and direct objects of action nominals are completely assimilated to noun phrase syntax) we find languages like Tamil (a Dravidian language) and Avar (a Northeast Caucasian language) where the internal syntax of the action nominal noun phrase, as far as subject and direct object are concerned, is like that of a sentence and different from that of a noun phrase. In Tamil, subjects have no inflection, while direct objects either have no inflection or take the suffix *-ai* (if definite and/or animate):

(122)    Nīṅkaḷ it-ai      cey-t-īrkaḷ
         you     this-DO  do-PAST-2PL
         'You did this'

Genitives take either no ending or one of the endings *-in*, *-uṭaiya*: the possibility of one of these endings, versus their impossibility with subjects or direct objects, is a sufficient criterion for distinguishing genitives from other uninflected noun forms. In the action nominal constructions, the genitive forms are excluded, and the morphology of subject and direct object is as in a sentence:

(123)   Nīṅkaḷ it-ai    cey-tal tarmam
        you    this-DO do-VN  right conduct
        'Your doing this is right'

In Avar, subjects of intransitive verbs and direct objects take no ending, while subjects of transitive verbs stand in the so-called ergative case:

(124)   Du-ca  ṭex̣  çal-ula
        you-ERG book read-PRES
        'You read the book'

With the action nominal, this same construction remains, although in non-derived noun phrases one would find genitive *du-r* 'your' or genitive *ṭox̣-ol* 'of the book' (cf. *dur ču* 'your horse'):

(125)   Du-ca  ṭex̣  çal-i    bugo çaq̇ čik̇ab iš
        you-ERG book read-VN is    very good thing
        'Your reading the book is a very good thing'

Having now examined the two poles – complete assimilation to noun phrase syntax (English) and complete retention of clause syntax (Tamil, Avar) – we shall go on to some further instances of complete assimilation to the internal structure of the noun phrase, and then on to some instances where assimilation to noun phrase syntax is only partial.

   b. *Russian.* As we showed above, one of the characteristics of English noun phrase syntax is the existence of two types of genitive, Saxon and Norman, the difference between which is utilized in action nominal noun phrases to a large extent to correlate with that between subject and direct object of a verb. This use of two genitives seems to be relatively rare among the languages of the world: it exists to a limited extent in German, though here there is a strong tendency for there to be only a preposed genitive or only a postposed genitive, largely irrespective of subject or direct object correspondence. An expression such as the following is rare:

(126)   Herrn Dührings Umwälzung der Wissenschaft
        'Mr Dühring's overturning of science'

Russian, on the other hand, has only one genitive construction, which usually follows its head noun. In certain styles it may precede, but this is a reflection of (relatively) free word order, and not, as in English or German, of a separate syntactic position. In an action nominal, a genitive can in principle correspond to either a subject or a direct object, so that one finds examples like the following, with either only a subject or only a direct object:

(127)   priezd soldat
        'the arrival of the soldiers'

(128)   razrušenie goroda
        'the destruction of the city'

Compare these with the sentences:

(129)   Soldaty priexali
        'The soldiers arrived'

(130)   Razrušili gorod
        'They (unspecified) destroyed the city'

What is impossible in Russian (and in many other languages), however, is the combination of subjective and objective genitive within a single action nominal noun phrase, as in English the *enemy's destruction of the city*. The equivalent string in Russian might seem to be one of the following:

(131)   razrušenie  goroda  vraga
        destruction of-city  of-enemy

(132)   razrušenie  vraga     goroda
        destruction of-enemy of-city

But although these are both well-formed in Russian, they do not mean 'the enemy's destruction of the city' but, respectively, 'the destruction of the enemy's city' and 'the destruction of the city's enemy', that is, in either case we have a head noun with a single genitive dependent on it, i.e. [[*razrušenie*] ([*goroda*] [*vraga*])] and [[*razrušenie*] ([*vraga*] [*goroda*])] rather than ([*razrušenie*] [*goroda*] [*vraga*]). In fact, there is *no* way of translating literally into Russian *the enemy's destruction of the city*: the greater restrictiveness of Russian noun phrase syntax, coupled with the fact that action nominals reflect noun phrase rather than sentence syntax, means that certain possibilities that are open to English are impossible here.

It is possible to translate *the enemy's destruction of the city* into Russian, namely as:

(133)  razrušenie goroda vragom
       destruction of-city  by-enemy

However, this corresponds more literally to 'the destruction of the city by the enemy' than to 'the enemy's destruction of the city': compare the discussion of 'passive' action nominals in section 2.1.1.1.3. (133) should be compared with the passive sentence:

(134)  Gorod byl razrušen vragom
       'The city was destroyed by the enemy'

In comparing the sentence in (134) with the action nominal in (133), we note that the sentence has a subject but no direct object, therefore the subject corresponds to a genitive in the action nominal noun phrase; *vragom* 'by the enemy' is neither subject nor direct object, and therefore remains unchanged in the action nominal noun phrase.

c. *Czech.* At first sight, Czech might seem to exhibit essentially the same pattern as (the genetically closely related) Russian: subjects of sentences are in the nominative case, direct objects in the accusative; genitives (typically posthead) occur both with non-derived nouns and with action nominals, in the latter case interpretable as corresponding to either the subject or the direct object of a verb; it is not possible to have both subjective and objective genitive qualifying the same action nominal, although 'passive' paraphrases are possible:

(135)  Starý vědec přišel
       'The old scientist arrived'

(136)  příchod starého vědce
       'the old scientist's arrival'

(137)  Upálili Jana Husa
       'They (unspecified) burnt Jan Hus'

(138)  upálení Jana Husa
       'the burning of Jan Hus'

(139)  Člověk vykořistuje člověka
       'Man exploits man'

(140)  *Člověka (GEN) vykořist'ování člověka
       'man's exploitation of man'

(141)  vykořist'ování  člověka člověkem
       'the exploitation of man by man'

However, there is one important difference in (non-derived) noun phrase syntax between Czech and Russian (and English): in Czech, wherever possible, the adnominal genitive is replaced, preferably, by a possessive adjective in *-ův* (stem *-ov-*) or *-in-*.[3] That is, the genitive form found in (142) is much less natural than the possessive adjective form seen in (143):

(142)   ?kniha ‹ vědce
        book    scientist(GEN)

(143)   vědcova   kniha
        scientist's book

Like other adjectives in Czech, *vědcova* is typically prenominal, and it agrees with its noun in number, case, and gender.

This same preference for possessive adjectives, subject to exactly the same restrictions as in non-derived noun phrases, carries over into action nominal noun phrases, in particular in correspondence with the subject of the corresponding verb (see further below). Although (136), i.e. *příchod starého vědce*, is the only possibility given the attribute on 'scientist', without this attribute the possessive adjective would be preferred:

(144)   ?příchod vědce

(145)   vědcův příchod
        'the scientist's arrival'

Since the prenominal possessive adjective and the postnominal genitive represent distinct syntactic positions in Czech, it is possible for both to occur with the same head noun. Just as in English one finds Saxon genitive$_1$ – action nominal$_2$ – Norman genitive$_3$ corresponding to subject$_1$ – verb$_2$ – direct object$_3$, so in Czech one finds possessive adjective$_1$ – action nominal$_2$ – objective genitive$_3$:

(146)   Leninova kritika mylných názorů oportunistů
        'Lenin's criticism of the erroneous views of the opportunists'

The difference between Czech noun phrase syntax (the possibility of prenominal possessive adjectives) and Russian noun phrase syntax (which virtually lacks this possibility) means that Czech has, for noun phrases, including action nominals, of the appropriate class, a syntactic possibility that is lacking in Russian. This possibility in Czech is very similar to the Saxon genitive in English, except that it is subject to the constraints mentioned in note 3.

Although we have illustrated the use of possessive adjectives in action nominals with Czech material, since the possibility for forming such adjectives is very widespread and productive in Czech, the same possibility does exist to a more limited extent in many other languages, including English and Russian, in particular with pronouns. Thus English has (pronominal) possessive adjectives like *my*, *your*: cf. Russian *moj*, *tvoj*. These can be used in correspondence with the subject of a verb, just like possessive adjectives in Czech, even where there is also an objective genitive present:

(147)   moe razrušenie goroda
        'my destruction of the city'

(The 'passive' action nominal is of course also possible, i.e. *razrušenie goroda mnoju* 'the destruction of the city by me'.) One slight complication in Russian is that some forms occupy an intermediate position between genitive and possessive adjectives: the third person forms *ego* 'his, its', *ee* 'her', *ix* 'their', unlike the first and second person forms, are morphologically genitives and retain some of the syntactic properties of genitives; however, they also have some of the syntactic properties of possessive adjectives, for instance in that they usually precede their head noun, and can co-occur with a postnominal genitive:

(148)   ego razrušenie goroda
        'his destruction of the city'

Just as in English the distinction between Saxon and Norman genitive correlates to some extent with that between subject and direct object, so in Czech the distinction between prenominal possessive adjective and postnominal genitive often corresponds to that between subject and direct object, as in (149–50).

(149)   matčina ztráta
        'mother's loss (of something)'

(150)   ztráta matky
        '(someone's) loss of (his) mother'

The preference for the genitive in (150) represents a difference between action nominal noun phrase syntax and non-derived noun phrase syntax, since in the latter the possessive adjective *matčin-* would invariably be preferred to the genitive *matky*, for example *matčina kniga* is greatly preferred to *kniga matky* for 'mother's book'. Overall in Czech, there is near identity, right down to idiosyncratic details, between the syntactic structure of action nominal noun phrases and non-derived noun phrases; the main exception is the utilization of the possessive adjective/postnominal genitive distinction to correspond to subject versus direct object, and here the structure of the action nominal noun phrase differs from that of other noun phrases in order the more closely to parallel the syntactic structure of a sentence.


2.1.2.1.3 *Subjects and objects only partially assimilate to NP syntax*
a. *Turkish.* We may now go on to languages where assimilation to noun phrase syntax in the action nominal construction is only partial. A clear example of this phenomenon is provided by Turkish. Sentences in Turkish have a subject in the absolute case (no ending) and a direct object in either the absolute case (if indefinite) or the accusative case (if definite) with the ending -*i*/-*i*/-*u*/-*ü* (variants here and below are vowel harmony variants); for the sake of simplicity, only definite direct objects are used in the examples below. Possession is always expressed with a possessive pronoun suffixed to the head noun; if there is a possessive noun it precedes the head noun in the genitive case (ending -*in*/-*in*/-*un*/-*ün*), so that the possession is in effect marked twice, as in the following example with a non-derived head noun:

(151)   Hasan-ɨn   kapɨ-sɨ
        Hasan-GEN door-his
        'Hasan's door'

In the action nominal noun phrase, there is assimilation to noun phrase syntax in so far as the subject of the sentence corresponds to a genitive attribute of an action nominal (with the appropriate possessive suffix on the action nominal); but sentence syntax is retained for the expression of the direct object, which remains in the absolute (indefinite) or accusative (definite) case:

(152)   Hasan gel-di
        Hasan come-3SG PAST
        'Hasan came'

(153)   Hasan-ɨn   gel-me-si
        Hasan-GEN come-VN-his
        'Hasan's coming'

(154)   Hasan mektub-u yaz-dɨ
        Hasan letter-DO   write-3SG PAST
        'Hasan wrote the letter'

(155)   Hasan-ɨn   mektub-u yaz-ma-sɨ
        Hasan-GEN letter-DO   write-VN-his
        'Hasan's writing of the letter'

In (155) it would not be possible to have genitive *mektub-un*. This is so even if the subject of the action nominal is not expressed:

(156)  mektub-u yaz-ma
       letter-DO  write-VN
       'the writing of the letter'

It is impossible to say *\*mektub-un yaz-ma(-si)*; in (156) there is, of course, no possessive suffix, given that the subject of the action nominal is completely unexpressed. Thus Turkish has a quite general correspondence rule:

> Subject of sentence = genitive of action nominal noun phrase
> Direct object of sentence = direct object of action nominal noun phrase

We may note in passing that a similar situation holds with the English gerundive nominal: this typically has verbal syntax, but does allow (in certain styles, require) noun phrase syntax in the expression of the subject, though not the object, in the (Saxon) genitive:

(157)  the enemy('s) destroying the city

b. *Classical Arabic.* Classical Arabic provides a similar example of partly nominal, partly verbal syntax of the action nominal. Subjects usually have the nominative ending -*u(n)*, direct objects the accusative ending -*a(n)*. (The qualification *usually* is because of certain morphologically irregular or otherwise defective types.) Genitives take the ending -*i(n)* and invariably immediately follow their head noun; when there is a following genitive, the definite article *al-* on the head noun is absent, although it is semantically definite:

(158)  al-xubzu
       the-bread

(159)  xubz-u    zayd-in
       bread-NOM Zaid-GEN
       'Zaid's bread'

With the action nominal, it is in principle possible (unlike Turkish) for both subjects and direct objects to stand in the genitive (though not both simultaneously), so that one can have ambiguous action nominals such as:

(160)  qatl-u    zayd-in
       killing-NOM Zaid-GEN

(160) can mean either 'Zaid's killing (of someone)' or '(someone's) killing of Zaid'. Where both subject and direct object of the action nominal are present (and only here), assimilation to noun phrase syntax is only partial, as in Turkish: the subject stands in the genitive, the direct object remains in the accusative:

(161)  Qatala zayd-un  muḥammad-an
       killed  Zaid-NOM Muhammad-ACC
       'Zaid killed Muhammad'

(162)  qatl-u      zayd-in   muḥammad-an
       killing-NOM Zaid-GEN Muhammad-ACC
       'Zaid's killing of Muhammad'[4]

In Classical Arabic, then, assimilation to noun phrase syntax, with respect to subjects and direct objects, is taken as far as possible: if there is only one such adjunct, it appears in the genitive. If there is more than one, they cannot all appear in the genitive, given the requirement that a given head noun can have only one (immediately following) genitive, and in such instances all but one of the adjuncts simply remain in the form consonant with sentence syntax.

c. *Written Modern Hebrew.* Written Modern Hebrew is similar to Classical Arabic in the partial assimilation of its action nominal to noun phrase syntax, but with one interesting complication: there are, not one, but three genitive constructions in the language. These may be schematized as follows:

(163)  a. *The 'bound' genitive ('construct'):*

$N_x$ '-of'  $N_y$
zkan       ha-iš
beard      of the man

b. *The šel genitive:*
$N_x$        šel $N_y$
ha-sakan   šel ha-iš
the-beard   of the-man

c. *The 'double' genitive:*
$N_x$ - 'of' - $PRO_y$  šel $N_y$
zkan-      o        šel ha-iš
beard of- his     of  the man
'the beard of the man'

The action nominal is similar to a simple noun phrase in its ability to occur with determiners, adjectives, and relative clauses. Here is an example (from Gordon 1977) which illustrates all three of these noun phrase concomitants:

(164)   ha-harisa          ha-gdola šel ha-ir      še   buca
        the-destruction the-big    of  the-city REL was performed
        bašana          še-avra
        in the year the-last
        'the big destruction of the city that was carried out last year'

The action nominal is also exactly like a simple noun phrase in that it can occur with either the subject or object in any of the three genitive constructions, as illustrated below (example from Berman 1976:70ff):

(165)   $N_y$ = subject
        a. $N_x$ '-of'        $N_y$
           knisat          yeled
           entrance of boy

        b. $N_x$        šel $N_y$
           knisa      šel yeled
           entrance of  boy

        c. $N_x$ '-of'        $PRO_y$ šel $N_y$
           knisat          -o     šel yeled
           entrance of-his    of  boy
           'the entrance of the boy'

(166)   $N_y$ = object
        a. $N_x$ '-of'        $N_y$
           bitul          ha-xoq
           cancellation of the-law

        b. $N_x$                 šel $N_y$
           ha-bitul            šel ha-xoq
           the cancellation of  the-law

        c. $N_x$ '-of'        $PRO_y$ šel $N_y$
           bitul          -o     šel ha-xoq
           cancellation of -its   of  the-law
           'the cancellation of the law'

Moreover, if *both* subject and object are present, *either* one may play the role of N in any of the three types of genitives (Berman 1976:71). However, in this case, as in Turkish and Classical Arabic, assimilation to noun phrase syntax is only partial: the participant which is *not* in the genitive relationship to the head noun must be marked by the very *sentential* case markers, the accusative *et* for the object in (167) and *al ydey* 'by' (the marker of the passive agent) for the subject in (168):

(167)  $N_y$ = subject
    a. $N_x$ '-of'    $N_y$
       dxiyat       dan *et*  ha-hacaa
       rejection of Dan ACC the-offer
    b. $N_x$          šel $N_y$
       ha-dixiya    šel dan *et* ha-hacaa
       the-rejection of Dan ACC the offer

    c. $N_x$         PRO$_y$ šel       $N_y$
       dxiyat       -o    šel dan *et*  ha-hacaa
       rejection of-his  of Dan ACC the-offer
       'Dan's rejection of the offer'

(168)  $N_y$ = object
    a. $N_x$ '-of'    $N_y$
       dxiyat-t      ha-hacaa *al ydey* dan
       rejection-of  the-offer by      Dan
    b. $N_x$          šel $N_y$
       ha-dxiya     šel ha-hacaa *al ydey* dan
       the-rejection of the-offer by      Dan

    c. $N_x$ '-of'    PRO$_y$ šel $N_y$
       dxiya-t      -a    šel ha-hacaa *al ydey* dan
       rejection-of-its  of the-offer by     Dan
       'Dan's rejection of the offer'

For extensive discussion, see Berman (1976) and Gordon (1977).

d. *Maori*. In the languages we have considered so far that have an overt distinction correlating with that between subjective and objective genitives, the overt distinction has been primarily syntactic, i.e. an existing syntactic distinction (prenominal versus postnominal genitive in English, adjectival versus genitival attribute in Czech) is utilized to make a distinction between subject and object. Another possibility is for an existing semantic distinction to be used to this end, as for instance in Maori (examples adapted from Biggs 1969:43–5).

We may start by presenting the general structure of the Maori action nominal, in its relation to active and passive sentences such as:

(169)  Ka patu te  tangata i  te  wheke
      PCL kill the  man    DO the octopus
      'The man killed the octopus'

(170)   Ka patua     te   wheke   e   te   tangata
        PCL kill(PASS) the octopus by the man
        'The octopus was killed by the man'

(Note that the usual word order in Maori is for a sentence-initial verb to be immediately followed by the subject.) The action nominal *patunga*, like English *killing*, does not overtly distinguish voice. In the action nominal construction, the subject (and only the subject) appears in the genitive, with the preposition *a* or *o*; the direct object remains with *i*, the passive agent with *e* (cf. section 2.1.1.1.3):

(171)   te   patunga a te   tangata i   te   wheke
        the killing   of the man       DO the octopus
        'the man's killing of the octopus'

(172)   te   patunga o te   wheke   e   te   tangata
        the killing   of the octopus by the man
        'the killing of the octopus by the man'

The important thing to note is that in (171) the genitive is constructed with *a*, whereas in (172) it is constructed with *o*. Quite generally in Maori, there is a semantic distinction between genitives with *a* and those with *o*, whereby the former indicates a more active relation of the possessor towards the possessed, whereas *o* indicates a more passive relation. For instance, 'the man's book' is *te pukapuka a te tangata* (the man can carry the book), but 'the man's canoe' is *te waka o te tangata* (the canoe can carry the man). An example closer to an action nominal would be the opposition between *te waiata a te tangata* 'the man's song' (i.e. the song that he composed) and *te waiata o te tangata* 'the song about the man'. This same opposition is maintained with action nominals: if a noun phrase is semantically a subjective genitive, it takes *a*, as in (171); if it is semantically an objective genitive, it takes *o*, as in (172).

The *a/o* opposition in Maori is semantic rather than syntactic. In particular, the *a* and *o* genitives do not have distinct syntactic positions, so that we cannot have a single head noun qualified by both an *a* and an *o* genitive, i.e.

(173)   *te   patunga *a* te   tangata *o* te   wheke
        the killing   of the man       of the whale

Moreover, in the action nominal both the *a* and *o* genitives correspond to a (surface) syntactic subject, *a* of an active sentence, *o* of a passive sentence; there is no direct relation between syntactic direct object and *o* genitive. For these reasons, we say that Maori utilizes a semantic, rather than a syntactic, distinction in correlation with the subjective/objective genitive distinction.

2.1.2.1.4 *Unexpressed subjects.* In apparently all languages with action nominalizations, it is possible to leave the subject unexpressed, the nominalization then referring to an abstract type of activity or state, as in English:

(174)    a. *Swimming* is good exercise
         b. *Lying on the grass* is forbidden
         c. *Criticism* is hard to take

In some languages, however, the nominalization takes a different form when the subject is expressed than when it is not. In Tagalog, for example, nominalizing the 'basic' (i.e., aspectless) form of a verb yields an abstract noun which cannot be particularized with an expressed subject:

(175)    a. Madali-ng *magsasalita*
            easy-LINK   speak(BASIC)
            'Speaking is easy'

         b. *Madali-ng   magsasalita   $\begin{cases} \text{niya} \\ \text{his} \\ \text{ni Pedro} \\ \text{of Pedro} \end{cases}$
            easy-LINK    speak(BASIC)

            $\left.\begin{array}{l} \text{'His} \\ \text{'Pedro's} \end{array}\right\}$ speaking is easy'

2.1.2.1.5 *Idiosyncrasies in valency of action nominals.* So far, we have been assuming that all syntactic characteristics of action nominals can be accounted for in terms of either the syntactic properties of the corresponding sentence, or the internal syntactic or semantic structure of the noun phrase in the language in question. Moreover, we have illustrated the successful application of this principle in a large number of instances in a wide range of language-types. For completeness, however, we must also note some instances where the syntax of the action nominal differs from that of both sentence and noun phrase. At the moment, these seem simply to be exceptions to the general principle; in some instances partial explanations may be forthcoming, though a fuller integration of most of these examples into our general account is a task for future research.

In the languages we examined above, the expression of the agent with a 'passive' action nominal was essentially the same as that of the agent with a passive verb. Compare, for example, *the destruction of the city by the enemy* with *the city was destroyed by the enemy*, both with *by the enemy*; although even in English the parallelism is not complete; for example alongside *a march by two thousand soldiers* there is no *it was marched by two thousand soldiers*. In some languages, the expression of the passive agent is regularly different as between sentence and verbal noun, without there being any reason internal to the syntax of other noun phrases for this discrepancy. In Italian, for instance, passive agents of verbs take the preposition *da* 'from, by':

(176)    La   città fu   distrutta   dal nemico
'The city  was destroyed by  the enemy'

With the verbal noun, *da* on its own is impossible; instead one must use *da parte di*, literally 'from (the) part of':

(177)    la distruzzione della città $\begin{cases} \text{da parte del nemico} \\ \text{*dal nemico} \end{cases}$
'the destruction of the city by the enemy'

(With the sentence, one can also say *La città fu distrutta da parte del nemico*, though the shorter version of (176) above is much more usual.) It is difficult to think of any good reason for this discrepancy: perhaps a more explicit coding of the agent is preferred in the more contracted expression of the action nominal, but at present this is purely speculative.

In German, the passive agent of a verb takes the preposition *von* 'by, of', whereas either *von* or *durch* 'through' is used with passive agents that are not strictly agentive (i.e. in particular, that are not animate, though are still not explicitly instrumental, for which the correct preposition in both active and passive sentences is *mit* 'with'):

(178)    Das Haus wurde vom Feind zerstört [*vom = von dem*]
'The house was destroyed by the enemy'

(179)    Das Haus wurde von/durch Bomben zerstört
'The house was destroyed by bombs'

(180)    Der Feind hat das Haus mit Bomben zerstört
'The enemy destroyed the house with bombs'

(181)    Das Haus wurde vom Feind mit Bomben zerstört
'The house was destroyed with bombs by the enemy'

With the verbal noun, the passive agent can only be expressed by *durch* (*mit* is, of course, retained for explicit instruments), although in sentence syntax *durch* is impossible for strictly agentive agents:

(182)    die Zerstörung des Hauses durch den Feind/*vom Feind
'the destruction of the house by the enemy'

(183)    Das Haus wurde vom Feind/*durch den Feind zerstört
'The house was destroyed by the enemy'

Again, we are unable to give a complete explanation for this discrepancy, though it is possible that the reason lies in the large number of other functions that the preposition *von* has in noun phrases: in particular, it expresses the genitival relation (in the written language only with certain morphologically definable noun phrases, in the spoken language much more generally). Since the agent construction with the 'passive' action nominal serves, to some extent, to remove the homonymy inherent in the existence of both subjective and objective genitives, this function would simply be nullified if the passive agent were constructed in the same way:

(184)    die Zerstörung von Städten
'the destruction of cities'

(185)    *die Zerstörung von Städten vom Feind
'the destruction of cities by the enemy'

(The noun phrase in (185) is, of course, possible, at least in the colloquial language, in the meaning 'the destruction of the enemy's cities'; since *der Feind* 'the enemy' has a morphologically explicit genitive, the written language would prefer in this sense *die Zerstörung von Städten des Feindes*.)

(186)    die Zerstörung von Städten durch den Feind
'the destruction of cities by the enemy'

As a last example, we may note the discrepancy between expressions of the passive agent with verbs and with action nominals in Welsh. The passive agent with verbs requires the preposition *gan* 'by, with', and *o* 'from' is not possible:

(187)    Gwerthwyd y    ceffyl gan y    ffermwr
was sold    the horse by  the farmer
'The horse was sold by the farmer'

With verbal nouns, however, one must use *o*, not *gan*:

(188)    gwrthodiad y    cynnig o'r gweinidog
rejection    the offer   the minister
'the rejection of the offer by the minister'

The only available explanation here seems to be historical: *gan* has over the history of Welsh replaced *o* in many of its uses (apart from locative 'from' and partitive 'of'), so that for instance Modern Welsh has *gan* for instruments, as in (189), where Middle Welsh has *o*, as in (190) (Evans 1970:204):

(189)  Lladdodd ef y   ddraig  gan  fwyall
      killed      he the dragon  with axe
      'He killed the dragon with an axe'

(190)  y drychu y  Freinc      llurugauc a   helmauc o    'e
      to cleave  the Frenchman armoured and helmeted with his
      uwyall deu vinyauc
      axe     two edged
      'to cleave the armoured and helmeted Frenchman with his double-edged axe'

Perhaps, then, the use of *o* in action nominals is a relic of the earlier more extensive use of *o*, in verbal constructions too.

A further set of instances where action nominal syntax deviates from both verbal and nominal syntax concerns 'irregular' syntactic expression of the object of an action nominal. As we saw in our discussion on valency in section 2.1.2.1, the expected situation is for an action nominal to take the same case/preposition/postposition as the verb to which it is derivationally related, unless there is a general rule in the language specifying that a certain type of verbal object regularly corresponds to a different kind of nominal adjunct (in particular, in many languages direct objects of verbs correspond to adnominal genitives in action nominal noun phrases). In many languages, however, we find that some action nominals obligatorily or optionally take a different object from the corresponding verb, without there being any regular principle of the direct object/adnominal genitive correspondence. In German, for instance, the verbs *lieben* 'love' and *hassen* 'hate' take a direct object (accusative case), whereas the action nominal *Liebe* 'love' requires the preposition *zu* 'to(wards)' and *Hass* 'hate' requires *gegen* 'against':

(191)  Peter liebt die Königin
      'Peter loves the Queen'

(192)  Peters Liebe zur Königin [*zur* = *zu der*]
      'Peter's love of/for the queen'

(In English, the nominal *love* may either retain the genitive, corresponding to a direct object, or take the preposition *for*; in German the former possibility is excluded, i.e. not *\*Peters Liebe der Königin*.)

(193)    Peter hasst den König
         'Peter hates the king'

(194)    Peters Hass gegen den König
         'Peter's hatred of the king'

Similar instances can be found in Russian, for example *ljubit'* + accusative 'to love', *ljubov'* *k* 'love (lit. towards)'; *nenavidet'* + accusative 'to hate', *nenavist'* *k* 'hatred'; *udivljat'sja* + dative 'to be surprised at', *udivlenie* + dative/*k*/*nad* 'surprise at' (with dative/ 'to'/'over'):

(195)    Andrej ljubit caricu
         'Andrey loves the tsarina'

(196)    ljubov' Andreja k carice
         'Andrey's love of/for the tsarina'

(197)    Andrej nenavidit carja
         'Andrey hates the tsar'

(198)    nenavist' Andreja k carju
         'Andrey's hatred of the tsar'

(199)    Andrej udivilsja ee kostjumu(DAT)
         'Andrey was surprised by her suit'

(200)    udivlenie Andreja ee kostjumu/k ee kostjumu/nad ee kost-
         jumom
         'Andrey's surprise at her suit'

In certain instances the lack of correspondence between the verbal and action nominal object seems to be purely idiosyncratic, a lexically conditioned irregularity. In many instances, however, the exceptional verbs do fall into a semantic class: for instance, Russian action nominals which exceptionally take *k* 'towards' are nearly all psychological predicates, verbs expressing someone's attitude towards something. The same is true of the German examples, except that here the kind of attitude is made more explicit, with *zu* 'to(wards)' for positive feelings and *gegen* 'against' for negative feelings. Thus there are at least subregularities here. Typically, such instances involve giving more explicit reference to the kind of semantic relation obtaining between the action nominal (and also the verb) and its object: cf. the suggestion above that there may be some tendency towards more explicit marking of the underlying subject in the action nominal construction.

Another piece of evidence pointing in the same direction concerns

German action nominals corresponding to verbs that take a genitive or dative object, for example *gedenken* + genitive 'commemorate', *danken* + dative 'thank', *widerstehen* + dative 'resist'. As noted above, action nominals are not permitted to take a genitive or dative object in German (except, of course, for the objective genitive corresponding to the accusative object of a verb). Where a verb takes such an object and has a derived action nominal, that action nominal usually takes a prepositional phrase: there seems to be no general rule for predicting which prepositional phrase, though the preposition is usually one that makes the relation of object to action nominal more explicit semantically, for example *Dank an* 'thanks to', *Gedenken an* 'remembrance of (literally: to)', *Widerstand gegen* 'resistance to (literally: against)':

(201)    Die Soldaten widerstehen dem Feind (DAT)
         'The soldiers resist the enemy'

(202)    der Widerstand (der Soldaten) gegen den Feind
         'the (soldiers') resistance to the enemy'

(203)    Der Mann dankt einem Freund (DAT)
         'The man thanks a friend'

(204)    der Dank (des Mannes) an einen Freund
         'the (man's) thanks to a friend'

(205)    Das Volk gedenkt der Toten (GEN)
         'The people commemorate the dead'

(206)    das Gedenken (des Volkes) an die Toten
         'the (people's) commemoration of the dead'

2.1.2.2 *Adverbs and adjectives.* Another difference between the syntactic combinations entered into by verbs and by nouns is that the former are normally qualified by adverbs, the latter by adjectives. As far as action nominals are concerned, the difference is particularly clear with manner adverbials: whereas verbs take manner adverbials, in many languages action nominals require the corresponding adjective, for example:

(207)    The enemy rapidly destroyed the city

(208)    the enemy's rapid destruction of the city

The same situation obtains in the Russian translation of these:

(209)    Vrag bystro razrušil gorod

(210)    bystroe razrušenie goroda vragom
'the rapid destruction of the city by the enemy'

However, the intermediate position of action nominals between verbs and nouns can be seen from the fact that in some languages both adverbials and adjectivals can be used in such constructions, as in the following examples from Colloquial Egyptian Arabic (Wise 1975:79–80):

(211)    mašy-ak        bisurʕa
         walking-your quickly
         'your walking quickly'

(212)    mašy-ak        is-sariiʕ
         walking-your the-rapid

In Polish, although the basic construction is for action nominals to take adjectives, examples with adverbs are often fully acceptable to native speakers, probably because Polish action nominals, unlike those in Russian and Czech (see 2.1.2.1.2), retain relatively many verbal categories. For example:

(213)    Konspiracja polega na chodzeniu cicho
         'The conspiracy depends on walking quietly'

Even in English, many native speakers find such constructions with manner adverbials tolerable, though clearly less preferable to versions with the corresponding adjective:

(214)    ?the enemy's destruction of the city rapidly

Other languages are even less tolerant, so that in Russian for instance it is quite impossible to use an adverb in:

(215)    *razrušenie bystro goroda    vragom
         destruction rapidly of the city by enemy

With other kinds of adverbials, where the morphological relation to corresponding adjectives is usually much less consistent, languages seem to be more tolerant of adverbs qualifying action nominals:

(216)    his departure tomorrow

(217)    ego ot"ezd zavtra (Russian)

(218)    safar-u bukra (Colloquial Egyptian Arabic)

Even here, however, there are language-particular restrictions, which seem not to have been well studied to date, for example there is a difference between Colloquial Egyptian Arabic and Russian:

(219)   tamalli tašğiil-ak       li-r-radiu (Colloquial Egyptian Arabic)
        always playing-your DO-the-radio
        'your always playing the radio'

(220    *tvoe čtenie  vsegda takix    knig   (Russian)
        your reading always of such books

The only grammatical equivalent in Russian would be with an adjective,
such as *postojannoe* 'perpetual', i.e.

(221)   tvoe postojannoe čtenie   takix    knig
        your perpetual    reading of such books

The possibility of adverbials qualifying action nominals is most
widespread when the action nominal is taken in its basic sense of
describing a fact or action, and is much less if at all possible when the
action nominal has a more concrete meaning. In the English examples
below, for instance, the adverbials are much more natural with *criticism*
in the sense of 'the fact that X criticized Y', than in the sense 'a piece of
critical writing':

(222)   John's criticism of Bill, sarcastically, surprised all those present

(223)   ?*John's criticism of Bill, sarcastically, appears on page 26

(Note that, even so, the adverb is reasonably natural only if separated
by pauses.)

(224)   John's criticism of the book before he had even read it was
        unfair

(225)   ?*John's criticism of the book before he had even read it
        appears on page 26

(Cf. Chomsky 1970:193–4.)


### 2.2 Nominalizations with no lexically derived noun

We have discussed at some length the 'action nominal', whose head is a
lexically derived noun. In languages which have morphological nominalization processes for creating lexical action/state nouns from verbs,
there will typically be an action nominal construction with the properties
we have described. However, some languages have no such morphological processes, and yet clauses can be nominalized and used in various
nominal contexts. Other languages may have a process creating

action/state nouns, and a separate, unrelated process for nominalizing clauses. For convenience, we will refer to this type of nominalization as 'clausal nominalization'. The characteristic feature of this type of nominalization is that there is no evidence in favor of viewing its head as a lexical noun. That is, the verb in such a clause typically has no nominal characteristics and often has such verbal characteristics as person and number, though it may be lacking in tense–aspect marking.

A good example of such a language is Mojave, a Yuman language of Arizona and California. Mojave has no action nominal construction, but it does have nominalized clauses. The verb in the nominalized clause differs from that in the corresponding simple sentence in that (i) it appears in a (non-regular) different form, and (ii) the otherwise obligatory tense marker is absent:

(226)   a.  *Simple sentence*
            ʔinʸeč ʔakor ʔ-isvaːr-k
            I       then  I-sing-TNS
            'I sang then'
        b.  *Nominalized clause functioning as subject*
            ʔinʸep ʔakor ʔ-suːvaːr-č ʔatay-pč
            me      then  I-sing-SUBJ much-TNS
            'My former singing was considerable (= I used to sing a lot)'

Comparison of the nominalized clause, italicized in (226b), with the simple sentence in (226a) reveals that in addition to the fact that the verb stem has a different shape and lacks tense marking, the subject of the clause appears in the accusative case, the first person marker ʔ- is still present, and a subject case marker is suffixed to the last element in the nominalization since it is functioning as the subject of ʔatay- 'much'. Thus, there are two important respects in which the 'clausal nominalization' exhibited in Mojave does not parallel the 'action nominalization' examined in the preceding section: (i) the subject of the Mojave nominalized clause appears not in a genitive or other oblique case but in the accusative case; (ii) the verbal category of 'person' is marked on the nominalized clause verb just as it is on the verb of a simple sentence. These two properties suggest that it is more appropriate in Mojave to view clauses as undergoing certain modifications which allow them to function as noun phrases rather than to think of the verb itself as having become a noun in such nominalizations. For an extensive discussion of nominalization in Mojave, see Munro (1976).

Clausal nominalization in Lakhota is accomplished by suffixing the article to a sentence. Thus compare the following sentences with their nominalized forms (Buechel 1939:314):

(227)  a. Unglapi
'We are going home'

b. *Unglapi*      *kin* iyonicip'ipi
we are going home the has pleased you
'Our going home has pleased you'

(228)  a. El cihipi
to I came you
'I came to you'

b. *El cihipi*    *kin* iyonicip'ipi
to I came you the has pleased you
'My coming to you has pleased you'

Here again, there is nothing noun-like about the verb in this nominalized clause; it undergoes no change whatsoever from its form in a finite sentence, and the nominalization is accomplished solely by the definite article.

Ancient Greek is similar. Thus, the noun phrase

(229)  to gnōthi     seauton
the know(IMP) yourself
'self-knowledge'

is formed by adding the singular neuter definite article *to* to the imperative clause *gnōthi seauton* 'know yourself'.

### 2.3 *Functions of nominalizations*
It is commonplace that a nominalization can occur wherever a noun phrase is called for. Thus, it is most natural for nominalizations to occur as subjects or objects of sentences or as objects of prepositions. Examples from English would be:

(230)  a. *His drinking too much* worried us

b. *Object*:
We didn't like *his drinking too much*

c. *Object of a preposition*:
We were sorry about *his drinking too much*

Nominalizations also often function in adverbial clauses together with a subordinating connector. For example: Luiseño, a Uto-Aztecan language, has such a strategy, at least for conditionals, where *-qala* is a general subordinating morpheme (see Davis 1973):

(231)  ʔári-up póy     ʔoy     pu   -ʔári-qala
kick-IMP him(ACC) you(ACC) 3 GEN kick-SUBORD
'Kick him if he kicks you'

Luiseño also exhibits a somewhat more rare function of nominalization: as a relative clause modifying a head noun (cf. also (14) above). A
good example of this function is the following sentence (Davis
1973:211):

(232)  Kiʔá·l-up niveʔ-qa   wíw       ŋa *nu-ʃŋaki pu-lóʔxa-ŋa*
       fly-PRES  be in-PRES acorn mush LOC my-wife 3GEN-make-LOC
       'There's a fly in the acorn mush my wife made'

There are two things to note about this sentence. First, there is a head
noun in this construction, *wíw* 'acorn mush', whose role as a locative
phrase in the main clause is clearly signaled by its locative suffix.
Second, the italicized nominalization can be seen to be structurally
identical to that in the preceding sentence, (231); evidence that it is a
nominalization comes from (i) the possessive prefix, characteristic only
of nouns, and (ii) the locative case marker. In fact if the head noun were
plural, the nominalization would be marked for plurality as well. Thus,
although this is not the only type of relativization possible in Luiseño, it
provides a clear case of a nominalization functioning as a relative clause.

It is not difficult to understand how a nominalization can function as a
relative clause: the nominalization and the noun with which it is in
construction can be thought of as two juxtaposed nominal elements
[NOM] [NOM], the modifying relationship between them being inferred by
the language-users (rather than being specified by the grammar, as it is
in languages with specific relative clause morphology), just as the
modifying relationship is inferred in a noun–noun compound such as
*tree-house*, in which the two nominal elements simply happen to be
single nouns.

An even more extreme example of the function of nominalization in
relative clause formation is provided by a language in which relativization is not structurally distinct from nominalization. A number of
languages of the American west and southwest are of this type (for
extensive discussion see Fauconnier 1971, Gorbet 1974, Munro 1976,
and Li and Thompson 1978), as well as Quechua, spoken in Peru (see
Weber 1978). Thus, in Diegueño, a Yuman language (see Gorbet 1974),
for example, both relative clauses and nominalizations are of the form:

(233)   NP[. . .V] – (DEM) – case

That is, in these languages, in which there is no structural head noun, it
may not be possible to distinguish a relative clause from a nominalization on the basis of their form alone. This time, which noun is to be

interpreted as the head noun is what must be inferred. Thus, consider the Diegueño relative clause and sentential object sentences below:

(234)  a. *Relative clause*
       [*I:pac 'wu:w*]-*pu-c*    ciyaw
       man  I saw-DEM-SUBJ sing
       'The man I saw sang'

       b. *Object clause*
       '*nʸa:-c* '-*i:ca-s*        [*puy  ta-'-nʸ-way*]-*pu-ɸ*
       I-SUBJ  I-remember-EMPH there PROG-I-be-there-DEM-OBJ
       'I remember that we were there'

Note that the demonstrative and case suffixes which mark clauses as being nominalized in this language are found on the italicized clauses in both (234a) and (234b), and there is no other formal difference between them. Hence our claim that in certain languages relativization is indistinct from nominalization.


## 3.0 Devices for forming nouns from nouns

We have so far been talking exclusively of nouns and noun phrases which are related to verbs or adjectives and to entire sentences. Are there any other sources for creating nouns and noun phrases in languages? We do not know of any languages which regularly derive nouns from any other category except other nouns; below we briefly give a few examples of this process.


### 3.1 *Abstract nouns*
In some languages, abstract nouns can be formed from more concrete ones. In Si-Luyana, for example, the prefix *u-*, which is the class prefix for the 'mass noun' class 14, can be added to human noun stems to form abstract nouns meaning 'the quality of being N' (Givón 1970: 79–80):

(235)  a. -nu       → u-nu
          person     humanity
       b. -ana      → u-ana
          child      childishness/childhood
       c. -lume     → u-lume
          male       virility/manhood

In English, serving this function are the Germanic suffixes -*dom*, as in *kingdom*, -*hood*, as in *childhood*, and -*ship*, as in *friendship*.

### 3.2 Concrete nouns: augmentative/pejorative/diminutive

Some languages allow nouns to be derived from other nouns where the new form denotes a larger, smaller, or less desirable version of the referent of the stem. Again, Si-Luyana is a rich source of examples (Givón 1970: 79–80):

(236)  a. si-fuba  → ka-fuba
          bone         small bone
       b. li-muna → ka-muna
          leaf         small leaf

(237)  a. n-de     → n-de-ana
          lion         lion-child = lion cub
       b. ka-bili  → ka-bili-ana
          hill         hill-child = little hill

(238)  a. mw-ana→ si-ana
          child        big/ungainly/naughty-child
       b. mu-tondo→ si-tondo
          tree         big/ugly/useless-tree

Reduplication is a process which, in language after language, is used to derive forms meaning diminution. Thus, in Nez Perce, for example, we find:

(239)  a. té·mul   → temulté·mul
          hail         sleet
       b. xóyamac→ xoyamacxóyamac
          child        small child

(For more discussion of reduplication see Moravcsik 1976.)

In Sundanese, reduplication of just the initial syllable of a noun plus the suffix -an results in forms meaning 'toy or false "noun"' (Robins 1959: 360):

(240)  a. mobil → momobilan
          car       toy car
       b. panon → papanonan
          eye       glass eye
       c. imah  → iimahan
          house     toy house/doll house

## 4 Summary

In this chapter we have discussed and illustrated the types of processes which languages have for creating nouns from verbs and adjectives and for forming noun phrases from entire propositions. The generalizations which we have arrived at can be summarized as follows:

1. Nouns can be formed from verbs and adjectives to designate either the name of an activity/state or the name of one of the arguments of that verb/adjective.
2. Nouns can also be derived from other nouns, but not from other categories.
3. Processes for forming nouns are likely to be non-productive and to involve a great deal of irregularity and unpredictability.
4. Languages differ as to whether their action nominals more closely resemble noun phrases or sentences in terms of the following parameters:
   (a) the number of verbal versus nominal categories shown by the head noun of the action nominal;
   (b) whether the nouns functioning as subject and object of the corresponding sentence are marked as genitive or oblique (i.e. more nominal) or with the case forms they would have in a full sentence (i.e., more verbal);
   (c) whether the adverb in the corresponding sentence appears as an adverb (i.e. more verbal) or as an adjective (i.e. more nominal).
5. In some languages derived noun phrases cannot be analyzed as having head nouns.

## NOTES

* We are grateful to Ruth Berman and Amnon Gordon for their helpful comments on the content of this chapter.
1 Lewis Carroll's 'un-birthday' notwithstanding.
2 This suggestion is due to Ruth Berman.
3 The qualification *wherever possible* is necessary because of the following restrictions on the formation of possessive adjectives. There is first of all a semantic restriction: only singular definite noun phrases allow possessive adjectives, i.e. there is no possessive objective alternative to the genitive in *kniha vědců* 'the scientists' book' or *kniha (jednoho) vědce* 'a scientist's book'. Secondly, there is a syntactic restriction: only unqualified nouns allow possessive adjectives, i.e. there is no alternative to the genitive in *kniha starého vědce* 'the old scientist's book'. Thirdly, there are idiosyncratic morphological restrictions, in that nouns of certain morphological classes simply do not form possessive adjectives, for example neuter nouns in *-ě* (stem *-ět-*) such as *dítě* 'child', so that there is no alternative to the genitive in *kniha dítěte* 'the child's book'. Where none of these restrictions applies, the possessive adjective is preferred to the genitive. We should also note that adjectives like *vědcův* are clearly possessive adjectives, meaning 'the scien-

tist's', and not relational adjectives of the type 'scientific', which are formally distinct from possessive adjectives in Czech: 'scientific book' would be *vědecká kniha*.

4 Certain other marginal possibilities are found in Classical Arabic, and noted by W. Wright (1898, Vol. 2:58–9), for example *qatlu muḥammad-in zayd-un*, with retention of the nominative subject rather than of the accusative direct object.

# Bibliography

Akmajian, A. and S. R. Anderson. 1970. On the use of the fourth person in Navajo, or Navajo made harder. *International Journal of American Linguistics* 36:1–8

Allen, W. S. 1956. Structure and system in the Abaza verbal complex. *Transactions of the Philological Society* 1956:127–76

Anderson, S. R. 1976. On the description of consonant gradation in Fula. *Studies in African Linguistics* 7:93–136

Anderson, S. R. 1977a. On mechanisms by which languages become ergative. In C. N. Li, ed. *Mechanisms of syntactic change*. Austin, University of Texas Press: 317–63

Anderson, S. R. 1977b. On the formal description of inflection. *Chicago Linguistic Society* 13:15–44

Andrade, M. J. 1933. Quileute. In F. Boas, ed. *Handbook of American Indian Languages, Part 3*. New York, Augustin: 149–292

Andrews, J. R. 1975. *Introduction to Classical Nahuatl*. Austin, University of Texas Press

Aoki, H. 1970. *Nez Perce grammar*. Berkeley, University of California Press. (University of California Publications in Linguistics, 62)

Arnott, D. W. 1970. *The nominal and verbal systems of Fula*. Oxford, Oxford University Press

Babby, L. H. 1975. A transformational analysis of transitive *-sja* verbs in Russian. *Lingua* 35:297–332

Bastuji, J. 1976. *Les relations spatiales en turc contemporain*. Paris, Klincksieck

Bateson, M. C. 1967. *Arabic language handbook*. Washington, Center for Applied Linguistics

Bender, B. 1969. *Spoken Marshallese*. Honolulu, University of Hawaii Press

Berman, R. A. 1976. On derived and deriving nominals in modern Hebrew. In Cole 1976:57–98

Bhat, D. N. S. 1978. *Pronominalization*. Poona, India, Deccan College

Biggs, B. 1969. *Let's learn Maori*. Wellington, New Zealand, Reed

Blake, B. J. 1977. *Case marking in Australian languages*. Canberra, Australian Institute of Aboriginal Studies

Boas, F., ed. 1911a. *Handbook of American Indian Languages, Part 1*. Washington, Government Printing Office. (Bureau of American Ethnology Bulletin 40,1)

Boas, F. 1911b. Tsimshian. In Boas 1911a:283–442

Boas, F. 1947. Kwakiutl grammar, with a glossary of the suffixes. Ed. by H. B. Yampolsky. *Transactions of the American Philosophical Society* 37:203–377

Boas, F. and E. Deloria. 1941. *Dakota grammar.* Washington, DC, Government Printing Office. (Memoirs of the National Academy of Science, 23,2)

Bondarko, A. V. 1971. *Vid i vremja russkogo glagola (značenie i upotreblenie). Posobie dlja studentov.* Moscow, Prosveščenie

Bonvillain, N. 1973. *A grammar of Akwesasne Mohawk.* Ottawa, National Museum of Man. (Mercury Series Ethnology Division Paper, 8)

Bowerman, M. 1981. *Beyond communicative adequacy: from piecemeal knowledge to an integrated system in the child's acquisition of language.* Palo Alto, Stanford University Press. (Papers and Reports on Child Language Development, 20)

Breen, J. G. 1976. Wangkumara. In Dixon 1976:336–9

Buechel, E. 1939. *A grammar of Lakota.* Saint Francis, S. Dakota, Rosebud Educational Society

Bull, W. E. 1960. *Time, tense, and the verb.* Berkeley, University of California Press. (University of California Publications in Linguistics, 19)

Bull, W. E. In preparation. *Morphology and morphophonemics*

Bybee, J. 1980. What's a possible inflectional category? Unpublished manuscript

Bybee, J. 1985. *Morphology: A study of the relation between meaning and form.* Amsterdam: John Benjamins

Campbell, A. 1959. *Old English grammar.* London, Oxford University Press

Chafe, W. L. 1970. *Meaning and the structure of language.* Chicago, University of Chicago Press

Chao, Y-R. 1968. *A grammar of spoken Chinese.* Berkeley, University of California Press

Chomsky, N. 1970. Remarks on nominalization. In Jacobs and Rosenbaum 1970:184–221

Chung, S. 1978. *Case marking and grammatical relations in Polynesian languages.* Austin, University of Texas Press

Cole, P., ed. 1976. *Studies in modern Hebrew syntax and semantics: the transformational-generative approach.* Amsterdam, North-Holland. (North-Holland Linguistic Series, 32)

Comrie, B. 1975. Causatives and universal grammar. *Transactions of the Philological Society* 1974:1–32

Comrie, B. 1976a. *Aspect.* Cambridge, Cambridge University Press

Comrie, B. 1976b. The syntax of action nominals: a cross-language study. *Lingua* 40:177–201

Comrie, B. 1976c. The syntax of causative constructions: cross-language similarities and divergences. In Shibatani 1976:261–312

Cooke, J. R. 1968. *Pronominal reference in Thai, Burmese and Vietnamese.* Berkeley, University of California Press

Costenoble, H. 1940. *Die chamoro Sprache.* The Hague, M. Nijhoff

Craig, C. G. 1979. Jacaltec: field work in Guatemala. In Shopen 1979:3–57

Davis, J. 1973. A partial grammar of simplex and complex sentences in Luiseño. Unpublished Ph.D. dissertation, University of California, Los Angeles

Davis, P. W. and R. Saunders. 1978. Bella Coola syntax. In E. Cook and J. Kaye, eds. *Linguistic studies of native Canada*. Vancouver, University of British Columbia Press: 37–65

Dixon, R. M. W. 1972. *The Dyirbal language of North Queensland*. Cambridge, Cambridge University Press

Dixon, R. M. W., ed. 1976. *Grammatical categories in Australian languages*. Canberra, Australian Institute of Aboriginal Studies.

Dixon, R. M. W. 1977. *A grammar of Yidiɲ*. Cambridge, Cambridge University Press

Doke, C. M. and S. M. Mofokeng. 1967. *Textbook of southern Sotho grammar*. Johannesburg, Longmans

Dorsey, J. O. and J. R. Swanton. 1912. *A dictionary of the Biloxi and Ofo languages*. Washington, Government Printing Office. (Bureau of American Ethnology Bulletin, 47)

Dowty, D. R. 1979. *Word meaning and Montague grammar: the semantics of verbs and times in generative semantics and in Montague's PTQ*. Dordrecht, Reidel. (Synthèse Language Library, 7)

Dumézil, G. 1967. *Études abkhaz*. Paris, Adrien-Maisonneuve. (Documents sur les langues et les traditions du caucase, 5)

Dumézil, G. 1975. *Le verbe oubykh: études descriptives et comparatives*. Paris, Klincksieck

Dyen, I. 1965. *A sketch of Trukese grammar*. New Haven, Conn., American Oriental Society. (American Oriental Society Essays, 4)

Ebeling, C. L. 1966. The grammar of literary Avar [a review article]. *Studia Caucasia* 2:58–100

Eliot, C. N. E. 1890. *A Finnish grammar*. Oxford, Clarendon Press

Evans, D.S. 1970. *A grammar of middle Welsh*. Dublin, Institute for Advanced Studies

Fauconnier, G. 1971. Theoretical implications of some global phenomena in syntax. Unpublished Ph.D. dissertation, University of California, San Diego

Fillmore, C. J. 1966. Deictic categories in the semantics of 'come'. *Foundations of Language* 2:219–27

Fillmore, C. J. 1975. *Santa Cruz lectures on deixis 1971*. Bloomington, Indiana University Linguistics Club

Fillmore, C. J. 1977. The case for case reopened. In P. Cole and J. M. Sadock, eds. *Syntax and semantics 8: Grammatical relations*. New York, Academic Press: 59–82

Forsyth, J. 1970. *A grammar of aspect: usage and meaning of the Russian verb*. Cambridge, Cambridge University Press

Frantz, C. 1973. Grammatical categories as indicated by Gadsup noun affixes. In H. McKaughan, ed. *The languages of the Eastern family of the East New Guinea Highland stock*. Seattle, University of Washington Press: 424–38

Fraser, B. 1976. *The verb–particle combination in English*. New York, Academic Press

Frei, H. 1944. Systèmes de déictiques. *Acta Linguistica* 4:111–29
Fromm, H. and M. Sadeniemi. 1956. *Finnisches elementarbuch I: Grammatik.* Heidelberg, Carl Winter
Givón, T. 1967. Some noun-to-noun derivational affixes. Santa Monica, Calif., System Development Corporation, Report #TM-3990/000/00
Givón, T. 1970. *The Si-Luyana language: a preliminary linguistic description.* Lusaka, University of Zambia. (Institute for Social Research, Communication 6)
Givón, T. 1971. Historical syntax and synchronic morphology: an archaeologist's field trip. *Chicago Linguistic Society* 7:394–415
Givón, T. 1972. Studies in ChiBemba and Bantu grammar. *Studies in African Linguistics*, Supplement 3:1–247
Goodwin, W. W. 1965. (1875). *Syntax of the moods and tenses of the Greek verb.* New York, St Martin's Press
Gorbet, L. 1974. Relativization and complementation in Diegueño: noun phrases as nouns. Unpublished Ph.D. dissertation, University of California, San Diego
Gordon, A. 1977. A unit grammar model of Hebrew. Unpublished M.A. thesis, University of California, Los Angeles
Greenberg, J. H., ed. 1966. *Universals of language.* 2nd edn. The Hague, Mouton
Greenberg, J. H., C. Ferguson and E. Moravcsik, eds. 1978. *Universals of human language. Vol. 4: Syntax.* Palo Alto, Calif., Stanford University Press
Gruber, J. 1965. *Studies in lexical relations.* Bloomington, Indiana University Linguistics Club
Hagège, C. 1977. Incorporation nominale et suffixation lexicale: essai de typologie et case particulier du comox (langue amerindienne de Colombie Britannique). *Bulletin de la société linguistique de Paris* 72:319–40
Haiman, J. 1980. *Hua: a Papuan language of the eastern highlands of New Guinea.* Amsterdam, Benjamins
Hale, K. L. 1967. Preliminary remarks on Walbiri grammar. Unpublished manuscript, M.I.T.
Hale, K. L. 1971. A note on a Walbiri tradition of antonymy. In D. Steinberg and L. Jakobovits, eds. *Semantics: an interdisciplinary reader in philosophy, linguistics and semantics.* Cambridge, Cambridge University Press
Harada, S. I. 1976. Honorifics. In M. Shibatani, ed. *Syntax and semantics 5: Japanese generative grammar.* New York, Academic Press: 499–561
Harris, A. 1976. Grammatical relations in modern Georgian. Unpublished Ph.D. dissertation, Harvard University
Harrison, S. P. 1976. *Mokilese reference grammar.* Honolulu, University of Hawaii Press
Haviland, J. B. 1979. How to talk to your brother-in-law in Guugu Yimidhirr. In Shopen 1979:160–239
Hill, J. H. and K. C. Hill. 1978. Honorific usage in modern Nahuatl. *Language* 54:123–54
Hjelmslev, L. 1972. (1935–7). *La catégorie des cas.* Munich, Wilhelm Fink
Hockett, C. F. 1966. What Algonquian is really like. *International Journal of American Linguistics* 32:59–73

Hook, P. E. 1983. The English abstrument and rocking case relations. *Chicago Linguistic Society* 19:181–94

Hopper, P., ed. 1982. *Tense and aspect: between semantics and pragmatics.* Amsterdam, Benjamins

Horne, E. C. 1961. *Beginning Javanese.* New Haven, Conn., Yale University Press

Horvarth, J. 1979. On the status of vowel patterns in modern Hebrew: morphological rules and lexical representations. Unpublished manuscript, University of California, Los Angeles

Hukari, T. 1976. Transitivity in Halkomelem. *Working Papers for the XI International Conference on Salishan Languages, University of Washington:* 69–119

Hukari, T. 1978. Halkomelem non-segmental morphology. *Working Papers for the XIII International Conference on Salishan Languages, University of Victoria:* 157–207

Hyman, L. 1979. *Aghem grammatical structure.* Los Angeles, University of Southern California. (Occasional Papers in Linguistics, 7)

Hyman, L. and D. Magaji. 1970. *Essentials of Gwari grammar.* University of Ibadan, Institute of African Studies. (Occasional Publications, 27)

Inènlikèj, P. I., V. P. Nedjalkov and A. A. Xolodovič. 1969. Kauzativ v čukotskom jazyke. In Xolodovič 1969:260–9

Inoue, K. 1979. Japanese: a story of language and people. In Shopen 1979:241–300

Isačenko, A. V. 1968. *Die russische Sprache der Gegenwart, Teil I: Formenlehre.* Halle, Max Niemeyer

Jacobs, R. and R. Rosenbaum, eds. 1970. *Readings in English transformational grammar.* Waltham, Mass., Ginn

Jacobsen, W. 1979. Noun and verb in Nootkan. In Efrat, ed. *The Victoria Conference on Northwestern Languages.* Victoria, British Columbia Provincial Museum: 83–153

Jakobson, R. 1957. Shifters, verbal categories and the Russian verb. In his *Selected writings* (1971). The Hague, Mouton, Vol. 2:30–147

Jespersen, O. 1965. (1924). *The philosophy of grammar.* New York, Norton

Josephs, L. S. 1975. *Palauan reference grammar.* Honolulu, University of Hawaii Press

Keenan, E. L. and E. Ochs. 1979. Becoming a competent speaker of Malagasy. In Shopen 1979:113–58

Kinkade, M. E. 1977. Singular vs. plural root in Salish. *Working Papers for the XII International Conference on Salishan Languages, Omak, Washington:* 147–56

Kleinschmidt, S. 1968. (1851). *Grammatik der grönländischen Sprache.* Hildesheim, G. Olms

Klokeid, T. J. 1976a. Encliticization in Nitinaht. *Working Papers for the XI International Conference on Salishan Languages, University of Washington:* 211–46

Klokeid, T. J. 1976b. Topics in Lardil grammar. Unpublished Ph.D. dissertation, M.I.T.

Kress, B. 1963. *Laut- und Formenlehre des isländischen*. Halle, Max Niemeyer

Kunene, E. 1974. Nominalization in Zulu. In Thompson and Lord 1974:107–29

Lafitte, P. 1962. *Grammaire basque*. Bayonne, Éditions des 'Amis du musée basque' et 'IKAS'

Lee, K-D. 1975. *Kusaiean reference grammar*. Honolulu, University of Hawaii Press

Lewis, G. L. 1967. *Turkish grammar*. Oxford, Clarendon Press

Li, C. N. and S. A. Thompson. 1978. Relativization strategies in Wappo. *Berkeley Linguistics Society* 4:106–13

Lyons, J. 1977. *Semantics*. Cambridge, Cambridge University Press

Macdonald, R. R. and S. Dardjowidjojo. 1967. *Indonesian reference grammar*. Washington, Georgetown University Press

Manley, T. 1972. *Outline of Sre structure*. Honolulu, University of Hawaii Press. (Oceanic Linguistics Special Publications, 12)

Marchand, H. 1969. *The categories and types of present-day English word formation*. 2nd edn. Munich, C. H. Beck

Matisoff, J. 1973. *The grammar of Lahu*. Berkeley, University of California Press. (University of California Publications in Linguistics, 75)

Matthews, P. H. 1972. *Inflectional morphology*. Cambridge, Cambridge University Press

Matthews, P. H. 1974. *Morphology: an introduction to the history of word structure*. Cambridge, Cambridge University Press

McCawley, J. D. 1968. Lexical insertion in a transformational grammar without deep structure. *Chicago Linguistic Society* 4:71–80

McCawley, J. D. 1971. Prelexical syntax. In R. J. O'Brien, ed. *Report of the 22nd Annual Round Table Meeting on Linguistics and Language Studies*. Washington, Georgetown University Press: 19–33

McCawley, J. D. 1981. *Everything that linguists have always wanted to know about logic, but were ashamed to ask*. Chicago, University of Chicago Press

McQuown, N. A. 1967. Classical Yucatec (Maya). In his *Handbook of Middle American Indians V: Linguistics*. Austin, University of Texas Press: 201–48

Merlan, F. 1976. Noun incorporation and discourse reference in modern Nahuatl. *International Journal of American Linguistics* 42:177–91

Meyerstein, Z. 1972. Czech deictics: pronouns and articles? *Linguistics* 91:17–31

Milner, G. B. 1956. *Fijian grammar*. Suva, Fiji Government Press

Mirikitani, L. T. 1972. *Kapampangan syntax*. Honolulu, University of Hawaii Press. (Oceanic Linguistics Special Publications, 10)

Mitchell, T. F. 1962. *Colloquial Arabic*. London, Hodder and Stoughton

Moravcsik, E. 1976. Reduplicative constructions. Unpublished manuscript, University of Wisconsin

Munro, P. 1976. *Mojave syntax*. New York, Garland

Murane, E. 1974. *Daga grammar*. Norman, University of Oklahoma, Summer Institute of Linguistics

Nash, D. G. 1977. A survey of ergativity in linguistics. Unpublished manuscript, M.I.T.

Nedjalkov, V. P., G. A. Otaina and A. A. Xolodovič. 1969. Morfologičeskij i leksičeskij kauzativy v nivxskom jazyke. In Xolodovič 1969:179–99

Nussbaum, L. N., W. W. Gage and D. Varre. 1970. *Dakar Wolof: a basic course.* Washington, DC, Center for Applied Linguistics

Osborne, C. R. 1974. *The Tiwi language.* Canberra, Australian Institute of Aboriginal Studies

Pawley, A. and T. Sayaba. 1971. Fijian dialect divisions: eastern and western Fijian. *Journal of the Polynesian Society* 86:405–36

Rassudova, O. P. 1968. *Upotreblenie vidov glagola v russkom jazyke.* Moscow, Moskovskij Universitet

Rastorgueva, V. S. 1964. A short sketch of the grammar of Persian. Trans. by S. P. Hill. *International Journal of American Linguistics* 30:Supplement

Reed, I. *et al.* 1977. *Yup'ik Eskimo grammar.* Fairbanks, University of Alaska, Alaska Native Language Center

Rigsby, B. 1975. Nass-Gitksan: an analytic ergative syntax. *International Journal of American Linguistics* 41:346–54

Robertson, J. 1976. The structure of pronoun incorporation in the Mayan verbal complex. Unpublished Ph.D. dissertation, Harvard University

Robins, R. H. 1959. Nominal and verbal derivation in Sundanese. *Lingua* 8:337–69

Rogers, J. H. 1975a. Non-TA verbs of Parry Island Ojibwa. *International Journal of American Linguistics* 41:21–31

Rogers, J. H. 1975b. Prediction of transitive animate verbs in an Ojibwa dialect. *International Journal of American Linguistics* 41:114–39

Rood, D. S. 1971. Agent and object in Wichita. *Lingua* 28:100–7

Rood, D. S. and A. Taylor. 1972. *Lakhota language course.* Boulder, University of Colorado, Lakhota Project

Sapir, E. 1911. The problem of noun incorporation in American languages. *American Anthropologist* 13:250–82

Sapir, E. 1912. The Takelma language of southwestern Oregon. In F. Boas, ed. *Handbook of American Indian languages, Part 2.* Washington, DC, Government Printing Office: 1–296. (Bureau of American Ethnology Bulletin 40,2)

Sapir, E. 1922. *Language.* New York, Harcourt and Brace

Sapir, E. 1930. Southern Paiute: a Shoshonean language. *Proceedings of the American Academy of Arts and Sciences* 65:1–296

Sapir, E. and H. Hoijer. 1967. *Phonology and morphology of the Navajo language.* Berkeley, University of California Press

Sapir, J. D. 1965. *A grammar of Diola-Fogny.* Cambridge, Cambridge University Press

Saunders, R. and P. W. Davis. 1975. The internal syntax of lexical suffixes in Bella Coola. *International Journal of American Linguistics* 41:106–13

Sayers, B. J. and H. B. Kerr. 1964. Wik-Munkan locative, temporal and demonstrative pronouns. In R. Pittman and H. B. Kerr, eds. *Papers on the languages of the Australian Aborigines.* Canberra, Australian Institute of Aboriginal Studies

Schachter, P. and F. T. Otanes. 1972. *Tagalog reference grammar*. Berkeley, University of California Press

Senn, A. 1966. *Handbuch der litauischen Sprache, I: Grammatik*. Heidelberg, Carl Winter

Shibatani, M. 1973. Semantics of Japanese causativization. *Foundations of Language* 9:327–73

Shibatani, M., ed. 1976. *Syntax and semantics 6: The grammar of causative constructions*. New York, Academic Press

Shopen, T. ed., 1979. *Languages and their speakers*. Cambridge, Mass., Winthrop

Shopen, T. and M. Konaré. 1970. Sonrai causatives and passives: transformational versus lexical derivations for propositional heads. *Studies in African Linguistics* 1:211–54

Silverstein, M. 1972. Chinook Jargon: language contact and the problem of multi-level generative systems, 1. *Language* 48:378–406

Silverstein, M. 1974. Dialectal developments in Chinookan tense–aspect systems: an areal–historical analysis. *International Journal of American Linguistics*, Memoir 29

Silverstein, M. 1976. Hierarchy of features and ergativity. In Dixon 1976:112–71

Skorik, P. J. 1961, 1977. *Grammatika čukotskogo jazyka*. 2 vols. Leningrad, Nauka

Sohn, H-M. 1975. *Woleaian reference grammar*. Honolulu, University of Hawaii Press

Story, G. L. and C. M. Naish. 1973. *Tlingit verb dictionary*. Fairbanks, University of Alaska, Alaska Native Language Center

Swadesh, M. 1939. Nootka internal syntax. *International Journal of American Linguistics* 9:77–102

Swanton, J. R. 1911. Tlingit. In Boas 1911a:259–304

Talmy, L. 1972. Semantic structures in English and Atsugewi. Unpublished Ph.D. dissertation, University of California, Berkeley

Talmy, L. 1975. Semantics and syntax of motion. In J. Kimball, ed. *Syntax and semantics 4*. New York, Academic Press: 181–238

Talmy, L. 1976a. Semantic causative types. In Shibatani 1976:43–116

Talmy, L. 1976b. Communicative aims and means. *Stanford Working Papers on Language Universals* 20

Talmy, L. 1978a. Figure and ground in complex sentences. In Greenberg *et al.* 1978:625–49

Talmy, L. 1978b. Relations between subordination and coordination. In Greenberg *et al.* 1978:487–513

Talmy, L. 1978c. The relation of grammar to cognition. In D. Waltz, ed. *Proceedings of TINLAP-2 (theoretical issues in natural language processing)*. Urbana, University of Illinois, Coordinated Science Laboratory

Talmy, L. 1982. Borrowing semantic space: Yiddish verb prefixes between Germanic and Slavic. *Berkeley Linguistics Society* 8

Talmy, L. 1983. How language structures space. In H. Pick and L. Acredolo, eds. *Spatial orientation: theory, research, and application*. New York, Plenum Press

Talmy, L. In preparation. How language structures its concepts. For *The Behavioral and Brain Sciences*

Tedeschi, P. and A. Zaenen, eds. 1981. *Syntax and semantics 14: Tense and aspect.* New York, Academic Press

Tereščenko, N. M. 1973. *Sintaksis samodijskix jazykov.* Leningrad, Nauka

Thompson, S. A. 1974. On the issue of productivity in the lexicon. In Thompson and Lord 1974. Also in *Kritikon Litterarum* 1975, 4:332–49

Thompson, S. A. and C. Lord. 1974. *Approaches to the lexicon.* Berkeley, University of California, Department of Linguistics. (UCLA Papers in Syntax, 6)

Topping, D. M. 1973. *Chamorro reference grammar.* Honolulu, University of Hawaii Press

Trepos, P. 1957. *Le pluriel breton.* Brest, Emgleo Breiz

Trepos, P. n.d. *Grammaire bretonne.* Rennes, Imprimerie Simon

Troubetzkoy, N. 1929. Notes sur les désinences du verbe dans les langues tchétchéno-lesghiennes. *Bulletin de la Société Linguistique de Paris* 29:153–71

Tryon, D. 1968. *Iai.* Canberra, Australian National University, Research School of Pacific Studies, Department of Linguistics. (Pacific Linguistics, B.8)

Vogt, H. 1971. *Grammaire de la langue géorgienne.* Oslo, Universitetsforlaget

Weber, D. 1978. Relativization in Huallaga (Huanuco) Quechua. Unpublished M.A. thesis, University of California, Los Angeles

Welmers, W. E. 1973. *African language structures.* Berkeley, University of California Press

Whorf, B. L. 1956. The punctual and segmentative aspects of verbs in Hopi. In his *Language, thought, and reality.* Cambridge, Mass., M.I.T. Press: 51–6

Wise, H. 1975. *A transformational grammar of spoken Egyptian Arabic.* Oxford, Blackwell

Wolkonsky, C. and M. Poltoratzky. 1961. *Handbook of Russian roots.* New York, Columbia University Press

Woodbury, H. 1975. Onondaga noun incorporation: some notes on the interdependence of syntax and semantics. *International Journal of American Linguistics* 41:10–20

Wright, W. 1898. *A grammar of the Arabic language.* 3rd edn. Cambridge, Cambridge University Press

Wurm, S. A. 1972. *Languages of Australia and Tasmania.* The Hague, Mouton. (Series Critica, 1)

Xolodovič, A. A. ed. 1969. *Tipologia kauzativnyx konstrukcij: morfologičeskij kauzativ.* Leningrad, Nauka

Young, R. A. 1971. *The verb in Bena-Bena: its form and function.* Canberra, Australian National University, Research School of Pacific Studies, Department of Linguistics. (Pacific Linguistics, B.18)

Zimmer, K. 1971. Some general observations about nominal compounds. *Stanford Working Papers on Language Universals* 5:C1–C21

Zwicky, A. 1977. On clitics. In W. Dressler and O. Pfeiffer, eds. *Phonologica 1976.* Innsbruck, Institut fur Sprachwissenschaft der Universität Innsbruck: 29–39. (Innsbrucker Beiträge zur Sprachwissenschaft, 19).

# Index

*Note:* References in this index are to all three volumes of *Language typology and syntactic description*. For ease of reference volume numbers are shown in bold type.

coreference in complementation, II 67, 68, 78, 82, 102, 126, 166
counterfactuality, II 195–7, 223, 237, 245–6, 276, 281–2, III 243, 245, 252–4
Cree (Algonquian: Canada, Montana), Plains, I 77, II 288, 297, 298–9, 344
cross-referencing, I 75–7, 106–8, 114, 123, 124
Crow (Siouan: Wyoming, Montana), II 264
Cupeño (Uto-Aztecan: California), I 249
Cushitic languages (Afroasiatic: North East Africa), III 181
Czech (Western Slavonic: Western Czechoslovakia), II 147, 151, 152, III 151, 280, 375, 376, 377, 397–8

Daga (Dagan, Papuan: Papua New Guinea), II 188
Dakota (Siouan: Central North USA), I 71–2, 82, 119, 145, II 39, 40
Danish (Germanic: Denmark), II 173, III 21, 178, 272
Dargwa (or Dargva, Northeast Caucasian: Southwestern USSR), III 197
dative case, III 184–5
dative-shift, I 282, 347–54
  universal rule in, I 352
declaratives, I 160, 162, 165–70, 223, 246, II 82
  dubitative, I 169–70
  emphatic, I 170
  inferential, I 169
  marked, I 165
  negative, I 159, 167
  putative, I 167–70
  unmarked, I 165–7
deixis, II 248–9, III 54, 103, 135, 149, 170, 178, 179, 259–308
  person deixis, III 259–77; fifth person deictics, III 262; fourth person deictics, III 262–3; gender deictics, III 269–70; person and number deictics, III 263–9; poly-focal deictics, III 268–9; portmanteau deictics, III 266–7; social status deictics, III 270–7; 'weak' deictics, III 262
  relative (relativized), II 260, 278, 301–7; in indirect discourse, III 302–5; spatial and time deictics, III 305–7
  spatial deixis, III 259, 277–95; additional dimension systems of, III 289–95; minimal systems of one-, two-, three-, four-term, III 280–8; person oriented and distance oriented three-tier systems, III 282–5; presentatives, III 279

temporal deixis, III 259, 295–301; in the lexicon, III 300–1; temporal demonstratives, III 297–9; the category of tense, III 300–1
deletion, III 59
derivation, notion of, III 162–4
  'zero', III 23
determiners, II 142, 161, 164, 167, 169, 192
  position of, II 145–6
detransitivization, II 322, 324, II 159, III 191, 320
Dibabawon (South Philippine, Austronesian: Philippines), II 217, 219
Diegueño (Yuman, Hokan: California), I 211–12, II 56, 162, 163, III 394–5
different subject markers, I 211–12
diminutives, III 163, 167, 170, 177–8
Diola (West Atlantic, Congo-Kordofanian: Gambia, Guinea Bissau), I 185, III 354, 355
disjunction, II 3, 4, 6, 17, 18, 21, 22, 25, 39–40
  open, II 24–5
dislocation, I 243, 244, 245, 246
Diyari (or Dieri, Pama-Nyungan: South Australia), I 105, 115–17, 132, 135, 145
Djeragan languages (Australian: Western Australia, Northern Territory), III 263
domain nouns, II 142, 161
double objects, I 90
Dravidian, I 66, 84
Duala (North Western Bantu, Congo-Kordofanian: Cameroon), I 362–3
Dutch (Germanic: Netherlands), I 198, 249, 273, 274, 275, 324–5, 332, 333
Dyirbal (Pama-Nyungan: Queensland, Australia), I 171, 288, II 24, 159, 161, III 132, 175, 182, 188, 192, 205, 291–2, 321, 327
  antipassives in, I 335–47, 353–4
  syntactic ergativity in, I 131, 134–5, 138, 144–7
Dzamba (or Bobangi, Northwestern Bantu, Congo-Kordofanian: Zaire, Congo, Central African Republic), II 151

Efik (Cross River Benue-Congo, Congo-Kordofanian: Nigeria, Cameroon), II 192
Egyptian, Ancient (Afroasiatic: Egypt), II 39
Ek-Nii (Chimbu, Papuan: Papua New Guinea), II 243, 267
ellipsis, anaphoric, II 67–8
enclitics, *see* clitics